T0338746

Cross–Industry Use of Blockchain Technology and Opportunities for the Future

Idongesit Williams
Aalborg University, Denmark

A volume in the Advances in Data Mining and
Database Management (ADMDM) Book Series

Published in the United States of America by
    IGI Global
    Engineering Science Reference (an imprint of IGI Global)
    701 E. Chocolate Avenue
    Hershey PA, USA 17033
    Tel: 717-533-8845
    Fax: 717-533-8661
    E-mail: cust@igi-global.com
    Web site: http://www.igi-global.com

Library of Congress Cataloging-in-Publication Data

Names: Williams, Idongesit, editor.
Title: Cross-industry use of blockchain technology and opportunities for
  the future / Idongesit Williams, editor.
Description: Hershey, PA : Engineering Science Reference, 2020. | Includes
  bibliographical references and index. | Summary: "This book provides
  research highlighting the possibilities inherent in blockchain for
  different sectors of the economy and the added value blockchain can
  provide for the future of these different sectors"-- Provided by
  publisher.
Identifiers: LCCN 2019057483 (print) | LCCN 2019057484 (ebook) | ISBN
  9781799836322 (hardcover) | ISBN 9781799836339 (paperback) | ISBN
  9781799836346 (ebook)
Subjects: LCSH: Blockchains (Databases)--Industrial applications. |
  Blockchains (Databases)--Economic aspects.
Classification: LCC QA76.9.B56 C76 2020 (print) | LCC QA76.9.B56 (ebook)
  | DDC 005.1/2--dc23
LC record available at https://lccn.loc.gov/2019057483
LC ebook record available at https://lccn.loc.gov/2019057484

This book is published in the IGI Global book series Advances in Data Mining and Database Management (ADMDM) (ISSN: 2327-1981; eISSN: 2327-199X)

British Cataloguing in Publication Data
A Cataloguing in Publication record for this book is available from the British Library.

For electronic access to this publication, please contact: eresources@igi-global.com.

Advances in Data Mining and Database Management (ADMDM) Book Series

David Taniar
Monash University, Australia

ISSN:2327-1981
EISSN:2327-199X

MISSION

With the large amounts of information available to organizations in today's digital world, there is a need for continual research surrounding emerging methods and tools for collecting, analyzing, and storing data.

The **Advances in Data Mining & Database Management (ADMDM)** series aims to bring together research in information retrieval, data analysis, data warehousing, and related areas in order to become an ideal resource for those working and studying in these fields. IT professionals, software engineers, academicians and upper-level students will find titles within the ADMDM book series particularly useful for staying up-to-date on emerging research, theories, and applications in the fields of data mining and database management.

COVERAGE

- Data Mining
- Heterogeneous and Distributed Databases
- Customer Analytics
- Web-based information systems
- Factor Analysis
- Profiling Practices
- Association Rule Learning
- Database Security
- Data Analysis
- Cluster Analysis

IGI Global is currently accepting manuscripts for publication within this series. To submit a proposal for a volume in this series, please contact our Acquisition Editors at Acquisitions@igi-global.com or visit: http://www.igi-global.com/publish/.

Titles in this Series

For a list of additional titles in this series, please visit:
http://www.igi-global.com/book-series/advances-data-mining-database-management/37146

Challenges and Applications of Data Analytics in Social Perspectives
V. Sathiyamoorthi (Sona College of Technology, India) and Atilla Elci (Aksaray University, Turkey)
Engineering Science Reference • © 2020 • 330pp • H/C (ISBN: 9781799825661) • US $245.00

Handling Priority Inversion in Time-Constrained Distributed Databases
Udai Shanker (Madan Mohan Malaviya University of Technology, India) and Sarvesh Pandey (Madan Mohan
Malaviya University of Technology, India)
Engineering Science Reference • © 2020 • 338pp • H/C (ISBN: 9781799824916) • US $225.00

Feature Extraction and Classification Techniques for Text Recognition
Munish Kumar (Maharaja Ranjit Singh Punjab Technical University, India) Manish Kumar Jindal (Panjab University
Regional Centre, Muktsar, India) Simpel Rani Jindal (Yadavindera College of Engineering, India) R. K. Sharma
(Thapar Institute of Engineering & Technology, India) and Anupam Garg (Bhai Gurdas Institute of Engineering
and Technology, India)
Engineering Science Reference • © 2020 • 300pp • H/C (ISBN: 9781799824060) • US $225.00

Neutrosophic Graph Theory and Algorithms
Florentin Smarandache (University of New Mexico, USA) and Said Broumi (Faculty of Science Ben M'Sik,
University Hassan II, Morocco)
Engineering Science Reference • © 2020 • 406pp • H/C (ISBN: 9781799813132) • US $245.00

Handbook of Research on Big Data Clustering and Machine Learning
Fausto Pedro Garcia Marquez (Universidad Castilla-La Mancha, Spain)
Engineering Science Reference • © 2020 • 478pp • H/C (ISBN: 9781799801061) • US $285.00

Big Data Analytics for Sustainable Computing
Anandakumar Haldorai (Sri Eshwar College of Engineering, India) and Arulmurugan Ramu (Presidency Univer-
sity, India)
Engineering Science Reference • © 2020 • 263pp • H/C (ISBN: 9781522597506) • US $245.00

Trends and Applications of Text Summarization Techniques
Alessandro Fiori (Candiolo Cancer Institute – FPO, IRCCS, Italy)
Engineering Science Reference • © 2020 • 335pp • H/C (ISBN: 9781522593737) • US $210.00

701 East Chocolate Avenue, Hershey, PA 17033, USA
Tel: 717-533-8845 x100 • Fax: 717-533-8661
E-Mail: cust@igi-global.com • www.igi-global.com

Dedicated to My Father Engineer Williams.

Editorial Advisory Board

Table of Contents

Detailed Table of Contents

Internet of Things (IoT) and blockchain technology-based information system (IS) can be used to improve tracking of goods and services in offering and build a collaborative operating environment among the business-partners of the manufacturing industry. In this process IS architecture plays an important role in storing, processing, and distributing data. Despite contributing to the rapid development of IoT applications, the current IoT-centric architecture has led to a myriad of isolated data silos that hinder the full potential of holistic data-driven decision-support applications with the IoT because of technical issues (e.g., standalone IoT applications suffer from security and privacy-related problems). This chapter presents a proof of concept of a hybrid enterprise information system architecture, which consists of IoT-based applications and a blockchain-oriented distributed-ledger system to support-transaction services within a multiparty global manufacturing (e.g., textile and clothing business) network.

Chapter 2

Blockchain technology (BCT) is becoming a common language across diverse geographical domains. BCT attempts to solve the fraud issues involved in financial transactions and government operations. E-governance is a convenient platform providing services to all connected citizens and inter-government sectors. Traditional centralization issues are addressed by decentralizing the stakes, keeping the transactions transparent on an open ledger–BCT. It works on the notion of disintermediation eliding the middle layers with the highest trust level. It can contribute to various e-government sectors, namely agriculture, property registrations, supply chain management, tax calculation, etc. BCT application for agriculture supply change management can provide assistance in crop plantation and delivery records. It can bring transparency in land registrations and tax management by maintaining immutable land records and simplified tax management preserving trust between various parties through smart contracts. This chapter focuses on BCT approaches for secured governance.

Chapter 3
  Adnan Ozsoy, Hacettepe University, Turkey
  Bahar Gezici, Hacettepe University, Turkey
  Necva Bölücü, Hacettepe University, Turkey
  Nurettin Bölücü, Hacettepe University, Turkey

Blockchain in government services has a wide range of application areas for various departments from legal document storage and management to healthcare benefits. Decentralized nature opens opportunities for a government that can achieve operations 24/7 and cut back office operations. A Blockchain system for government offers a potential solution to legacy pain points and establishes a secure storage for citizens and businesses. It also reduces intensive paper processes, excessive managing costs, and potential corruption and abuse. Instead, it greatly increases security of digital services and more importantly trust in the government. This chapter provides a detailed review of Blockchain solutions for three major government services: land registry, GDPR, and healthcare. For each service, a state-of-the-art is given, followed with the technical details of use cases and potential improvements for current problems.

Chapter 4
  Dhanalakshmi Senthilkumar, Malla Reddy Engineering College (Autonomous), India

Blockchain and artificial intelligence are two disruptive technologies in the today's world; Blockchain can connect data storage and data users from multiple domains, and different kinds of analytics applications run on top of the data in artificial intelligence techniques. So that Blockchain technology provide the excellent backbone for the development of artificial intelligence algorithms, it is useful to secure the data input from multiple data storage locations and to have whatever applications running on top of the data in a Blockchain visible to everyone. The concept of Blockchain technology and artificial intelligence techniques together develop interesting uses cases and nice applications. When paired with Blockchains, AI is better understood by humans, operates more efficiently, and the blockchains in general more efficiently. AI and Blockchain together support B2B environment and getting better outcomes.

Chapter 5
  Sourav Banerjee, Kalyani Government Engineering College, India
  Debashis Das, University of Kalyani, India
  Manju Biswas, Kalyani Government Engineering College, India
  Utpal Biswas, University of Kalyani, India

Blockchain-based technology is becoming increasingly popular and is now used to solve a wide range of tasks. And it's not all about cryptocurrencies. Even though it's based on secure technology, a blockchain needs protection as well. The risks of exploits, targeted attacks, or unauthorized access can be mitigated by the instant incident response and system recovery. Blockchain technology relies on a ledger to keep track of all financial transactions. Ordinarily, this kind of master ledger would be a glaring point of vulnerability. Another tenet of security is the chain itself. Configuration flaws, as well as insecure data storage and transfers, may cause leaks of sensitive information. This is even more dangerous when there are centralized components within the platform. In this chapter, the authors will demonstrate where the disadvantages of security and privacy in blockchain are currently and discuss how blockchain technology can improve these disadvantages and outlines the requirements for future solution.

Chapter 6

Samuel Agbesi, Aalborg University, Copenhagen, Denmark
Fati Tahiru, Ho Technical University, Ghana

The administration of lands in Ghana has been a major issue in the past years that has resulted in parties seeking arbitration to determine the rightful owners and others resulting in death because of the land-guard menace. The main issues in land administration in Ghana include modification and falsification of land records, difficulty in authenticating the ownership of land property, sales of land property to more than one customer, and lack of transparency in land transactions. This chapter examines the application of Blockchain in land administration in Ghana to solve the issues of unauthorized modification of land records, difficulties in proven ownership of land properties, and the lack of transparency in land transactions. The proposed solution is based on Ethereum Blockchain technology using a smart contract. The solution used a non-fungible token to represent land properties as a digital asset that can be traded on the proposed solution. The proposed solution provides integrity, immutability, provenance, and transparency in land administration.

Chapter 7

İsmail Yıldırım, Hitit University, Turkey

New technologies that will be developed in the future will determine the place of Blockchain technology in our lives. It is certain that blockchain technology, which has the potential to be used in every field from smart phones to the health sector, will be a technology that will be frequently encountered in the future rather than simply being used in some sectors. What will determine the areas of use of Blockchain technology and how much it can be used depends on what future security, cost, and speed it can do. Blockchain, which can be used in the insurance sector, will help to keep track of accidents, material, and moral losses during the insurance period and keep track of all records very easily. It is expected that this technology, which is expected to be useful in eliminating the minute information problems in the insurance sector, can be very helpful in preventing insurance frauds, and it is expected to have a preventive effect in defrauding insurance and citizens. This chapter discusses how blockchain technologies will transform the insurance sector and their future uses.

Chapter 8

Ezer Osei Yeboah-Boateng, Ghana Technology University College, Ghana
Stephane Nwolley, Jnr., Npontu Technologies Ltd., Ghana

Technology innovation creates value and competitive advantage. Blockchain has been used to resolve existing problems and offer efficient operations. Blockchain is applied in education, healthcare, automation, etc. Blockchain with permanence and reliability attributes has created trust in digital assets with high integrity and availability to leverage on innovative transactions. Indeed, a plethora of blockchain use cases and value propositions are documented. That notwithstanding, there is dearth of literature on transforming some legacy systems and creating value. To harness the potential, a deeper understanding of use cases and future opportunities is imperative. So, how can blockchain be harnessed for best value creation? What strategies could be adopted by SMEs to leverage? The study explicated on taxonomy of use cases in taxation, e-voting, AI and IoT, and analyzed some value creation perspectives to identify opportunities, in particular, smart contracts used to enforce regulatory compliance. It implies that blockchain use cases could create future opportunities for SMEs.

Chapter 9

Cephas Paa Kwasi Coffie, University of Electronic Science and Technology of China, China
    & All Nations University College, Ghana
Hongjiang Zhao, School of Management and Economics, University of Electronic Science
    and Technology of China, China
Benjamin Kwofie, Koforidua Technical University, Ghana
Emmanuel Dortey Tetteh, University of Electronic Science and Technology of China, China
    & Koforidua Technical University, Ghana

Contracts have emerged as an appropriate expanse for the application of Blockchain to eliminate human mediation perceived to be mired by weaknesses. Smart contracts date back to the 1990s, but the proposed Blockchain technology makes it a great force economically. Beyond the transactional processing qualities of blockchain, industries envisage the technology to resolve divergent human-related complications with traditional contracts. Per literature, smart contracts offer superior economic value with respect to legality, formation, deployment, execution, and cost. These qualities of smart contract ensure performance and eliminate risk. Criticised on the inhumane aspect of the technology in terms of contract amendments and the current influx of foreign-based blockchain companies in Africa limiting indigenous design considerations, the application of smart contracts in continent could be hindered by contract renegotiations strongly embedded in cultural values of empathy. Nonetheless, a trade-off would resolve the contractual bottlenecks in Africa.

Chapter 10

Idongesit Williams, Aalborg University, Denmark

This chapter explains the role and how interoperability standards and compatibility standards will enable the development of cross-chain blockchain networks. Blockchain currently lacks standardization. There are different initiatives aimed at facilitating interoperability between different blockchains. But if there are no uniform interoperability and compatibility standards, that will cause a problem for the development of cross-chain blockchain networks. In the EU, there is an initiative to facilitate a continental cross-chain blockchain network. Interoperability and compatibility standards are an integral aspect of the initiative. This chapter uses the case of the EU as a basis for explanation on how blockchain service providers can work together to develop these standards.

The blockchain digital technology holds immense possibilities for the growth and development of developing economies such as Ghana. Since the emergence of blockchain technology, many developing economies have as yet to tap into its limitless possibilities with Ghana being no exception. In this chapter, the authors explore the possibilities for the blockchain for SMEs in developing economies like Ghana with a view to identifying the properties of a blockchain ecosystem that will facilitate their development, adoption, and use by SMEs.

The Mobilization Decision theory provides an insight into why mobilization occurs and the factors that result in mobilization. In the last decade, blockchain technology has been touted as a technology that facilitates trust between unknown parties. Trust is at the core of all human interaction, be it commercial or social. However, the global adoption of blockchain is low. At a global scale, relatively few organizations have mobilized blockchain to either handle or support their organizational processes. In order to understand why this is the case, the mobilization decision theory is used to explain why the global adoption of blockchain is low and what needs to change to facilitate its widespread adoption at a global scale.

Foreword

The Internet is revolutionizing the world by influencing how innovations cater to human needs. This revolution is a continuous process as new techniques and technologies are emerging to cater for the needs of citizens and organization. The speed of the revolution accelerates as the years go by, resulting in the prolific transformations in the 21st century. One of such technologies that has been a catalyst to the Internet revolution are wireless communication technologies. These technologies have bridged distance and enabled remote collaboration in the delivery of different services in different sectors of the economy. These wireless technologies has enabled the utilization of voice-based commands in the service delivery processes. We are aware of voice- command services in our cars and homes. These wireless services arc delivered using newer digital technologies such as Internet of Things (IoT), augmented reality and Blockchain etc.

These digital technologies operate either independently or collaboratively over wireless networks, presenting new market value to the customer. In this book, the focus is on the Blockchain technology. Blockchains, a digital technology, has been popularized by cryptocurrency applications. Today, Blockchain is being deployed in collaboration with other technologies such as Big data, IOT etc. to deliver value to companies in different vertical economic sectors. The cross-industry adoption of Blockchain is low since Blockchain is still a developing technology. There is the need for inspiration on how this development can be achieved. This book serves as a starting point to that process. This book presents a unique understanding and learning prospect on Blockchain technologies and opportunities in several industries. The book visualizes the various ways and possibilities of applying Blockchain technologies to facilitate trust in the delivery of e-governance, land use, supply chain management, artificial intelligence and the financial sectors in Small and Medium Sized Enterprises (SMEs) and developing countries.

The contributing authors have adopted practical approaches towards discussing issues. There is also a special focus on security and privacy issues related to Blockchain. The practical approach and special focus enables the reader to identify challenges and opportunities in the delivery of Blockchain within their Domain. It also enables readers adopt a Do-it-yourself approach towards customizing Blockchain to enable the security and Privacy of the nodes in the Blockchain.

The book is written by experts in their respective field, which provides diversity to approaches presented in the book. Readers of this book will be equipped with deep understanding on new ways of managing applications based on Blockchain technology in different industries.

Prashant Dhotre
Associate Professor at Department of IT
Savitribai Phule Pune University, Pune, India

Preface

Blockchain technology has been around for some time now. The cryptographic technic, data storage and network topology of the technology has been around much longer. But the synergy of these three facets of Blockchain has resulted in a technology that facilitates transparency, trust, secured data storage, and data immutability. These attributes do not exist in current cloud-based technologies, databases and identity management technologies that provide similar services to Blockchains. Hence, this makes Blockchain a unique technology.

Initially Blockchain technology gained traction for the delivery of cryptocurrencies. Today, it is a technology used in different sectors of the economy to enable either transparent transactions, data storage or trust-driven business ecosystems. Examples of industries utilizing Blockchain include the supply-chains in the automotive industries, manufacturing industries, tourism industries, shipping industries etc. However, the level of utilization of Blockchain in these industries is low. Furthermore, the global economy is interlinked because of globalization; this implies that sectoral services are not just vertical but horizontal as well. For example, financial institutions enable payment and revenue sharing across different industries in different sectors collaborating to deliver an economic good. Another example is the role of the digital technology provider who offers cloud-based services to different stakeholders in different industries who collaborate. The existence of these horizontal services implies that Blockchains has to evolve in order to cater for these possibilities.

Hence, the question this book answers is what can be done to enable more adoption of Blockchains in the vertical sector services? In addition, how can Blockchain be configured to also cater for the horizontal sector services? To answer these questions, this book provides practical suggestions on the configuration of the technology based on industry based technical parameters, service requirements and legal requirements and requirements needed for organizational readiness.

The primary target of this book are organizations that will or are adopting Blockchain and Blockchain service providers. This book will help different organizations in different industries identify the prospect of using Blockchain in their organizations. The book highlights how organizations can deal with the technical limitations that makes it challenging to deploy Blockchains in their organizations and ecosystem. Due to the limitation for space, this book does not cover all sectors, however the authors have provided practical insights on how Blockchains can be configured to enable the delivery of different services that can be applicable in different sectors of the economy. The benefit this book provides is the focus on how organizations in developing economies can also benefit from the advice provided in the book. For Blockchain service providers, this book is a valuable feedback on the challenges organizations face in the delivery of Blockchain and suggestions for future Blockchains. One of the issues identified is in this Book is the fact that existing Blockchain platforms do not support organizational processes in certain industries. It is obvious that the approach adopted by Blockchain service providers is aimed at disrupting existing business models using Blockchains. However, that approach seems not to be working. Most organizations using Blockchains do not want a disruption in their current business models and ecosystems. Furthermore organizations seem to prefer other technologies competing with Blockchain. Hence there is the need for a more user, organizational and ecosystem friendly Blockchain for certain industries. Blockchain service providers will also benefit from the technical suggestions provided in the book. The secondary but not less significant target of the book are academics, researchers, policy makers, standards organizations, public administrators and consultants.

This book is written in a language that the relevant target audience will understand. The writing style is a mixture of academic research, reviews and expert opinions. This is deliberate to ensure that the message outlined in this book is transmitted to relevant stakeholders in a language they will understand. To facilitate this writing style, experts on the technical aspect of Blockchain; service delivery using Blockchain; organizational operations and deployment of Blockchain; and ICT and society; were invited to contribute. Twenty-eight authors from India, the UK, Denmark, Turkey and Ghana contributed to the book. The book has 12 chapters. A brief description of each chapter is as follows

Chapter 1: This chapter presents a high-level description of Internet of Things (IoT) based information system alongside blockchain technology to improve global manufacturing supply chain operations. The chapter describes how these technologies (i.e. IoT and blockchain) can complement each other in different aspect of manufacturing (e.g. textile and clothing industry) supply chain functions, bringing in transparency, efficiency, and cost reduction

Chapter 2: This chapter describes how Blockchain technology can enable various e-government sectors namely, Agriculture, Property registrations, Supply Chain Management, Tax calculation, etc. BCT application for agriculture supply change management can provide assistance in crop plantation and delivery records. It can bring transparency in land registrations and tax management by maintaining immutable land records and simplified tax management preserving trust between various parties through smart contracts.

Chapter 3: This chapter provides a detailed review of Blockchain solutions for three major government services; land registry, GDPR and healthcare. For each service a state-of-the-art is provided, followed by technical details of each use cases, and potential improvements for current problems.

Chapter 4: This chapter describes how Blockchain and Artificial Intelligence solutions can work together to deliver different use case applications.

Chapter 5: In this chapter, the authors demonstrate the security and privacy disadvantages on Blockchain platforms. They further provide technical solutions on how Blockchain technology can be upgraded and improved to deal these disadvantages. They also outline the technical requirements needed for the future solution.

Chapter 6: This chapter described how Blockchain could be used to manage land administration. The chapter proposes an Ethereum blockchain technology solution using smart contracts. The solution uses a Non-fungible token to represent land properties as digital assets that can be traded on the platform. The proposed solution provides integrity, immutability, provenance, and transparency in land administration.

Chapter 7: This chapter discusses how Blockchain technologies will transform the insurance sector and their future uses.

Chapter 8: This chapter discusses how Blockchain can be harnessed for value creation purposes by SMEs. The discussion provides insights into strategies that SMEs to create value with Blockchain. These strategies are supported by examples of similar Blockchain value creation processes for taxation, e-voting, AI and IoT. The crux of the strategies is the utilization of smart contracts that are enforced using different forms of regulatory compliance.

Chapter 9: This chapter analyses the readiness for African SMEs towards the utilization of smart contracts. Contracts have emerged as an appropriate expanse for the application of Blockchain to eliminate human mediation perceived to be mired by weaknesses. Smart contracts date back to the 1990's, but the proposed Blockchain technology makes it a great force economically. Beyond the transactional processing qualities of Blockchain, industries envisage the technology to resolve divergent human-related complications with traditional contracts. Per literature, smart contracts offer superior economic value with respect to legality, formation, deployment, execution, and cost. These qualities of smart contract ensure performance and eliminate risk. Criticised on the inhumane aspect of the technology in terms of contract amendments and the current influx of foreign-based Blockchain companies in Africa limiting indigenous design considerations, the application of smart contracts in continent could be hindered by contract re-negotiations strongly embedded in cultural values of empathy. Nonetheless, a trade-off would resolve the contractual bottlenecks in Africa.

Chapter 10: This chapter explains the role/and how interoperability standards and compatibility standards will enable the development of Cross-chain Blockchain networks. This chapter uses the case of the EU as Basis for explanation on how Blockchain Service Providers can work together to develop these standards. Furthermore, the chapter highlights how such standards could generate positive network effect, which will result in the widespread adoption of cross-chain Blockchain networks.

Chapter 11: This chapter explores the possibilities for the Blockchain for SMEs in developing economies like Ghana. The exploration is performed towards identifying the properties of a blockchain ecosystem that will facilitate their development, adoption and use by SMEs.

Chapter 12: This chapter explores why the global adoption of Blockchain is low. The mobilization-Decision theory is used to provide an explanation as to why organizations are not adopting Blockchain. The chapter further provides recommendations and insights, based on the Mobilization-Decision theory, on what Blockchain services providers should do to remedy the situation.

Readers of this book will not only gain knowledge about the current state of Blockchains and how to solve practical problems related to Blockchains; but also they will gain inspiration on how to facilitate cross-country industry adoption and utilization of Blockchains. They will also be inspired to conduct research and find solution to areas of deficiency of the Blockchain technology. Such areas include, the technical, process/operations and service delivery.

The production of this book was made possible by the Editorial Team at IGI who, in the last 30 years, have published highly rated books. In addition, we sincerely thank everyone, who contributed in making this book possible.

Idongesit Williams
Aalborg University, Denmark

Acknowledgment

The editor specially thanks the contributors to this book: Kamalendu Pal, Hongjiang Zhao, Jyoti Malhotra, Nagesh Jadhav, Rajneeshkaur Sachdeo-Bedi, Rekha Sugandhi, Sambhaji Sarode, Adnan Ozsoy, Bahar Gezici, Necva Bölücü, Nurettin Bölücü, Dhanalakshmi Senthilkumar, Sourav Banerjee, Debashis Das, Cephas Paa Kwasi Coffie, Manju Biswas, Utpal Biswas, Samuel Agbesi, Fati Tahiru, İsmail Yıldırım, Ezer Osei Yeboah-Boateng, Stephane Nwolley, Jnr, Benjamin Kwofie, and Emmanuel Dortey Tetteh, for their immeasurable contribution to make this book a success. It has been a privileged to work with you on the dissemination of knowledge in this area of research.

The editor is also grateful to the Editorial Advisory Board, the team of peer reviewers and the Editorial Team from IGI for their assistance in making this book a reality. The editor is grateful to the assistant development editor from IGI and the project managers for the book, Courtney Tychinski and those who collaborated with her for their immense contribution, guidance, and supervision in the course of this project.

Chapter 1
Information Sharing for Manufacturing Supply Chain Management Based on Blockchain Technology

Kamalendu Pal

ⓘ https://orcid.org/0000-0001-7158-6481

City, University of London, UK

ABSTRACT

Internet of Things (IoT) and blockchain technology-based information system (IS) can be used to improve tracking of goods and services in offering and build a collaborative operating environment among the business-partners of the manufacturing industry. In this process IS architecture plays an important role in storing, processing, and distributing data. Despite contributing to the rapid development of IoT applications, the current IoT-centric architecture has led to a myriad of isolated data silos that hinder the full potential of holistic data-driven decision-support applications with the IoT because of technical issues (e.g., standalone IoT applications suffer from security and privacy-related problems). This chapter presents a proof of concept of a hybrid enterprise information system architecture, which consists of IoT-based applications and a blockchain-oriented distributed-ledger system to support-transaction services within a multiparty global manufacturing (e.g., textile and clothing business) network.

INTRODUCTION

In recent decades, many global manufacturing industries, such as automotive, pharmaceutical, apparel, consumer electronics, started to operate globally in extending the geographical boundaries of their business operations. At the same time, global manufacturing business today appreciates the value and consequence of building an effective supply chain as part of organizational proliferation and profitability. A manufacturing supply chain is a cooperative business network of facilities and distribution options that perform the functions of material procurement, the transformation of these materials into intermediate

DOI: 10.4018/978-1-7998-3632-2.ch001

and finished products, and distribution of these finished products to customers (Pal, 2017). Supply Chain Management (SCM) aims at improving the allocation, management and control of logistical resources and their operational issues.

The operational structure of the manufacturing supply chain can vary from industry to industry. For example, there are a handful of computer manufacturers, but only a few microchips sellers dominate at their tier in personal computer manufacturing supply chain networks. The automotive industry has few final-stage assemblers, but many manufacturers for most parts. In recent year aircraft manufacturing giant – Boeing need to resynchronize its supply chain, and decisions made now by tier-three and tier-four suppliers will affect Boeing's 2021 production rate. Yet uncertainty makes decision-making difficult for owners and executives in the supply chain. This results in 'mixed supply-based' approach in the manufacturing industry. The actual application of a mixed supply-based approach has been established in the textile and clothing industry. Thus, rather than contracting either cost-effective overseas manufacturers or responsive domestic suppliers, the mixed supply-based approach can be used to optimize the manufacturing supply requirements and supplier selection is often driven by corporate policy and market demand.

Much manufacturing company product and service operates in supply chain networks that interconnect hundreds of suppliers, wholesalers, logistics service providers, and distribution channels with physical operations located around different continents. The operational environment in which global manufacturing businesses are collaborating with their suppliers and customers have recognized interoperability of information systems as importance. The need to address this change becomes even more important when considering that new paradigms such as the Internet of Things (IoT) and its ability to capture real-time information from different aspects of manufacturing business processes by using RFID tags and sensors-based data communication networks. In this process enterprise information system architecture plays an important role in storing, processing, distributing data and relevant information.

Despite the growing potential to apply IoT in manufacturing supply chain management systems, there are many challenges need to be resolved. For instance, IoT-related technical issues experienced when operating at the whole manufacturing business level, such as security, authenticity, confidentiality, and privacy of all business-partners. From an IoT vulnerability perspective, practitioners and academics consider security to be the most important issue. Existing security solutions are not well suited because current IoT devices may consume a significant amount of energy and may have significant information processing overhead. Also, problems such as counterfeiting, physical tampering, hacking, data theft might raise trust concerns among manufacturing supply chain business partners.

Appropriate protection must be developed to leverage the value and enhance the trust of connected IoT devices in manufacturing supply chains. For example, blockchain technology now offers several potential solutions to address known issues related to IoT. A blockchain is a distributed network for orchestrating transactions, value, and assets between peers, without the assistance of intermediaries. It also commonly referred to as a 'ledger' that records the transaction. Another way to view a blockchain is as a configuration of multiple technologies, tools and methods that address specific problems. With the adopting of blockchain technology, manufacturing businesses aim to enhance information transparency and improve trust in their supply chains while supporting the interoperability among the networked supply chain exchange partners. As a result, it has gained considerable attention from academics, practitioners, manufacturers who seek to combine IoT with other technologies. At the same time, developments are in progress to integrate blockchain technology with IoT solutions, leading to novel structure of modern manufacturing supply chains, a new partnerships, as well as new way of collaboration and value creation across manufacturing networks.

This chapter presents how manufacturing companies can leverage IoT in combination with block-chain technology to streamline their manufacturing supply chains business processes. When combined, these enabling technologies will help global manufacturing companies to overcome problems related to data acquisition and integrity, address security challenges, mitigate traceability concerns, and reduce information asymmetry. In the following sections, the chapter reviews IoT-based information system in the context of an apparel manufacturing supply chain business case and present an architecture to store data and process these data in a service oriented platform to get nearly real-time information for operational decision making purpose.

The rest of this chapter is organized as follows. Section 2 uses a simple apparel manufacturing supply chain business case. Section 3 describes the background knowledge about the global textile industry. It also explains different paradigms of the ICT world, which are used for business processes automation. Section 4 presents the proposed three-layer framework for an information system. Section 5 explains the emerging issue in blockchain based information system's deployment. Section 6 reviews related research works. Section 7 provides an overview of future research directions. Finally, Section 8 concludes the chapter by discussing relevant research challenges.

OVERVIEW OF APPAREL MANUFACTURING SUPPLY CHAIN

Textile and clothing industries are an integral part of the world economy and society. In a global economy privileged access to natural resources, capital, trained human resources, and even access to markets are not enough to gain a competitive advantage for any apparel enterprise. Moreover, the future of world textile manufacturing, in a vision of 'Gandhian Engineering' based economy (Prahalad & Mashelkar, 2010) needs cost-effective production methods to cater the constantly evolving demands of its customers. In this way, a profound globalization effect is currently shaping the future of global apparel manufacturing industry. In a typical apparel manufacturing chain, raw materials are purchased from suppliers and products are manufactured at one or more production plants (Pal, 2019). Then they are transported to intermediated storage facilities (e.g. warehouse, distribution centres) for packing, loading and shipping to retailers or customers. In this way, an apparel manufacturing supply chain consists of business entities in the chain and these are suppliers, manufacturers, distributors, retailers, and customers (Pal, 2017). In many industries (e.g. apparel), manufacturing and logistics supply chains are challenged by their increasing complexity and the need for higher flexibility to meeting individual customer requirements (Pal, 2020).

Based on mandatory national and international policies, transparency in the textile and clothing industry is often limited to the '*made in*' label. Since this tag usually refers to the last, most important aspect of the clothing production process, it may lose sight of important steps taking place before that point. While the garment industry has been under a microscope in recent years, especially when it comes to 'fast fashion', shoppers are becoming increasingly conscious and want to know more about where their products come from. As conscious customers demand sustainability and integrity on large scale, new transparency solutions are gaining attraction all along the textile supply chain, ideally from farm to retail. Transparency-enabling systems – besides promoting a fairer and cleaner fashion industry – represent also a tool that helps brands to combat the proliferation of counterfeit goods, recognized by Apparel Fashion Business as one of the biggest threats to the global fashion industry.

Secured traceability implies not only the ability to identify, capture, and share required information on product transformation throughout the supply chain, but also the ability to ensure the security of the traceability data. Due to information asymmetry and lack of transparency, textile and clothing industries often face challenges in implementing and maintaining enough traceability. The supply chain actors find it difficult to identify and track the suppliers and sub-suppliers involved. Additionally, the opaque and largely untraceable structure of the supply chain has enabled the easy intrusion of counterfeits. Hence, a secured traceability system is imperative to ensure that the required traceability data are captured and shared among supply chain actors, thereby allowing the tracking and tracing of the products in the supply chain. Further, a secured traceability system helps organizations in various decision-making processes and protects customers from counterfeits.

In this way, product and service provision is getting importance in the apparel industry. Flexibility and adaptability are the crucial characteristics of today's short-lived fashion clothing, where fashion trends and customer demands change in the blink of an eye. Moreover, there exists another layer of complexity in current apparel manufacturing network, which is attributed to the geographical separation of the contributing suppliers and manufactures; and efficient information sharing mechanism within the business partners along the global supply chain operations. In this way, sharing, storing and processing of apparel supply chain data requires secure information systems architecture. Apparel manufacturing supply network data could be analyzed for locating the areas with problems so that proper operating instructions could be provided by the logistics controlling management teams.

Modern information and communication technologies (ICTs) often regarded as the catalyst to improve supply chain information sharing ability. Information sharing across textile manufacturing networks is based on linking unique identifications of objects – tagged using RFID transponders or barcodes – with records in supply chain database management systems. In this process, Electronic Product Code Information Services (EPCIS) is the most relevant industry standard. Internet of Things (IoT) is one of the most promising technological innovations, is used now-a-days in apparel manufacturing. In simple, RFID tags, sensor technology, and relevant data communication networking provision form the concept of IoT. The IoT is a concept in which the digital world of information technology integrates seamlessly with the real world of things. This real-world becomes easily accessible through modern computers and data communication networked devices in the apparel manufacturing business. In recent decades, IoT technology is used heavily in apparel manufacturing business processes - inventory management, warehousing, and transportation of products, automatic object tracking and supply chain management. With access to precise information, apparel supply chain operational managers can perform their analysis on a nearly real-time basis and can take appropriate strategic decisions.

Figure 1. RFID tagging level at different stages in the apparel manufacturing network

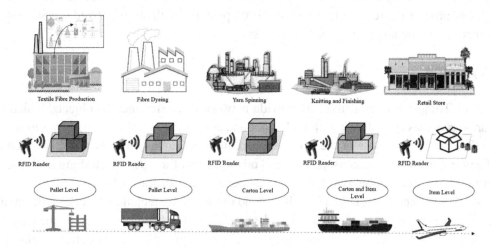

Despite contributing to the rapid development of IoT applications, the current IoT-centric architecture has led into a myriad of isolated data silos that hinders the full potential of holistic data-driven business applications with the IoT. Moreover, standalone IoT application systems face security and privacy related problems. The blockchain technology has introduced an effective solution to the IoT based information systems security. A blockchain enhance IoT devices to send data for inclusion in a shared transaction repository with the tamper-resistant record and enables business partners to access and supply IoT data without the intervention of central control and management. This chapter presents a blockchain-based design for the IoT applications that brings secure distributed data management to support transactions services within a multi-party global apparel business network, as shown in Figure 1.

BACKGROUND INFORMATION

In recent decades, it has become a significant tendency for the apparel industry to adopt decentralization as a new manufacturing paradigm. At the same time, advantages in data analysis give more insights into apparel production lines, thus improving its overall productivity. This enables more efficient operations and facilitates the shift from mass to customized production. This section presents a brief review of important aspects of service-oriented computing, the IoT based information system, and provide an introduction on the blockchain technology.

Service Oriented Computing

Service oriented computing platforms are mainly hosted in large-scale data centre environments that are empowered by the data communication networks. The consolidation and centralization of data centres, however, yield an increased distance between clients and services. This arrangement creates different outcomes in high variability in latency and bandwidth. To address this issue, particularly with regards to resource-intensive and interactive applications, decentralized service-oriented computing architectures, namely cloudlets, have emerged. Cloudlets are small-scale data centres that are situated nearer to users and can mitigate low latency and high bandwidth guarantees. This research embraces this locality-aware data storage and processing trend and brings it to its full potential with decentralized access control layer which ensures ownership and secure sharing of data.

IoT Ecosystems

The Internet of Things (IoT) is a smart worldwide network of interconnected objects, which through unique address schemes can interact with each other and cooperate with their neighbours to reach common goals. The primary purpose of the IoT is to share information acquired by objects, which reflects the manufacture, transportation, consumption and other details of textile and clothing industries detail. The gathered information can be used for effective operational decision making.

The prompt and effective decision not only depend on reasoning techniques but also the quality and quantity of data. Every major apparel manufacturing paradigm has been supported by the advancement of Information Technology (IT) and its applications. For example, the wide adoption of enterprise resource planning (ERP) and industrial business processes automation made flexible apparel manufacturing systems feasible. It includes the technologies for computer-aided textile design, computer-aided garment development, and computer-aided process planning made computer integrated apparel manufacturing practical. In developing enterprise systems (ESs), more and more enterprises rely on the professional providers of IT software service to replace or advance their conventional systems. Therefore, it makes sense to examine the evolution of the IT infrastructure and evaluate its impact on the evolution of apparel business process automation paradigms, when a new IT (e.g. blockchain technology) becomes influential.

Blockchain Technology

A blockchain is defined as a "digital, decentralized and distributed ledger in which transactions are logged and added in chronological order to create permanent and tamperproof records". Essentially, it is a novel mechanism for storing, securing and sharing data between multiple nodes in a network. A blockchain breaks away from the traditional centralized approach by managing chain data across a distributed and interlinked network of nodes. The main characteristics of blockchains are shared recordkeeping, immutability, decentralization, distributed trust, multiple-party consensus, independent validation, tamper evidence, and tamper resistance. The term blockchain gained its popularity as the output of a combination of configured technologies, tools and methods underpinning the cryptocurrency - Bitcoin. Bitcoin is a decentralized digital currency based on an open system of computer networks and online communication protocols and was the first successful application built on an online blockchain.

Blockchains can be configured to encrypt and store on-chain or off-chain data and record timestamped transactions. Furthermore, they can automate agreements through the utilization of smart contracts to run procedures based upon a set of conditions, terms, and rules that participants in the system have agreed upon. A blockchain platform can support multi-party exchange relationships in global supply chains by authenticating participant identities, authorizing their access and enhancing recordkeeping of transactions. This capability is possible by cryptographic mechanisms and recursive hashing of blocks. Each block contains a header and a body, the former of which contains the hash of the previous block, thus connecting the individual blocks. Any attempt to tamper with a block necessitates that the headers of previous and consecutive blocks be changed accordingly to avoid detection, and it gets progressively more difficult to tamper with as the chain gets longer. Since their pervasiveness and distributed nature characterize IoT networks, a centralized approach to collecting, storing, and analyzing all relevant supply chain data may cause delays and lead to a situation often referred to a single point of failure. A blockchain, therefore, has the potential to address the challenges mentioned above and provide supply chain exchange partners with trust based on decentralization. The lack of centralized controls in blockchains ensures a high-level of scalability and robustness by using resources of all involved nodes and eliminating many-to-one traffic flows.

Figure 2. A simple blockchain structure

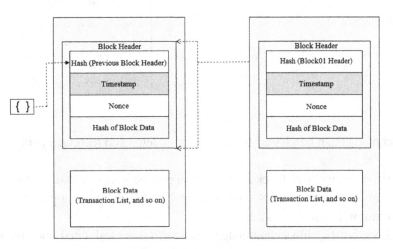

Blockchain is a distributed data structure comprising a chain of blocks. Blockchain acts as a distributed database or a global ledger that maintains records of all transactions on a blockchain network. The transactions are time-stamped and bundled into blocks where each block is identified by its cryptographic hash. The blocks form a linear sequence where each block references the hash of the previous block, forming a chain of blocks called the '*blockchain*'. A blockchain is maintained by a network of nodes and every node executes and records the same transactions. The blockchain is replicated among the nodes in the blockchain network. Any node in the network can read the transactions. Figure 2 shows the structure of a blockchain.

Blockchain technology, at its core, features an immutable distributed ledger, a decentralized network that is cryptographically secured. Blockchain architecture gives participants the ability to share a ledger, through peer-to-peer replication, which is updated every time a block of the transaction is agreed to be committed.

The technology can reduce operational costs and friction, create immutable transformation records, and enable transparent ledgers where updates are nearly instantaneous. It may also dramatically change the way workflow and business procedures are designed inside an enterprise and open-up new opportunities for innovation and growth.

Figure 3. Structural parts of a blockchain

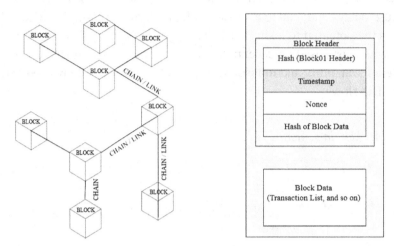

Blockchain technology can be viewed from a business, legal and technical perspective:

- From a business perspective, blockchain is an exchange network that facilitates the transfer of value, assets, or other entities between willing and mutually agreeing participants, ensuring privacy and control of data to stakeholders.
- From a legal perspective, blockchain ledger transactions are validated, indisputable transactions, which do not require intermediaries or trusted third-party legal entities.
- From a technical perspective, blockchain is a replicated, distributed ledger of transactions with ledger entries referencing other data stores (for additional information related to ledger transactions). Cryptography is used to ensure that network participants see only the parts of the ledger that are relevant to them, and that transactions are secure, authenticated and verifiable, in the context of permission business blockchains.

A blockchain is a historical record of all the transactions that have taken place in the network since the beginning of the blockchain. In general, a blockchain system consists of several **nodes**, as shown in Figure 4, each of which has a local copy of a **ledger**. In most systems, the nodes belong to different organizations. The nodes communicate with each other in order to gain agreement on the contents of the ledger and do not require a central authority to coordinate and validate transactions.

The process of gaining this agreement is called ***consensus***, and there are a few different algorithms that have been developed for this purpose. Users send transaction requests to the blockchain in order to perform the operations the chain is designed to provide. Once a transaction is completed, a record of the transaction is added to one or more of the ledgers and can never be altered or removed. This property of the blockchain is called ***immutability***.

Cryptography is used to secure the blockchain itself and the communications between the elements of the blockchain system. It ensures that the ledger cannot be altered, except by the addition of new transactions. Cryptography provides integrity on messages from users or between nodes and ensures operations are only performed by authorized entities.

Figure 4. Components of a generalized blockchain

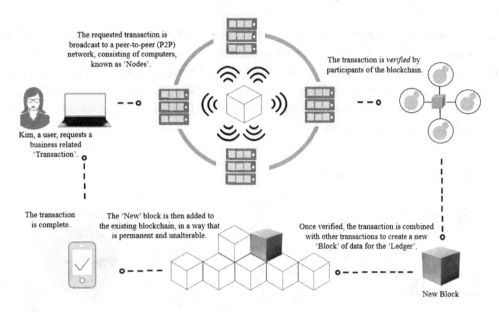

The authority to perform transactions on a blockchain can use one of two models, ***permissioned*** or ***permissionless***. In a permissioned blockchain, users must be enrolled in the blockchain before they can perform transactions. The enrollment process gives the user credentials that are used to identify the user when he or she performs transactions. In a permissionless blockchain, any person can perform transactions, but they are usually restricted from performing operations on any data but their own.

Most business-oriented blockchains include the ability to use ***smart contracts***, sometimes called ***chaincode***. A smart contract is an executable software module that is developed by the blockchain owners, installed into the blockchain itself and enforced when pre-defined rules are met. When a user sends a transaction to the blockchain, it can invoke a smart contract module which performs functions defined by the creator of that module. Smart contracts usually can read and write to local data stores which is separate from the blockchain itself and can be updated when transactions occur. The business logic contained in a smart contract creates or operates on business data that is contained in this persistence data store.

In a simple blockchain, every node is identical, and every copy of the ledger is identical. However, more complex blockchains allow differences in the nodes and the ledgers. Some blockchains support the concept of ***subchains***, which are sometimes called ***channels***.

Subchains are logically separate chains that occupy the same physical blockchain. Each subchain may be owned by a different entity and may be accessible to a different set of users. Nodes may be set up so that some nodes participate in certain subchains and not in other subchains. The result of this configuration is that the ledger on some nodes will contain transactions for that subchain while the ledgers on other nodes will not. Another variation on the basic blockchain is one in which nodes are assigned specific purposes instead of being identical in their function. This configuration may be used to optimize performance since the system can be faster if every node does not have to perform every operation required for a transaction on the chain.

Automated Transactions and Smart Contracts

An important character of blockchain technology is its automated smart contract. In a smart contract, the transactions will execute only when the predefined conditions are met. This possibility widely known as a "Smart Contract" creates the option of automated financial transactions. The "contract" is defined in software and stored in the blockchain. Once agreed between the parties, the execution of the "contract" is entirely automated, with no need for third-party authority and no possibility of modification. The steps of a smart contract are shown in Figure 5.

Figure 5. Concept of blockchain contract

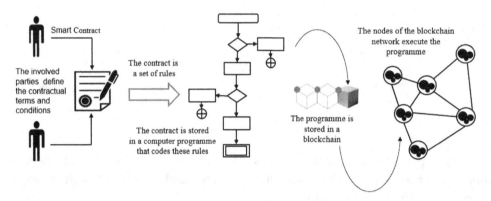

Blockchain is one of the most hyped innovation these days, and it has been gaining a lot of attention as an information technology to be widely adopted in various areas (e.g. automated payments, trace and track transactions, information sharing among business partners) in the global manufacturing business. Since its inception in 2008 (Nakamoto, 2008), blockchain continued to emerge as a disruptive innovation that will revolutionize the way business community interact, automate different types of information exchange in the context of global supply chain management.

The blockchain technology can reduce operational costs and friction, create transformation records that are immutable, and enable transparent ledgers where updates are nearly instantaneous. It may also dramatically change the way workflow and business procedures are designed inside an enterprise and open-up new opportunities for innovation and growth.

One of blockchain's direct benefits is that it provides a possible solution to identity management. Blockchain can be used in a manufacturing supply chain network to know who is performing what actions. Moreover, the time and location of the actions can be determined.

Blockchain provides a valid and effective measurement of outcomes and performance of key supply chain management business activities. Once the inputs tracking data are on a blockchain ledger, they are immutable. Other suppliers in the supply chain network can also track shipments, deliveries, and progress. In this way, blockchain produces trust among suppliers. By getting rid of middleman auditors, the efficiency of business processes can be improved, and costs can be reduced. Individual suppliers can perform their checks and balances on a nearly real-time basis.

Blockchain also enhances the ability of an accurate way of measuring product quality during transportation. For example, by analyzing data on the travel path and duration, stakeholders in a manufacturing supply chain can know whether the product was in a wrong place or whether it remained in a location for too long. Blockchain can provide traceability history of a product and by doing this counterfeit product can be traced with ease. In this way, the blockchain-based information system may give the customers confidence that the product is genuine and of high quality and make them significantly more willing to purchase the manufactured item.

Academics and practitioners have advocated blockchain as the biggest innovation in computer science (Tapscott, 2016). The World Economic Forum (WEF, 2015) proposes blockchain to be among six computing "mega-trends" that are likely to shape the world in the coming decades. It is worth to consider the industrial advantages of blockchain application in key manufacturing supply chain activities. Researchers have begun to grapple with this nascent trend of blockchain deployment in different organizational objectives, and particularly the use of various information system architectures using blockchain technology in conjunction with other information technologies (IoT, Service Oriented Computing, and so on) for manufacturing business process automation.

ENTERPRISE INFORMATION SYSTEM ARCHITECTURE

Service oriented computing (SOC), and IoT applications are key technologies that will have a huge impact in the next decades for apparel manufacturing supply chain management. This section describes how SOC technology will improve efficiencies, providing new business opportunities, address regulatory requirements, and improve transparency and visibility of global apparel manufacturing activities.

Figure 6. Enterprise information system architecture for an apparel business

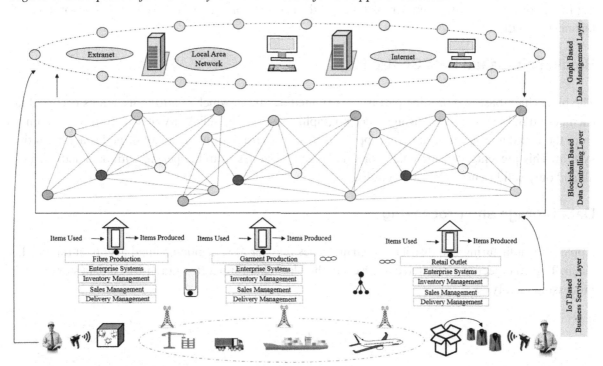

Table 1. The research issues of combing IoT with blockchain technology

Internet of Things (IoT)	Blockchain Technology
Scalability	IoT devices such as sensors have limited computing capability, which is both difficult and computation point of view costly to enhance performance. Again, the blockchain technology has a decentralized architecture without central control. The rights and obligations of any node in the blockchain are the same, and each node has a complete record of transactions. In order to assess effectiveness and scalability of IoT-based blockchain technology, early implementation and performance evaluation are important research challenge.
Security	With the proliferation of global apparel business exchange partner relationships, textile and clothing industries are driven to protect their data and information as well as the integrity of their physical objects to protect against theft and different types of illicit trade including diversion and counterfeiting. In addition, blockchain-based information systems can transform the potential advantages of IoT and bridging the difference of device-data interoperability while keeping security and privacy intact.
IoT data storage	There are research issues regarding design decisions of IoT data streams, storage and processing applications.

The IoT systems allow capturing real-time manufacturing business processes data from plant-level operational environment. The enterprise architecture for distributed apparel manufacturing supply network used for current research is shown in Figure. 6. This architecture mainly consists of three layers: (i) IoT-based service, (ii) blockchain-based data controlling, and (iii) data storage and processing part.

IoT-based Service Layer

The development of the IoT has created many devices, such as sensors, interconnected and interoperable devices for data collection and exchange. The data obtained from the IoT can make apparel manufacturing more convenient through numerous types of decision-making at all its levels and areas of apparel business activities.

Blockchain-based Data Controlling

The blockchain-based controlling part is a distributed database, which record transactions occurred in each period in blocks, chained using of cryptographic hashes. The reliability of such a structure comes from the fact that every transaction is approved by a consensus of the majority of nodes acting in the system. This prevents any single node or small group of nodes from tampering with data and ensures all and only valid transactions are recorded.

Data Storage and Processing

Apparel manufacturing and distribution chain nodes register as semantic-enabled agents in the blockchain. Tagged objects are registered as assets in the blockchain supported graph-based data storage and processing facility.

Emerging Issues in Blockchain Based Application Deployment

The acceptance of IoT-based technological solution, the use of Electronic Product Code (EPC) for individual products identification purpose, as well as of EPC global network for nearly real-time data gathering, object tracking and different types of business services providing a greatly improve accuracy for supply chain operation management (Pal, 2019).

Blockchain-based technologies allow for the decentralized aggregation of vast amounts of data generated from IoT devices and ensure that benefits are shared more equitably across supply chain exchange partners. Some of the research issues (e.g. scalability, security, and traceability) are highlighted in Table 1.

Blockchain facilitates machine-to-machine interaction where sensors and IoT devices attached to machinery will be synchronized, resulting in high flexibility and collaboration with exchange partners. The importance of this new capability lies in the secure communication, confidentiality, and integrity of the exchange transactions. Users can transact with the machine directly and engage in on-demand manufacturing services by sending transactions to a registered machine. Blockchain-based distributed ledgers that harness smart contracts enable the embedding of business logic covering a wide range of purposes such as payment conditions, product acceptance, smart inventory replacement, predictive maintenance, and repairs.

By combining blockchain technology and IoT, business information exchange partners gain new and timely insights into their supply chain in real-time with more precise and reliable information about key processes, events, and product attributes – such as quality, performance and availability. This fusion of IoT and blockchain technology can help to enhance end-to-end traceability and enable rapid recall capabilities of unsafe goods. As a result, exchange partners will be informed about the products, potential risks, and the preventative and corrective actions needed for sustaining enough flow of safe products to the final consumers.

RELATED RESEARCH WORKS

Academics and practitioners identified industrial business processes, particularly supply chain and logistics management, are important areas for deploying IoT based information system applications (Atkore, Iera & Morabito, 2018) (Gubbi et al., 2013). IoT based industrial information systems can enhance the competitiveness of enterprise through more effective tracking of the flow of raw materials, leading to improve the effectiveness and efficiencies of business processes (Shroud, Ordieres & Miragliotts, 2014). In the context of globalized business practice, with multiple collaborating-partners based supply chains, IoT-based applications enhance to facilitate the sharing of more precise and timely information relevant to production, quality control, distribution and logistics (Chen, Guo & Bao, 2014). However, researchers expressed their concern regarding standalone IoT-based applications along with global supply chain management (Pal, 2020). The main concerns were raised on the issues of standalone IoT systems security and privacy.

Different hybrid information system architectures (e.g. IoT with blockchain, cloud based IoT and blockchain technology) have been proposed by the research community. A blockchain enhances IoT-based applications tamper-resistant characteristics. In recent years, different blockchain-based information management systems have been reported by researchers. For example, IBM has developed a new blockchain-based service that is designed to track high-value items through complex supply chains in a secure cloud-based application system (Kim, 2016). Another exemplary industrial application is a fine-wine Provence-tracking service, known as the Chai Wine vault, developed by London-based Company Ever ledger (Finextra, 2016) in business-partnership with fine-wine expert Maureen Downey. Blockchain-based digital identification tools for physical property and packaging have been reported for enhancing high-value parts for supply chain management (Arrear, 2017). An innovative anti-counterfeit application, called Block Verify, is designed and deployed for tracking anti-counterfeit products (Hulse apple, 2015) to create a sustainable business world. A start-up company from Finland (i.e. Kouvola) in partnership with IBM, developed a smart tendering application for the supply chain management. The reported application is built on an automatic blockchain-based smart contract (Banker, 2016). Another blockchain-based smart contract, called SmartLog, the application was launched by Kouvola in recent years (AhIman, 2016).

In recent decades, due to globalization manufacturing supply chain networks are going through an evolutionary change through continued digitization of its business practices. These global manufacturing chains are evolving into value-creating networks where the value chain itself turns into an important source of competitive advantage. At the same time, developments are in progress to integrate blockchain technology with other innovative technological solutions (e.g. IoT-based applications, cloud-based solutions, and fog computing-based automation), leading to novel structures of modern apparel manufacturing supply chains, new types partnerships, holistic mechanisms of collaboration and value enhancing applications for the global apparel business. The reported research in this chapter is one of these values creating applications, which explains the adoption of IoT-based item description and use in blockchain infrastructure, in order to reap the combined advantages for future-generation apparel business supply chain management.

FUTURE RESEARCH DIRECTIONS

Beyond geographical boundaries, the combination of blockchain with IoT can be delayed by both regulatory uncertainties and the lack of industry standards. Although blockchain technology could enhance peer-to-peer connectivity between supply chain exchange partners, the integration of blockchain and IoT challenges some of the institutional assumptions common in international business. Indeed, harmonization (or 'equivalency' between sovereign states) of data protection laws remains a problem, while stronger industry self-regulation to govern and control the access to data and organize their transmission both nationally and globally is a requirement. It is still unclear how disparate blockchain technologies and systems will interoperate with each other and integrate with other technological artefacts. This is compounded by the existence of unreliable and inefficient transmission standards and protocols that clog the arteries of information sharing between the exchange partners. Additionally, an IoT environment is inherently dynamic, unpredictable and affected by the ever-changing laws and regulations related to security and other interoperability requirements. Such sudden variability and chaotic nature necessitate new laws and regulations in the manufacturing business world. In future, this research will review most of these challenges and will try bringing together potential solutions for naïve manufacturing operational managers.

CONCLUSION

Today's textile and clothing supply chain face significant volatility, uncertainty and complexity imposed by a dynamic operating environment. Changes in customer buying pattern – the demand for lower price, higher service levels, mobile commerce and so on – necessitate customer intelligence and varying fulfilment models. These have introduced significant stress on apparel manufacturing supply chain networks, compelling clothing businesses to revisit their supply chain design strategies. It includes the deployment of appropriate information systems that enhance supply chain execution. In such scenarios, enterprise information systems architecture plays a very important role.

This chapter presents a hybrid enterprise information systems architecture, which consists of IoT applications and a blockchain-based distributed ledger to support transaction services within-in a multi-party global apparel business network. The IoT is a smart worldwide network of interconnected objects, which through unique address schemes can interact with each other and cooperate with their neighbour to reach common goals. The data obtained from the IoT applications along apparel business processes can make operational decision-making much easier. However, standalone IoT application systems face security and privacy related problems.

Security and business organizational issues tend to enhance the need to build an apparel manufacturing supply chain management system leveraging blockchain ledger technology. Regardless of the particularities of the specific textile manufacturing supply chain related application, blockchain can offer a wide range of advantages. By registering and documenting a product's (e.g. cotton, fibre, textile cloths) lifecycle across the manufacturing supply chain nodes increases the transparency and the trust of the participating business-partners. Finally, the chapter presents the research proposition outlining how blockchain technology can impact important aspects of the IoT system and thus provide the foundation for future research challenges.

REFERENCES

AhIman. (2016). *Finish city partners with IBM to validate blockchain application in logistics.* https://cointelegraph.com/news/finish-city-partners-with-ibm-to-validate-blockchain-application-in-logistics

Atzori, L., Iera, A., & Morabito, G. (2010). The Internet of Things: A survey. *Computer Networks, 54*(15), 2787–2805. doi:10.1016/j.comnet.2010.05.010

Banker, S. (2016). *Will blockchain technology revolutionize supply chain applications?* https://logisticsviewpoints.com/2016/06/20/will-block-chain-technology-revolutionize-supply-chain-applications/

Chen, I.-R., Guo, J., & Bao, F. (2014). Trust management for service composition in SOA-based IoT systems. *Proceedings of the IEEE Wireless Communications and Networking Conference (WCNC),* 3444-3449.

Finextra. (2016). *Everledger secures the first bottle of wine on the blockchain.* https://www.finextra.com/pressaritcle/67381/everledger-secures-the-first-bottle-of-wine-on-the-blockchain

Gubbi, J., Buyya, R., Marusic, S., & Palaniswami, M. (2013). Internet of Things (IoT): A vision, architectural elements, and future directions. *Future Generation Computer Systems, 29*(7), 1645–1660. doi:10.1016/j.future.2013.01.010

Hulseapple, C. (2015). *Block Verify uses blockchains to end counterfeiting and making world more honest.* https://cointelegraph.com/news/block-verify-uses-blockchains-to-end-counterfeiting-and-make-world-more-honest

Inera, A. (2017). *Bosch, Cisco, BNY Mellon, other launch new blockchain consortium.* https://www.reuters.com/article/us-blockchain-iot-idUSKBN15B2D7

Kim, N. (2016, July). IBM pushes blockchain into the supply chain. *Wall Street Journal.*

Nakamoto. (2008). *Bitcoin: A peer-to-peer electronic cash system.* Academic Press.

Pal, K. (2017). Supply Chain Coordination Based on Web Services. In H. K. Chan, N. Subramanian, & M. D. Abdulrahman (Eds.), *Supply Chain Management in the Big Data Era* (pp. 137–171). Hershey, PA: IGI Global Publication. doi:10.4018/978-1-5225-0956-1.ch009

Pal, K. (2019). Algorithmic Solutions for RFID Tag Anti-Collision Problem in Supply Chain Management. *Procedia Computer Science,* 929-934.

Pal, K. (2020). Internet of Things and Blockchain Technology in Apparel Supply Chain Management. In H. Patel & G. S. Thakur (Eds.), *Blockchain Applications in IoT Security.* Hershey, PA: IGI Global Publication.

Prahalad, C. K., & Mashelkar, R. A. (2010). Innovation's Holy Grail. *Harvard Business Review, July-August Issue, 88*(7/8), 132–141.

Shrouf, Mere, & Miragliotta. (2014). Smart factories in Industry 4.0: A review of the concept and of energy management approached in production based on the Internet of Things paradigm. *Proceedings of the IEEE International Conference on Industrial Engineering and Engineering Management,* 679-701.

Tapscott, D. (2016). *How will blockchain change banking? How won't it?* https://www.huffingtonpost.com/don.tapscott/how-will-blockchain-change_b_9998348.html

World Economic Forum. (2015). *Deep shift technology tipping points and societal impact survey report.* http://www3.weforum.org/docs/WEF_GAC15_Technological_Tipping_Points_report_2015.pdf

KEY TERMS AND DEFINITIONS

Block: A block is a data structure used to communicate incremental changes to the local state of a node. It consists of a list of transactions, a reference to a previous block and a nonce.

Blockchain: In simple, a blockchain is just a data structure that can be shared by different users using computing data communication network (e.g., peer-to-peer or P2P). Blockchain is a distributed data structure comprising a chain of blocks. It can act as a global ledger that maintains records of all transactions on a blockchain network. The transactions are time stamped and bundled into blocks where each block is identified by its *cryptographic hash*.

Cryptography: Blockchain's transactions achieve validity, trust, and finality based on cryptographic proofs and underlying mathematical computations between various trading partners.

Decentralized Computing Infrastructure: These computing infrastructures feature computing nodes that can make independent processing and computational decisions irrespective of what other peer computing nodes may decide.

Immutability: This term refers to the fact that blockchain transactions cannot be deleted or altered.

Internet of Things (IoT): The internet of things (IoT), also called the Internet of Everything or the Industrial Internet, is now technology paradigm envisioned as a global network of machines and devices capable of interacting with each other. The IoT is recognized as one of the most important areas of future technology and is gaining vast attention from a wide range of industries.

Provenance: In a blockchain ledger, provenance is a way to trace the origin of every transaction such that there is no dispute about the origin and sequence of the transactions in the ledger.

Supply Chain Management: A supply chain consists of a network of *key business processes* and facilities, involving end users and suppliers that provide products, services and information. In this chain management, improving the efficiency of the overall chain is an influential factor; and it needs at least four important strategic issues to be considered: supply chain network design, capacity planning, risk assessment and management, and performances monitoring and measurement. Moreover, the details break down of these issues need to consider in the level of individual business processes and sub-processes; and the combined performance of this chain. The coordination of these huge business processes and their performance improvement are the main objectives of a supply chain management system.

Warehouse: A warehouse can also be called storage area and it is a commercial building where raw materials or goods are stored by suppliers, exporters, manufacturers, or wholesalers, they are constructed and equipped with tools according to special standards depending on the purpose of their use.

Chapter 2
Redefining Trust and Disinter–Mediation With Blockchain in E–Governance

Jyoti Malhotra

iD https://orcid.org/0000-0002-1147-4549

*MIT Art, Design, and Technology University,
India*

Nagesh N. Jadhav

*MIT Art, Design, and Technology University,
India*

Rajneeshkaur Sachdeo-Bedi

*MIT Art, Design, and Technology University,
India*

Rekha Sugandhi

iD https://orcid.org/0000-0003-1349-6773

*MIT Art, Design, and Technology University,
India*

Sambhaji Sarode

*MIT Art, Design, and Technology University,
India*

ABSTRACT

Blockchain technology (BCT) is becoming a common language across diverse geographical domains. BCT attempts to solve the fraud issues involved in financial transactions and government operations. E-governance is a convenient platform providing services to all connected citizens and inter-government sectors. Traditional centralization issues are addressed by decentralizing the stakes, keeping the transactions transparent on an open ledger–BCT. It works on the notion of disintermediation eliding the middle layers with the highest trust level. It can contribute to various e-government sectors, namely agriculture, property registrations, supply chain management, tax calculation, etc. BCT application for agriculture supply change management can provide assistance in crop plantation and delivery records. It can bring transparency in land registrations and tax management by maintaining immutable land records and simplified tax management preserving trust between various parties through smart contracts. This chapter focuses on BCT approaches for secured governance.

DOI: 10.4018/978-1-7998-3632-2.ch002

INTRODUCTION

Blockchain technology (BCT), referred broadly as a distributed and fixed ledger system, tracking the transaction details and data interchange among the decentralized network is one of the assured technologies for the future. BCT employs the notion of disintermediation wherein, the middle layers are completely elided with the highest level of security and confidence. Therefore, it saves time, money, and provides direct benefits to the users with ease.

Blockchain is the next big attestation in the growth of Industry providing an easier platform to complete the tasks without interposing third-party applications. BCT threads multiple transaction blocks which are connected with each other. In BCT, an addition of a new block is based on the following events:

1.   Triggering the transaction or multiple transactions:

The transaction activity is bundled in the block along with the transaction information.

2.   Transaction verification: Confirm the transaction details such as date/time, amount, asset, ownership, and the transaction size.
3.   Store the transaction on the block: Post verification, the transaction is recorded on the block.
4.   Hash the block: A unique hash code is assigned to each block and is finally added to the chain of the blocks and is publicly visible.

BCT makes every person accountable for the work they do and avoids any disputes among them. BCT can contribute to various sectors namely, Healthcare, Agriculture, Property and vehicle registrations, Supply Chain Management, Digital Identity, Energy Markets, Financial services such as banking and tax calculation, content management covering the working of land and vehicle registration, and many more as shown in Figure 1. Every sector works on the tri-stage principle which comprises- managing the trust consent between stakeholders, exchanging data, and formulating the indices for further referral.

The extensive umbrella that can be enclosed in BCT is e-governance. E-Governance is a strong and convenient platform that provides government services to all connected entities like citizens, public sectors and even inter-government sectors. E-Governance includes services, as shown in Figure 2, are related to client property dealings, public surveys and census data management, financial and tax records, human resource management, etc (Moon, 2002). The major stakeholders or entities involved in the implementation and execution of these services majorly include government officials, authorities in the form of an automated system governed by local laws, citizens, other parallel ministries and third-parties like financial sectors, vendors and contractors. Currently, the e-Governance framework supports the government-intermediate-citizen model of communication for exchanging information, for doing transactions that may or may not involve financial transactions. At every level, however, this model proves expensive to citizens in terms of delay and financial overburden. Secondly, the trust involved in these transactions may be compromised in lieu of middlemen involved.

Figure 1. Blockchain Technology Framework

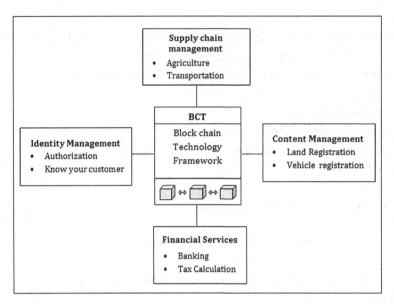

Figure 2. e-Governance Services

All the e-Governance services are facilitated with the help of various Information and Communication Technologies (ICT). The organization of the chapter is distributed in the following sections –

1. E-Governance Features and Implementation Challenges
2. Blockchain in Agriculture
3. Blockchain in the future of tax
4. Blockchain in land registrations
5. Conclusion

E-GOVERNANCE FEATURES AND IMPLEMENTATION CHALLENGES:

The design aspects for these services involve IT solutions that can cater to wide user communities with well-defined authorities (Government IT Initiatives, 2019), (CIOReview Team, 2019). The framework also demands constant monitoring and maintenance of the solutions. The desirable features of e-Governance services include:

1. **Accommodating Varied End-User Types**: Each unit has its own set of processes and operating standards. IT-enabled online services involving these parties lead to major design constraints on plug-n-play applications.
2. **Conformance To Changing Government Norms And Regulations:** The services thus provided should be regularly modified in the business logic so as to conform to all changes in government laws and regulations from time-to-time.
3. **Ever-Increasing User-Base:** The common citizens are increasingly getting technology-aware and have growing access to the latest ubiquitous devices. Therefore, their expectations and needs for technology-based solutions are constantly increasing.
4. **Border-Less Transactions:** Growing global business transactions necessitate the need for a platform that allows seamless and secure transactions across territorial borders. The internationalization of business norms is, therefore, a very important feature of e-Governance systems.
5. **The Digital Form Of Data:** It is easier to maintain a history of transactions and the related documented proof in digital form. It also makes it convenient and efficient to retrieve legacy data as well.
6. **Transparency In Transactions**: Most of the ICTs in E-Governance have been built on centralized systems that maintain data mapped to the digital identity of the involved parties. Designing them requires systems to have data maintained on centralized servers. Centralization facilitates data consistency for all stakeholders, but it also has its drawbacks. The major drawback of centralized systems is the susceptibility to tampering and failures. This issue can be addressed by decentralizing the stakes, keeping the transactions transparent and by implementing an open auditing system.
7. **Maintaining Evidence Of Transactions**: It is desirable to maintain transparency in all transactions, so that breach of trust can be controlled leading to secure and fool-proof outcomes
8. **Data Consistency**: Dealing with data duplication and integrity becomes a humongous challenge when it has to be maintained/shared across platforms and different units. The possibility of a data breach also highly increases when different departments refer to and use client information. The risks hike especially when the information needs to be updated from time to time.

9. **Faster Transactions**: The typical services communication model involves sequences of transactions involving government, intermediaries and the citizens. A particular service transaction may involve more than two or three entities there-by increasing hop-levels causing delay and financial overburden for the transaction.

Blockchain Technology can be an appropriate framework for the implementation of these features and challenges. BCT implementations have shown remarkable advancements in various trustworthy use cases and, E-Governance is one of them. For instance, establishing trust in the entities involved in an e-Governance transaction is one useful feature of BCT. Furthermore, this also contributes to reducing corruption in providing services to needy citizens. All eligible citizens will be benefited from the services by digitally proving their identity. In citizen-centric services, proving the identity of the end-beneficiary is a big challenge since the e-Governance system works on a two-way communication model. In this regard, BCT can help in certifying the identity of origin and proof of delivery in distinct abnormal situations.

The attractive BCT features that make it an obvious choice for upgrading the implementation of e-Governance services are (CIOReview Team, 2019), (Ministry of Electronics and Information Technology, 2019):

1. **Ability To Deal With Huge Data:** The Blockchain network can be implemented with the blocks contain actual data or with links to the actual data. Therefore, while working with large data repositories, the actual data need not necessarily be put on the network. Instead, the blocks in the network will contain IDs to the actual data.
2. **Decentralized Services**: The BCT transactions carried out in a decentralized environment ensure that all transactions are consensus-based where the participant nodes are kept transparently aligned to all the sequences of communication carried out in a contract.
3. **Immutable Transactions**: The Blockchain network ensures that the action once committed cannot be recalled. Therefore the transactions between the people and the government are immutable, thereby mandating a foolproof method to legalize the communications.
4. **Faster Services And Outcome**: Currently, the e-Governance framework supports the government-intermediate-citizen model of communication for exchanging information and making financial transactions. At every level, however, this model proves expensive to citizens in terms of delay and financial overburden.
5. **Disintermediation**: Secondly, the trust involved in these transactions may be compromised in lieu of middlemen involved. To counter this, BCT works on the notion of disintermediation wherein, the middle layers are completely elided with the highest level of security and confidence. Therefore, it saves time, money, and provides direct benefits to users with ease. Furthermore, this also contributes to reducing corruption in providing services to needy citizens.
6. **Stakeholders' Pay-Offs**: Each eligible citizen will be benefited from the services by proving their identity digitally. BCT makes every person accountable for the work they do and avoids any disputes among them.
7. **Identity-Protection**: In citizen-centric services, proving the identity of the end-beneficiary is a big challenge since the e-Governance system works on a two-way communication model. In this regard, BCT helps in certifying the identity of origin and proof of delivery in distinct abnormal situations. It is one of the assured technologies for the future and it has shown remarkable advancements in various trustworthy use cases.

Many organizations are adopting this persistent technology for making their business faster, secure, and reliable. Governments of the USA, Norway, Sweden, UAE, Ghana, South Korea, India, and many more have already pioneered Blockchain happenings in various aspects (Ølnes, Jansen, 2017),(Chung, 2015),(Suberg, 2019). Potential uses of BCT in governance covers a wider umbrella of identity management, asset management, financial services, and supply chain tracking. Figure 3 shows the generic BCT model applied to any Governance. The authenticity of the information can be verified directly by accessing the records from the Blockchain. Any modifications or alterations are time-stamped and are known to everyone. It has brought the trust through the system rather than depending on middlemen or software services and has shown a new way to make people accountable for their online activities. BCT not only removes the intermediate barriers but also makes every online entity accountable for each action they perform.

Figure 3. Blockchain Technology Framework for e-Governance services

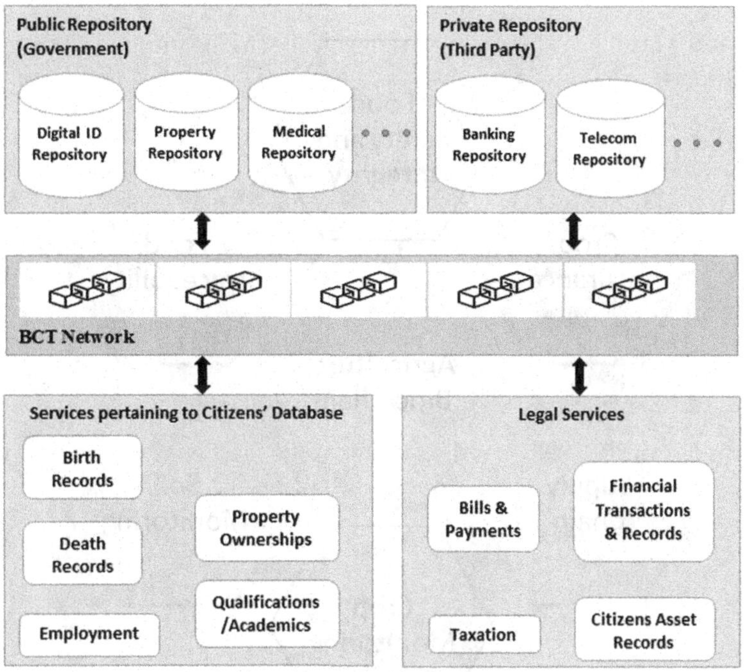

This chapter reflects the relevance of Blockchain with respect to agriculture, tax management, and land registrations. The crop or agriculture supply change management can provide great assistance in maintaining the unyielding records from the plantation of the crop, to its delivery to the market or to the customers. Such systems will increase the trust among the customers about agricultural products and their safety. BCT can bring transparency in land registrations by maintaining immutable records of sell-and-buy deeds for lands. It will also help in safekeeping digital records in case of natural calamities or disasters. Furthermore, BCT can be utilized to simplify the property registrations, and tax management with reference to the decentralized ledger; maintaining a trust relationship between various authorities and administrative domains. Smart contracts of BCT can contribute to calculating all the taxes and their payments in real-time reducing the risks of fraud and errors. Tampering of the property records can be violated by registering those as Blockchain transactions and maintaining their originality and ownership using smart contracts.

BLOCKCHAIN IN AGRICULTURE

With the proliferation of technological advancement, Blockchain technology is not only limited to financial, banking and healthcare domain but it can also be applied to other domains like E-governance. Agriculture is a less explored area as far as Blockchain is concerned. Blockchain technology provides a distributed and secure way of transaction which is an important aspect of agriculture Blockchain. The following are the areas of agriculture (refer Figure 4), which can be considered in Blockchain implementation.

Figure 4. E-governance-Agriculture and Blockchain

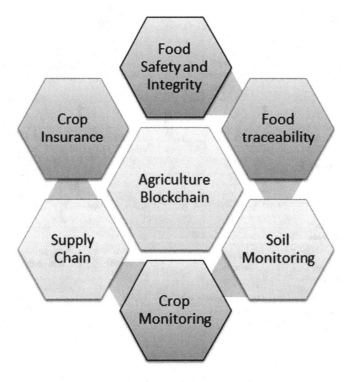

1.   Food Safety and Integrity

Most of the world's population falls sick because of contaminated food. As per the World Health Organization's (WHO) statistics, almost 1 in 10 people in the world fall ill due to consumption of contaminated food. Food safety deals with processing and storing food in a sanitized manner. Falsely labeled food items, long-distance shipping, processing delay at hubs contribute to reduced food safety. Blockchain can provide a transparent and efficient solution for food safety. The food integrity is concerned with the dependable exchange of the food in the supply chain. Implementation of Blockchain will bring transparency in food exchange also tracking the origin of the product will become easy (Andreas, Agusti, Francesc, & Prenafeta, 2019)

2. Food Traceability

The food industry is growing rapidly; however, it suffers from key challenges in the food supply chain like traceability, transparency, and liability. The Blockchain technology can help the companies to address these issues. The customers can easily find out the producer of the food, how it was produced and where it comes from. It can increase trust among the consumers of the industry. Walmart and Kroger are the first companies to implement Blockchain technology in supply chains.

3. Soil and Crop Monitoring

Internet of things (IoT) enabled devices are used to collect the sensory information from soil and crop in real-time. The collected information cannot be directly stored on the Blockchain. The information needs to be processed before it becomes part of the Blockchain. The latest machine learning algorithms can be applied to extract useful information, which can be stored in Blockchain for the use of all the stakeholders of the agriculture chain.

4. Crop Insurance

In crop insurance, the crucial fact is to settle the insurance claim. It involves lots of paperwork, on-field inspections and loss calculations. This may lead to a delay in claim settlement. Farmers in developing countries have a rolling financial cycle. They invest profit gained from one crop into the next crop. The delayed claim settlement process can distress the farming business. The use of Blockchain technology will reduce paperwork as well as claim settlement duration (Ledger Insights, 2019).

Many researchers have contributed to integrating Blockchain technology in the field of agriculture. In (Lin, Y.P. et al., 2017) Yu-Pin Lin et. al. have reviewed to ICT enabled BlockchainGe system. E-agriculture system with Blockchain concepts can provide transparency in agricultural data management. The key challenge in the use of Blockchain for ICT is scalability and high latency in the network. (Lan Ge et al., 2017) have done the pilot study in the use of Blockchain for agriculture and food. The use of Blockchain in the agri-food industry will help in reducing the burden on third parties for the certification of the food product. Implying BT will help in dealing with the risk of food adulteration and fraudulent labels certifying bad quality food products. They have demonstrated the use of proof of work for food certification in a concrete way. (Henry Kim and Marek Laskowski, 2018) have discussed the key challenges in agriculture addressing applications like food safety, local economy, and sustainable agriculture and agriculture finance.

In (Leng Kaijun et al., 2018) have proposed a dual chain agriculture resource public Blockchain. They have used transaction chain and user information chain for designing a Blockchain. Paper also focuses on security mechanisms for public domain Blockchain. (Daniel Tse et al., 2017) in their article discussed the information security of the food supply chain in detail. They have used empirical research methods and demand analysis for food supply chain Blockchain. The article demonstrates the decentralized authentication model for the food supply chain. The use of Blockchain technology can improve the supply chain effectively. This is been demonstrated by (Casado-Vara et al., 2018) in their research work.

The proposed multi-agent system can provide a solution for logistical problems in the supply chain. The smart contracts are used for buying and selling products.

(Papa Semou Faye, 2017) has proposed Blockchain for transparency and monitoring in agriculture trade. Blockchain will help in re-establishing trust in agriculture products. (Caro et al., 2018) have explained a layered AgriBlockIoT solution for food traceability in agriculture supply chain management. The solution is developed on the top of existing Blockchain implementations like Ethereum and Hyperledger Sawtooth. IoT devices are used for collecting information from various sources. Thus, it can be seen that the Blockchain technology helps in re-establishing trust in agriculture products.

Inspired from (Akash Takyar, 2019), the system as demonstrated in Figure 5 can be considered as one of the use cases supporting agriculture and Blockchain.

Figure 5. Agriculture Blockchain Use case

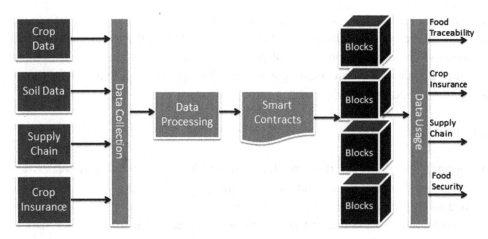

The process starts with the collection of data using IoT enabled devices from various resources. The collected data need to be processed in order to apply suitable machine learning approaches to extract the desired information. The next step is to develop smart contracts and Blockchain creation. The data on the Blockchain can be used to infer the required information and alterations as users need (refer to Table 1).

Table 1. Steps for Agriculture Blockchain

1. Collect the data from various sources like IOT enabled devices etc.
2. Process the data using existing pre-processing algorithms
3. Create smart contact for digital verification of the transactions
4. Hash the data and store it on Blockchain
5. Create Blockchain with hashed data
6. Exploit data stored on the Blockchain

BLOCKCHAIN: THE FUTURE OF TAX

This section covers the aspect and importance of BCT in regard to yet another compulsory e-governance service i.e. tax system which is imposed by the state or country on the individuals or businesses to the cost of goods or any transaction. Blockchain technology has the power to disrupt and redefine the taxation system in a better way against existing accounting systems by generating the smart contract. Introducing the Blockchain in the taxation system invites the major changes in the government databases and network systems. It will not only affect any particular sector but instead, it will also bring major changes in all areas of governmental activities. Mainly, it affects the legal systems, laws, intellectual property, and legal identities at a great extent. Though it seems difficult to implement it at the initial stages; considering the infrastructure cost but can be useful for the long run. Developing automated tax processes will help all involved stakeholders. Presently, in the developed countries payroll systems are digitalized but are vulnerable to many threats due to intermediaries involved. Blockchain would be an appropriate solution to address and assure the trust among the parties.

In case of the payroll tax, as soon as any institute issues the salary to any employee, spontaneously tax amount will be paid to the government without the involvement of any third party for ensuring the trust with the help of Blockchain. These involved steps can be viewed as follows:

1. The employer credits the salary to its employee account.
2. Using the Blockchain system, tax amount and social security amount are calculated with the help of smart contract technology.
3. Calculated tax is automatically transferred to Government.
4. Consequently, the payroll tax process becomes faster, cost efficient and effective cash-flow.

Presently, tax systems are paper-heavy and labor-intensive which makes auditing complicated and results in legal disputes. Few countries have made changes such as SAF-T in Europe and real-time electronic invoicing in South America. For instance in India, at present two taxes such CGST and SGST are calculated and paid to different governments, namely, Central Government and State Government. It is the responsibility of the concerned party to take care and ensure that it should be paid timely. In this regard, the institution has to hire services from a third trusted party to do the needful. Sometimes it leads to human errors, frauds, or delays in making the tax payment to concern government authorities. (Ernest, Marcjanna, Piotr, 2017). Therefore, it is essential to implement the system which takes efficient care with the highest degree of trust. Hence, Blockchain is the most suitable technology to design a trustworthy automatic model to do it.

In the case of transfer pricing, laws of transfer pricing are different in each country. A smart contract can take care of cross border transactions between involved parties. It becomes easy to track, helps in minimizing the risk and maintain the transparency among involved parties. (Jurgen G, 2018).

The idea of bringing the Blockchain in taxation system is not limited to:

1. Prevent a vast amount of papers in the taxation system
2. Reduce dependency heavily on third parties for the tax collection
3. Make it entirely digital
4. Make automatic calculations
5. Create code that itself becomes the witness for the obligation of any party if arises

Figure 6. Blockchain-based Tax system

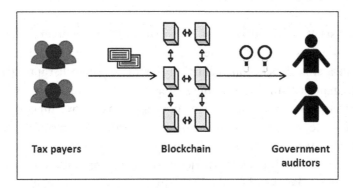

In tax systems, the filing process is very tedious due to constant changes in regulations executed by the government. It delays making the tax payments in time due to difficulty in understanding the new complicated system (Bulk, 2018). Therefore Blockchain in Taxation provides the following benefits:

1. Reduces the administrative burdens, saves time, and reduces the cost of accounting services.
2. All transactions are executed in real-time
3. Due to the smart contract, all the transactions are tamper-proof and transparent
4. Immediate understanding of company's finance
5. No delays in money transfer between business and government
6. No waiting period for returns due to real-time calculation time to time
7. Reduces fraud

Based on the survey of Blockchain solutions in taxation systems, it is observed that (Pokrovskaia, 2017) discussed how the taxation process would be developed automatically by avoiding the human interference at the regional and global level. The process of tax payment can speed up with the help of Blockchain technology; it will make the transaction(s) to the concerned authority with applicable rules and regulations in respective jurisdictions. It not only helps in removing the in-between barriers but also reduces the chances of manual taxation errors and saves time to a great extent which improvises the overall system performance. In (Z. Lu, etc all, 2019) proposed the Bis: A Novel Blockchain-based Bank-tax Interaction System in Smart City model to address the higher credit costs and difficulties in controlling risks. It ensures the openness of tax data in an inter-enterprise bank tax interactive business system. While addressing this challenge it assures the security and trustworthiness of tax data for enterprises. The fabric framework is used to make it more secure and reduces the additional overheads. The coalition chain such as a super-book is built for making authorized transactions to prevent unauthorized access. In (Filip Fatz, 2019) discussed various current challenges to address the compliance problem and their violations; therefore, in this article authors have proposed the technique using BT to achieve the different solution objectives. The solution objectives are defined on the basis of removing the barriers or hurdles occur during the taxation process. It mainly focused the compliance and noncompliance issues related to auditing the taxation. Presently, if something goes wrong during audit then auditing entity is held legally liable instead of addressing the issues digitally with automation for preventing in future. The improvising manual system is a very hectic process; thus, it is the need for present systems for the smooth functioning of the taxation system.

Figure 6 shows the working of Blockchain-based taxation (Charles, 2018). It illustrates how every individual is connected to the Blockchain network for making payment timely without any tedious process. The Blockchain network maintains the track of each person in the blocks and uses it for retrieving the necessary information for a particular purpose.

Furthermore, government organizations can verify the records as a part of the audit process. It saves the time to process the tax and immediate refunds will be credited if applicable. This brings the complete distributed approach to make the taxation system digitized with a greater level of security. Figure 7 describes how the Blockchain-based taxation system eliminates the intermediates to make timely processing (Tarasenko, 2019) of tax payments. This system is highly essential to make the payment of the tax amount transparent. It clearly shows the transparency in executing the tax amount timely and hassle-free. Therefore, adopting the Blockchain-based system is nowadays a necessity.

Figure 7. Blockchain-based taxation system versus Traditional taxation system

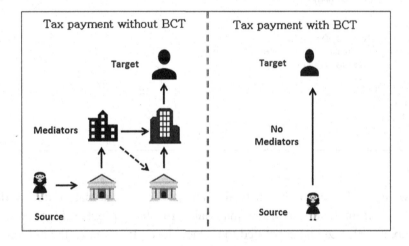

In this section, let us understand how Blockchain contributes to the role of calculating the goods tax and pays to the government. Let us consider the example of the Indian government of tax payment. Goods and Service Tax (GST) comprises Central-GST and State-GST. Both are applicable to every goods and service that are being sold or offered respectively at various levels.

Figure 8. Blockchain in Tax payment

Table 2. Smart contract for Tax Payment

```
contract IncomeTax {
// Model a incomeTax
struct incomeTax {
uint Salary;
uint Tax;
uint eduCess;
string public ownerName;
address SGST;
address SGST;
address government;
address landDetails;

constructor () public {
incomeTax(GST);
}
Function incomeTax(uint _salary) payable public{
If (_salary < 250000){
        Tax = eduCess;
}
If (_salary > 250000 && _salary < 500000){
        Tax = eduCess + (_salary - 2500000) * 1;
}
If (_salary > 500000)
        Tax = eduCess + (_salary - 2500000) * 15;
// Accordingly cases can be put for remaining slabs for tax calculations
// Calculate and Pay SGST & CGST as per rules
government.transfer(CGST_Tax);
government.transfer(SGST_Tax);
employee.transfer(_salary);
//Code is for illustration purpose only
}
}
```

Figure 8 shows how Blockchain automatically adjusts the tax calculation during the payment. It reduces the overheads from the origin of raw material to finish the product. In a traditional system, at every stage, the tax is collected and submitted to the next level. It increases the burden on the government to return back to concern stakeholders after verification. Finally, the tax amount is collected from the consumer. Using Blockchain technology the additional calculations of tax during the payment process are completely reduced with the help of a smart contract. The smart contract reduces the layering overheads and fraud cases drastically.

Smart contract contributes for better planning, fewer frauds, and efficient economy (Thomas, 2019). The association of tax collection and government benefit can be related as:

1.   More collection of costs leads to Greater tax share to the government
2.   Adequate information primes Efficient planning
3.   Better transparency guarantees Minimal fraud cases

Therefore, the effective implementation of smart contracts allows the transferring of tax efficiently and a more trustworthy manner to the government. Here we present the Smart contract for "incomeTax" and it cited in Table 2 as described in the following steps:

1. Create a custom type structure incomeTax describes the tax payment calculation process and indicates that how tax is calculated. The distribution of tax payments for CGST and SGST can be designed as per government rules and can be transferred accordingly.
2. Create a function incomeTax illustrates the tax calculations.
3. Transfer tax to the government

Smart contract – *"IncomeTax"* can be further extended to integrate consumer-government by adding new fields to the structure for CGST and SGST functions (e.g. string supplier_name, string type, uint tax_payments, etc). New functions can be added for –

1. Tax calculation at goods origin to consumer layers
2. Immediate refund process
3. On-time tax processing
4. Tax amount bifurcation to concern government authorities
5. Tax transfer

BLOCKCHAIN IN LAND REGISTRATION

This section explores the primary role of Blockchain technology to improvise content management of land records focusing on aspects such as privacy, record authenticity, land ownership, and secured buy-sell deeds.

Land or property ownership is one of the valuable and targeted areas where fraud or disputes can materialize very easily. Components involved in land content management can include -

1. Property/land details
2. Ownership rights associated with land
3. Multiple ownership
4. Buy-sell deed
5. Rental agreement
6. Bank loan details
7. Tax payment
8. Insurance coverage

These ownership and land exchange information is recorded by the land governance to document the asset profile for tax payment and later usage. This documentation becomes messy and is easily liable for fraud with thousands of records. In the traditional land registry system; these records are either stored as a manual paper-based ledger or on the cloud storage database; manual records are highly exposed for mutations and theft, while cloud storage is vulnerable to the security breach and meddling. This traditional registry method can clue various land frauds and can get altered. For instance, in the land exchange transaction, the seller can lead to sell the same piece of land to more than one buyer and fraud them on the monetary terms. Moreover, tenants or middlemen or brokers can tamper the land records to claim asset ownership and share(s). Furthermore, a group of rowdy punk can privilege the possession of an unattended land portion. Thus the old-style process of maintaining the land records is –

1. Not transparent to everyone.
2. Easily mutable and liable for any alterations.
3. Time-consuming in recording the registration information and authenticating the same.
4. Less secure and less coordinated; prone to security breaches and tampering.

Blockchain can steer a ubiquitous and matured decentralized ledger (Peiró, Martinez, 2017) and accelerate the process of storing land registry transactions. These records can be handled with permission and public Blockchain (Androulaki, Barger, Bortnikov, Cachin, Christidis, De Caro, & Muralidharan, 2018); wherein only authorized users can upload or modify the transactions and are viewed publicly.

(Thakur et.al, 2019) explores the application of BCT in the administration of land details in India. The author addresses various issues in the existing process of recording the land registry and presents the importance of Blockchain to overcome them through favored technology platforms- Ethereum and smart contracts. Authors also point to various challenges in implementing Blockchain in developing countries such as proof of concepts, lack of experts, fear in the minds of personnel due to irreversible nature of transactions, latency issues of the network and many more. In yet another article (Bamasag et.al. 2020), the authors discover the role of tamper-proof Blockchain technology in real-life activities including real estates, and intellectual property. It highlights the process of storing the property details over the Blockchain and uses its security in uploading the official documents, transfer the land ownership, selling the land, reserving and buying the land. (Hudson & Sloan 2019) articulates the risks involved in co-owned or jointly owned registered lands. The author highpoints the importance of a distinctive Blockchain approach to make the process not easily accessible and vulnerable. As the details are recorded on the secured blocks, BCT prevents the risks of mistaken identity, imitating the dead owner, property transfer without the consent of the co-owner to maintain the correctness of the land details. In (Phan & Mentzer 2019), the authors address the common issues, challenges, frauds, security, privacy related to BCT and real-time applications. The author points out the importance of Blockchain technology in financial services, supply chain, and integrity parameters.

With respect to land registration, post literature review we found that, in BCT, with the transaction blocks, every change in the land details and ownership of land trading can be recorded as a new transaction block in the ledger. Thus, as it lessens the ability to interfere with the records. Landowners or buyers can automatically verify the ownership and eligibility to sell-buy the property. Buy-sell deed transactions can be recorded on the secured Blockchain platform; these transactions can also be verified by the bank for sanctioning the loan for the authorized personnel and real-time programmed payments.

Smart contracts (Bhargavan et.al, 2016), code agreements of predefined rules help to understand the partakers and edge a detailed digital transaction. These auto-run contracts contribute to preventing the frauds on the open ledger and efficiently deal the access rights between the partakers. The legal steps involved in land registry transactions such as- ownership rights, sale deeds, rental agreements, and bank payments can be easily coded using smart contracts. Smart contracts can be written in various programming languages (The Blockchain Council, 2019) such as C++, Solidity, Javascript, Java, and Golang. With respect to land registration, here we present the smart contracts for:

1. Uploading land ownership details
2. Buy-sell deed activities on the Blockchain

Figure 9. Uploading land ownership details

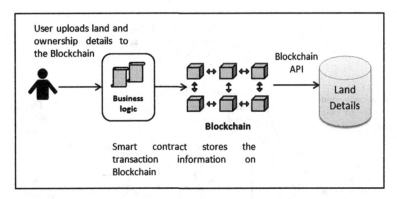

The examples quoted here address the smart contract written in Solidity (Ethereum Revision 7709ece9, 2019).

Table 3. Smart contract for uploading the details

```
contract LandDepartment {
struct LandRecord { // Model a LandRecord
     uint landID;
     string public ownerName, landAddress, landDetails;
     uint ownerIdentity;
     uint landValue;
}
mapping(address => LandRecord) public lands;
address[] public landAccts;

constructor () public {
uploadLand(LandRecord);
}
function uploadLand (address _address, uint _landID, string _ownerName, string _landAddress, string _landDetails, uint _
ownerIdentity, uint _landValue) public {
     var land = landAccts[_address];
     land.landID = _landID;
     land.ownerName = _ownerName;
     land.landAddress = _landAddress;
     land.landDetails = _landDetails;
     land.ownerIdentity = _ ownerIdentity;
     land.landValue = _landValue;
     landAccts.push(_address); //push the new land record address to the array of landAccts.
}
function viewLands() view public returns (address[]) {
     return landAccts;
}
function viewSpecificLand(address spec) view public returns (uint, string, string, string, uint, uint) {
     return (lands[spec].landID, lands[spec].ownerName, lands[spec].landAddress, lands[spec].landDetails, lands[spec]. ownerIdentity,
lands[spec].landValue);
}
}
```

Figure 10. Buy-Sell Deed activities on the Blockchain

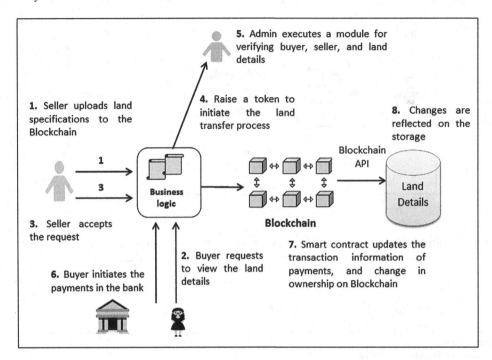

Figure 9 highlights the process of uploading land ownership details on the secured ledger with the help of smart contracts and Blockchain transactions. User uploads the land specifications and ownership details through the front-end client interface; these details are further fetched by business logic to write a smart contract storing the transaction information on the Blockchain as quoted in Table 3. Later, the details are uploaded to the land details storage through Blockchain Application Programming Interface (API) and LevelDB/CouchDB (Androulaki et. al, 2018); for further querying and fetching.

Smart contract – *"LandDepartment"* cited in Table 3 is described in the following steps:

1. Create a custom type structure *LandRecord* to define the land record storing the details such as – land identifier, owner name, land address (house number, town, city, state, country, pin code), land details (area, insurance, loan, tax, land type-agricultural/nonagricultural), owner identity (ID proof) along with land's market value.
2. *Map* a <key, value> pair of land with its address i.e. lands are referred by their addresses.
3. Create an array of *landAccts* to store all the land accounts of the ledger.
4. Create a function *uploadLand()* to upload land details entered by the user.
5. Create a function *viewLands()* to view all land records.
6. Create a function *viewSpecificLand()* to view the details for a specific land.

Figure 9 can be further extended to sketch the trusted buy-sell deed as drafted in Figure 10. The process schemes involved between seller, buyer, and land registry database along with the business logic of Blockchain in different steps is as mentioned below:

1.   Seller, Jack uploads land specifications and ownership details to the Blockchain.
2.   Buyer, Anna learns about the land and requests the view rights for the land specifications.
3.   Jack accepts Anna's requests to view the land details.
4.   Jack through the business logic raises a token to start the verification and complete the authentic land transfer process.
5.   Admin fetches the transaction details through smart contract(s) and verifies the identity of the buyer and seller. Land details are also validated for ownership and correctness.
6.   Upon successful user verification and land validation; Anna obtains a token to initiate the payment through a registered bank.
7.   Bank validates the identity of Anna through a smart contract and releases the payment in Jack's account.
8.   Every doings in the trade are plotted in the block transaction through a smart contract.
9.   To sum up, the Blockchain API reflects the changes in the land details storage.

Smart contract – *"LandDepartment"* can be further extended to integrate buy-sell trust deed by adding more fields in the structure namely (e.g. string current_owner, string joint_owner, string deed, uint payments, etc). New functions can be added for –

1.   Requesting landowner to sell the property
2.   Displayed advertisements by the owner to sell the property
3.   Buy the property
4.   Requesting bank to sanction the loan
5.   Loan transfer
6.   Transformation of ownership
7.   Modifying the insurance coverage, and many more as per the requirements.

Smart contracts can be written to address every other transactions relating to land registry including multiple ownership, rental agreement, tax payment, insurance coverage, etc. without involving any intermediaries to avoid any tampering as these transactions can be tracked and are unalterable. Thus, Blockchain can be considered as the relevant and professional practice in various e-governance services plotted in the chapter leading minimum or no fraud in its working.

CONCLUSION

The chapter summarizes the use of Blockchain technology in agriculture systems, tax calculation, and land registration, which can be automated using a complete distributed network. A smart contract addresses the problem of the center point of failure in the present distribution network by incorporating the mirror images of data across the network. It achieves the high reliability of confidential information at various distributed nodes with high integrity. In e-Governance use cases, maintaining the information across the network is an essential task to make the routine operation smooth with minimum manual overheads. The traditional systems have many drawbacks for processing the documents at different stages which incurs the time-consuming overheads thus Blockchain could be the best alternative for replacing the existing system to fasten processing the documents for achieving better outcomes. The use of distributed ledgers provides distinctive prospects to the agriculture sector. The use of smart contracts introduces trust among the buyers and sellers to excel exchange of information, transparency and traceability, which in turn is an essential factor for the agricultural sector. In the future it is needed for e-Governance, agricultural sector to understand the importance of Blockchain technology, identify the potential and opportunities and prepare for the upcoming BCT revolution. Few of them highlighting the concerns for replacing the traditional techniques with BCT are as follows:

1.   Faster and involves less manual work
2.   Immutable
3.   Improved trust through smart contracts
4.   Transactions are time-stamped; avoiding land frauds and providing a smart and scalable solution.

REFERENCES

Androulaki, E., Barger, A., Bortnikov, V., Cachin, C., Christidis, K., De Caro, A., & Muralidharan, S. (2018). Hyperledger fabric: a distributed operating system for permissioned Blockchains. In *Proceedings of the Thirteenth EuroSys Conference* (p. 30). ACM. 10.1145/3190508.3190538

Bamasag, O., Munshi, A., Alharbi, H., Aldairi, O., Altowerky, H., Alshomrani, R., & Alharbi, A. (2020). Blockchain and Smart Contract in Future Transactions—Case Studies. In *Decentralised Internet of Things* (pp. 169–198). Cham: Springer. doi:10.1007/978-3-030-38677-1_8

Bambara, J. J., Allen, P. R., Iyer, K., Madsen, R., Lederer, S., & Wuehler, M. (2018). *Blockchain: A Practical Guide to Developing Business, Law, and Technology Solutions* (Rev. ed.). McGraw-Hill Education.

Bhargavan, K., Delignat-Lavaud, A., Fournet, C., Gollamudi, A., Gonthier, G., Kobeissi, N., & Zanella-Béguelin, S. (2016). Formal verification of smart contracts: Short paper. In *Proceedings of the 2016 ACM Workshop on Programming Languages and Analysis for Security* (pp. 91-96). ACM. 10.1145/2993600.2993611

Bulk. (2018). *How Blockchain can transfer the world of indirect tax*. Retrieved from https://www.ey.com/en_gl/trust/how-Blockchain-could-transform-the-world-of-indirect-tax

Caro, M. P., Ali, M. S., Vecchio, M., & Giaffreda, R. (2018). *Blockchain-based traceability in Agri-Food supply chain management: A practical implementation. In IoT Vertical and Topical Summit on Agriculture - Tuscany* (pp. 1–4). Tuscany: IOT Tuscany.

Casado-Vara, Prieto, Prieta, & Corchado. (2018). How Blockchain improves the supply chain: case study alimentary supply chain. *Procedia Computer Science, 134*, 393-398. doi:10.1016/j.procs.2018.07.193

Charles. (2018). *Blockchain and HR: How They Intertwine*. https://hropenstandards.org/wp-content/uploads/2018/04/Charles-St-Louis.pdf

Chung, C. S. (2015). *The Introduction Of E-Government In Korea : Development Journey, Outcomes And Future*. Retrieved from https://www.cairn.inforevue-gestion-et-management-public-2015-2-page-107.htm

CIOReview Team. (2019). *India Looks To Blockchain For E-Governance*. Retrieved November 4, 2019, from https://www.cioreviewindia.com/news/india-looks-to-Blockchain-for-egovernance-nid-3284-cid-135.html

Dhillon, V., Metcalf, D., & Hooper, M. (2017). *Blockchain-Enabled Applications: Understand the Blockchain Ecosystem and How to make it Work for You* (Rev. ed.). Gent, Belgium: Academia Press. doi:10.1007/978-1-4842-3081-7

Ethereum Revision 7709ece9. (2019). *Solidity language documentation*. Retrieved from https://solidity.readthedocs.io/

Fatz. (2019). Towards Tax Compliance by Design: A Decentralized Validation of Tax Processes Using Blockchain Technology. *2019 IEEE 21st Conference on Business Informatics (CBI)*, 559-568.

Frankowski, Barańsk, & Bronowska. (2017, Dec.). *Blockchain technology and its potential in taxes*. Deloitte.

Ge, L., Brewster, C., Spek, J., Smeenk, A., Top, J.L., Diepen, F.V., Klaase, B., Graumans, C., & Wildt, M.D. (2017). *Blockchain for agriculture and food: Findings from the pilot study*. Academic Press.

Government I. T. Initiatives. (2019). Retrieved November 4, 2019, from https://www.gsa.gov/technology/government-it-initiatives

Hudson, S., & Sloan, B. (2019). *Death, Lies, and Land Registration*. Hart Publishing. doi:10.5040/9781509921409.ch-016

Insights, L. (2019, October). *Iota Launches Decentralized Industry Marketplace Miranda Wood*. Retrieved from https://www.ledgerinsights.com/iota-decentralized-industry-marketplace/

Jurgen, G. (2018). *Introducing Blockchain Technology to the world of Tax*. Retrieved from https://medium.com/@jurgeng/an-introduction-to-Blockchain-technology-tax-567e536767ec

Kamilaris, A., Fonts, A., & Prenafeta-Boldú, F. X. (2019). The rise of Blockchain technology in agriculture and food supply chain. Trends *Food Science & Technology, 91*, 640-652. doi:10.1016/j.tifs.2019.07.034

Kim, H. M., & Laskowski, M. (2018). Agriculture on the Blockchain: Sustainable Solutions for Food, Farmers, and Financing (December 17, 2017). In D. Tapscott (Ed.), *Supply Chain Revolution*. Barrow Books.

Leng, K., Bi, Y., Jing, L., & Fu, H.-C. (2018). Research on agricultural supply chain system with double chain architecture based on Blockchain technology. *Future Generation Computer Systems, 86*, 641-649. doi:10.1016/j.future.2018.04.061

Lin, Y.-P., Petway, J. R., Anthony, J., Mukhtar, H., Liao, S.-W., Chou, C.-F., & Ho, Y.-F. (2017). Blockchain: The Evolutionary Next Step for ICT E-. *Agriculture. Environments, 4*, 50.

Lu, Z. (2019). Bis: A Novel Blockchain based Bank-tax Interaction System in Smart City. *2019 IEEE Intl Conf on Dependable, Autonomic and Secure Computing, Intl Conf on Pervasive Intelligence and Computing, Intl Conf on Cloud and Big Data Computing, Intl Conf on Cyber Science and Technology Congress*, 1008-1014. 10.1109/DASC/PiCom/CBDCom/CyberSciTech.2019.00183

Ministry of Electronics and Information Technology. (2019). *Government of India | Home Page*. Retrieved November 4, 2019, from https://meity.gov.in/

Moon, M. J. (2002). The Evolution of E-Government among Municipalities: Rhetoric or Reality? *Public Administration Review, 62*(4), 424–433. doi:10.1111/0033-3352.00196

Ølnes, S., & Jansen, A. (2017). Blockchain Technology as s Support Infrastructure in e-Government. *Lecture Notes in Computer Science, 10428,* 215–227. doi:10.1007/978-3-319-64677-0_18

Papa, S.F. (2017). *Use of Blockchain Technology in Agribusiness: Transparency and Monitoring in Agricultural Trade*. Academic Press.

Peiró, N. N., & Martinez García, E. J. (2017). Blockchain and Land Registration Systems. *European Property Law Journal, 6*(3). doi:10.1515/eplj-2017-0017

Phan, L., Li, S., & Mentzer, K. (2019). *Blockchain Technology and The Current Discussion on Fraud.* Academic Press.

Pokrovskaia, N. N. (2017). Tax, Financial and Social Regulatory Mechanisms within the Knowledge-Driven Economy. Blockchain Algorithms and Fog Computing for the Efficient Regulation. *2017 XX IEEE International Conference on Soft Computing and Measurements (SCM).* 10.1109/SCM.2017.7970698

Suberg, W. (2019, December 19). *First Government Blockchain Implementation For Russia.* Retrieved November 4, 2019, from https://cointelegraph.com/news/first-government-Blockchain-implementation-for-russia

Takyar, A. (2019, January). *Blockchain in Agriculture - Improving Agricultural Techniques.* Retrieved from https://www.leewayhertz.com/Blockchain-in-agriculture/

Tarasenko. (2019). *Private Blockchain vs traditional centralized database.* https://merehead.com/blog/private-Blockchain-vs-traditional-centralized-database/

Thakur, V., Doja, M. N., Dwivedi, Y. K., Ahmad, T., & Khadanga, G. (2019). Land records on Blockchain for implementation of land titling in India. *International Journal of Information Management, §§§,* 101940.

The Blockchain Council. (2019). *An authoritative group of experts and enthusiasts who are evangelizing the Blockchain Research, Development, Use Cases, Products and Knowledge for the better world.* Retrieved from https://www.Blockchain-council.org

Thomas. (2019). *How Blockchain technology could improve the tax system.* Retrieved from https://www.pwc.co.uk/issues/futuretax/how-Blockchain-technology-could-improve-tax-system.html

Tse, D., Zhang, B., Yang, Y., Cheng, C., & Mu, H. (2017). Blockchain application in food supply information security. *2017 IEEE International Conference on Industrial Engineering and Engineering Management (IEEM),* 1357-1361. 10.1109/IEEM.2017.8290114

Chapter 3
Blockchain Technology Applications in Government

Adnan Ozsoy
https://orcid.org/0000-0002-0302-3721
Hacettepe University, Turkey

Bahar Gezici
Hacettepe University, Turkey

Necva Bölücü
Hacettepe University, Turkey

Nurettin Bölücü
Hacettepe University, Turkey

ABSTRACT

Blockchain in government services has a wide range of application areas for various departments from legal document storage and management to healthcare benefits. Decentralized nature opens opportunities for a government that can achieve operations 24/7 and cut back office operations. A Blockchain system for government offers a potential solution to legacy pain points and establishes a secure storage for citizens and businesses. It also reduces intensive paper processes, excessive managing costs, and potential corruption and abuse. Instead, it greatly increases security of digital services and more importantly trust in the government. This chapter provides a detailed review of Blockchain solutions for three major government services: land registry, GDPR, and healthcare. For each service, a state-of-the-art is given, followed with the technical details of use cases and potential improvements for current problems.

INTRODUCTION

Governments play an important role as a central authority that provides infrastructures necessary for its citizens. These infrastructures range from physical establishments like roads, highways, bridges, and sewage systems to administrative structures like juridical system, police department, municipalities,

DOI: 10.4018/978-1-7998-3632-2.ch003

and many other offices that add value to the daily lives of citizens. Technology acts as an important catalyst to the establishment of these infrastructures. This is because technology tools that are created by Information and Communication Technologies serves as the backbone to any system (infrastructure inclusive). With the growing size of the information and the recent capabilities to extract crucial knowledge from chunks of information makes data the most valuable asset of any system. Considering the responsibilities of the government, among others, the protection of lives and properties is one of the highest priorities of government. Since government gather almost any information about a citizen, protecting this information and building trust among citizens about how this information is used is also very crucial responsibility of a government.

A technology designed to build trust between different stakeholders is Blockchain. This is a disruptive technology because it is new, not an upgrade of any technology and can replace existing database technologies. Blockchain technology provides auditability with its distributed architecture, secure storage and immutability of information using crypto functions. Blockchain also provides continuous service with its decentralized structure. From this perspective, Blockchain is a remarkable technology that will be of value in the digitalization of services provided by the government. This effort will boost the confidence of citizens on how governments handle their data. As a result of the capabilities of Blockchain, many government organizations around the world use Blockchain for different scenarios.

This chapter describe how Blockchain provides the solutions that were not possible before for three government agencies. These agencies are namely, Land Registry, General Data Protection Regulation, and Healthcare. For each of these areas, the chapter will provide a discussion on the shortcomings of the current Blockchain solutions and propose a new model that can improve the current solutions.

BLOCKCHAIN FOR LAND REGISTRY

Blockchain has been a major attraction as an alternative system to the current land registration methods. It promises immutability, decentralization, transparency and trusted records of a wide variety. Many governments have started piloting Blockchain technology for their land registration system at different levels. A Land registration system can be described as a system that organizes and records the ownership of a title, facilitate transactions and prevent unlawful disposal. This system is relevant today because a growing population of the modern world is rapidly increasing in the last decades. Currently the estimated total worth of lands without any evidence of ownership valued at $20 trillion (Francisco, 2018). Hence land registration will grow and it is becoming one of the most important aspects of modern society. Governments have started exploring the advantages of Blockchain technology due to its ability to manage financial transaction, transfer asset and record keeping capabilities. Blockchain is a digital network which allow the storage of digital information across the network of computers. The decentralization of record by Blockchain makes it less vulnerable to corruption or human error.

State-of-the-Art

There are several studies on Blockchain with respect to its usage of record keeping and land registration by governments. These studies discuss the advantages of this technology as compared to the lack of transparency and vulnerability of the current systems.

Lemieux (2017) presents a synthesis of several cases. Lemieux identifies three distinct design patterns of Blockchain solutions which explains different solutions with respect to record keeping and the long-term preservation of records. Lemieux further provides a discussion on three unique and atomistic solutions with unique design patterns for unique challenges. These systems are; "Mirror type" solution, "Digital Record type" solution and "Tokenized type" solution.

1.   **Mirror Type**: In this type of solution, which is a pilot project for land registration solution initiated by the Brazil government, Blockchain system preserve the digital fingerprints of the original documents and does not create or store the land registration documents. This solution aims to ensure and improve the integrity of the records by recording the hashes of the original records and provide ability to compare these hashes.

2.   **Digital Record Type:** In this type of solution, which is used in a pilot project in Sweden, the Blockchain system does not only mirror the fingerprints, it actively creates the records on chain as smart contracts. Swedish land registration system uses Esplix and Postchain (Postcain, 2018) to create smart contracts and record it in the Postchain ecosystem. Users use Esplix to define smart contracts and execute each property transfer. Each new transaction creates a block to be recorded in the Postchain system. The Postchain keeps system available for saving and accessing the data. It also enables secure replication of data between "consortium" of databases, but it also incorporates the distribution and redundancy of a Blockchain. According to Lemieux, this solution is the most innovative among all. This type of recordkeeping system captures not only records but also the assets represented on chain via linking method. These assets can represent the land or any other value.

Spielman (2016) works with the Blockchain-based record keeping systems that exams a growing American city called Davidson County, Tennessee, USA where 95 of 3143 counties are located. Spielman discusses how Blockchain technology may change the way real estate title transactions are processed. He proposes a Smart Property system which can create a contract of sorts in a decentralized system of exchange for any asset. Generating a smart property concept allows trading in circumstances where there is less trust and will reduce fraud and cost.

3.   **Tokenized Type**: By "coloring" a token to represent an asset, it can be exchanged on the Bitcoin Blockchain. With Smart properties, other administrative benefits such as necessary digital signatures of buyers, sellers, land administrators can be included the Blockchain system. In (Hearn, 2011), author argues on how usage of Blockchain technology may change the way real estate title trans-actions are handled and about the cost of these benefits and challenges. Goldman Sachs report reveals Blockchain technology has the potential to save 2-4 billion dollars cost in the U.S. by reducing errors and manual efforts (Schneider et al, 2016). Blockchain system has the potential to eliminate transaction risks, reduce title-searching time and make it more transparent, and with unique keys it reduces the human input errors such as misspelling.

Blockchain Usage

Most of these approaches for land registration using Blockchain rely on the trust that money will be transferred after the agreement. These solutions proposed are mainly for generating a decentralized system that decreases the time it takes to process the transfer and also for reducing the interaction with the government and organizations. One missing component in previous works would be a dedicated crypto-currency/token which will help enormously in data transfer. This token can be used as the main trade asset for land transactions. A dedicated token can also be used to overcome most of the digital attacks such as double spending and unauthorized transfers.

Double-spending is the issue of spending the same coins more than once. For a transaction to be successfully inserted to the chain, it requires that it be verified by the miners using Proof of Work mechanism which prevents double-spending. The Blockchain protocol uses the irreversible transaction methodology. So, when a transaction is sent to the network it cannot be canceled, though it can be rejected by the miners. Although double-spending is not possible for Blockchain, it is possible to generate a transaction which will not be verified by the miners but the service or good are delivered before verification. Double-spending is unique to the currencies where a centralized system is lacking and verification takes time and requires more than one verification.

Double spending is achieved by canceling the transaction after getting the service or in this case the money in real life. With a token model, there will be no interaction outside the digital world and canceling a transfer would cancel the transaction for both ends so no fraud can be achieved by canceling a transaction.

The Token Model

Here, we propose a land registry model on top of blockchain which will consist of the following items:

1. A Blockchain Network.
2. Smart contracts generated by the government or organizations.
3. Users (buyers and sellers)
4. A token developed for asset or land transfer.
5. An off-chain data storage.

In this model, there are three roles; the "Buyer", "Seller" and "Smart Contract". Smart contract is an account that creates and receives transactions, generated by the government or organization. The complete data is held in an off-chain storage with the data pointers in the network. When a buyer demands to buy an asset, he/she creates a transaction with the information about the money he/she is willing to pay and with other necessary information needed for the smart contract. Smart contract then processes the transaction, to find out whether the contract is valid by checking the off-chain storage, it then creates the contract and sends it to seller. When the seller receives the transaction, he/she can either approve the transaction and sign it or reject the transaction and requests for a new transaction. Finally, smart contract generates a transaction information for the buyer about the seller response.

For the model, there are 4 main transaction methods:

- t_req: Request to buy a property from a seller, with the definition of amount of money.
- t_cont: Generated contract with respect to the information in the t_reg.
- t_sign: Reply for the transaction with either an approval or denial.
- t_info: Information transaction of the" Seller's response.

This model is a transparent model, every node in the network can check the state of a land from the off-chain storage and its history. There are several options for storing the data. One possible solution is data storage in the Blockchain at every node but considering the size of the storage, computational difficulties and potential problems associated with forking but storage of the lands registration data in the Blockchain is questionable. Storing the complete land registration and transactions data would be possible for off-chain storage and Inter Planetary File System (IPFS) (Benet, 2014) can be used with data pointers kept on-chain.

BLOCKCHAIN FOR GENERAL DATA PROTECTION REGULATION

The General Data Protection Regulation (GDPR) is a new European Union (EU) data protection law going into effect in May 2018 (https://gdpr-info.eu/). GDPR imposes new data protection requirements for processing personal data, by data controllers and data processors. These requirements introduce new rules that regulate legal status of personal data. The challenge of GDPR-compliance is verification that is controlled by a supervisor or some sort of authority. It is difficult to ensure that data controller adheres to the GDPR. Moreover, it is harder for the owner of the data to monitor his/her personal data. These problems provide the possibility for the synergy of the GDPR and Blockchain in order to develop GDPR-compliant frame works to prevent security problems.

While, Blockchain is a new technology that has a high potential for ensuring the compliance of the GDPR, some questions must be defined in the given solutions. In GDPR, there are three different roles, Data subject (DS), Data Controller (DC) and Data Processor (DP). In Blockchain, Data Subjects write their own transactions. However, in GDPR, data is written by data controller and data controller's role is not compatible with Blockchain because of the decentralization of Blockchain. One major problem in Blockchain integration is how these roles will be defined within the Blockchain. As Blockchains are immutable, it is difficult to rectify or remove personal data already stored in Blockchain networks. Another GDPR based problem with Blockchain based solutions is how erasure or update procedures will be defined in the proposed models. Blockchain is also characterized by anonymity. Personal data is defined as information related directly to a living person who should be identified or identifiable. The GDPR applies does not permit the nonconsensual processing of personal data unless it has been anonymized.

Frameworks in previous studies provide some solutions to these issues. There are two sides to this subject. There are developers who use Blockchain to develop new product and services and lawyers who settle questions about compatibility of GDPR (Cate et al. 2018, Fabiano et al. 2018, Finck 2018, Ramsay 2018). In this section, authors summarize several studies that propose models that will enable the application of the GDPR to Blockchain. Furthermore, the authors propose a new framework for a GDPR-compliant personal data platform for mobile applications. The goal of the proposed framework is to preserve the legal requirements of GDPR when using Blockchain. In this framework, it is ensured that only designated DS and DC have permissions to create, update, and withdraw consents, and DP can process personal data by given permissions.

General Data Protection Regulation

The main goal of GDPR is adjusting a set of standardized data protection laws across all the member countries across the European Union. This regulation is essential to make it easier to ensure privacy and extend data rights for EU residents. It also helps EU residents understand personal data use.

GDPR defines some requirements for data protection and privacy:

1. Data processing requires consent of the person.
2. To ensure privacy, data is collected in a private way.
3. Data can only be transferred for EU citizens.

To ensure these requirements, three main roles are defined in GDPR Article 4. As below:

1. DS: authorizes a data controller to access his/her personal data.
2. DC: collects and determines the purposes and means of the processing of personal data. They are also responsible for determining their legal authority to obtain that data.
3. DP: processes personal data only on behalf of the controller. The data processor is usually a third party external to the company.

Some features of Blockchain that are incompatible in GDPR:

1. Immutability: "Right to be forgotten" is the requirement of GDPR that allows data subject to have their data deleted upon request that is contrary with Blockchain.
2. Data Controller role: In Blockchain, Data subjects write their own data. However, data controller has right to write personal data with given permissions by data subject in GDPR. For this reason, data controller role is not directly compatible with Blockchain.
3. Anonymization: While data must be related with alive person that should be identified or identifiable that is specified in Article 4. in GDPR, anonymization is a Blockchain property.

STATE-OF-THE-ART

Blockchain is used in other areas besides cryptocurrencies over the last few years. Especially, the features of Blockchain can be used for managing digital assets such as health records (Azaria et al, 2016), and personal data (Zyskind et al, 2015).

There are several studies that analyze the relationship between Blockchain technology and GDPR. The studies discuss the technological aspects of Blockchain systems, in different industries and value chains such as energy distribution, compliance of block chain technology, on GDPR. The US National Institute of Standards and Technology's (NIST) (Yaga et al, 2018) report that the technology is hyped but not understood.

In literature, a few studies do focus on Blockchain based GDPR compliment personal data management systems using smart contracts. Thornton (2018) published a report that focused on the challenges and advantages of Blockchain in the implementation of the GDPR. The challenges were on the legality in the processing personal data when it comes to the right of cancellation, erasure, and forgotten, accuracy principle of personal data. This implies ensuring the accuracy, storage limitation, and integrity and confidentiality. Thorton (2018) divided the compatible framework solutions into two groups: Cryptographic Hash and Private Channels.

Truong et al. (2019) design a platform for personal data management, which is GDPR-compliant. This platform is strengthened by using Blockchain and smart contract technologies to sustain decentralized systems. It also provides a system for service holders and owners of personal data. Hyperledger Fabric, a Linux Foundation framework for permissioned Blockchain, was selected for the platform. As off-chain, an honest Resource Server (RS) is used for data storage in this framework. The proposed platform ensures Service Node System (SNS) clients rights and SNS provider's obligations. The authors analyzed the models on GDPR-compliance, threads and performance of systems.

Zyskind and Nathan (2015) describe a decentralized personal data management system that gives the data owner control over their data. The conversion of Blockchain into an automated access-control manager that puts third parties away is ensured with an implemented protocol. The system is composed of Blockchain and off-chain as data storage and it is implemented on Blockchain. The privacy issues with respect to personal data (data ownership, data transparency, auditability and Fine-grained access control) are ensured by system.

Wang et al. (2018) propose a control scheme for decentralized storage systems. This scheme provides a fine-grained access through Ethereum framework and Interplanetary File System (IPFS)(Benet, 2014).

Neisse et al. (2017) propose three contracts for data accountability and origin tracing that ensure GDPR (4.2) compliance. The contracts are written for a certain controller where data subject creates a contract specifically for each data controller. Additionally, contracts are also written for specific data where each subject's data is shared among all other data controllers. Finally, contracts are provided for multiple data subjects where the data controller identifies how data from different subjects are treated from the controller.

Wirth and Kolain (2018) propose a methodology that is an architectural blueprint designed using legal requirements. Their proposed blueprints show solutions that comply with the principle of Privacy-by-Design (Art. 25 GDPR). A single legal requirement is integrated into a Blockchain-enabled architecture based on GDPR.

The main drawbacks of these studies are 1) only conceptual approach were presented and 2) the challenges of GDPR compliance for smart contracts were not addressed.

An Alternative Model on Blockchain

In this section, authors introduce a framework for the Blockchain-based GDPR compliment personal data management mobile platform. Authors begin with an overview of this new framework. The architecture of the framework is given in Figure 1.

Figure 1. Overall architecture of the proposed framework

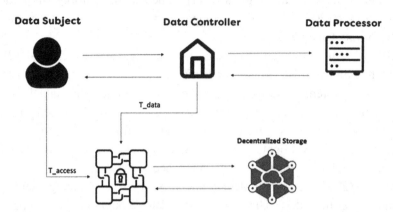

In this framework, three main roles are depicted using GDPR terminologies:

1. User - Data Subject - an entity that is a person who downloads and uses the application owns the personal data (DS in GDPR terminology)
2. Data Controller - an entity that collects and manages personal data (DC in GDPR terminology)
3. Data Processor - an entity that processes personal data for its own services (DP in GDPR terminology)

These roles are represented as a Blockchain node within the framework. Authors assume that DC and DP nodes should be located within the borders of the EU. While authors add constraint on locations of DC and DP, there are no restriction for DS.

Authors design two types transactions for the Blockchain: T_{access} and T_{data} in the framework. T_{access} is used for access control management and T_{data} is used for data storage and retrieval. A new block is formed and added to the existing Blockchain after a new DS enrolled to the mobile platform, or information sharing between DS, DC, and DP.

As illustrated in Figure 1, the DS entity engages with the framework when he/she installs an application that uses the proposed platform for the protection of his/her privacy. After signing, a new DS entity is generated and sent, with the permissions, to the Blockchain in a T_{access} transaction. The sensor of the phone, to whom the personal data belongs, to DS and encrypted using an encryption key, collects the data. The encryption key is sent to the Blockchain in a T_{data} transaction in a manner that a data pointer is stored in the Blockchain and the reference data stored in off-chain.

As depicted in Figure 2, DS is granted access only to perform T_{access} transactions. An authorized DC receives all data from DS and record data pointer of the data with T_{data} transaction. This data is transferred to the Blockchain and also sent to the off-chain. The DP interacts with DC to request data; DC checks the permissions stored in the Blockchain; If DP has permissions to get the personal data belongs to DS; DC gets the data pointer from Blockchain and retrieve the data from off-chain with data pointer and forward to DP. DS has the right to monitor the access of his/her data. When DS wants to monitor logs, he/she sends request to DC and the DC forwards the logs to DS. In the framework DS can change the permissions of DC and DP with T_{access} transaction.

A sequence diagram of granting a consent for a DP is given in Figure 2. DS requests for consent to provide data. DC checks the permissions of DP. If DP has permissions to monitor the personal data, DC accepts the request by providing his/her digital signature t_{DC}. DC sends the query with digital signature t_{DC} and retrieves data pointer. In Blockchain system, Policies and logs are updated. Finally, data is retrieved from off-chain by reference data pointer and sent to DP. The response is transmitted DC, DS, and DP.

Figure 2. Process of granting consent for a DP

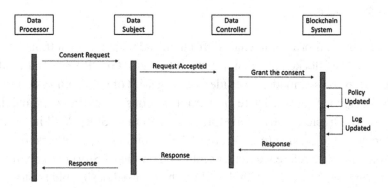

After the DP receives request to monitor personal data and grants consent, the steps to accessing personal data begins. Sequence diagram of accessing personal data, stored in an RS, by a DP is given in Figure 3. When DP wants to access personal data, corresponding smart contract that stores permissions for DP is invoked and if DP has permission to access to personal data, his/her request is accepted and *en_pointer* is returned and DP sends his/her *en_pointer* to DC. Finally, DC get the data pointer from Blockchain and retrieve the data from off-chain with data pointer and forward to DP.

Figure 3. Sequence diagram of accessing personal data stored in an RS by a DP

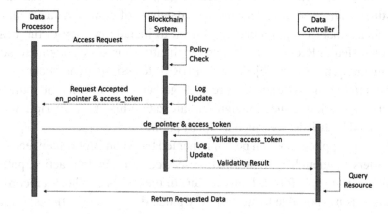

Blockchain Protocols

As mentioned earlier in the chapter, authors define two transactions in Blockchain: T_{access} and T_{data}. T_{access} transactions allow DS to change permissions granted to DC and DP by sending a protocol *POLICY*. The protocol sends empty sets when a DS enrolls the system. An empty set revokes all access-rights. After enrolling, DS have right to change the permissions that are stored in Blockchain.

T_{data} transactions are used for read/write operations. With *CheckPolicy* protocol the permissions are checked for DC and DP. If the permissions are granted, the DC gains right to get data with T_{data} transaction and sends to DP.

Off-Chain Data Storage

Here authors provide a brief information what is off-chain and what model authors use in their platform. Storage of personal data in Blockchains is not compatible with GDPR (Zyskind et al, 2015), because of security bridges. All proposed models consider the necessity of off-chain systems (Yaga et al, 2018; Truong et al, 2018; Wang et al, 2018). There are various options for storing personal data: conventional DBMS (e.g. MongoDB, Oracle), distributed storage system (e.g. Storj (Wilkinson et al, 2014), IPFS (Benet, 2014)), storage cloud service (e.g. Azure, AWS). In this study, authors use Storj for off-chain data storage and store only data reference (data pointer) on on-chain. Storj is an open-source file storage system that uses encryption, file shading, and a Blockchain-based hash table to store files in a peer-to-peer network. The advantages of this system is that it is cheaper, private and provides faster cloud file storage. It also prevents security problem by blocking accessing file of third parties.

BLOCKCHAIN FOR HEALTHCARE

Sharing personal health data is vital for smart medicine as it promotes both medical providers and research. Nevertheless, most medical research and data are warehoused in different medical institutions, which lead to the decentralization of medical data. Obtaining comprehensive health records from different medical institutions is a major challenge for patients. Breaking the information landmass in health data is a significant difficulty that needs a resolution. Blockchain technology has the potential to address this difficulty by providing a single, secure, decentralized database of clinical data for all patients.

As in all other areas, there is the fundamental need to include privacy in the health sector at the highest level. Personal Health Records (PHRs) are applications used by patients to access and control their medical information. The critical objective for PHRs is to assist patients securely and appropriately collect, track, and control their entire medical records gathered from different sources. These records consist information of visitation to the clinician, immunization history, prescriptions history, physical movement data provided by IoT devices such as smart phone devices, etc.

Personal health record applications can be implemented based on Blockchain technology which provides privacy and offers a patient health information service securely. In practice, patients can get help from different medical service platforms. However due of the absence of health record sharing between different institutions, it is not possible to successfully guide doctors and patients to provide a more accurate diagnosis. However, sharing personal medical data and a control mechanism for accesses based on the Blockchain can show a great improvement over the current healthcare industry.

State-of-the-Art

Several studies offer solutions that allow patients greater access to and control over their health data. These solutions include facilities towards contributing to their record, choosing the healthcare provide the intend to handle their records and share parts of their anonymized health records with research organizations. Many factors contribute to the difficulty of providing and controlling access to healthcare data as described below.

One of the early works in this domain is by Kim et al. (2016) where a mobile application for healthcare data distribution is implemented. They suggest a simple method that guarantees which the patients secure the possession of their personal healthcare data and control access of other persons to the data but is limited to patient and doctor.

Petersen et al. (2016) discuss how challenges with interoperability elude the computation rate. They present a Blockchain-based methodology for sharing patient records. This method trades a particular centralized source of confidence in favor of network consensus and establishes consensus on proof of structural and semantic interoperability, but did not indicate the access control.

Zhang et al. (2016) reports the adoption of Blockchain in the community network area but they did not not provide comprehensive benefits of Blockchain. Ivan (2016) argues Blockchain as a new approach to secure medical data storage, implementation difficulties, and a plan for transitioning incrementally from existing technology to a Blockchain solution. Xia et al. (2017) suggest MeDShare, which is a system that handling health data sharing between medical big data keepers in a trustless environment. The system is based on Blockchain and aims to deliver data provenance, auditing, and control for shared health records in cloud mines.

Roehrs et al. (2017) offer a distributed architecture model called OmniPHR which searches a solution for recurrent requirements in the adoption of PHR through patients and healthcare providers. This model offers a design for users to obtain a single sight of patient medical records with scalability, elasticity, and interoperability. Nevertheless, the model needs more assessments, primarily about security, privacy, and integration with other systems.

Omar et al. (2017) present a MediBchain protocol that is a patient-centric medical data management system by using Blockchain as a means of storage and privacy management. Anonymity is guaranteed via the cryptographic utilities to protect the patient's record.

Liang et al. (2017) plan and develop a healthcare system on mobile devices. The system offers personal health data collection, sharing, and collaboration among people and healthcare providers, as well as insurance firms. For scalability and performance concerns, a tree-based data processing and batching method are used to handle huge data sets. The data of personal health data is gathered by the mobile platform.

Fan et al. (2018) suggest a Blockchain-based data management system called MedBlock. This system proposes to handle patients' information. They is a method using Blockchain, which can preserve and guarantee users' privacy as an embedded feature in their record. This method is by applying the combination of access control protocol and encryption. However, there are some challenges in this study. For example, the data integrity feature outcomes is immutable as data cannot be altered or deleted once stored in the Blockchain. Nevertheless, if healthcare data is stored, then such personal data would come under the protection of privacy laws. Generally, no one would allow personal data to be saved forever. Besides, Healthcare data, such as imaging and treatment plans, are huge datasets and relational that requires searching. How well Blockchain technology can handle both necessities is still unclear.

Chen et al. (2018) design a storage scheme to cope with personal medical data constructed on Blockchain and cloud storage. Moreover, a service framework to share medical records is designated. In addition, the features of the medical Blockchain are presented and evaluated over a comparison with traditional systems.

In addition to the academic papers, there are also company websites providing Blockchain-based personal health data records. YouBase is an open-source protocol that aims to address key problems currently in the health data world: security, authenticity, share ability (Robinson et al, 2016). YouBase at the consumer-level provides options to more traditional data storage service areas, which are unavoidably controlled by a third party. This protocol lets individuals maintain their data and identity through different networks they use daily and share whenever they want. There are four repositories available for YouBase (https://github.com/YouBase).

Emrify Personal Health Record is a decentralized personal health record platform that allows the user to share their personal health data with anybody they choose by using a regenerative access code (Emrify, 2018). Now, the app is accessible for both IOS and Android with thousands of registered users and hundreds of downloads every month. This company has revealed new concepts such as health passport, health registry, health portal, etc. in Blockchain technology. There is one repository for this app (https://github.com/vikas1188/Emrify).

Patientory is a patient-centered protocol supported by Blockchain that is changing the manner healthcare stakeholders cope with digital medical data and cooperate with clinical care teams (McFarlane et al, 2017). It is using the Ethereum network for healthcare storage, but records privacy is greatly dependent on the cryptography approaches.

MintHealth is a worldwide, distributed health platform that aligns healthcare stakeholders around the common goal of patient authorization (Samir et al, 2018). It is presenting two tokens on the Ethereum Blockchain: Vidamints and the MintHealth Security Token. Here is Github repository of MintHealth (https://github.com/MintHealth/Vidamints).

MedRec is a record managing system concentrating on EMRs via smart contracts (Azaria et al, 2016). This system provides patients a widespread, immutable record and easy access to their medical data through providers and treatment sites. Leveraging single Blockchain properties, MedRec succeeds authentication, confidentiality, accountability and data sharing, but increases privacy concerns. Github link is provided by (https://github.com/mitmedialab/medrec).

MyMEDIS is a novel medical data storage and access system (Kovach et al, 2018). It gives control to patients over their medical records and health-related data. It is also making data directly accessible everywhere. The system operates distributed storage technology for redundancy and availability, and strong cryptographic encryption to guarantee the confidentiality of the content uploaded in the form of medical records, diagnostic imaging or IoT data.

BurstIQ is a worldwide network of industries and people connected through the power of Blockchain. The objectives of this application are empowering people, expanding health access, engaging care providers, establishing the authoritative secure data record, etc. Github code repository is https://github.com/BurstIQ/biq-token-crowdsale.

Medicalchain is a distributed platform that facilitates users to give conditional access to diverse healthcare agents like doctors, hospitals, laboratories, pharmacists and insurers to cooperate as they see suitable (Albeyatti, 2018). Each communication with their medical data is auditable, transparent and secure. During this procedure, the patient's privacy is protected in every period. However, there might be some unexpected or malicious attacks with Medicalchain, since it is based on the Ethereum protocol. Github link of Medicalchain is (https://github.com/medicalchain).

Iryo Network is a zero-knowledge personal health record database platform that is resistant to all attacks, with an anonymous query interface (Iryo, 2017). It practices Blockchain permission controls for health record admission and tokens to incentivize end-users' consent enabling artificial intelligence (AI) research.

Case Studies

In this section, Blockchain-based two well-known and highly cited applications, MedRec and Medichain will be described in detail.

MedRec: The article by the researchers at Massachusetts Institute of Technology recommends that the Blockchain be used to record medical data. Researchers who created a system based on the Ethereum platform called MedRec, in which the test results, medicines, assays and all other medical data can be recorded, thus making it clear that the confusion between the health institutions will be eliminated and the patient's file load will be reduced.

Electronic health records may help to centralize patient data to some extent, but sensitive information may be difficult to share with various healthcare providers, such as healthcare professionals because EHR platforms are not standardized across organizations. Therefore, MedRec aims to improve electronic medical records and to solve the problem of time, money and recurrence of patients' records. Medical records of a patient are usually distributed between the polyclinic, clinics, and laboratories. A Blockchain-based health record; it can be read and updated from various services and locations and includes a note about who did each adding or updating in the record. A patient can take the data and choose who to share it with. Thus, one-stop access to all medical history is provided to patients and health institutions. If patients wish to give access to their personal medical records, they will be provided anonymously to use the data for research purposes. The researchers claim that with MedRec, physicians and patients can easily access the patient's health history, and even if the records of the patient is changed, the patient's treatment regimen will not reduce the efficiency of the treatment process. It is a small scale private Blockchain with extensive, specific APIs that focuses on Blockchain solutions to prevent patients to share data with the institutions they allow under their own controls and to prevent counterfeiting on prescriptions and there is a data sharing authority with off-chain content synchronization.

Obviously, data on patients have been stored in digital media rather than physical records, but most healthcare organizations keep data only visible to staff in the same organization so that these records are not up-to-date compared to MedRec. However, MedRec also offers great advantages in terms of privacy and security. Although the patients in MedRec form part of a large pool of data, as long as the patients do not have permission, people who examine the database, except for the physicians involved, will only be able to see the health information and not know who owns it. In other words, they will not see which patient belongs to the disease or test results.

To sum up, with the outdated technology used in hospitals throughout the world, patient records and medical diagnosis can cause unnecessary workloads. MedRec is a good example of the contribution of the Blockchain in the field of health.

Technical Information About MedRec

MedRec propose to address the four key problems: 1) slow access to fragmented medical data; 2) system interoperability; 3) patient agency; 4) improved data quality and quantity for medical research. Raw medical data is not stored on the Blockchain, instead; they assemble references to data and encode these as hashed pointers onto a Blockchain ledger.

A Proof of Authority Blockchain developed as a part of **Go-Ethereum** client and **Solidity** are used as opposed to PyEthereum and Serpent libraries that were used in MedRec 1.0. This system gives an improvement in the case of privacy and scaling properties of transactions. Proof of authority is used to append blocks where authorities are hospitals and caregivers who are included in the system. MedRec 1.0 created a small-scale privacy Blockchain and it did not build on the live Ethereum network. Different than MedRec 1.0, MedRec 2.0 is *a network not a service*. Providers can join that network and make the data accessible on-demand at the request of patients. This gives an advantage in case of providing a cross-provider, interaction mechanism, and patient-oriented interface.

Ethereum supports Private Blockchain and the use of *"Smart Contracts"*. Smart contract structures are stored in the Blockchain. Relate the references to the owner of the data and the references to separate them and to separate the record retrieval locations. This enables an immutable data lifecycle log that allows later control. The content of a *raw medical record* is never stored on the Blockchain directly, however, it is securely kept in the obtainable data storage of providers. Instead, metadata as a set of pointers to the locations of medical data is encoded in the smart contracts. The records inside the smart contract have a cryptographic hash. The reason for this is to form the basis of the original content, so give a control against possible tampering.

MedRec prioritizes usability by introducing a designated contract that brings together user references to all patient-provider relationships and thus provides a single reference point to check for updates to the medical history. That is, it provides a regular data sharing task by updating the viewing permissions on the associated data pointers. It offers a common interface with the pointers for patient data collected in smart contracts on the Blockchain, with which the patients select their data and whom they share. Users are alerted by a notification system that is provided by the interface when a new record is sent or shared on behalf of the user. Identity confirmation is handled by public-key cryptography that maps ID to the Ethereum address. Data exchange among patient and providers database will be "off-chain" and this handles by a syncing algorithm.

In this implementation, there are three types of contracts that structures and navigates a large amount of records as shown in Figure 4.

1. Registrar Contract (RC) is implemented to map identification strings for participant to their associated Ethereum address.
2. Patient-Provider Relationship Contract (PPR) is distributed among two nodes in a system while storing and managing medical records by one node for the other. Data content of this contract is "owner", "access info", "EMR queries & hashes", "permissions" and "mining bounties". The PPR expresses a collection of data pointers that involves a query string and related permission of access which find the records held via a provider. To facilitate patients to share their medical records with the other users, a hash table like a dictionary that maps addresses of viewer's to queries. Each of these queries can identify a percentage of the patient's data to give access to a third-party viewer.

Figure 4. MedRec Network Design
(Courtesy of Azaria et al, 2016)

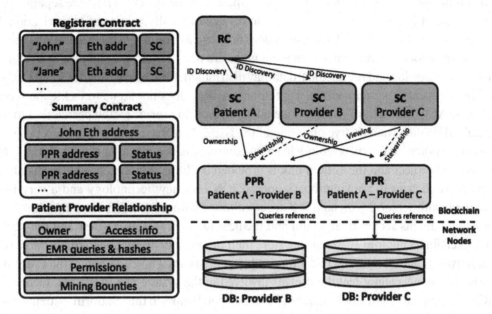

3. Summary Contract (SC) keeps a list of references to PPRs. This list represents all of the previous participants and their engagements in the system with other nodes. It consists of Ethereum address, PPR address, and status. The patient controls acceptation, rejection or deletion of relationships, so it gives full control over which records in their history they wish to acknowledge. A MedRec usability criterion is satisfied by this feature: good indicators to fragmented records are drawn together in a single, dedicated location.

It is important to highlight that the contracts are only used to provide pointers: the records are handled off-chain and the database queries return the records themselves.

In the system design, there are Backend library, Ethereum client, Database gatekeeper and EMR manager software components as an off-chain structure. There is integration between a prototype of these components and a database. It is managed in the course of their web UI. In Blockchain contracts, interoperability protocol is defined, and this protocol is employed like any user interface and provider backend implementations can contribute to the system.

Patient nodes hold a similar fundamental mechanism as providers in this system. A local device (PC or a phone) can be used to perform this implementation. Databases can role simply like a cache of medical patient data. In the MedRec Blockchain system, miners are incentivized to participate in the network. When a Blockchain is used to track cryptocurrency transactions, the miners that provide computing power to verify the data are given some crypto money as a reward. In the MedRec system, which will require miners to verify patient records in large areas, miners will be rewarded, but this award will not be monetary. The miners who verify the data on drug and general health will be able to view the health information from the permitting patients provided that the personal information of the patients is reserved. This will enable large companies to develop new medicines or treatments to acquire important data for the products they are developed by taking on the role of the miner.

In the case of security and robustness, MedRec gives a robust model guarantees to avoid a single point of failure that relies on the many nodes that are participating in the system. There are separate providers and entries are stored in these providers and patient databases locally; copies of authorization data are stored on each node in the network. This system does not have a central location for a content attack that can aim at a target, which is a very important issue in the era of cyber-attacks and data leaks. Since, both the global authorization log and raw medical data stay distributed. Individual provider databases' security is managed by the local IT system admin. Therefore, MedRec does not argue to tackle the security for these databases. Also, the right of users to take advantage of this service, "the permission to use their personal data" when they want to give up is one of the issues MedRec is not trying to solve. It is necessary to address the potential for vulnerability in smart contracts, especially after the DAO attack. MedRec is an open-sourced project and the Github link is provided as: https://github.com/mitmedialab/medrec.

MediChain: Medichain is a revolutionary approach, a very new technology and a very important approach to the health sector. Medichain is a decentralized platform to safely store health-related data. They ensure that patients secure their health and medical records. It is also a new and life-saving ICO based on Blockchain technology. Patients can store their data in a convenient geographic area off-chain (outside the network) and give access to doctors and specialists anywhere. Although the EMR system is quite important, patients cannot feel themselves involved in the system due to the fees incurred during use. MediChain completely removes the question marks, and thanks to this platform, patients will not be charged any fees when using the EMR system in medical facilities. Medical System components such as doctors, hospitals, and patients could insert data into a compliant cloud. The Blockchain infrastructure stores necessary information such as pointers and rules with anonymity, while the actual data itself is stored off-chain in a cloud backend. Data seeking parties such as researchers and pharmaceutical companies would access the data as big data in a fully anonymized form. Considering the data of the World Health Organization, it has also made the project important to initiate a solution process against the top ten diseases. Patients with medical records of the MediChain Platform's EMR system will be able to share information without the need for names to find solutions to their various diseases.

Based on the problem, a patient's medical records, such as treatment, surgery, medication, etc., are written randomly on one page of a book and are not recorded in a database. This form of traditional and unusable data storage does not work very well in cases where some medical intervention is required, because of the absence of historical data from the disease, the absence of trauma records, and the exact time during which the medication and treatment are not known. Besides, sometimes patients' information is mixed and this may have bad results. The main reason for keeping the data very reliable and accurate is that it is vital for the protection of the patient's health. Wrong and routine health records are shown to be the third-largest cause of death in today's world. Although these data are stored digitally in the computers of different hospitals, there is always the possibility that uninformed and malicious people will interfere with this data. Also, each hospital has a separate data logging system, and there is no uniformity between them, cannot integrate each other in a patient's treatment of this information from a medical center to transfer to another problem brings with it. Technology development and knowledge accumulation in the globalizing era have brought with it the ability to store these health data more easily and faster with the help of advanced technological computers and tools. Deaths resulting from inaccuracy and loss of health records can now be reduced by the Blockchain technology platform called MediChain.

Technical Information about MediChain

The MediChain company focuses on eight areas that it believes will improve the health sector: a model where resource use and risks can be estimated, population management, drug, and medical vehicle safety management, disease and treatment heterogeneity, sensitive drug and clinical decision support, quality of care and performance measurements, public health, and research applications. Dr. Mark Baker, CEO of MediChain, thinks that analytical prediction, especially in the health sector, can work.

There are many classes of data, which can be defined as raw user data, interpretations and diagnosis and structural data. Shortly;

1. Raw user data keeps a financial value that the patient has such as EMR records, lab test results, etc.
2. Interpretations and diagnosis come from the patient data and are sustained by other participants such as doctors, hospitals or automated systems.
3. Structural data can categorize datasets, which is used anonymously through cryptographic hashes to insurance companies, commercial researchers or academic scientists in the Blockchain ecosystem.

Data control will be in the patient and security will be in the Blockchain. Security of the personal data within the Blockchain is ensured by three levels of security as shown in Figure 5.

Figure 5. The architecture of MediChain
(Courtesy of Albeyatti, 2018)

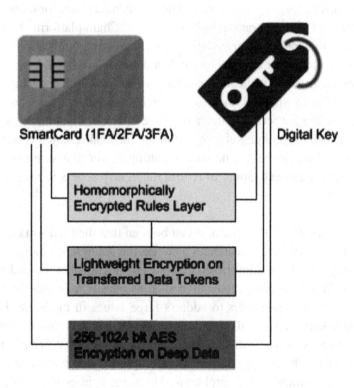

1. Homomorphic encryption is an encryption type that allows processing/computation on encrypted data. This is a fundamental prerequisite for allowing patients to check in detail about their data and to make sure that their privacy is controlled in detail.
2. Lightweight Symmetric Cryptography on transferred data tokens guarantees deep data security by giving anonymity that Blockchain does not have.
3. 256-1024 bit AES Encryption on Deep Data

Now when new patients are added to a patient because of surgery, consultation or prescription, the patient will be able to independently decide what to add to his or her record with an application. Medichain allows safe and precise transmission of the received and collected data from the patients to the doctors working in the healthcare sector. The patient's medical data will quickly be passed into the hands of the attending doctor without any changes thereby saving time. Thus, the exchange of health data between patients and the healthcare sector will be highly secure. Medichain uses the best in Blockchain encryption technology, which is transparent, accountable, linked to the privacy policy and manages data sharing. MediChain is platform-independent and provides APIs but uses built-in technologies like Smartcards to provide robust info about either patient or doctor identity.

1. MediChain Token: represents the value of the optional patient data blocks. The token of the Medichain system is based on the MCU Ethereum ERC-20 standard. BTC and ETH are the currencies to be accepted during ICO. During the ICO, Medichain will distribute their tokens to investors. These icons can be used to trade on the Medichain platform. Some of these icons can be used for; buying digitally communicated health services, voting by laboratories, the health network, and academic institutions to determine future research, and ultimately used in services for payment of medical data. MCU is the official token of MediChain. The MediChain token comes with many advantages. This token can be used to make transactions on the MediChain platform. You can take advantage of MCU reductions to handle your transactions in a smaller amount, and you can carry out your transactions without paying for medical research and data.
2. Mining: Data contractors and medical researchers are the main miners. They sell authorized data to insurers etc. Similar to MedRec, medical researchers are incentivized to perform the miners' role. Therefore, they can get access to the anonymized data for epidemiological studies. As a significant part of Medichain, an integral role within the medical research community is engaged in the protocol. Researchers deliver the necessary mining power to assure safety in the system and support the Blockchain authentication. In return, they grasp access to very valuable anonymized medical data as transaction fees.

There is also a social benefit of Medichain. It can be seen that the platform can provide significant income flow to participants. Medical researchers who use the anonymous patient medical data stored in Blockchain fund the system. Population-based unreported patient data provided advances against the first ten diseases of the World Health Organization such as obesity, diabetes, hypertension and heart failure. Population data allows researchers to address large issues in medicine. Patients hiding their medical records in Medichain's EMR will be able to share their anonymous information to help them find improvements to diseases such as obesity, diabetes and heart failure. When patients prefer and share their data, they support research breakthroughs that can help people who are able to improve their own health and who suffer from similar health problems. The same applies to commercial interests, such as drug development. However, pharmaceutical companies pay wages when they want to get this data. Research institutions using patient data will then pay Medichain using the tokens distributed to Medichain and pay the data to the Blockchain and, most importantly, the health institutions that load them. Basically, everyone wins, researchers can fold big data at a lower cost, and system users are rewarded for enriching the system with new data.

In terms of Privacy, Medichain maintains the privacy of health data and offers these records to the patients. Unlike the old traditional health record-keeping system, which is easily accessible by all, the patient is given the opportunity to identify people who have access to the medical data. These records are only available to the patient's health service providers, such as hospitals, doctors, etc. access is available on request. Otherwise, access is not possible. Medichain also helps companies engaged in medical work to mediate pharmacies and doctors to give improper contact to drug providers by specialists working in the medical community. This feature of Medichain is a bridge between different computers and databases in different places. While the patient's data on this decentralized platform are examined for health testing and examination, and the patients are consulted by the doctors, the Medichain token will be paid to the doctors. Services are provided to patients and doctors free of charge.

Moreover, medical Blockchain also enables key information to be entered into the off-chain. Medichain stresses that it is one of the most important benefits of the off-chain direction of the system. The Blockchain ecosystem indexes highly sensitive patient data using an encryption database maintained by an almost undistorted computer network. In addition, the patient's permission is required to get access to certain encryption keys.

The system also helps solve a number of failures that cause vital errors. In late February 2018, UK Health Minister Jeremy Hunt announced that the government would do everything in its power to reduce the number of deaths because of the government's prescription or misuse of patients. This was followed by the announcement of the results of the state-sponsored research and the emergence that the deaths of 22,000 people in the country could be due to these errors. Moreover, general practitioners, hospitals, nursing homes, and pharmacists can make 237 million mistakes each year. Doctors, who enter the Medichain platform, including those from other hospitals, or patients with smart cards, enter the information in the same Blockchain.

One of the problems that Medichain has experienced while integrating the Blockchain technology into the health sector is the processing speed. Ethereum has only 20 processing capacity per second compared to the Visa card system with a processing capacity of 24,000 per second. In order to solve this problem, Medichain team is designing a new system that allows the healthcare Blockchain to be processed in parallel which can increase the transfer speed of medical data by 14,400 times.

Bitcoin has some scaling problems and Medichain tries to address these problems as well. In the Bitcoin network, a client keeps the whole transaction history and more transactions processed on the network cause growing the size faster. In addition, Blockchain transactions normally recorded only once every 10 minutes and this will cause some problems with doctor-patient interactions and medical devices that are synchronizing daily or more often.

In addition, In Blockchain, it is standard practice to wait up to 50 minutes after each new record appears, as records are regularly retracted to increase the security of payments. It will not be applicable to sequential medical procedures in the clinic or hospital.

To address this problem, Medichain architecture needs an enhanced approach. One is divided into *index Blockchain*, each chain is divided into horizontal sector Blockchain that hold data for a particular set of diseases, and vertical patient Blockchain. Thus, each disease will have its own Blockchain related to a specific disease that can be found in it and to the research community dealing with these diseases by academics and companies. By applying horizontal Blockchain, each patient-doctor interaction would, therefore, have to get access to only one storage for each consultation. Medichain is also open-sourced project and the Github link is provided as: https://github.com/medichain.

An Alternative Model on Blockchain

In this section, we propose a secure, scalable, private permissioned and public permissionless Hybrid Blockchain architecture. The system consists of six entities, namely patients, hospitals, clinical laboratories, data providers, data analyst and insurances.

System Entities

1. **Patients:** have an agency on their own health record. Whenever (s)he wants, they can grant permission about their health data such as stewardship, viewing, etc. Patients are responsible for data accessing mechanism that (s) he can accept, delete or reject the requests.
2. **Hospitals**: provide some diagnosis or interpretations on patient data and under the patient permission, they can share medical treatments, laboratory or test results by a third parties.
3. **Clinical Laboratories:** exchange health data with doctors, pathology groups, patients or insurers when necessary in a secure way.
4. **Data Providers**: can provide and request health data. By getting health data, they can give suggestions and provide new treatments. Also, they can provide health data to patients, clinicians or insurers etc.
5. **Data Analyst**: requests patient data for logging or notification patient to share own data.
6. Insurances: to make relevant plans or strategies, they request accesses to health data. They also interact with medical laboratory or another unit of hospitals and guarantee charming payments.

Data Types

1. Raw user data indicates that the patient has such as EMR records, lab test results, etc.
2. Diagnosis data is extracted from the patient data and is provided to third parties such as doctors, hospitals, data providers etc.

System Overview

To talk about the system design, the authors proposed a hybrid Blockchain that covers the advantages part of the public and private Blockchain. The hybrid Blockchain enables an open system that can be audited, builds trust among transactions and protects the privacy of data in the private Blockchain. In a hybrid Blockchain, the private Blockchain can differentiate among transactions for public use and give these transactions to the public Blockchain for open access. Hybrid solution transactions are treated by the nodes in the network and validated by all other nodes. This provides a way to sustain the immutability of the previous transactions. While allowing external node validation of transactions, it also keeps the data secure. Data placed into a transaction history of a particular node is not shared with the network.

Figure 6. Personal Health Record Modeling

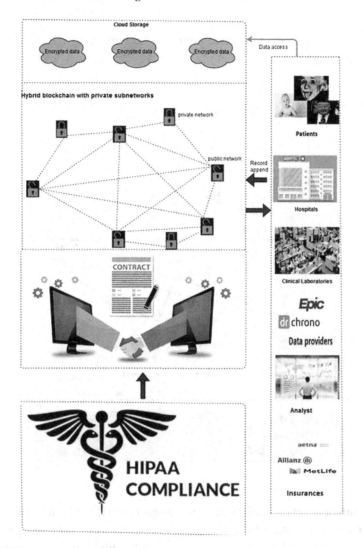

In summary, Hybrid Blockchain accomplishes the immutability of a public Blockchain with the data security of a private Blockchain. Figure 6 shows a general scenario for the personal health record.

To handle scalability issues, raw data and diagnostic data are held in off-chain and by using this system that integrates between pointers in Blockchain and data in the cloud. Blockchain only stores smart contracts and references to data. Every request for data and the necessary data access is recorded on the Blockchain. According to this system, each data request needs permission from the owner of the data through a decentralized permission management protocol.

On the other hand, certain health information must be held securely and not publicly released to the rest of the network. In order to guarantee privacy and security, the SHA256 algorithm will encrypt the data before uploading it to the cloud by the system entities. Lastly, HIPAA compliance is important for this system. The proposed method gives a faster and easier approach to HIPAA compliance. Thus, a pre-certified HIPAA compliant cloud can be used to store all off-chain data.

Smart Contracts

A relational set of contracts are used to encode pointers. Authors review smart contract structure with three-level as shown in Figure 7.

Figure 7. Smart Contracts structure

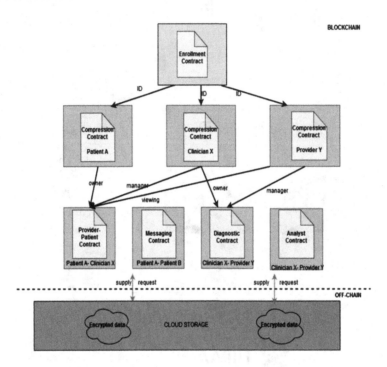

1. **Enrollment Contract:** acts as a dictionary and maps user IDs to their public key.
2. **Compression Contract:** holds a history of transactions. By using relationships' status, established time of relationships or approved relationships are stored in this contract. There are different relationships between different entities such as for the diagnostic contract between Clinician X- Provider Y only allows owning data with each other and does not allow other entities to view or read it.
3. **Providers' Relationship Contracts:** include four types of contracts. Each contract specifies special data or entities with their own permission. For example, some cancer patients do not want everyone to see their health data publicly. So, in Diagnosis contract the clinician and patient nodes can be linked while giving some permission on diagnosis data privately. Another contract is a messaging contract that links between two patients who have some experiences on the same diseases and they share their experiences or difficulties about those diseases. They might not share this information with another third party, so it is private just for the patients.

CONCLUSION

Public sector organizations around the world are moving away from uncertain and inefficient centralized systems and maintaining their systems on an auditable, fully transparent and collaborative structure offered by Blockchain. While existing systems are insecure and costly due to their central structures, Blockchain networks offer safer structures.

Blockchain based systems contribute to the digital government process in many ways. First, it can protect data, streamline processes, and reduce fraud, waste and abusive activity while improving trust and accountability. In this model, citizens, corporations and government resources are secured through cryptography functions and shared in a distributed ledger. The distributed architecture eliminates a single point of failure and prevents disruption in government services.

Although Blockchain solutions offer very useful features in government services, it is not expected that a recent transition from existing systems to Blockchain based systems will be complete without sufficient maturity in Blockchain frameworks.

REFERENCES

Albeyatti, A. (2018). *White paper: MedicalChain*. MedicalChain self-publication.

AlOmar, A., Rahman, M. S., Basu, A., & Kiyomoto, S. (2017, December). Medibchain: A Blockchain based privacy preserving platform for healthcare data. In *International conference on security, privacy and anonymity in computation, communication and storage* (pp. 534-543). Springer. 10.1007/978-3-319-72395-2_49

Azaria, A., Ekblaw, A., Vieira, T., & Lippman, A. (2016). Medrec: Using Blockchain for medical data access and permission management. *2016 2nd International Conference on Open and Big Data (OBD)*, 25–30.

Benet, J. (2014). *IPFS - Content Addressed, Versioned, P2P File System*. arXiv preprint arXiv:1407.3561

Berberich, M., & Steiner, M. (2016). Blockchain Technology and the GDPR-How to Reconcile Privacy and Distributed Ledgers. *Eur. Data Prot. L. Rev.*, 2(3), 422–426. doi:10.21552/EDPL/2016/3/21

Burts, I. Q. (2017). *Bringing Health to Life Whitepaper*. Retrieved from: https://www.burstiq.com/

Cate, F. H., Kuner, C., Lynskey, O., Millard, C., Loideain, N. N., & Svantesson, D. (2018). Blockchain versus data protection. *International Data Privacy Law*, 8(2), 103–104. doi:10.1093/idpl/ipy009

Chen, Y., Ding, S., Xu, Z., Zheng, H., & Yang, S. (2019). Blockchain-based medical records secure storage and medical service framework. *Journal of Medical Systems*, 43(1), 5. doi:10.100710916-018-1121-4 PMID:30467604

Damani, Verma, Harbour, Gross, Nigam, Lalwani, & Daniels. (2018). *Healthcare Ecosystem*. White Paper. Retrieved from: https://www.minthealth.io

Emrify Inc. (2018). *Health Passport: a decentralized personal health record platform to deliver trusted health information to the right hands at the right time anywhere in the world.* Retrieved from: https://www.emrify.com/hit/assets/Whitepaper.pdf

Fabiano, N., & Fabiano, S. L. (2018). Blockchain and Data Protection: the value of personal data. IMCIC 2018-9th International Multi-Conference on Complexity, Informatics and Cybernetics.

Fan, K., Wang, S., Ren, Y., Li, H., & Yang, Y. (2018). Medblock: Efficient and secure medical data sharing via Blockchain. *Journal of Medical Systems, 42*(8), 136. doi:10.100710916-018-0993-7 PMID:29931655

Finck, M. (2018). Blockchains and data protection in the European union. *European Data Prot. L. Rev., 4*(1), 17–35. doi:10.21552/edpl/2018/1/6

Francisco, J. (2018). *Blockchain land registry to help resolve ownership problems.* Retrieved from: https://businessBlockchainhq.com/business-Blockchain-news/Blockchain-land-registry-to-help-resolve-ownership-problems/

Hearn, M. (2011). Smart property. *Bitcoin Wiki, 5.* https://en.bitcoin.it/wiki/Smart_Property

Iryo. (2017). *Global participatory healthcare ecosystem - Whitepaper.* Retrieved from: https://iryo.io/iryo_whitepaper.pdf

Ivan, D. (2016, August). Moving toward a Blockchain-based method for the secure storage of patient records. In *ONC/NIST Use of Blockchain for Healthcare and Research Workshop.* Gaithersburg, MD: ONC/NIST.

Kim, H., Song, H., Lee, S., Kim, H., & Song, I. (2016, July). A simple approach to share users' own healthcare data with a mobile phone. In *2016 Eighth International Conference on Ubiquitous and Future Networks (ICUFN)* (pp. 453-455). IEEE.

Kovach, A., & Ronai, G. (2018). *MyMEDIS: a new medical data storage and access system.* Academic Press.

Lemieux, V. L. (2017, December). A typology of Blockchain recordkeeping solutions and some reflections on their implications for the future of archival preservation. In *2017 IEEE International Conference on Big Data (Big Data)* (pp. 2271-2278). IEEE. 10.1109/BigData.2017.8258180

Liang, X., Zhao, J., Shetty, S., Liu, J., & Li, D. (2017, October). Integrating Blockchain for data sharing and collaboration in mobile healthcare applications. In *2017 IEEE 28th Annual International Symposium on Personal, Indoor, and Mobile Radio Communications (PIMRC)* (pp. 1-5). IEEE. 10.1109/PIMRC.2017.8292361

McFarlane, C., Beer, M., Brown, J., & Prendergast, N. (2017). *Patientory: A Healthcare Peer-to-Peer EMR Storage Network v1.* Addison, TX: Entrust Inc.

Neisse, R., Steri, G., & Nai-Fovino, I. (2017). A Blockchain-based approach for data accountability and provenance tracking. In *Proceedings of the 12th International Conference on Availability, Reliability and Security* (p. 14). ACM. 10.1145/3098954.3098958

Peterson, K., Deeduvanu, R., Kanjamala, P., & Boles, K. (2016, September). A Blockchain-based approach to health information exchange networks. In *Proc. NIST Workshop Blockchain Healthcare* (*Vol. 1*, pp. 1-10). Academic Press.

Postchain - the first consortium database. (2018) Retrieved from: https://chromaway.com/products/postchain/

Ramsay, S. (2018). *The General Data Protection Regulation vs. The Blockchain: A legal study on the compatibility between Blockchain technology and the GDPR*. Academic Press.

Robinson, J., & Kish, L. (2016). *Youbase White Paper*. Retrieved from: https://www.youbase.io/

Roehrs, A., da Costa, C. A., & da Rosa Righi, R. (2017). OmniPHR: A distributed architecture model to integrate personal health records. *Journal of Biomedical Informatics*, *71*, 70–81. doi:10.1016/j.jbi.2017.05.012 PMID:28545835

Schneider, J., Blostein, A., Lee, B., Kent, S., Groer, I., & Beardsley, E. (2016). *Blockchain: putting theory into practice*. Profiles in Innovation Report.

Spielman, A. (2016). *Blockchain: digitally rebuilding the real estate industry* (Doctoral dissertation). Massachusetts Institute of Technology.

Thornton, G. (2018). *GDPR& Blockchain - Blockchain solution to general data protection regulation*. Technical report.

Truong, N. B., Sun, K., Lee, G. M., & Guo, Y. (2019). *GDPR compliant personal data management: A Blockchain-based solution*. arXiv preprint arXiv:1904.03038

Wang, S., Zhang, Y., & Zhang, Y. (2018). A Blockchain-based framework for data sharing with fine-grained access control in decentralized storage systems. *IEEE Access: Practical Innovations, Open Solutions*, *6*, 38437–38450. doi:10.1109/ACCESS.2018.2851611

Wilkinson, S., Boshevski, T., Brandoff, J., & Buterin, V. (2014). *Storj a peer-to-peer cloud storage network*. Academic Press.

Wirth, C., & Kolain, M. (2018). Privacy by Blockchain design: a Blockchain-enabled GDPR-compliant approach for handling personal data. In *Proceedings of 1st ERCIM Blockchain Workshop 2018*. European Society for Socially Embedded Technologies (EUSSET).

Xia, Q. I., Sifah, E. B., Asamoah, K. O., Gao, J., Du, X., & Guizani, M. (2017). MeDShare: Trust-less medical data sharing among cloud service providers via Blockchain. *IEEE Access: Practical Innovations, Open Solutions*, *5*, 14757–14767. doi:10.1109/ACCESS.2017.2730843

Yaga, D., Mell, P., Roby, N., & Scarfone, K. (2018). *Blockchain technology overview. Technical report*. National Institute of Standards and Technology. doi:10.6028/NIST.IR.8202

Zhang, J., Xue, N., & Huang, X. (2016). A secure system for pervasive social network-based healthcare. *IEEE Access: Practical Innovations, Open Solutions*, *4*, 9239–9250. doi:10.1109/ACCESS.2016.2645904

Zyskind, G., & Nathan, O. (2015, May). Decentralizing privacy: Using Blockchain to protect personal data. In *2015 IEEE Security and Privacy Workshops* (pp. 180-184). IEEE.

Chapter 4

Cross–Industry Use of Blockchain Technology and Opportunities for the Future:
Blockchain Technology and Aritificial Intelligence

Dhanalakshmi Senthilkumar
https://orcid.org/0000-0003-0363-5370
Malla Reddy Engineering College (Autonomous), India

ABSTRACT

Blockchain and artificial intelligence are two disruptive technologies in the today's world; Blockchain can connect data storage and data users from multiple domains, and different kinds of analytics applications run on top of the data in artificial intelligence techniques. So that Blockchain technology provide the excellent backbone for the development of artificial intelligence algorithms, it is useful to secure the data input from multiple data storage locations and to have whatever applications running on top of the data in a Blockchain visible to everyone. The concept of Blockchain technology and artificial intelligence techniques together develop interesting uses cases and nice applications. When paired with Blockchains, AI is better understood by humans, operates more efficiently, and the blockchains in general more efficiently. AI and Blockchain together support B2B environment and getting better outcomes.

INTRODUCTION

Blockchain is a digitized and decentralized system for facilitating secured transactions. These transactions are stored in ledgers similar to the traditional ledger. This ledger can store and manage transactions. Once transactions are completed, these completed transactions are stored in blocks and recorded chronologically in a transparent setup. (Rohitha, 2018). The Blockchain technology has been made popular by cryptocurrencies. Cyrptocurrencies such as Bitcoin use Blockchain to maintain a public

DOI: 10.4018/978-1-7998-3632-2.ch004

ledger for every single transaction (Chikara, 2019). Hence, Blockchain technology is the foundation of Cryptocurrency technique. Therefore, Blockchain is a concept and bitcoin is the implementation of that concept. Nevertheless, Blockchain is equipped with digital signatures, which enables secure transactions. Security in Blockchains is enabled by the utilization of public &private keys inorder to solve puzzles on cryptographic hash functions (Yaga, Mell, Roby & Scarfone, 2018).

Blockchain technology is the next generation of the internet (Rohitha, 2018). It is not a centralized data systems. Rather this is a system of decentralized distributed database systems. Hence, the ledger can be distributed all around the world (ibid). Bitcoin demonstrates how the decentralization is implemented using Blockchain. Bitcoin is a peer-to-peer digital currency developed using Blockchain, The peer-to-peer network consists of nodes. Each node verifies and validates the legitimacy of payments before a transaction is completed. Hence, there is no need for intermediaries (such as banks) in the Bitcoin payment process (Agrawal, 2019).

Although Blockchain has been used for Cryptocurrencies, it has value for enhancing the performance of other technologies. An example of such a technology is Artificial Intelligence. Artificial Intelligence (AI) enables the implementation of computer systems that can solve independently and intelligently. It influences operational processes in workplaces. These processes are enabled via the building of machines capable of performing intelligent tasks. (Yessi Bello Perez, 2019). The machines operate by receiving and executing commands generated from data gathered, analyzed, interpreted and reinterpreted by algorithms powering the machines. This enables the machine to act independently and efficiently with limited human supervision (Budko, 2018). AI uses different techniques to enable machine intelligence. These techniques include the use of neural networks, support vector machines, natural language processing, fuzzy logic, robotics and machine learning etc., (Marwala & Xing, 2018). These techniques are data driven, and the security and encryption of such data is important. The compromise of such data will have consequence on the intelligent operation of the machine. This is where Blockchain comes into play.

Blockchains will enable the storage of encrypted AI data in a distributed, decentralized, & immutable ledger format. The data collected and stored in Blockchain can be used to facilitate the decision-making ability of the machine within the AI engine or system. The synergy between Blockchain and AI will ensure the availability of data storage and power resources to the overall network. This synergy will reflect a combination of two network approaches, which are the centralized (for AI), and Decentralized (Blockchain) network approaches (Gonfalonieri, 2018). Industries that have utilized both technologies in their production processes have realized that they synergy presents a unique and powerful pair which further contributes to the growth within that industry (Daley, 2019). Therefore, this chapter provides very basic explanations of both technologies and how they can work together.

BACKGROUND

In this section, an overview of Blockchain technology and artificial intelligence, with its concepts, applications and its use cases will be discussed. Blockchain technology, as mentioned earlier, is a digitized, decentralized, distributed ledger that can be used for different kinds of transactions. These transactions occur in a decentralized on peer-to-peer (P2P) network. The structure of Blockchain technology is represented by data structure concepts of pointers (information of the variable pointing to one another) and linked lists (with help of pointer each block points to specific data and link, that contains the sequence of blocks) (Lastovetska, 2019).

In general, a Blockchain is a continuously growing list of records called blocks. The blocks are sequential with each block holding a complete list of transaction records. Each block consists of a block header and transactions (block body). The set of transactions are replicated to all nodes in the network (Paul, 2019). Subsequent blocks point to previous blocks, but these block share only one parent block. This parent block is the beginning of the block called "the genesis block". The parent block has no parent block. Miners create these blocks. Metadata verification is utilized to ensure the validity of a block in block header. In order to construct the block header in the metadata, the mining node needs to fill the fields that contains:

1. The version of block header (4 bytes),
2. The previous block header hash (32 bytes),
3. The merkle root hash (32 bytes),
4. The timestamp(4 bytes) and,
5. The nBits, and nonce (4 bytes) (Zheng, Xie, Dai, Chen & Wang, 2017).

The rest of a block contains transactions. Depending on the choice of a miner any number of transactions could be bundled into a block (Paul, 2019). In order to authenticate the validation of transactions, asymmetric key cryptography mechanisms is used (Zheng, Xie, Dai, Chen & Wang, 2017).

The blocks can be classified into three types namely; the main branch blocks (current main Blockchain simply extend the most blocks, part of the longest chain), the side branch blocks (some blocks reference a parent block, part of the longest chain), and orphan blocks (which are not part of the main chain) (Paul, 2019).

Figure 1. Basic Blockchain Representations
(Gupta & Sadoghi, 2018)

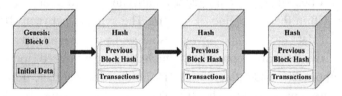

The Blockchain technology has four characteristics. The Blockchain network consists of:

1. The ledger: The ledger provides full transactional history,
2. The secure characteristic: The Blockchain technology is secured using cryptographic mechanisms,
3. The shared (consensus): The ledger is shared among multiple participants, and
4. The distributed (decentralization) characteristic: The Blockchain technology consist of distributed nodes that make up the Blockchain network (Yaga, Mell, Roby & Scarfone, 2018).

The representation of the Bitcoin transaction process is represented in Figure.1. When Bitcoin transactions are initiated in the Blockchain, each bitcoin transactions are verified and approved by resources in the peer-to-peer bitcoin network. However, in traditional databases, transaction record are combined in one block with other transactions. However, in Blockchain, each transaction have a period. Within the period when the block is incomplete, timestamps are allocated to it to avoid duplication. The completed block is placed throughout the network. Once approved, then it is added to the chain of blocks in the sequence. The validation process ensures that data is added in correct order an that all participants access latest version (Knezevic, 2018). These blocks are added every 10 minutes after that they verified by miners with help of consensus mechanisms, each entry in the blocks are secured by cryptographic mechanisms (Agarwal, 2019).

MAIN FOCUS OF THE CHAPTER

Blockchain Basics

A quick recap. So far, in this chapter, it has been highlighted that Blockchain is a kind of distributed ledger, where the data is stored in blocks and the blocks are aligned in one continuous chain. Each block is sealed by a hash function, this type of public ledger technique. The distributed ledger is public because it is visible to all participants. The ledger can store document, transactions, images and other digital assets. A ledger has entries and transactions; it can be organized like a chain of blocks, and new entries can be appended at the end of block. Each block has the hash of previous block. If changes are made to the block, the hash of all subsequent blocks also changed as well (Xu, Weber, &Staples, 2019).

Blockchains are visually represented in rows and columns. Each row represents distinct transactions. The first, second, third columns respectively represents the transaction's timestamp, transaction's details & the stored hash of the current transaction and previous transactions. These columns of transaction enables the verification of the data at any point, and possible to tracking the transaction history (Pierro, 2017) (Anascavage & Davis, 2018).

The most prominent use case of Blockchain is Bitcoin. Bitcoin is a completely decentralized, peer-to-peer, permissionless transaction systems (Satoshi, 2008). It is a cryptocurrency. When trade happens on the bitcoin network, the transactions are written on a Blockchain ledger. A bitcoin address mathematically corresponds to a public key based on ECDSA (Elliptic Curve Digital Signature Algorithm) algorithm.

Bitcoin transactions are also represented in rows and columns. The decentralization of the network implies that every node has access to the same transaction represented in the rows and columns. The delivery of bitcoin transactions using a public ledger enables direct transaction between parties in the network. Therefore, third parties that are not nodes in the network can neither control nor interfere with the transaction. The form of service delivery on Bitcoin platforms enable money transfer for users of bitcoin cryptocurrency (Yli-Huumo, Ko, Choi, Park & Smolander, 2016).

Types of Blockchains

There are three types of Blockchains. These are; Public Blockchain, private Blockchain and consortium or federated Blockchain. The public and private Blockchain have similar characteristics but differ in their application and their format for concensus. Both are decentralized, peer-to-peer networks with digitally stored the signed transactions (Bernard, 2018).

1. **Private Blockchain:** A private Blockchain is a private property owned by either an individual or an organization (Iftemi, 2018). The rights to access or modify the database is managed by a central authority. The authority validates blocks. This authority also has the mandate to authorize new nodes into the database as well as authorize the modification of the database (Agrawal, 2019).

2. **Public Blockchain:** A public Blockchain is not restricted. Anyone can participate in either reading, writing or auditing the Blockchain. This type of Blockchain is open &transparent in that anyone can review and validate the Blocks (Agrawal, 2019). The characteristics of the public Blockchain are as follows:

   a. It is an open network where nodes can join and leave as they please without requiring permission from anyone.

   b. All nodes in the network can verify each new piece of data added to the data structure. These data structures include blocks, transactions, and effects of transactions.

   c. Its protocol includes an incentive mechanism that aims to ensure the transparent validation of transactions. Successfully validated transactions are included in the ledger and the invalid transactions are rejected (Xu, Weber, & Staples, 2019).

   Cryptocurrency platforms are examples of public Blockchain. This type of Blockchain stores a single type of data. As an open platform, new participants can join & maintain the network. They also have the possibility of accessing the transaction database in order to analyze all information in Blockchain network. This type of Blockchain network is decentralized network, and it is a backbone of cryptocurrency (Iftemi, 2018).

3. **Consortium Blockchain**: Consortium Blockchains are open to the public, but not all data is available to all participants or nodes within the Blockchain (El Moutaouakil, & Richard, 2017). Consortium Blockchain the blocks are validated based on predefined rules. Consortium Blockchains are partly decentralized (ibid). This is because it has the properties of both public and private Blockchains. This Blockchain, just like the public and private Blockchains happens operates on the basis of consensus (Iftemi, 2018).

Table 1. Purpose of Public, Private and Consortium Blockchains

Public Blockchain	Private Blockchain	Consortium Blockchain
No Centralized Management	Single Organizations	Multiple Organizations
Permissionless Systems	Permissioned Systems	Permissioned Systems
Large Energy Consumption in consensus mechanisms	Low Energy Consumption in consensus mechanisms	Low Energy Consumption in consensus mechanisms
Long Transaction Systems	Short Transaction Systems	Short Transaction Systems
PoW, PoS, PoA Consensus Algorithms Supported	Supported for Voting or Multi Party Consensus Algorithms	Supported for Voting or Multi Party Consensus Algorithms
Can make transactions for anyone	Anyone can't make transactions	Consortium can make transactions only for selected members
Can run the BTC/LTC full node with anyone	Anyone can't run full node	consortium can run a full node with Selected members
review/audit the Blockchain for anyone	Anyone can't review/audit the Blockchain	review/audit the Blockchain for selected members
Low Efficiency	High Efficiency	High Efficiency

(Iftemi, 2018 & Agrawal, 2019)

Blockchain Categories

Blockchain networks are categorized either as permissioned, permissionless, or the consortium models (Yaga, Mell,Roby & Scarfone,2018). The permissionless model is also known as public internet systems (ibid). In this model, anyone can publish a new block as well as participate in the Blockchain. An example includes Bitcoin and Ethereum. The permissioned model is also known private internet systems (Yaga, Mell,Roby & Scarfone,2018). In this model, only authorized users can publish blocks. The Consortium model is also a permissioned Blockchain networks (ibid). The network is deployed for a group of organizations or an individual authorized users or entities can read/write/audit the transaction (Yaga, Mell,Roby & Scarfone,2018).

1. **Permisionless Blockchain:** In Permissionless Blockchain any user can create a mode and interact with other nodes in the Blockchain network (Kadiyala, 2018). Public Blockchains are permissionless Blockchain. Permissionless Blockchains are also decentralized ledger platforms. The nodes in the network do not require authorization to read or write into the ledger. Where new nodes can sign up without authorization a platform. All members have the right to add and validate the transactions as well as create smart contracts on the network. An example of such validation process is the Proof of work and Proof of stake (Yaga, Mell, Roby & Scarfone,2018). The key characteristic of permissionless systems includes decentralization, the use of digital assets, transparency, anonymity, governance, tokens, and scalability & performance (Dob, 2018).

2. **Permissioned Blockchains**: The permissioned Blockchain can either be a centralized or decentralized network. It is a closed ecosystem and the participants in the network are well defined. Private Blockchains are likely to be employed as private Blockchains (Kadiyala, 2018). This is because it is easy to share trusted information as secure context; enable efficient information exchange; and to record transactions in consortium networks (Kadiyala, 2018).

Permissioned Blockchains are preferred for centralized organizations (Dob, 2018). Here, authorized users maintain the Blockchain. Owners of permissioned Blockchain networks exercise tight control and restrict their Blockchain to be used within their organizations, (Yaga, Mell, Roby & Scarfone,2018). Corda, and Quorum are examples of permissioned Blockchain (Gupta, 2018). The characteristics of permissioned Blockchain include: varying decentralization, transparency & anonymity, privacy, tokens, scalability & performance, and Governance (Kadiyala, 2018 & Dob,2018).

Table 2. Difference between Permissionless and Permissioned Blockchains

Permissionless Blockchains	Permissioned Blockchains
Anyone can access and create data	Closed ecosystems (all participants defined)
Anyone can publish smart contracts	Decentralization and transparency varies
Anyone can run a node	Only preapproved entities can run node
100% Transparency	No tokens given to nodes as incentive
Relatively high level of anonymity	No anonymity
Performance is slow	Performance is drastically increased
Scaling is a massive challenge	Scaling is drastically increased
Monetary incentives to nodes (miners)	Mining is not required

(Gupta, 2018)

Consensus Mechanisms in Blockchain

Decision making on Blockchain platforms are based on consensus. The mechanisms for consensus are inbuilt in Blockchains and they enable transparency among the nodes during transactions on the Blockchain. This consensus protocol are highly suited for business requirements of modern applications (Asayag, Cohen, Grayevsky, and Leshkowitz, 2018). The consensus mechanisms enables the transparent validation of new data entries.

The consensus mechanisms are evident in permissionless and permissioned Blockchains. In the permissionless systems publish all nodes have to validate the transaction before a Block is added to the Blockchain. In the permissioned systems consensus mechanisms are instituted between the authorized nodes. Generally, consensus mechanisms provide a level of trust between publishing nodes.

Several consensus models are used in Blockchain networks (Yaga, Mell, Roby, & Scarfone, 2018). The consensus mechanism implemented in a way that it does not only validate the transaction but enable the creation of simple transaction ledgers as well as maintain a history of transactions (Porat, Pratap, Shah & Adkar, 2017). The most popular and widely consensus models are Proof of Work (PoW) and Proof of Stake (PoS).

1. **Proof of work:** Proof of work is a consensus model mainly used in Bitcoin systems. The Bitcoin consensus model operate in a manner that all nodes confirm transactions & produce relevant blocks to the Blockchain (Anwar, 2018). The consensus mechanism prevents double utilization of digital asset. Hence, there is a verifiable guarantee of trust within the network. The guarantee of trust for the single utilization of a digital asset is called nonce (Hassan, Ali, Latif, Qadir, Kanhere, Singh, & Crowcroft, 2019).

In the PoW process, the hash value of the block header in each node of network is calculated (Zheng et al, 2017). The main principle behind the PoW is to solve complex mathematical problems and easily give out solutions, and also takes 10 minutes to create a new block (Anwar, 2018). Miners that are able to solve these mathematical challenges validate the transaction enabling other nodes to add this block to their Blockchains (Zheng et al, 2017).

2. **Proof of Stake**: Proof of Stake consensus models mainly deals with the drawbacks of proof of work algorithm (Anwar, 2018). In that model every block, get validated, before it is added to the Blockchain. PoS systems is still in its development phase (Hassan, 2019). In the PoS have to prove the ownership of the amount of currency (Zheng et al, 2017). This Blockchain networks use the amount at stake to determine if new blocks will be added to the Blockchain (Yaga et al., 2018). Compared to PoW, PoS saves energy and is more effective, and it doesn't require high energy resources (Zheng, 2017).

ARTIFICIAL INTELLIGENCE

Artificial Intelligence (AI) is a branch of computer science, which deals with building smart machines, capable of performing tasks that typically requires human intelligence (Schroer, 2019). Human intelligence is designed to perform different sets of tasks (Daley, 2019). In order to advance AI systems, natural language processes, machine learning and deep learning, are utilized. They are creating a paradigm shift in new industry, as Intelligent Machines are gradually replacing humans in industrial productions. Therefore, AI is the core, endeavor to replicate or simulate human intelligence in machines.

AI can be broadly classified into two categories, namely the Type-1 and Type-2 AI. The Type-1 technique is based on capabilities of the programmed machine. The Type-2 techniques is based on the functionalities of the programmed machines. The Type-1 technique can be classified as either weak or narrow AI, and Strong AI (Speiser, Mulherin, King & Clark, 2017). The Type-2 technique can be classified as reactive machines that are limited in, memory, theory of mind and self-awareness (Hintze, 2016).

Type-1 or Weak AI (narrow AI), focuses on narrow tasks; it has no power of perception and this system is designed and trained for a particular task. Its focus is narrowly defined to a specific problem, and it is able to perform dedicated task with intelligence. Most AI around us today are Narrow AI (Ghosal,2019). Good examples of Narrow AI are Siri and Alexa (Speiser, Mulherin, Kin & Clark, 2017). Conversely, for Strong AI, the systems intellectual capability and functionality is equal to humans (Speiser et al, 2017). In most cases, it is better at performing tasks than humans, hence it is called super AI (Speiser et al, 2017).

The Type-2 as mentioned earlier is based on functionalities. The first functionality is interactive reactivity. This is visible in reactive AI machines. Reactive AI machines are the most basic forms of AI. They do not store memories or past information to future actions. They only react as programmed. An example of reactive machines is Google's AlphsGo. The second functionality is that limited recollection. Based on this functionality, the machine can use past experience stored in its memory. However this memory is limited and the duration of data storage is also limited. An example of such Machines can be found in self-driving cars. The third functionality is that of self-awareness. This is the Theory of the mind. Such AI machines do not exist at the moment, but there are efforts being made to develop this type of AI. Such AI should be able to understand human emotion, beliefs, thoughts, and expectations and also interact socially like humans. And the final functionality self –awareness; these AI machines are smarter than human mind (its complete human being), main thing to understand the human intelligence (Chethan Kumar, 2018).

DISCUSSION

Blockchain Technology and AI Integration

The Artificial intelligence concept was conceived in the 1950s, but it did not find mainstream popularity until 1990's and early 2000s (Nesbitt, 2019). The sharp interest in AI began in 2016-2017. Coincidentally, Blockchain also experienced a sharp interest in 2017-2018. Both technologies then were in the experimental stages. AI and Blockchain are both innovative technologies. Blockchain stores data in an encrypted and an immutable format, while AI derives intelligence from data driven algorithms (Namahe, 2018). Hence, AI and Blockchains complement each other.

AI and Blockchains complement each other in three different ways;

1. AI requires encryption, which Blockchain provides;
2. Blockchain enables the tracking, understanding and explanation of decisions made by AI,
3. AI can manage Blockchains more efficiently than humans or conventional computers (Marr, 2018).

Compared to centralized technologies, Blockchain technology makes safer and more transparent data transaction processes (Budko, 2018). Conversely, AI is a revolutionary technology that can learn by analyzing and discovering patterns in massive amounts of data (Makridakis, Polemitis, Giaglis & Louca, 2018). These two techniques serve to enhance the capabilities of each other, and also provide better opportunities for oversight & accountability (Marr, 2018).

Blockchain for AI Applications

As mentioned previously, AI has the potential of managing Blockchains. The tasks that can be performed by AI on Blockchain include: facilitating the smart computing power of Blockchains; the creation of diverse data sets; data protection; data monetization; and Trusted AI decision making processes using Blockchain (Banafa, 2019). These potentials relate to the influence of Blockchain on AI applications and Algorithms.

Blockchain for AI Algorithms

There are different applications where Blockchain is utilized to facilitate AI algorithms in a service delivery process. Examples of such initiatives include SingularityNet, Deepbrain chain and Matrix AI.

1. SingularityNET: SingularityNET provides a global AI network. SingularityNET is a decentralized market place for AI services. These services exchange for other AI services or cryptocurrency. The singularityNET cryptocurrency is called AGI tokens. These AI services are delivered in decentralized market. The agreement between buyer and seller are embedded in the lines of code, AI services operating the search requirements are called agent (Bharadwaj, 2019). The features of SingularityNet

are; interoperability, data sovereignty & policy, modularity, and scalability. SingularityNET securely host the public and private Blockchains, but run the AI application on top of a private Blockchain on top of its singularity-networking platform (Geortzel, 2017).

2. DeepBrain Chain: DeepBrain Chain is providing an AI computing platform with the help of Blockchain. Their concept is based on artificial neural network technique with machine learning and deep learning techniques. The main objective of deepbrain chain are to ensure that artificial neural network operations are decentralized and distributed over global Blockchain nodes. Each individual node is interconnected with the help of Blockchain. Transactions in the Blockchain network is via smart contracts. The design of the smart contract, the data provider & data training parties are physically separated thereby protecting their privacy, and important features of Deepbrain chain. The computing nodes can be adjusted dynamically according to the user application in amount of calculation.

3. MATRIX AI: MATRIX is the latest artificial intelligence technology to deliver on the promise of Blockchain. It is a platform, which incorporates Blockchain and AI to enable the realization of an Intelligent Blockchain. It is an open source, intelligent Blockchain platform, but it is used to automatically self-optimize the Blockchain network, and support smart-contracts & machine learning services. The matrix project was officially launched on September 2016. AI Bayesian inference machine design completed on January 2017, and Blockchain design based on artificial intelligence completed on May 2017. The objectives of MatrixAI are; the automatic generation of smart contracts and secured smart contracts. The Features of Matrix AI include the auto-coding of intelligent contracts; AI-powered cybersecurity system; adaptive Blockchain parameters; value-added green mining, and dynamic delegation network. The Matrix AI basically utilized the combination of proof of stake and proof of work in Blockchain consensus protocol (Tao, Ma, Tian & Han, 2018.)

Integrating Blockchain Technology with Artificial Intelligence

The synergy of Blockchain and AI, has been applied to upgrade different industries such as: food supply chain logistics, health care record, financial security, media, and medical scan records for diagnosis (Daley, 2019).

Table 3. Key Features and benefits of Integration with Blockchain and AI

Benefits of AI and Blockchain Integration	AI	Blockchain
Enhanced Data Security	Centralized	Decentralized
Improved Trust on Robotic Decisions	Changing	Deterministic
Collective Decision Making	Probabilistic	Immutable
Decentralized Intelligence	Volatile	Data Integrity
High Efficiency	Data, Knowledge, and Decision-Centric	Attacks Resilient

(Salah, Rehman, & Nizamuddin, 2019)

There are different examples where AI and Blockchain were utilized in different selected sectors. Some of these examples of companies in certain industries that utilizes the synergy of Blockchain and AI in their service delivery are:

1. **FINALZE**: Finalze is a software platform, build the applications to improve civil infrastructure.
2. **CORE SCIENTIFIC**:Core Scientific in this process upgrading business infrastructure.
3. **BURSTIQ**: They have created a health wallet to holistically manage patient's data & learn more about specific disease,.
4. **VIA**: VIA is the world's largest energy companies. They use the Blockchain/AI tools to facilitate a more effective use the company's energy data.
5. **FIGURE:** This platform streamlines the home loan process for finding the consumer credit products,
6. **CYWARE LABS**: It is an AI/Blockchain based tool. This tool is used for mobile threat intelligence, secured messaging and incident reporting platform,
7. **CHAINHAUS**: Its useful for education and marketing firm,
8. **VERISART**: This platform certifies and verify works in real time. They also create tamper proof certificates for ensuring credit and immutability,
9. **VYTALYX**: It is a health tech company, storing medical information on a Blockchain, and relevantly search for medical data.
10. **STOWK**: It is useful for business operations, data access and IT governance,
11. **MOBS**: It is useful for selling and buying of Smartphone videos,
12. **LIVEEEDU**: This is an online Project Based Learning platform.
13. **NEUREAL**: This is an engine used for predictions. It is used to predict everything from stock market to google searches.
14. **COINGENIUS**: This is an AI-driven cryptocurrency trading platform that gives advanced forecasting,
15. **BOTCHAIN** - Botchain ecosystems runs applications on distributed network, it's also work with healthcare industry,
16. **BLACKBIRD.AI**: This company rates the credibility of news content. It constantly scans the references, websites, social media pages, fake articles inorder to ensure that the content is truthful and credible.
17. **GAINFY**: It is a healthcare platform, these devices to improve the industry experience (Daley, 2019).

CONCLUSION

Bitcoin cryptocurrency systems run on Blockchain technology. Blockchain technology serves as internet applications and network environment. The Blockchain systems provide security, privacy and transparency to all users. Blockchain technology & artificial intelligence provide benefits to the society, and more innovation to the industry. Combination of these two technologies developing their applications, and researchers exploring their knowledge, both technologies provide huge benefits to the society.

REFERENCES

Agrawal, H. (2019). *Understanding Blockchain Technology: What is Blockchain and how it works.* Retrieved August 12, 2019, from https://coinsutra.com/Blockchain/

Anascavage, R., & Davis, N. (2018). *Blockchain Technology: A Literature Review.* https://papers.ssrn.com/sol3/papers.cfm?abstract_id=3173406

Anwar, H. (2018). *Consensus Algorithms: The Root of the Blockchain Technology.* Retrieved August 25, 2108, from https://101Blockchains.com/consensus-algorithms-Blockchain/#1

Asayag, A., Cohen, G., Grayevsky, I., & Leshkowitz, M. (2018). *Helix: A Scalable and fair Consensus Algorithm.* https://pdfs.semanticscholar.org/0d19/de4e8c825164e1306b362ce6a1d43e1c5480.pdf

Banafa, A. (2019). *Blockchain and AI: A Perfect Match?* Retrieved May 6, 2019, from https://www.bbvaopenmind.com/en/technology/artificial-intelligence/Blockchain-and-ai-a-perfect-match/

Bernard, R. (2018). *Private vs. Public Blockchain: What are the Major Differences?* Retrieved December 17, 2018, from https://medium.com/luxtag-live-tokenized-assets-on-Blockchain/private-vs-public-Blockchain-what-are-the-major-differences-d92a504f3a4a

Bharadwaj, R. (2019). *AI in Blockchain – Current Applications and Trends.* Retrieved August 13, 2019, from https://emerj.com/ai-sector-overviews/ai-in-Blockchain/

Budko, D. (2018). *How Blockchain can Transform Artificial Intelligence.* Retrieved February 13, 2018, from https://dzone.com/articles/how-Blockchain-can-transform-artificial-intelligence

Buren, W. V. (2017). *The Potential of Blockchain Technology Application in the Food System.* https://www.beefresearch.org/CMDocs/BeefResearch/.../Potential of Blockchain.pdf

Chethan Kumar, G. N. (2018). *Artificial Intelligence: Definition, Types, Examples, and Technologies.* Retrieved August 31, 2018, from https://medium.com/@chethankumargn/artificial-intelligence-definition-types-examples-technologies-962ea75c7b9b

Chikara, A. (2019). *Introduction to Blockchain Technology.* Retrieved October 8, 2019, from https://www.3pillarglobal.com/insights/introduction-to-Blockchain-technology?unapproved=124382&moderation-hash 71e3560ea105cf114152a7d186sc24c# comment-124382

Daley, S. (2019). *Tastier Coffee, Hurricane Prediction and Fighting The Opioid Crisis: 31 Ways Blockchain & Ai Make A Powerful Pair.* Retrieved September 24, 2019, from https://builtin.com/artificial-intelligence/Blockchain-ai-examples

Dinh, T. N., & Thai, T. (2018, September). AI and Blockchain: A Disruptive Integration. *IEEE Computer Society, 51*(9), 48–53. doi:10.1109/MC.2018.3620971

Dob, D. (2018). *Permissioned vs Permissionless Blockchains: Understanding the Differences.* Retrieved July 17, 2018, from https://blockonomi.com/permissioned-vs-permissionless-Blockchains/

El Moutaouakil, S., & Richard, C. (2017). *Blockchain, a catalyst for new approaches in insurance.* PWC.

Fenwick, M., & Vermeulen, E.P.M. (2018). *Technology and Corporate Governance: Blockchain, Crypto, and Artificial Intelligence.* Retrieved November 7, 2018, from https://papers.ssrn.com/sol3/papers.cfm?abstract_id=3263222

Ghosal, M. (2019). *What Is AI - Weak AI and Strong AI with examples.* Retrieved July 26, 2019, from https://spotle.ai/feeddetails/What-Is-AI-Weak-AI-Strong-AI-with-examples-Key-disciplines-and-applications-Of-AI-/3173

Goertzel, B. (2017). *SingularityNET: A decentralized, open market and inter-network for AIs. Thoughts, Theories & Studies on Artificial Intelligence (AI).* Research.

Gonfalonieri, A. (2018). *Blockchain + AI: Towards Mode Decentralization & Less Data Oligopoly.* Retrieved July 16, 2018, from https://medium.com/predict/Blockchain-ai-towards-more-decentralization-less-data-oligopoly-e0a2b2781082

Gupta, N. (2018). *Permissionless Blockchain vs Permissioned Blockchain – What's Your Pick.* Retrieved September 14, 2018, from https://akeo.tech/blog/Blockchain-and-dlt/permissionless-permissioned-Blockchain

Gupta, S., & Sadoghi, M. (2018). Blockchain Transaction Processing. Springer International Publishing AG. *Part of Springer Nature, 2018.* doi:10.1007/978-3-319-63962-8_333-1

Hassan, F., Ali, A., Latif, S., Qadir, J., Kanhere, S., Singh, J., & Crowcroft, J. (2019). *Blockchain and the Future of the Internet: A Comprehensive Review.* https://arxiv.org/pdf/1904.00733.pdf

Hintze, A. (2019). *Understanding the four types of Artificial Intelligence.* Retrieved November 14, 2018, from https://www.govtech.com/computing/Understanding-the-Four-Types-of-Artificial-Intelligence.html

Iftemi, A. (2018). *Exploring the different types of Blockchain.* Retrieved July 9, 2018, from https://blog.modex.tech/exploring-the-different-types-of-Blockchain-10395da93a51

Kadiyala, A. (2018). *Nuances between Permissionless and Permissioned Blockchains.* Retrieved February 18, 2018, from https://medium.com/@akadiyala/nuances-between-permissionless-and-permissioned-Blockchains-f5b566f5d483

Knezevic, D. (2018). Impact of Blockchain Technology Platform in Changing the Financial Sector and Other Industries. *Montenegrin Journal of Economics. 14*(1), 109-120.

Lastovetska, A. (2019). *Blockchain Architecture Basics: Components, Structure, Benefits & Creation.* Retrieved January 31, 2019, from https://mlsdev.com/blog/156-how-to-build-your-own-Blockchain-architecture

Makridakis, S., Polemitis, A., Giaglis, G., & Louca, S. (2018). Blockchain: The Next Breakthrough in the Rapid Progress of AI. *Robotics & Automation Engineering Journal, 2*(4), 1-12.

Marr, B. (2018). *Artificial Intelligence and Blockchain: 3 Major Benefits of Combining These Two Mega-Trends.* Retrieved March 2, 2018, from https://www.forbes.com/sites/bernardmarr/2018/03/02/artificial-intelligence-and-Blockchain-3-major-benefits-of-combining-these-two-mega-trends/#3ce781f64b44

Marwala, T., & Xing, B. (2018). *Blockchain and Aritificial Intelligence*. University of Johannesburg. Auckland Park. Republic of South Africa. https://arxiv.org/pdf/1802.04451

Nakamoto, S. (n.d.). *Bitcoin: A peer-to-peer electronic cash system*. https://bitcoin.org/bitcoin.pdf

Namahe. (2018). *How to Actually Combine AI and Blockchain in One Platform*. Retrieved July 7, 2018, from https://hackernoon.com/how-to-actually-combine-ai-and-Blockchain-in-one-platform-ef937e919ec2

Nesbitt, A. (2019). *Blockchain Technology & Artificial Intelligence — Unmasking the Mystery at the Heart of AI*. Retrieved January 20, 2019, from https://medium.com/datadriveninvestor/Blockchain-technology-artificial-intelligence-unmasking-the-mystery-at-the-heart-of-ai-b1e930a59937

Patel, A. (2018). *How Blockchain and artificial intelligence complement each other*. Retrieved November 21, 2018, from https://jaxenter.com/Blockchain-artificial-intelligence-152001.html

Paul. (2019). *Everything you need to know about Blockchain architecture*. Retrieved May 22, 2019, from https://www.edureka.co/blog/Blockchain-architecture/

Perez. (2019). *Blockchain and AI could be a perfect match – here's why*. Retrieved February 5, 2019, from https://thenextweb.com/hardfork/2019/02/05/Blockchain-and-ai-could-be-a-perfect-match-heres-why/

Porat, A., Pratap, A., Shah, P., & Adkar, V. (2017). *Blockchain Consensus: An analysis of Proof-of-Work and its applications*. https://www.scs.stanford.edu/17au-cs244b/labs/projects/porat_pratap_shah_adkar.pdf

Rohitha, E. P. (2018). *An Introduction to Blockchain Technology*. Retrieved July 5, 2018, from https://dzone.com/articles/an-introduction-to-Blockchain-technology

Salah, K., Rehman, M.H., Nizamudddin, N., & Al-Fuquaha, A. (2019). Blockchain for AI: Review and Open Research Challenges. *IEEE Access, 7*, 10127-10149. doi:10.1109/ACCESS.2018.2890507

Salman, S. (2019). *Why Artificial Intelligence Needs to breath on Blockchain?* Retrieved Mar 14, 2019, from https://towardsdatascience.com/why-artificial-intelligence-needs-to-breath-on-Blockchain-354d7b7027c6

Schroer, A. (2019). *Artificial Intelligence. What is Artificial Intelligence? How Does AI Work?* Retrieved August, 29, 2019, from https://builtin.com/artificial-intelligence

Speiser, M., Mulherin, G., King, K., & Clark, S. (2017). *Artificial Intelligence and Blockchain*. Available: https://nacm.org/pdfs/gscfm/Artificial_Intelligence-Blockchain.pdf

Tao, O., Ma, K., Tian, E., & Han, S. (2018). *Matrix Wallet App is Online*. Retrieved April 2018, from https://www.matrix.io/

Xu, X., Weber, I., & Staples, M. (2019). *Architecture for Blockchain Applications*. Springer International Publishing. doi:10.1007/978-3-030-03035-3

Yaga, D., Mell, P., Roby, N., & Scarfone, K. (2018). *Blockchain Technology over Overview*. National Institute of Standards and Technology Internal Report 8202. https://nvlpubs.nist.gov/nistpubs/ir/2018/NIST.IR.8202.pdf

Yli-Huumo, J., Ko, D., Choi, S., Park, S., & Smolander, K. (2016). Where Is Current Research on Blockchain Technology?—A Systematic Review. *PLoS One*, *11*(10), e0163477. doi:10.1371/journal. pone.0163477 PMID:27695049

Zheng, Z., Xie, S., Dai, H. N., & Wang, H. (2017). An Overview of Blockchain Technology: Architecture, Consensus, and Future Trends. *IEEE 6th International Congress on Big Data Congress*.

KEY TERMS AND DEFINITIONS

Artificial Intelligence: Artificial intelligence is the simulation of human intelligence processes by machines, especially computer systems. These processes include learning (the acquisition of information and rules for using the information), reasoning (using rules to reach approximate or definite conclusions) and self-correction.

Assets: Anything that can be transferred.

Bitcoin: Bitcoin is a complete decentralized peer to peer and permission less cryptocurrency, it's a form of electronic cash system with completely decentralized; cannot be any central party for ordering or recording or controlling your currency like bank or government.

Blockchain: Blockchain is a decentralized computation and information sharing platform which enables multiple authoritative domains that do not trust each other to cooperate coordinate and collaborate in a rational decision-making process.

Blocks: A block is a collection of data. And each piece of data is added to the Blockchain by connecting one block after another in a chronological way, much in the same way a row of a spreadsheet follows another row.

Consensus Model: A process to achieve agreement within a distributed system on the valid state. It's otherwise called consensus algorithm, consensus mechanisms and also consensus method.

Cryptocurrency: Cryptocurrencies are a subset of digital currencies that rely on cryptographic techniques to achieve consensus, for example Bitcoin and ether. Nodes are network participants in a distributed ledger

Distributed Ledger: A distributed ledger is a database that is spread across different computer systems, countries or organizations. Records are stored one after the other in a continuous ledger. Distributed ledger data can be either "permissioned" or "un-permissioned."

Double Spend: An attack where a Blockchain network user attempts to explicitly double spend a digital asset.

Ethereum: Ethereum is a platform that allows distributed, decentralized applications such as smart contracts to run on a virtual machine on top of a Blockchain network.

Genesis Block: A genesis block is the very block on a Blockchain with no previous block before it.

Hash Function: A cryptographic hash function allows one to easily verify that some input data maps to a given value. This is used for assuring integrity of transmitted data and is the building block for providing message authentication. Hash functions are related to (and often confused with) check digits, fingerprints, and other verification tools.

Hash Pointer: A cryptographic hash pointing to a data block. Hash Pointer lets you verify that the previous block of data has not been tampered.

Ledger: A record of transactions

Mining: The act of solving a puzzle within a proof of work consensus model

Peer-to-Peer (P2P): Peer-to-peer is a system where participants on a network interact with each other directly without needing to go through a centralized system or intermediary.

Permissioned Blockchain: It works in open environment and large network of participants, so the participants do not need to reveal their own identity, the users do not need to reveal their own identity to other peers. It's something called private model. In a permissioned Blockchain, only a restricted set of users have the rights to validate the block transactions.

Permissionless Blockchain: Here anyone can join the network, participate in the process of block verification to create consensus and also create smart contracts. Permissioned Blockchains do not have to use the computing power-based mining to reach a consensus since all of the actors are known.

Private Blockchain: A private blockchain is a permissioned blockchain. Permissioned networks place restrictions on who is allowed to participate in the network and in what transactions.

Public Blockchain: A public blockchain is a permissionless blockchain. Anyone can join the Blockchain network, meaning that they can read, write, or participate with a public Blockchain.

Chapter 5
Study and Survey on Blockchain Privacy and Security Issues

Sourav Banerjee
Kalyani Government Engineering College, India

Debashis Das
https://orcid.org/0000-0003-4422-3196
University of Kalyani, India

Manju Biswas
Kalyani Government Engineering College, India

Utpal Biswas
University of Kalyani, India

ABSTRACT

Blockchain-based technology is becoming increasingly popular and is now used to solve a wide range of tasks. And it's not all about cryptocurrencies. Even though it's based on secure technology, a blockchain needs protection as well. The risks of exploits, targeted attacks, or unauthorized access can be mitigated by the instant incident response and system recovery. Blockchain technology relies on a ledger to keep track of all financial transactions. Ordinarily, this kind of master ledger would be a glaring point of vulnerability. Another tenet of security is the chain itself. Configuration flaws, as well as insecure data storage and transfers, may cause leaks of sensitive information. This is even more dangerous when there are centralized components within the platform. In this chapter, the authors will demonstrate where the disadvantages of security and privacy in blockchain are currently and discuss how blockchain technology can improve these disadvantages and outlines the requirements for future solution.

INTRODUCTION

The evolution of Blockchains (or integrated ledger technology) has been likened to the growth of the Internet. As a result, there have been remarks and discussions about the ability of technology to disrupt

DOI: 10.4018/978-1-7998-3632-2.ch005

various sectors such as healthcare, the public sector, energy, manufacturing and, in particular, financial services (Grut, 2016). This means the emergence of evolved suppliers to evolved industrial sectors. Blockchain is popular today, but there are still critics who challenge the technology's scalability, safety, and sustainability.

If one assumes a peripheral device that does not have a single point of error and is resilient to the cyberattacks that make news these days. This is the value presented by Blockchain. This value is enabled by the shared ledger, which today is used for cryptocurrencies like Bitcoin and Ethereum, which challenges the conventional model of server/client architecture. Bitcoin has become the first application developed using Blockchain in 2009. A safe decentralized currency exchange system eliminated the use of internal intermediaries. Recently, in other areas, Blockchain has proved its worth (Dickson, 2016). It could be said that Blockchain is the continuation of centuries of cryptography and safety studies and breakthroughs. This breakthrough offers a completely distinct strategy towards saving data and performing tasks, making it particularly appropriate for settings with strong safety demands and mutually unidentified performers. Participants who are already acknowledged by the ledger validate and process requests within a permitted Blockchain transaction.

Technologies based on Blockchain are becoming common. Today Blockchain serves a broad variety of functions and not everything has to do with cryptocurrencies. Blockchain technology is the main component in the establishment of business operations that can be used in the manufacturing sector. In the Internet of Things (IoT) networks, scalability governance applications, cryptocurrencies, and many other areas, the Blockchain technique is also being applied. Therefore, Blockchain is now a vital and cutting-edge element for a whole range of enterprises. However, Blockchain can itself be subjected to multiple hazards based on security-driven metric. This is because Blockchains include confidential data regarding particular participants, businesses resources and services, therefore it is essential to provide extensive security. This chapter will demonstrate areas of disadvantages towards safety and privacy in Blockchain. This chapter also will discuss how Blockchain technology can improve safety and privacy as well as outlines future difficulties and problems.

BLOCKCHAIN TECHNOLOGY

Blockchain is a decentralized computation and information sharing platform that enables us to connect multiple authoritative domains where no one can trust each other in order to cooperate, collaborate and coordinate with each other in an intelligent decision-making process. Figure 1 shows that Blockchain is also a data structure which stores all the ordered set of block-organized transactions (Zheng et al., 2017). The first block of the Blockchain is called genesis block. A block in a Blockchain can contain only a single transaction or more.

Figure 1. Blockchain's data structure representation
(Kumar, 2018, Chakraborty, 2018)

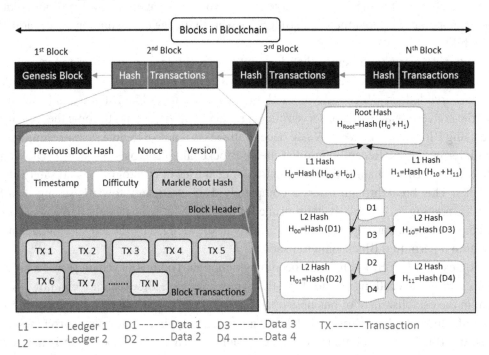

Once, there was a traditional way of sharing information and this environment was and 'is' still centralized. The main problem with this type of environment is that of the single point of failure. This implies that if the central node crashes then all other nodes, which are connected, with the central node are disconnected. In a Blockchain, every node maintains a local copy. This copy, which is identical to the original copy and updated in the global information sheet as it is distributed within the database (Nakamoto, 2008) with well-built constancy support. In this database, once data is inserted within the Blockchain ledger, then no one is able to alter this data in the future and that way that data is tamper-proof (Al-Saqaf&Seidler, 2017). Figure 2 represents the main requirements towards building a reliable Blockchain architecture and infrastructure. Blockchain is like a public ledger therefore the following aspects ought to be considered in its design(Chakraborty, 2018):

1. **Protocols for Commitment:** This ensures that every valid transaction from users are committed and included in the Blockchain within a finite time. Whenever a new transaction is committed at that time, the protocol for commitment ensures that, if valid, the transaction is committed to an existing public ledger or Blockchain otherwise the entry will not be added to Blockchain.
2. **Consensus:** Consensus is an essential element in the Blockchain framework. This framework makes sure that each local copy is consistent with each other across the nodes in the network thereby ensuring that everyone (node) has the most updated copy.
3. **Security:** Thirdly, safety is essential in the transaction processes. All the data within the Blockchain are assumed to be tamper-proof and must be validated. This ensures that there are no malicious nodes within the Blockchain network. This is because, as mentioned earlier, the data inserted into a public ledger or inside the Blockchain is now distributed to individual clients and everyone

maintains their local copy of the Blockchain. In that local copy, that individual cannot tamper but upgrade the data and retransmit the data within the network. But inorder for the transaction to be validates, the other nodes should be convinces that the broadcasted information is not malicious or a false information from the database. So, in this way security needs are ensured.

4. **Privacy and Authenticity:** The final aspect is privacy and authenticity. As information is coming from different clients and we are putting that information into the Blockchain and a copy of the Blockchain is accessible to every client and so privacy and authenticity need to be ensured.

Figure 2. Requirements to the Blockchain Solution
(Chakraborty, 2018)

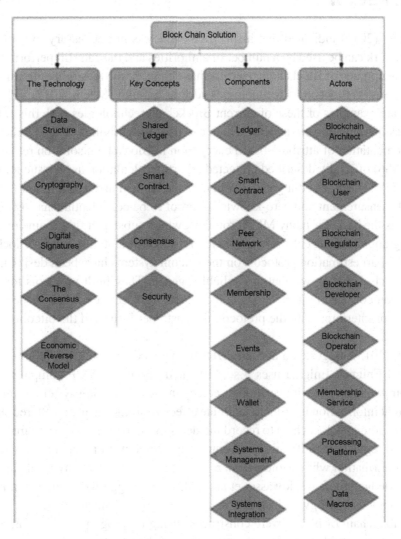

A Blockchain is a scheme that enables consumers to create a public agreement without the influence of a specific third party. This is represented in the deployment of Bitcoin. Today the technology provides a broad range of applications and many comparable schemes have been developed for various transactions. Obviously, digital currencies are commonly used and goods without brokers can either be traded or shared.

Therefore, Blockchain is a technology of value in today's modern economy therefore, ensuring secure transactions as well as the privacy of relevant stakeholders on the platform is crucial. However, the simplicity of the structure of a Blockchain helps us identify its weaknesses with respect to privacy and security. Currently, privacy and security in Blockchain is enables by its support for digital signature (Ikeda, 2018) policy and the proof of work. Both elements have distinct security and privacy signifiers. But they are not enough as there are problems that need to be resolved with Blockchain security.

LITERATURE REVIEW

Lewko and Waters (2011) indicated that a specified agency is not necessary to encrypt attributes. A decentralized network can be used by a number of authorities and the can still perform the same tasks as they do today. The upgrade of Blockchain overtime has enhanced the feasibility for utilizing the technology in different sectors. Blockchain technologies such as Steemit (Steem, 2017), IPFS (Benet, 2015), SAFE Network, are examples of these of current Blockchain technologies with this enhanced abilities. In these examples, participants on the Blockchain can trust the activities of the public authorities even though the implementation of attribute-based encryption in Blockchain solution remains a challenge.

Yao (1982, 1986) officially described protected bipartite calculation as an issue for the millionaires. Goldreich et al. (1987) suggested a generalization of the Multi-Party Calculation (MPC), presuming that all inputs of measurement and zero-knowledge proof to be confidential sharing components. This generalization was the basis for many MPC protocols, which subsequently became more effective.

MPC is being applied in recent years to maintain user confidentiality within Blockchain schemes. The reliable multi-part estimation protocols on the Bitcoin systems have been designated and enforced by Andrychowicz et al.(2014), without any reliable agency. They built protocols for safe multi-party lotteries. Their protocols ensure justice to genuine clients irrespective of their dishonest behavior. If a customer violates or interferes with the protocol, the customer loses and the bitcoins are transferred to the real customers.

Zyskind et al. (2015) suggested a decentralized framework for Symmetric Multiprocessing (SMP) computing, called Enigma. Enigma uses a sophisticated variant of SMP computation to ensure the privacy of its computing model with verifiable secrecy in the exchanging system. Enigma also encodes confidential mutual information in order to facilitate effective storage using an altered shared hash table. Moreover, it uses a foreign Blockchain to record incidents in a corruption-resistant manner and the peer-to-peer network to regulate identification and entry. Like Bitcoin, Enigma autonomously controls and protects private information while avoiding the requirement of a trustworthy third party and its dependence. Zero-knowledge proofs (Goldwasser et al., 1985) were suggested at the beginning of the 1980s as another encryption technology with strong, data conservation characteristics.

The first reliable chain of blocks were constructed using cryptography. (Haber& Stornetta, 1991). In 1993, there was a proposal to improve the efficiency of the Blockchain by integrating Merkle trees and placing a number of documents into a single block. Sahai & Waters (2004) suggested the notion of attribute-based authentication (Fuzzy Identity Based Encryption). Since then there have been proposals for a number of extensions to the baseline Attribute Bases Encryption (ABE) (Chase, 2007, Jung et al., 2013). The proposal called for the inclusion of ABE with multiple authorities for the joint generation of private key users, which will assist random predicates. Attribute-based encoding (Garg et al., 2013, Gorbunov et al., 2013) is very potent, However, few apps to date operate with this form of encoding. This is because both key ideas are not understood even though its execution is effective. ABE is yet to be utilized for real-time operations in a Blockchain. An ABE system (Gorbunov et al., 2013) was suggested as a way of applying ABE in Blockchains in 2011. In order for both technologies to work together, using their own off-chain on the conduct of virtual devices, Arbitrum (Kalodner et al., 2018) has proposed a system that encourages and require verifiers to check the digital contract signature. Arbitrum is built as an effective challenge-based protocol aimed at defining and incentivizing deceitful participants in order for the dishonest members to complain about the conduct of virtual machines. The off-chain validation motivation system for digital computers has greatly enhanced the scalability and security of intelligent agreements.

AN OVERVIEW OF THE BLOCKCHAIN SECURITY & PRIVACY

Everyday cybersecurity attacks emerge, although older risks exist, ready to attack again. Unfortunately Blockchain technology is not the pinnacle of cybersafety, but a powerful tool for hardening networks. If the process breaks into a hierarchical network at one clear failure point, the Blockchain uses its abilities superbly. In the case of higher transaction rates, Blockchain is a platform operates alongside technologies such as Internet of Things (Atlam & Wills, 2018), smart grids, used currency system and smart contracts (Kosba et al., 2016).

Figure 3. Various Security Risk Areas of Blockchain

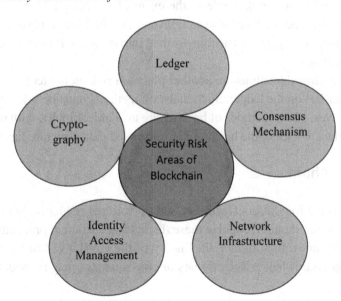

Key Security Risk Areas of Blockchain

- **Ledger:** The ledger is used to register all transactions and changes in the status of the data. This ledger is distributed by smart design and shared between the nodes. Two significant hazards generally threaten the independence of the folder: (a) unauthorized entry into the ledger; and (b) unauthorized, improper or illegal operations recorded on the ledger.
- **Identity Access Management (IAM):** A successful IAM program requires participants and users to identify themselves and have the correct allowances. Authorizations to review transactions on the ledger can include read or write permissions.
- **Consensus Mechanism**: Let us move on to a consensus process that is essential to the legitimizing transactions. Since no formalized protocols exist, it is very contextual to establish a consensus mechanism; furthermore, it is really a stressful environment. The problem here is that everybody has to be inspired and accountable towards maintaining the integrity of the ledger. Smart contracts are seen as an optional requirement prior to the transfer, authentication, and confirmation of transactions as well as the adjustment of the information status. Two samples of well-known cryptocurrency consensus frameworks to explain threats in this domain are a) Proof-of-Work (PoW) (b) Proof-of-Stake (PoS).
- **Network Infrastructure:** *T*he network infrastructure is required for both Blockchain and Distributed Ledger Technology (DLT) DLT naturally has its own risks. However, it is still important to maintain the DLT infrastructure. Similar threats can be detected in the case of nodes being stopped or the ability to manage an attack-good anticipatory hazard. If the incident occurs, reducing this risk is essential. The second scenario is a complete system disaster. Backups and reliable business models will reduce this risk. Blockchain, as implemented with Bitcoin, is more vulnerable to a distributed Denial of Service (DDoS) attack. Nonetheless, the network is often smaller and potentially more vulnerable in the event of private DLTs, if not built properly. The convergence with other networks poses the last threat in the area of network infrastructure. At a certain level, the ledger may have to be transformed into other areas of the company depending on how it is implementated.
- *Cryptography*: Hashing algorithms are another potential risk on the technical side of the specific identification of hashes on the ledger. Such malware methods must be selected to satisfy the overall security objectives. Many methods of hacking are available. Finally, with respect to the features and purposes of the DLT used, the hashing algorithm and data structure has to be selected.

The Risks of Blockchain

Although Blockchain technology offers flexibility and operational reduction in cost, it has several associated risks. Organizations should recognize these threats and sufficient precautions adopted in order to take advantage of this innovation. In fact, the history of the legislative frameworks and their consequences is necessary to acknowledge. Such threats or consequences may be widely divided into three groups (Santhana, 2019):

- **Standard Risks**: Blockchain introduces organizations to threats analogous to those associated with current business operations. Furthermore, Blockchain establishes complexities for which companies are required to be responsible.
- **Value Transfer Risks**: Blockchain facilitates the sharing of ownership in a peer-to-peer network without a central authority. The exchanged digital assets could be related to land, identification, or data. The marketing strategy opens the negotiating groups to the same threats that centralized technologies also encounter.
- **Smart Contract Risks**: Smart contracts may possibly encrypt digital assets related to domain-specific enterprise, legal and financial agreements on a Blockchain. However it can also contribute to the threat of lack of privacy exposing the non-digital copies of the asset to Blockchain stake-holders with access to the digital assets themselves.

Blockchain Security Issues

A Blockchain derives its safety advantages from its nodes, which are decentralized in nature, where each node has a copy of validated transactions. As a result, one of the parties cannot alter the ledger. If there is an alteration before the transaction is committed to the Blockchain all the other process nodes have to commit to the change. Nevertheless, all public Blockchains are susceptible to 51% attacks. An assault of 51 percent attack happens when an attacker (or hacking group) consumes over 50% of the computing power of the Blockchain. It helps the attacker to engage in double coin investment; stops certain miners from making frames, and removes transactions entirely. The 51% are also the major network component of the Blockchain, hence they can control the entire Blockchain. In larger Blockchains with fewer miners, the risk is higher because the computational capacity needed to control 51% is greater. In contrast, certain Blockchain systems are susceptible in the case of a 34 percent assault by IOTA Tangle. As a result, since the Blockchain software is distributed, anyone can gain control over the Blockchain, with only 34 percent of network risk. Other security problems (Meng et al., 2018) plague the broader crypto culture. Hence, protection of transaction or exchange is also a critical issue.

Blockchain Privacy Issues

If a ledger is open, everyone is available on the platform has access to every transaction ever registered on the Blockchain. That does not necessarily mean, of course, that anyone can recognize you. The very reality that such data is accessible on the public front is in tension with lengthy-standing norms, specifically in the economic, various legal and medical fields.

Security Management of Blockchains

Blockchain safety can be described as a defense against central, external, malicious and unintended attacks to transaction data and information in one block (any type of data). Generally, risk identification, threat prevention, effective threat mitigation utilizing security policies, equipment, and IT infrastructure are included in this defense. Below are some important security concepts and principles (Joshi et al., 2018):

- **Penetration Security:** It is a technique involving multiple data protection corrections. This supports the idea that data protection is more effective across multiple layers than in a single safety layer.
- **Maximum Prerogative:** Access to information is limited to the lowest possible level in this approach, thereby improving a high degree of trust.
- **Vulnerabilities Detection**: This chapter verifies and manages vulnerabilities through Identification, Authentication, Modification, and Patching.
- **Risk Management:** By detecting, assessing and managing threats, this approach measures danger within a system.
- **Patches Control:** By purchasing, reviewing and deploying updates, this technique patches the faulty part as software, program, operating system, firmware, etc...

Blockchain technology implements a number of techniques to ensure transaction information protection and block details irrespective of the block's use as well as results. Some use the authentication method for data security, for instance, for bitcoin, Tschorsch and Scheuermann (2016)explained in detail how information was securely encrypted and decrypted using a blend of a public and private key. Blockchain's other best idea is that the most genuine chain. It reduces security risks related to major attacks (Li et al., 2017)and bending issues for 51 percent. Since the longest chain is real, the other attacks come to nothing as orphaned forks end up being.

Privacy Management of Blockchains

Confidentiality is the willingness of a particular individual or group to recline itself, and therefore to communicate itself with discernment. Blockchain security ensures that transfers can be carried out without revealing identity data. In the same period, confidentiality encourages a client to be reliable by revealing oneself discerningly without displaying his / her actions throughout the network. It is the goal of improving security in Blockchains to make the copying or using of cryptoprofile of other users extremely difficult by other users. When using Blockchain technology, an unmeasurable amount of variance can be seen. Some common features(Zyskind et al., 2015) are especially important and summarized as follows:

- **Data Sorting Stored:** Flexibility to save all forms of data is offered by Blockchain. The perspective on privacy in Blockchain varies between personal and corporate data. While the rules on privacy apply to personal data, stricter rules concerning privacy apply to sensitive and organizational data.
- **Distribution of Inventory:** The network nodes that store full Blockchain copies are called complete nodes. The total nodes together with the Blockchain only function and contribute to information redundancy. This information redundancy provides support for two key functions, accountability, and authentication, of the Blockchain technology. The degree of openness and verifiability for the application is defined by the consistency of systems with information minimization.
- **Only in the Append:** The information from prior frames cannot be changed undetected in the ledger. In some instances, the only function applied to Blockchain does not restrict the right of users to correct, especially when data is wrongly registered. There is a need to pay special consideration when granting privileges to Blockchain technology to information topics.

- **Private vs. Public Blockchain**: Blockchain's simplicity is impressive from a security perspective. In an advanced level, restricted block information can be encoded in order to allow licensed users to access conditionally because every node in the network has a copy of the whole Blockchain.
- **Licensed and Allowed Blockchain Forms**: Both clients are permitted to enter information in principle for open and licensed Blockchain applications. Allowing trustworthy mediators to be returned affects the transfer of authority over the network.

Digital Payments Privacy and Security Requirements

The following seven forms of transactions are generally classified in this Section as security and privacy necessity.

- **Ledger Continuity of Organizations:** Due to the different structure and business processes of financial institutions and the involvement of manual procedures, arbitration, clearance and liquidation processes between financial institutions not only contribute to high transaction costs from the customer and history of the business side of the financial institutions, but it also is prone to errors and discrepancies.
- **Transactions Accuracy:** Various intermediaries handle shares, bonds, banknotes, vouches of profits, store receipts and other resources when using online transactions for equity or asset management. Not only does it raise transaction costs but it also threatens to misfile and manipulating credentials intentionally. Therefore, the process should maintain the validity of transactions and stop the degradation of transactions.
- **System and Information Availability:** Online users should at anytime and anywhere be able to retrieve payment information. The accessibility here applies both to the rates of the process and of the payment. Even in case of such a web threat, the device must work properly at a root level. Transaction information can be obtained without being unachievable, incoherent, or fraudulent at the stage of the transaction by individual accounts.
- **Double Spending Avoidance**: A major challenge in the exchange in electronic money is the avoidance of double-spending, including investing more than once in a distributed network. Credible central third parties are responsible for checking in a hierarchical system whether or not a digital currency has been spent twice already. Strong protection protocols and countermeasures are needed for transactions carried out in a decentralized network environment, to avoid double-spending.
- **Transaction Confidentiality**: People tend to have a minimum report of their payments or account details in an online trading process in most commercial transactions. Such minimum protection requires (1) no unauthorized person may access payments details; (2) no user information may be exposed to others without his or her authorization by the system administrator or the individual in the network; (3) all user data should be maintained and transmitted regularly and safely, even in the face of unforeseen malicious cyber-attacks or vulnerabilities. In many non-financial cases, this secrecy is important.
- **User Identity Confidentiality**: It can cost a high amount for repetitive user authentication due to the difficulty of efficient and safe exchange of user data between various financial institutions. The disclosure threat of the identification of consumers by some intermediaries often falls indirectly. However, in some situations, one or both parties to the agreement can fail to notify the other Group of its true identity.

- **Transaction Unlinkability**: While confidentiality of identification (not exposing true identity), consumers must allow that their purchases cannot be connected together. Since all client transactions are connected, certain data about the consumer can be readily derived, such as the balance of the account, the amount and duration of the transactions. With the use of statistical data on purchases and accounts, along with certain background data on an individual, curious or adversaries, the true identity of the consumer can be devoured with absolute confidence.

Security Properties of Blockchain

All advancements in encryption and Bitcoin development and implementation are key elements in the protection of Blockchain. In 1991, cryptography was used for the first time for the stable chain of blocks (Haber&Stornetta, 1991). The Blockchain was built to guarantee a range of intrinsic safety qualities such as reliability, deceptive tolerance, DDoS resistance, pseudonymity, and dual-spending intrusion protection. Nonetheless, extra security and privacy properties are required to use Blockchain for safe shared storage (Zhang et al., 2019).

- **Consistency**: The definition of continuity as a decentralized global leader in Blockchain refers to the fact whether all participants have the same file concurrently. The topic of reliability has caused some contentious debate. Some people argue that Bitcoin schemes just offer potential reliability (Wattenhofer, 2016), which is low. Another statement that Bitcoin maintains solid coherence and not potential coherence (Sirer, 2016). The potential consistency is a coherence framework suggested by finding a compromise between the reliability and stability of high-performance computing systems. This formally guarantees that all duplicate changes are disseminated lazily and every reading access to an information object inevitably receives the last actual value if no fresh updates are provided to the item (Vogels, 2009). The time taken to make the system nodes compatible may not be established for ultimate reliability. Therefore, stable information ultimately means that, changes take time to be repeated in addition, and when anyone reads from a copy which is not modified (because Replicas are inevitably updated), then there is a possibility that outdated data will be returned. The clear continuity paradigm of the Blockchain network system ensures that all nodes have the same database at one point and all future read / write transactions will wait for the commit of this upgrade while the decentralized ledger is being modified with new data. The main challenge to reliability is that the price of service (with respect to latency / availability) is too large for all situations to be acceptable. The major task of reliability is how the uncertainty generated by stalemate information can be avoided.
- **Tamper-Resistance:** Tamper- resistance refers to the resistance of users or opponents, whether they are a system, a product or other logic / physical objects, to any intentional manipulation of an entity. Database security ensures that all the data on transactions recorded in the database may not be changed during and after the block creation process. In general, the mining nodes generate new blocks in a Bitcoin system. There might be two possibilities for modifying the transaction information:
  - Miners can attempt to modify the details of the transaction received; or
  - Adversaries can try to alter the data stored on the ledger.
  - A miner may try to modify the payee's address of the payment to himself for the first kind of fraud. Such an attempt cannot, however, be accomplished because a stable Hash element,

such as SHA-256, compresses all transactions and then signatures them using a safe signature algorithm such as ECDSA in a Bitcoin network. The payment is then sent for validation and authorization by mining throughout the network. Several miners can, therefore, obtain and take over the transaction in a non-deterministic manner. Whenever a miner updates some details about the contract, certain entities can notice it when verifying the signature by using the public keys of the payer, as without a private key the miner cannot establish a legitimate signature of the changed records. The protected signature algorithm is believed to be enforceable. An adversary may fail to change any of the historical data held on the ledger to trigger the second type of abuse. The explanation is that the shared database infrastructure of Bitcoin utilizes two security techniques: a hash reference, a cryptographic protocol and network-wide support for encryption and Blockchain validation. In fact, everybody has a decentralized version of the database in the Bitcoin network. A competitor has trouble switching all copies throughout the network.

- **Resistance to DDoS Attacks**: The DoS intrusion on a server is a denial of service attack. It is the form of a cyberattack that disrupts Internet services thereby disrupting the host's server or network asset to the host. DoS attacks are targeted at overloading the servers and networks by overwhelming superfluous programs, thereby blocking legal resources from being fulfilled (Mahjabin et al., 2017). DDoS intrusion applies to a decentralized DoS attack, namely that the incoming flood attack on a target arrives from several different sources spread over the Web. A DDoS attack can penetrate and attack another machine with security vulnerabilities or weaknesses using some individual device. A DDoS attacker could submit huge amounts of data to a website hosting a collection of such compromised machines or send spam to specific e-mail addresses (Mahjabin et al., 2017). This makes it very difficult to stop attacks easily by cranking every origin one by one.

- **Resistance to Double-Spending Attacks**: The Bitcoin network double-dollar assault refers to a specific issue unique to digital currency payments. Remember that the double-filing assault can be viewed as a general security issue due to the relatively easy replication of digital information. In general, for digital token transactions such as virtual currencies, an owner can replicate the digital token and submit multiple tokens to several beneficiaries in the same way. Inconsistency due to the transfers of multiple digital tokens is a major security risk to the double-spending problem. In order to prevent double spends, Bitcoin utilizes an agreement log to determine and check the validity of each payment. By including all transactions in the database, the Consensus protocol requires everyone to collectively review the transactions in a block prior to entering the block into the global ledger, assuring that the recipient of every payment uses only the bitcoins he has legally owned, However, each payment is signed using a protected digital signature algorithm through its recipient. It makes sure that the verifier will easily detect this if someone substantiates the payment. The integration of signed payments with digital signatures and the open inspection of liberal democratic transactions means the Bitcoin network can be immune to double-spending.

- **Resistance to the Majority (51%) Consensus Attack: The risk of corruption in the majority agreement** process has alluded to this assault. One such threat, in particular in connection with double spending, is sometimes assigned to like a 51% attack. In the presence of hostile miners, for instance, the 51 percent assault can take place. For example, if a miner controls over 50% of the computing power required to maintain the Blockchain, the distributed ledger of all cryptocurrency trades. One instance of a 51-percent assault maybe when a mining team collaborates to conspire, e.g. to collect the miners ' votes for verification. When one dominant user or team of conspiring users manage the Blockchain, various privacy and security threats, like the unauthorized transfer of bitcoins to some destination wallet(s) may be initiated, restoring legitimate transactions such as never happened, etc.

- **Pseudonymity**: The pseudonym implies a hidden state of identification. Bitcoin hashing for public keys for a node (user) on the network addresses in the Blockchain. By using the public key Hash as a pseudo-identity, users can communicate with the program without exposing their real name. The email used by a client can therefore, be seen as a pseudo-identity. To order to protect the real name of the consumer, we must consider the device as private property. Moreover, users can produce somany addresses as they like, equivalent to a person's preferred ability to create multiple bank accounts. While pseudonymity is possible through the use of public keys to obtain a poor level of anonymity, there are still concerns that users are detected.

- **Unlinkability:** Unlinking implies that the association between two observable network objects with high confidence cannot be identified. Anonymity applies to the confidential or undefined situation. While Bitcoin's Blockchain guarantees that pseudonymity protects the confidentiality of user identification by providing pseudo-identity, it does not guarantee users unlinkability. Only if the client still uses his pseudo-identity to communicate with the program can the full privacy of a Client be secured by maintaining both pseudonymity and unlinkability. Unlike unlinking, de-anonymization assumption attacks that merge a user's activities to reveal the actual user identity in the context of the contextual information [68] are challenging to initiate. Concretely, a client may have a variety of pseudonymous addresses in Bitcoin like networks. Nonetheless, this does not give users complete confidentiality, as each transfer is recorded on the ledger of sender and receiver addresses and can be tracked free of charge by anyone using its sender and receiver's relevant emails. Through a simple statistical study of the addresses used in Bitcoin transactions, anyone can connect the client payment to other transactions involving his accounts. For example, evaluating the sum and a total number of bitcoins on a senders account may easily be obtained. Additionally, multiple accounts that transact from a single IP address can be connected. More seriously, if the connection between your bitcoin address and the user's real-world identification is revealed, a user could lose confidentiality and privacy for all transactions connected to your Bitcoin address. However, in light of the open nature of the digital ledger, everyone can try to execute this type of attack anonymously or illegally without even letting the intended client know that she is targeted or that her true identity is exposed. Therefore, the Bitcoin implementation achieves pseudonymity, but not unlinkability, and thus not absolute privacy specified by an unlinkable pseudonym.

- **Transaction Privacy and Data Protection**: Blockchain data privacy relates to the rights that Blockchain is able to confidentially protect for all of its information and private data. For example, the smart contract administration, derivative works and the digitalization of company and corporate registries can be used through Blockchain. Not unexpectedly, the protection of payment data, such as transaction details (e.g. transaction sums in bitcoin), and addresses, is a valuable authentication asset popular in all Blockchain applications. Sadly, Bitcoin networks do not endorse this protection property the details and addresses of a contract are publicly visible in Bitcoin, even though the username is not the real identity but the senders or receivers. We believe that the ability to maintain private transaction contents helps to reduce the possibility that pseudonyms are connected to the actual user's identities. This is essential in order to facilitate the exchange of needs rather than the whole network. This is important. In addition, Blockchain networks use intelligent contracts to perform complex transactions, such as Ethereum, need (1) details from each contract and the program that it operates on publicly-specific data, and (2) that all miners replicate the output of each contract. This refers to data leakage. For instance, a user creates a smart contract to pass some ETH to another user at some point in time. This opponent could reveal and connect the portion to his real identity if he has background information on one of the two groups. It is thus important that enhanced privacy protection frameworks for intelligent contracts be designed and implemented.

In conclusion, data protection work over recent decades has shown the threats of privacy leakage as a consequence of several inference attacks that link confidential transaction data and / or a pseudonym to the real identity of actual users, given the use of the same pseudonym (Dupont, 2015). A loss of privacy may contribute to a violation of payment information's confidentiality. Thus, the secrecy and security of Blockchain and its implementations including financial payments or private data are a serious concern.

Privacy and Security Techniques Used in Blockchain

This section gives a detailed overview of a number of strategies for improving the security and privacy of existing and prospective Blockchain networks.

- **Mixing:** Bitcoin's ledger does not ensure a user's anonymity: transactions use pseudonyms and can be publicly checked, so anybody can connect the transaction of the client to their other transactions by merely evaluating the address they used in Bitcoin exchanges. More importantly, it may allow the transaction's address to leak all its transactions if connected to a user's real-world identity. Mixing services (or tumblers) were therefore designed to avoid the association between users' accounts. Mixing is, basically, a spontaneous swap of coins between users and other client coins, so the observer is unaware of the possession of these coins. Nevertheless, coin stealing is not covered by these mixing services. This segment discusses two of these mixing services and analyzes their privacy and security.
  - *Mixcoin:* Mixcoin (Bonneau et al., 2014), which allows for an anonymous transaction on Bitcoin and cryptocurrencies-like bitcoin in 2014, was introduced by Bonneau et al. Mixcoin expands its privacy to enable multiple participants to combine coins concurrently in the protection of active opponents. Mixcoin provides privacy similar to traditional messaging mixes to protect against aggressive opponents. Mixcoin utilizes a transparency system to prevent theft, which reveals that consumers can rationally utilize Mixcoin without taking bitcoins by rewards.
  - *CoinJoin:* CoinJoin (Maxwell, 2013) has been suggested for Bitcoin transactions in 2013 as an alternate authentication process. The notion of a shared fee motivates this. If a client wants to pay, he or she will seek another consumer, who also wants to pay, and in agreement, they make a joint fee. The combined transfer decreases dramatically the likelihood that inputs and outputs are related in a single transaction and that a particular client monitors the exact course of cash flow. CoinJoin encourages people to arrange mutual payment transfers. The first phase of mixing systems (e.g. SharedCoin (Moniz et al., 2006), for example) utilized hierarchical databases that allowed customers to rely on the service provider not to cheat and permit someone else to snatch bitcoins. In light of the single failure point, central

banks may be at risk of confidentiality leaks because they will hold transaction records and record all joint payment participants.

- **Anonymous Signatures:** Many versions have been created for digital signature technologies. Several signature mechanisms themselves can provide the signatories with anonymity. These signature systems are classified as secret signatures. Group signature and ring signature are previously proposed under anonymous signing schemes and are the two key and most popular anonymous signature strategies.

  ○ *Group Signature:* Initially proposed (Chaum & van Heyst, 1991) a group signature is a cryptographic system. In the case of a group, each participant may secretly sign a letter for the entire group with his personal secret key. Each individual with a public key may verify and validate the signature produced, ensuring that a group member's signature will be used in the message signature. The signing verification process shows nothing of the true identity of the signatory except the group's membership. The group signature has a group leader that helps to introduce group members, to negotiate with disagreement, and to identify the initial signatory. A licensed body must be formed or revoked under Blockchain, and new members are dynamically introduced to the group and certain participants are excluded/withdrawn from the group. Since a group leader is needed to set up the group, the group signature is appropriate for Blockchain consortiums.

  ○ *Ring Signature:* Ring signature can be obtained by signing any group member (Rivest et al., 2001). The word "ring signature" derives from the ring design signature algorithm. If it is hard to determine what member of the group uses the key to sign the email, then a ring signature becomes anonymous. For two main ways, ring signatures vary from group signatures: First, the signer's real identity cannot be shown in the event of a conflict in a ringing signature system as the ring signature does not include group members. Second, the ring signature can be used for the public ledger. CryptoNote (van Saberhagen et al., 2012) is one of the common implementations of the ring signature. This adopts the ring signature to protect the relationship between the sender's payment addresses.

- **Homomorphic Encryption (HE):** Influential authentication is homomorphic encryption (HE). It can explicitly execute those forms of calculations on ciphertext to ensure that, when the calculated output is decrypted, the operations conducted on the encrypted data produce the same results as those performed with the same network operations. There are several cryptosystems that are partly homomorphic (Paillier, 1999, Rivest et al., 1978) and completely homomorphic (Gentry, 2009, van Dijk et al., 2010). Homomorphic cryptographic methods can be used to keep informed through the network without substantial changes to Blockchain properties. It means that the Blockchain information is encrypted in order to address existing ledger privacy concerns. The use of homomorphic cryptography provides privacy rights which allow for immediate exposure for auditing and other uses to encrypted data through public Blockchain such as employee allowances management. Ethereum's smart contracts offer homomorphic authentication on Blockchain information to improve confidentiality and control.

- **Attribute-Based Encryption (ABE):** Attribute-based encryption (ABE) is a cryptographic system in which the cipher text attributes are encoded by the secret key of a client and are the distinguishing and governing variables. The encrypted data can be decrypted using the user's secret key if its attributes are compatible with the ciphertext attributes. The resistance to collaboration is an important safety function of ABE. That means that a malicious person cannot control all information, including data that can be decrypted using his own private key unless he shares with others. For example, permissions can be expressed in a Blockchain by owning access tokens. The unique rights and privileges related to the token are available to all network nodes that have some token given to them. This token offers a way to monitor who has certain characteristics and the licensed entity that distributes this token should do this algorithmically and consistently.

- **Secure Multi-Party Computation:** Enigma utilizes a de-central SMP computing mechanism to guarantee the confidentiality of its computational model by a verifiable information sharing system. Enigma often codes mutual confidential information for secure processing by using an altered aggregate hash table. The MPC template describes a multi-partner protocol that enables them to jointly execute any computation about their personal data entries without violating the privacy of their input. This enables opponent to know nothing about an authenticable party's input but about the result of a joint computation. The popularity of using MPCs for democratic elections, private procurement, and shared access to information has rendered most real-world problems a common solution. For 2008 it was MPC's first large-scale operation in Denmark to fix an auction problem (Bogetoft et al., 2009).

- **Non-Interactive Zero-Knowledge (NIZK) Proof:** A zero-knowledge proof is another authentication technique that has powerful properties that protect privacy. The fundamental idea is that a structured proof can be designed to confirm that a system with some internally identified user-input could yield publicly available outcomes without any other data being revealed. That is, a certifier may prove that some assumptions are accurate by supplying the verifier with useful information.

- **The Trusted Execution Environment (TEE) Based Smart Contracts**: TEE is considered an implementation system if the code is completely isolated and effective in preventing other software applications or operating systems from controlling or knowing the status of the program. The eXtensions Intel Security Guard (SGX) is a symbolic TEE technology Ekiden (Cheng et al., 2018) is, for instance, an SGX-based smart contract protection solution. The Ekiden estimate was isolated from the agreement. This conducts smart contract estimation on off-line nodes in TEEs and uses a system for remote certificates to verify the right execution of on-line nodes in computers. Consensus nodes are used to maintain the network and need not require trustworthy equipment. Enigma utilizes TEE for users to build secret smart contracts with a hierarchical credit rating algorithm in its current version. Many considerations such as account numbers and forms, payment history and product use are weighted for credit calculation.

- **Game-Based Smart Contracts:** Quite recent development described by TrueBit (Teutsch&Reitwießner, 2017) and Arbitrum were game-based solutions for smart contract evaluation. TrueBit provides an online testing system to determine if a computer assignment has been carried out successfully or not. TrueBit presents incentives that allow users to check computing tasks and to search for vulnerabilities so that an intellectual agreement can reliably execute a computing function with verifiable properties.

DISCUSSION

In order to maintain security and privacy within a robust Blockchain network certain considerations should be in place.

- Blockchain's security and privacy panacea is not one single technology. The correct safety and confidentiality strategies should be selected in accordance with security and private standards as well as considering the scope of the software. In fact, this functions much better than using a single technology to combine multiple technologies. For example, Enigma, integrates cutting edge SMPC and TEE hardware cryptographic technologies with Blockchains in order to perform computation on encrypted data on a scale.
- There is no innovation without flaws or in all ways good. If a complex system includes new technologies, it always creates certain complications and new forms of abuse. It calls for careful consideration of the drops and potential damages done to Blockchains by adding certain security and privacy strategies.
- Combining safety protection with productivity is always a balance. Those techniques are required that enhance Blockchain security and privacy while supporting the realistic implementation and success of Blockchain applications.

REQUIREMENTS FORFUTURESECURE BLOCKCHAIN SOLUTION

Begin with the creation of a threat framework for a stable Blockchain approach that can resolve multiple enterprises systems, compliance, infrastructure, and system risks. Define security controls based on the following 3 criteria that minimize risk and threats (Arunkumar& Muppidi, 2019):

1. Enforcement of specific Blockchain protection controls
2. Use of traditional security checks.
3. Enactment of Blockchain commercial monitors.

Enforcement of Specific Blockchain Protection Controls

- *Deal with the runtime environment for the Blockchain solution as a vital infrastructure:* All necessary safety practices must be implemented. The certification of industry standards should be adopted and enforced.
- *Partition and implementation of good name spacing practices to control access:* Channels and name spacing are essential to partition the system so that the virtual resources of all the network participants can be shared. Name spacing allows exposure to the digital assets on the network to be controlled. The working approach can also help to save money, as improvements will need to be reworked later.
- *Definition and application of acceptable corporate endorsement policies:* The Blockchain approach utilizes endorsement policies to identify the conditions to be satisfied to ensures the legitimacy of the requested transaction, the number of signatures needed, and which organizations are included in the examples. Such strategies should be subject to a smart contract that will lead to the protection of the enterprise network and either any cryptocurrencies or information associated with the agreement.
- *Enforce identification and access restrictions on the Blockchain system:* Identify policies that guarantee the correct person's right level of access for proper use. New members should be integrated into correct identification and control processes within the Blockchain platform. Every

data exfiltration (malicious operation carried out using various techniques) should also be avoided by the deportation process. Audit reports and control procedures should be introduced to warn a suspicious behavior administrative unit so that it can be alleviated.

- *Enforce the hardware security module (HSM):* For safe Blockchain identification keys, it is important to use an HSM. It's also necessary to make sure that every entity in the HSM where the keys are stored has its own partition. HSM guarantees the safety of the keys by keeping Blockchain identification data. The HSM partition system guarantees each entity to do partition function on each specific partition with segregated organizational privileges and responsibilities (crypto officers, crypto clients, super executives, etc.).

- *For increasing activities use privileged access management (PAM) approach:* Use a PAM system to guarantee that modules are accessible for administrative and change management purposes by authorized clients with the correct permissions. This is particularly important because the system can have confidential information, like client and member fee transactional details. Through code rotation and effective division of tasks, a PAM approach should be introduced. It is also important to set end-to-end logging to monitor entry-to-departure movements.

- *Using policies and procedures for API security in order to secure API transactions:* APIs are the instant messenger's type among Blockchain resolution components. APIs must be guarded against any abuse and confined to the purpose of the transaction. Although API protection covers a range of things, the detection, configuration and authorization of all APIs should be subject to the three main controls.

- *Take advantage of privileged access and use a confidentiality warehouse:* The Blockchain approach has many modules, which deal with client and API transactions. Some of these transfers have a fixed key set, such as keys, tokens, and attestations. Such keys need to be kept in a secure warehouse, so access should be restricted depending on use at runtime.

- *Embrace a data identification system of data/information safeguard:* define and label corporation, legal and technical data in order to protect data and confidentiality by implementing effective information security management. Data registration for all Blockchain system participants must be applied on a continuous basis.

- *Using sensitive information software that protects confidentiality:* using approved ledger technology, where privacy is a design norm, and control the data protection of members. Therefore, implement security protections that mask transaction details such as the name and specifics of the transaction author.

- *Secure apps from bugs and data protection:* Leverage DevOps to optimize software functional testing over the life cycle of the development In line with the information identification study, it is also essential to enforce data security on different levels.

- *Enact accessibility control in smart contracts:* Smart contracts are a key component in the Blockchain system and implement policies consistent with business goals, which ensures that all smart contracts must be protected in every way. Close consideration should be paid to access regulation to the management of the intelligent contract period, smart access within the smart contract and the coordination between smart contracting systems or applications.

- *Leverage Trusted Platform Modules (TPMs) to enforce important code:* Many software elements are essential and trustworthy platform modules should be used in these critical components. It allows storing HSM-enabled cryptography. These often permit the execution of privacy-preserving chain codes to avoid execution by the node manager without detection.

- *Secure internal and external communications:* Make sure that certain network interactions between communicating components both internally and externally go through a highly secure system. This can be achieved using shared and generic TLS solutions.

Using Traditional Security Checks

- *To maintain a stable production of technology, device testing, and the appropriate safety protocols, using corporate security guidelines and systems:* both organizational rules, standards, and common security mechanisms should be used. It guarantees continuity, quality, comfort, and productivity of service.
- *Enact user's onboard identification and access protection capabilities:* use IAM tools for encryption, access control, and information identity processing.
- *Authentication of the multi-factor remit:* multi-factor authentication (MFA) with default IAM instruments to allow access to the Blockchain. No exceptions, companies, and managers need to use MFA.
- *Using effective cryptographic key / certificates management:* To handle the number of keys in the Blockchain system including Blockchain Identity keys, TLS internals, existing TLS certificates and domain certificates, use the efficient, secure key management software.
- To handle local TLS keys use powerful internal PKI solution.
- Make appropriate judgments for existing TLS certificates of the Certification Authority.
- *Leverage protection events and event management:* Organizations must provide network participants with security event updates, or pick event information for each participant. Security incident and event management (SIEM) across all structural elements are vital.
- *Leverage hardware security:* Use the HSM unit for the storing of essential key data. While the advocated system has several participants, HSM and its effects have to be determined by the advocated design. The system needs a growing transparent protocol to use HSM.
- Storage keys with limited access to members in correct partitions.
- *Enact protection of implementation:* the application of safety precautions for each element guarantees that somehow the end solution has no safety breaches.
- *Regulate the safety of networks:* network infrastructure protection and system information are essential. The infrastructure on which the Blockchain technology is implemented must be protected, including all software and hardware elements.
- *Conduct rigorous penetration testing and vulnerability evaluation:* ensure full penetration checks are performed at each stage of solution delivery. In order to solve these problems, it is necessary to undertake susceptibility evaluations at a scale of the company and of the process as a whole.

EnactBlockchain Commercial Monitors

- *Defining and applying information governance:* Ensuring safety protection is enforced through different policies, frameworks for access control and monitoring.
- Defining the exclusive service law to ensure consumers have clarity and protection to conflict laws and legal disputes regardless of the location where they have been positioned.
- *Ensure compliance and regulatory controls:* Accountability is an essential component and every organization has its own specific demands, guided by its compliance officers. This is why it is

important that each participant or vendor's responsibility in the event of a violation of protection is clearly established. Confirm process and software reviews to ensure the reduction of this threat.

- *Defining, scoping and carrying out functional controls*: A Blockchain implementation requires a full set of protection protocols to be collected and monitored once the development, construction, and deployment measures have been completed.

CONCLUSION

Thanks to the open network and peer-to-peer design of Blockchain technology, it is widely recognized and much utilized and discussed. It is a technology that can support various industries and applications. An overview of Blockchain security and privacy is proposed through this chapter with a detailed survey by first examining the Blockchain architecture and its key components and characteristics. Then the authors try to emphasize on the security and privacy issues in the different areas of use of Blockchain technologies. It assumes that Blockchain will quickly become a widespread and well-known trend with the rate of their development and growth. A couple of decades ago, Blockchain could be associated with the Internet. Since the heart of the Blockchain is stable and cooperative, this software will increasingly push other essential devices that need security and non-repudiation. Although some drawbacks remain in Blockchains and many groundbreaking implementations are hard to implement and Blockchain would probably become the platform to be established by everyone.

REFERENCES

Al-Saqaf, W., & Seidler, N. (2017). Blockchain technology for social impact: Opportunities and challenges ahead. *Journal of Cyber Policy.*, *2*(3), 338–354. doi:10.1080/23738871.2017.1400084

Andrychowicz, M., Dziembowski, S., Malinowski, D., & Mazurek, L. (2014). *Secure Multiparty Computations on Bitcoin* (pp. 443–458). SP.

Arunkumar, S., & Muppidi, S. (2019). *Secure your Blockchain solutions*. Retrieved from https://developer.ibm.com/articles/how-to-secure-Blockchain-solutions/

Atlam, H. F., & Wills, G. B. (2018). Technical aspects of Blockchain and IoT. *Advances in Computers*. doi:10.1016/bs.adcom.2018.10.006

Bayer, D., Haber, S., & Stornetta, W.S. (1993). *Improving the Efficiency and Reliability of Digital Time-Stamping*. Academic Press.

Benet, J. (2015). *IPFS - Content Addressed, Versioned, P2P File System*. Retrieved from https://arxiv.org/abs/1407.3561

Bogetoft, P., Christensen, D. L., Damgård, I., Geisler, M., Jakobsen, T. P., Kroigaard, M., . . . Toft, T. (2009). Secure Multiparty Computation Goes Live. FC, 325–343.

Bonneau, J., Narayanan, A., Miller, A., Clark, J., Kroll, J. A., & Felten, E. W. (2014). Mixcoin: Anonymity for bitcoin with accountable mixes. In *Financial Cryptography and Data Security - 18th International Conference, FC 2014, Revised Selected Papers 8437* (pp. 486-504). Springer Verlag. 10.1007/978-3-662-45472-5_31

Chakraborty, S. (2018). *Introduction to Blockchain – II (History). Blockchain architecture design and use cases.* Retrieved from https://nptel.ac.in/courses/106/105/106105184/

Chase, M. (2007). *Multi-authority Attribute Based Encryption.* Doi:10.1007/978-3-540-70936-7_28

Chaum, D., & van Heyst, E. (1991). Group Signatures. In D. W. Davies (Ed.), Lecture Notes in Computer Science: Vol. 547. *Advances in Cryptology -EUROCRYPT '91. EUROCRYPT 1991.* Berlin: Springer.

Cheng, R., Zhang, F., Kos, J., He, W., Hynes, N., Johnson, N.M., Juels, A., Miller, A., & Song, D. (2018). *Ekiden: A Platform for Confidentiality-Preserving, Trustworthy, and Performant Smart Contract Execution.* CoRR abs/1804.05141

Dickson, B. (2016). *How Blockchain can help fight cyberattacks.* Retrieved from https://techcrunch.com/2016/12/05/how-Blockchain-can-help-fight-cyberattacks/

DuPont, J., & Squicciarini, A. C. (2015). Toward De-Anonymizing Bitcoin by Mapping Users Location. CODASPY, 139–141.

Garg, S., Gentry, C., Halevi, S., Sahai, A., & Waters, W. (2013). *Attribute-Based Encryption for Circuits from Multilinear Maps.* Academic Press.

Gentry, C. (2009). Fully Homomorphic Encryption Using Ideal Lattices. STOC, 169–178.

Goldreich, O., Micali, S., & Wigderson, A. (1987). How to Play any Mental Game or A Completeness Theorem for Protocols with Honest Majority. *STOC*, 218–229.

Goldwasser, S., Micali, S., & Rackoff, C. (1985). The Knowledge Complexity of Interactive Proof-systems. *STOC*, 291–304.

Gorbunov, S., Vaikuntanathan, V., & Wee, H. (2013). Attribute-based Encryption for Circuits. *Proceedings of the Forty-fifth Annual ACM Symposium on Theory of Computing In STOC*, 545–554.

Grut, O. W. (2016). *WEF: Blockchain will become the 'beating heart' of finance.* Retrieved from http://uk.businessinsider.com/world-economic-forum-potential-of-Blockchain-in-financial-services-2016-8

Haber, S., & Stornetta, W. S. (1991). How to time-stamp a digital document. *Journal of Cryptology*, 3(2), 99–111. doi:10.1007/BF00196791

Ikeda, K. (2018). Security and Privacy of Blockchain and Quantum Computation. *Blockchain Technology: Platforms, Tools and Use Cases*, 199–228. doi:10.1016/bs.adcom.2018.03.003

Joshi, A. P., Han, M., & Wang, Y. (2018). A survey on security and privacy issues of Blockchain technology. American Institute of Mathematical Sciences, Kennesaw State University. doi:10.3934/mfc.2018007

Jung, T., Li, X. Y., Wan, Z., & Wan, M. (2013). Privacy preserving cloud data access with multi-authorities. INFOCOM, 2625–2633.

Kalodner, H., Goldfeder, S., Chen, X., Weinberg, S. M., & Felten, E. W. (2018). Arbitrum: Scalable, private smart contracts. USENIX Security, 1353–1370.

Kosba, A., Miller, A., Shi, E., Wen, Z., & Papamanthou, C. (2016). *Hawk: The Blockchain Model of Cryptography and Privacy-Preserving Smart Contracts*. Paper presented at 2016 IEEE Symposium on Security and Privacy (SP). 10.1109/SP.2016.55

Kumar, A. (2018). *Is Blockchain a Linked List like Data Structure?* Retrieved from https://vitalflux.com/Blockchain-linked-list-like-data-structure

Lewko, A., & Waters, B. (2011). Decentralizing Attribute-based Encryption. EUROCRYPT, 568–588.

Li, X., Jiang, P., Chen, T., Luo, X., & Wen, Q. (2017). A survey on the security of Blockchain systems. *Future Generation Computer Systems*. doi:10.1016/j.future.2017.08.020

Mahjabin, T., Xiao, Y., Sun, G., & Jiang, W. (2017). A survey of distributed denial-of-service attack, prevention, and mitigation techniques. *International Journal of Distributed Sensor Networks*, *13*(12), 155014771774146. doi:10.1177/1550147717741463

Maxwell, G. (2013). *CoinJoin: Bitcoin privacy for the real world.* bitcointalk.org

Meng, W., Tischhauser, E. W., Wang, Q., Wang, Y., & Han, J. (2018). When Intrusion Detection Meets Blockchain Technology: A Review. *IEEE Access: Practical Innovations, Open Solutions*, *6*, 10179–10188. doi:10.1109/ACCESS.2018.2799854

Moniz, H., Neves, N. F., Correia, M., & Verissimo, P. (2006). Experimental Comparison of Local and Shared Coin Randomized Consensus Protocols. SRDS, 235-244.

Nakamoto, S. (2008). *Bitcoin: A Peer-to-Peer Electronic Cash System.* www.Bitcoin.org

Paillier, P. (1999). Public-key Cryptosystems Based on Composite Degree Residuosity Classes. EUROCRYPT, 223-238.

Rivest, R. L., Shamir, A., & Adleman, L. (1978). A Method for Obtaining Digital Signatures and Public-key Cryptosystems. *Commun. ACM, 21*(2), 120-126.

Rivest, R. L., Shamir, A., & Kalai, Y. T. (2001). *How to Leak a Secret.* ASIACRYPT. doi:10.1007/3-540-45682-1_32

Sahai, A., & Waters, B. (2004). *Fuzzy Identity-Based Encryption.* Doi:10.1007/11426639_27

Santhana, P. (2019). *Risks posed by Blockchain-based business models.* Retrieved from https://www2.deloitte.com/us/en/pages/risk/articles/Blockchain-security-risks.html

Sirer, E. G. (2016). *Bitcoin Guarantees Strong, not Eventual, Consistency.* Retrieved from http://hackingdistributed.com/2016/03/01/bitcoin-guarantees-strong-not-eventual-consistency/

Steem. (2017). *An incentivized, Blockchain-based, public content platform.* Retrieved from https://steem.com/SteemWhitePaper.pdf

Teutsch, J., & Reitwießner, C. (2017). *TrueBit: A scalable verification solution for Blockchains.* Academic Press.

Tschorsch, F., & Scheuermann, B. (2016). Bitcoin and beyond: A technical survey on decentralized digital currencies. *IEEE Communications Surveys and Tutorials*, *18*(3), 2084–2123. doi:10.1109/COMST.2016.2535718

van Dijk, M., Gentry, C., Halevi, S., & Vaikuntanathan, V. (2010). Fully Homomorphic Encryption over the Integers. EUROCRYPT, 24-43.

van Saberhagen, N., Meier, J., Juarez, A. M., & Jameson, M. (2012). *CryptoNote Signatures.* Academic Press.

Vogels, W. (2009). Eventually consistent. *Commun. ACM, 52*(1), 40-44. Doi:10.1145/1435417.1435432

Wattenhofer, R. (2016). *The Science of the Blockchain* (1st ed.). CreateSpace Independent Publishing Platform.

Yao, A. C. (1986). How to Generate and Exchange Secrets. *SFCS*, 162–167.

Yao, A. C. (1982). Protocols for secure computations. SFCS, 160–164.

Zhang, R., Xue, R., & Liu, L. (2019). Security and Privacy on Blockchain. *ACM Computing Surveys*, *52*(3), 1–34. doi:10.1145/3316481

Zheng, Z., Xie, S., Dai, H., Chen, X., & Wang, H. (2017). An Overview of Blockchain Technology: Architecture, Consensus, and Future Trends. *2017 IEEE International Congress on Big Data (BigData Congress)*, 557-564. doi: 10.1109/BigDataCongress.2017.85

Zyskind, G., Nathan, O., & Pentland, A. (2015). Enigma: Decentralized Computation Platform with Guaranteed Privacy. *Computer Science*.

Zyskind, G., Nathan, O., & Pentland, P. (2015). Decentralizing privacy: Using Blockchain to protect personal data. Security and Privacy Workshops (SPW), 180–184.

Chapter 6
Application of Blockchain Technology in Land Administration in Ghana

Samuel Agbesi
https://orcid.org/0000-0002-9527-1924
Aalborg University, Copenhagen, Denmark

Fati Tahiru
https://orcid.org/0000-0003-0874-0428
Ho Technical University, Ghana

ABSTRACT

The administration of lands in Ghana has been a major issue in the past years that has resulted in parties seeking arbitration to determine the rightful owners and others resulting in death because of the land-guard menace. The main issues in land administration in Ghana include modification and falsification of land records, difficulty in authenticating the ownership of land property, sales of land property to more than one customer, and lack of transparency in land transactions. This chapter examines the application of Blockchain in land administration in Ghana to solve the issues of unauthorized modification of land records, difficulties in proven ownership of land properties, and the lack of transparency in land transactions. The proposed solution is based on Ethereum Blockchain technology using a smart contract. The solution used a non-fungible token to represent land properties as a digital asset that can be traded on the proposed solution. The proposed solution provides integrity, immutability, provenance, and transparency in land administration.

INTRODUCTION

Blockchain technology, which was first developed for the sole purpose of digital currency has now been applied successfully in other application domains, such as real estate, voting, food safety, etc. Blockchain use cases have been extended beyond digital currency transactions (Brakeville, & Perepa,

DOI: 10.4018/978-1-7998-3632-2.ch006

2018). Blockchain technology is been explored in the supply chain industry to track the flow of goods and payments and to ensure transparency in the supply chain (Brakeville et al, 2018). Furthermore, it brings trust, transparency, and auditability in democratic elections (Williams, & Agbesi, 2019) and also "allow securities trades to be settled in minutes rather than days" in the financial sector (Brakeville et al, 2018). The use of blockchain is also been studied to help resolve the numerous challenges that exist in land administration in Ghana. Because in general, blockchain can hold a verifiable transaction that has ever occurred which can solve the risk of double-spending, manipulation of land records and fraud. Double-spending in this context is in terms of selling a piece of property to multiple parties. In this chapter, we will discuss the challenges of land administration in Ghana and look at how blockchain technology can be used to mitigate these challenges. The chapter will introduce the blockchain concepts and discuss how Ethereum blockchain technology using smart contracts can be used to conceptualize blockchain-based land administration architecture.

Land administration can be defined as the process of determining, recording, and disseminating of information about ownership, value, and use of land (Vos, Beentjes, & Lemmen, 2017). It is a "system that is used to locate and identify a real property and to keep a record of past and current data regarding ownership, value, and use of that property" (Stefanović, Pržulj, Ristic, & Stefanović, 2018). The administration of lands in Ghana has been a major issue in the past years which has resulted in parties seeking arbitration to determine the rightful owners and sometimes resulting in death because of the Land-guard menace. The main issues in land administration in Ghana include modification and falsification of land records, difficulty in authenticating the ownership of land property, sales of land property to more than one customer, and lack of transparency in land transactions. But with the advancement and success of blockchain technology in the cryptocurrency domain, it is of the view of the authors that this blockchain technology can be used to resolve the problems enumerated above.

Figure 1. Blockchain-based Land registration
(Esatya, n.d.)

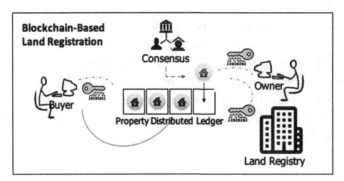

The blockchain technology can be used, as shown in figure 1, by both buyers, owners and government agencies such as survey and mapping, land registration and land valuation to validate land properties and determine the rightful owners.

The problems identified in the administration of land in Ghana can be broadly categorized into three main components, first and foremost is the unauthorized modification of data at the different department in the land sector. The processes involved in the acquisition of landed properties and their related resources requires the engagement of different department in the lands commission. As part of the public sector reforms program and the Ghana Land Administration Projects, the Lands Commission was remodeled to now comprise of four divisions which are Survey and Mapping, Land Registration, Land Valuation, and Public and Vested Land Management. The remodeling is intended to increase efficiency and effectiveness. However, there have been instances where records of land title at the land registration differ from what is stored at the survey department and vice versa, and these happened as a result of data tampering or improper synchronization of records at the various institutions involved. Secondly, the identification of the rightful owner of the land and its related resources is also a problem, since it is easier to forge land documents. Getting to know who owns the title to a parcel of land is a major problem confronting the land sector. The entities that own land in Ghana are the Chiefs or Stools, Families, individual and the State. Due to the multiple sales of lands by some of these entities, there has been the emergence of illegal private security service providers who employ violence means to protect land and landed property in exchange for payment from land-owners in Ghana. These groups are popularly known as 'land guards', and their operations are considered dangerous to landowners who do not have the financial capabilities or resources to engage their services. (Darkwa and Attuquayefio, 2012) Some landowners abandon their lands for the other party for fear of being killed. There are lots of legal suits in connection with the 'land guard' menace in Ghana. Lastly. Due to the perceived nature of fraud involved in the land acquisition process, people are reluctant to invest in landed properties, and the lack of transparency in land sales/ lease transactions has resulted in land conflicts cases at the various court of arbitration. Hence this chapter examines how blockchain technology can be applied to land administration in Ghana to provide the needed integrity, provenance and transparency in land transactions.

BLOCKCHAIN TECHNOLOGY

Overview of Blockchain

Before the introduction of blockchain as a solution to the double-spending problem, other inventions were made to solve the double-spending problem. One such solution was the establishment of a consistent P2P network by users to disable unauthorize users/systems from attacking the system. Another solution that could not stand the test of time is the quorum systems. This system works in such a manner that a transaction can only be executed if most of the nodes vote to execute it. However, the quorum system is susceptible to the Sybil attack, where bad nodes take control of the network with false information. That is, the attacker subverts the reputation system of a peer-to-peer network by creating many pseudonymous identities or nodes and uses them to gain access to most of the nodes that form the P2P network (Kaushik, Gola, Khan, & Rathore, 2016). But the introduction of bitcoin, a blockchain technology, by Satoshi Nakamoto in 2008, has brought a new dimension of solving the issue of double-spending, and have also brought about the technology and infrastructure to build solutions and system that provides trust, transparency, and immutability.

There have been varied definitions of blockchain, depending on which field (Economist, Legal, Political or Technology) you are coming from. A blockchain, according to Brakeville and Perepa, (2018) "is a tamper-evident, shared digital ledger that records transactions in a public or private peer-to-peer network" is also as a decentralized, distributed database which is shared across multiple nodes on a P2P network (Hackernoon, 2019), or chain of transactions stored in a block where each block is linked together using a cryptographic hash function to prevent any modification of the stored data. The transactions in the block must be signed digitally by the sender to provide its authenticity (Hackernoon, 2019). The use of these cryptographic protocols, such as encryption and digital signature, on the stored data in blockchain makes it temper-resistance and immutable (ConsenSys, 2019; Hackernoon, 2019). Blockchain distributed ledger technology (DLT), according to Brakeville, and Perepa (2018), is revolutionizing the way organizations conduct business transactions.

In the blockchain, transactions represent individual activities such as transfer of digital or physical assets, records, etc. (Brakeville, & Perepa, 2018). The transaction data is signed and distributed by participants on the network. Nodes are the individual computers that connect to the network and full nodes perform verification of all blockchain rules (Brakeville et al 2018; ConsenSys, 2019). The nodes process the data in the ledger and verify it. Blocks contain transactional records. Blocks are linked to each other using a cryptographic technique, with each block containing the hash of the previous block, a timestamp and transaction data (Brakeville et al 2018; ConsenSys, 2019; Hackernoon, 2019). There are several blockchain technology implementations, notable among them is Bitcoin, Ethereum, Hyperledger, Litecoin, etc. In this chapter, we shall discuss Bitcoin and Ethereum blockchain since they are the leading blockchain technologies in the market now.

Features of Blockchain

In our definitions and discussion in the previous section, we identified some features of blockchain that need further discussion.

1. **Decentralized:** A decentralized blockchain is a blockchain architecture where no single person or entity has control over the network (Hackernoon, 2019), that is, "it does not have to rely on a central point of control" (Lisk, n.d.). In a decentralized blockchain network, all node has a copy of the blockchain database, and no node has the authority of the data. Updating and accepting new transactions into the blockchain is achieved through consensus (Lisk, n.d). Decentralization brings transparency and security while giving power to users (Hackernoon, 2019).

2. **Node**: A node in a blockchain network is all the connected devices that participate in the P2P network (ConsenSys, 2019). The function of a node is to "support the network by maintaining a copy of a blockchain and, in some cases, to process transactions" (Lisk, n.d), depending on the type of node. A node could be a light node, full node, and mining node; where light node only participate in the network by sending and receiving messages in the form of transactions, full nodes on the other hand stores the entire copy of the blockchain database, validate transactions and also responsible for the propagation of the blockchain to other nodes on the network to ensure consistency and trust on the blockchain platform (Beedham, 2019). Miners nodes are basically responsible for producing valid blocks to be added to the blockchain, they confirm blocks that are to be added to the blockchain through the process called "mining" (Beedham, 2019).

3. **Block**: A block is an essential component of blockchain technology, and its primary purpose is to record transactions (ConsenSys, 2019). In the bitcoin domain, a block contains a maximum of 2000 transactions, with an average size of a bitcoin block being 1MB (ConsenSys, 2019). When transactions are created, they are stored in a block which is then is added to the blockchain (Williams, & Agbesi, 2019). A typical block structure is made up of the header and the data section. The header contains the hash of the previous block, a timestamp, the block height, and the nonce value. While

the data section holds that actual transaction such as the amount being sent, the sender's address and the recipient address if we are working with the bitcoin blockchain.

4. **Distributed Ledger Technology (DLT):** DTL is a technology where the ledger information is replicated among all the nodes on the p2p network. It is important to state the blockchain is not DTL and DTL is not a blockchain but combining the two technology gives you the full power and functionalities of blockchain technology (ConsenSys, 2019). With a distributed ledger, the blockchain database is replicated and shared and synchronized among the full nodes participating in the network (Brakeville et al 2018).

5. **Peer-to-Peer Network:** P2P network in blockchain provides security and robustness in the network and the model adopted by blockchain technology (ConsenSys, 2019). The general concept of a P2P network is that all devices, called nodes, participating in the network has equal rights and access. Within the blockchain network, the P2P protocol allows all nodes to hold an identical copy of the blockchain database, where approval of new transactions is done through a consensus mechanism (Hackernoon, 2019)

6. **Immutability:** Immutability is a property of blockchain that ensures that data stored on the blockchain cannot be altered or changed (Hackernoon, 2019). This immutability property is achieved through the application of a cryptographic hash function, where a block stores the hash value of the previous block. What this implies is that once a transaction is added to the blockchain and secure with a hash function it is permanent. In theory, the only way anyone can make changes to the data store in the block is for the block containing the data and subsequent blocks to be re-hashed after the data has been changed. But this is extremely complicated since re-calculating the hash values for all the affected blocks requires a lot of computational power (ConsenSys, 2019; Hackernoon, 2019).

7. **Provenance:** Provenance is a concept that provides the historic account of assets or properties. The assets or property could be in this context, a land property. According to Devan (2018), data provenance is a historic record of any piece of data or asset. That is, "data provenance systems track changes that are made to data, where data originates and moves to, and who makes changes to it over time".

8. **Tamper-Resistance:** Temper-resistance is where an attempt to alter a block can be detected and addressed due to the immutability properties of the blockchain (ConsenSys, 2019; Hackernoon, 2019). The issue is that once data in a block is altered the hash values of all the blocks on top of it will change because of how each hash value of a block is stored in the block linked to it, and it means the adversary must change all the hashes of the blocks after it.

9. **Consensus**: The consensus mechanism in the blockchain allows nodes in a p2p network to have the right to validate and accept a transaction base on a consensus rule. The consensus is the process where all nodes on the network agree on the same state of the blockchain (Lisk, n.d). There are several consensus protocols, notable ones are Proof-of-Work (PoW) and Proof-of-Stake (PoS). PoW was introduced in Bitcoin blockchain and used widely by cryptocurrency blockchain applications. The PoW requires miners solving a complex mathematical problem in other to create a new block to be added to the blockchain. PoS is a consensus algorithm, mostly used in Ethereum blockchain, which was developed due to the inefficiencies in the PoW. With PoS the creation of a new block is based on how much stake a node has in the network. That is "the probability of creating a block and receiving the associated rewards is proportional to a user's holding of the underlining token

or cryptocurrency on the network" (Lisk, n.d). PoS is more energy-efficient and secure compared to PoW because it does need huge electricity which results in less cost.

Private, Consortium and Public Blockchain

In deciding to implement a blockchain system one must decide whether to have a private, consortium or public blockchain. So far most of the examples we have cited, such as Bitcoin, and Ethereum are public blockchain network, which means anybody can join the network.

1. **Private Blockchain:** A private blockchain is a permission blockchain system, which means nodes are granted permission before they can join the private blockchain network (ConsenSys, 2019). Most often, the performance of private blockchain is much better than public blockchain because private blockchain does not rely on any proof-of-work to establish consensus (ConsenSys, 2019).
2. **Consortium Blockchain:** A consortium blockchain is a shared permission blockchain. A consortium blockchain may comprise of a group of companies that regulate and operate the blockchain, and they allow certain members to be nodes (ConsenSys, 2019). Like the private blockchain, nodes must be granted permission before they can join the network and each node can validate a transaction.
3. **Public Blockchain:** A public blockchain is an open and permissionless blockchain, and nodes do not need permission to join. All you must do is to download the blockchain software onto your device and you are ready to join (ConsenSys, 2019). With a public blockchain, anyone connected to the network can see the ongoing transaction as well as past transactions.

Bitcoin vs Ethereum

Once we have some understanding of the basic features of blockchain technology, we will now discuss the Ethereum and Bitcoin blockchain framework and determine which framework will be suitable for our prototype.

1. **Bitcoin Framework:** Bitcoin blockchain was developed as the basis for the digital currency eco-system (Antonopoulos, 2014). Bitcoin is a digital currency, launched in 2009 as the first cryptocurrency used in the blockchain technology. Bitcoin is also the currency that is traded on the bitcoin platform. Bitcoin runs as a distributed P2P network, hence there is no central authority, and the coins are created through a process called "mining" (Antonopoulos, 2014). The main components of a bitcoin network consist of a decentralized p2p system, a public ledger, a consensus rule and a consensus algorithm, PoW (Antonopoulos, 2014). One important point developers of blockchain apps should be aware is that, since bitcoin was created for a digital payment network, it uses for developing any application beyond cryptocurrency apps, comes with some constraints and limitation (Antonopoulos, & Wood, 2018), and this led to the development of other blockchain frameworks like Hyperledger and Ethereum.
2. **Ethereum Framework:** Ethereum, as compared to Bitcoin, was created as a general-purpose blockchain framework and not for only digital currency payment systems, which means it does not have the limitations and constraints that come with Bitcoin blockchain framework. According to Antonopoulos et al (2018), "Ethereum is an open-source, globally decentralized computing infrastructure that executes programs called smart contracts", and it allows blockchain developers

to build powerful decentralized applications known as DApps (Antonopoulos et al, 2018). A smart contract is a small piece of logic or code that can interact with an Ethereum blockchain (ConsenSys, 2019). Ethereum digital currency, ether, is integral and necessary for performing operations on the Ethereum platform. Ether is intended as a utility currency that is used to pay for gas fees for transactions on the platform (Antonopoulos et al, 2018).

As has established, Ethereum is a general-purpose programmable blockchain framework that runs a virtual machine (Antonopoulos et al, 2018; ConsenSys, 2019). Ethereum is classified as a "Turing complete", which implies that it can run as a general-purpose computer (Antonopoulos et al, 2018). Ethereum blockchain has a memory, compare to Bitcoin blockchain, that can store both code and data and it is capable to track the state change over time (Antonopoulos et al, 2018). The state change is triggered by a transaction and operation of Ethereum Virtual Machine (EVM) ConsenSys, 2019). EVM is one of the unique features of Ethereum blockchain, and that makes Ethereum a general purpose-computer.

Overview of Ethereum Blockchain Framework

Form the previous comparison between Bitcoin and Ethereum, it is obvious Ethereum blockchain frameworks provide more flexibility and resources in building general-purpose applications, it can allow developers to code complex logic using the smart contract. In our proof-of-concept (POC) of the blockchain-based Land administration system, we will use Ethereum blockchain technology to conceptualize our proposed solution. Hence, in this section, we shall get into some basic concepts and functionalities that will be used in our POC. The main components of the Ethereum framework as described by Antonopoulos et al (2018) are:

1. P2P network, addressable on TCP port 30303, and runs a protocol called ÐƐVp2p. ÐƐVp2p is a set of network protocols that constitute the Ethereum p2p network. Ð is a letter from old English, pronounced "eth".
2. Transactions, a network message such as a sender, receiver, value, and data payload.
3. A data structure, that stores the state of Ethereum locally in each node as a database.
4. A consensus algorithm, such as the Proof-of-Stake (PoS)
5. Clients, software that connects to other nodes on an Ethereum network. These clients allow you to join the Ethereum network, create and run smart contracts.

Ethereum Tools

1. Wallet: In using Ethereum, there are tools that we need to help us explain the POC, among them, is a wallet, smart contract. A wallet is a client application that is used by a user to manage an account on the blockchain network, and it also holds the private keys that are used to make transactions (Antonopoulos et al, 2018). One of such wallets is MetaMask, which will be used to demonstrate our POC. There are other wallets such as Jaxx, MyEtherWallet and Emerald Wallet which will not be discussed in this chapter.
2. Solidity: Solidity is an object-oriented programming language that is used in Ethereum to implement our smart contract. And as we have already discussed a smart contract a code that is written and deployed on an Ethereum p2p network. There several smart contract programming languages such

as LLL, Viper, Lvy, Serpent, etc., available but we shall demonstrate our solution in solidity. The smart contract will hold the land administration codes that will be deployed onto the blockchain.

Tokenization

An important feature in blockchain and Ethereum is tokenization. In a blockchain network, anything from idea, service, assets, etc. can be represented as a token. Tokenization is the process of turning physical assets into digital tokens (O'Neal, 2019) which can be transferred to another person, traded and stored on the blockchain system (Etoro, 2019). A token is used to represent a unit of value in the digital space (ConsenSys, 2018). In Ethereum blockchain the implementation of tokens is done in smart contract code. There are two main types of a token; that is fungible and non-fungible tokens.

1. Fungible Tokens (FT): Fungible tokens are tokens that represent digital assets where individual tokens are equivalent to the other. Fungible tokens are interchangeable; for example, bitcoin is fungible because the value of 1 bitcoin is the same 1 bitcoin being held by another customer. Fungibility also allows a token to be broken into smaller tokens and have the same value. For example, if we have 20 bitcoins, which is a fungible token, we can divide this token into smaller denominations and still have the same value. I can give part of the bitcoins to someone and retain the balance. The main characteristics of fungible tokens are (Oxcert, 2018):
    a. They are interchangeable, and this implies you can exchange a token of the same type and value.
    b. Fungible tokens are divisible
    c. ERC-20 is used for creating fungible tokens on Ethereum blockchain.
2. Non-Fungible Tokens (NFT): NFT began with the Implementation proposal in 2017 by Ethereum (Oxcert, 2018). Non-Fungible Token (NFT) uniquely represents an asset, assets that have unique characteristics (Curran, 2019). It allows assets or goods with unique characteristics to be represented as a token to be traded and stored on the blockchain network. Because NFT represents a unique asset it cannot be replaced or interchanged by another NFT, it is a unique token and is different from all other tokens, and it is not divisible (Oxcert, 2018). ERC-721 is used to issue NFT on Ethereum blockchain.

BLOCKCHAIN AND LAND ADMINISTRATION

In the introduction section, we describe the problem associated with land administration in Ghana, which includes unauthorized modification of land information, difficulties of proving the rightful owner of land assets and the lack of transparency in a land transaction. Furthermore, we have also examined the fundamental properties of blockchain technology and discussed how Ethereum blockchain technology can be used to design a blockchain-based land administration system to address the current challenges and to provide the needed integrity, provenance and transparency in land transactions in Ghana. In this section, we are going to examine how blockchain technology can be used to solve the three major challenges identified in the chapter.

Unauthorized Modification

One of the major issues in land administration in Ghana is the ease at which land records can be altered, this is as a result of improper and inaccurate storage of land records and how these records are being stored in traditional centralized database at the various institutions (Themistocleous, 2018), such as Survey and Mapping Department, Land Registration, and Land Valuation department. As such, when there are any disputes about land properties and the need to verify and confirm ownership, these departments often provide different records of ownership, because there is no data synchronization among these departments. So how can blockchain be used to address these issues? One property of blockchain technology is its immutability, that is, data stored on a blockchain cannot be changed or altered; and secondly, blockchain technology is based on a decentralized peer-to-peer (p2p) system, which means different departments do not need to keep different data about land properties. With the decentralized p2p network same copy of the land information will be kept by the various department that is connected to the blockchain network, hence any changes will reflect in all the copies of the data held by the various nodes connected to the network. And all unauthorized changes will be detected and prevented from saving permanently onto the database.

Prove of Ownership of Land Properties

Another issue is how to prove the ownership of a land property at any point in time. Currently, it is difficult to prove the various stages a land property has gone through in terms of change of ownership. Several land litigations in Ghana now is as a result of customers buying lands from people who do not hold the right to land. But with blockchain, the entire history of the land properties, which includes all the changes of ownership will be stored and can be tracked. This is the concept of data provenance. If potential buyers can trace and verify the rightful owner of land property customers will not fall victim to buying lands from fraudsters. It will also prevent selling one piece of land to more than one customer.

Lack of Transparency

Transparency in a land transaction is another major challenge in land administration in Ghana. There is a lack of trust among parties involved in land transactions since there is not enough information on the land property. Notwithstanding the sought of due diligence a customer does, there is usually less information available to help make an informed decision on the acquisition of land property, even is the purchase is from a registered real estate agency. But using blockchain technology, because there is a permanent history of an immutable record of each land property, customers can easily obtain all the information needed before making any decision to acquire a property.

The use of blockchain in land administration in Ghana can provide enormous opportunities and benefits in the land administration ecosystem.

Figure 2. Stakeholders in the Blockchain Land Administration System (Markunas, 2019)

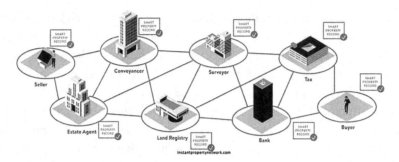

As shown in figure 2, the use of blockchain technology in land administration will benefit both, sellers, estate agents, land registry, surveyors, banks and buyers. The technology will provide the needed transparency among these various stakeholders (Markunas, 2019), and increase trust among these parties.

In the next section, we conceptualize our blockchain technology and discuss how the proposed design can solve the challenges in land administration in Ghana.

DESIGN SOLUTION

Proposed Architecture

The main challenges in the land administration in Ghana as discussed in the previous section includes unauthorized modification of land records, proof of ownership, and transparency. These challenges impact on integrity, immutability, and trust in land transactions and record. Our focus is to conceptualize a blockchain technology that can provide a transparent, tamper-proof and immutable land transaction that can bring trust among the various stakeholders.

As shown in table 1, the main stakeholders that will participate in the blockchain-based land administration system will include the government agencies, which include land registration department, survey and mapping, and land valuation, and seller and buyers. The seller encompasses chiefs, public and private owners who own properties that are for sale.

Table 1. Land Administration Stakeholders

Stakeholders	Roles	Node Type
Land Registration	Validate transaction	Full Node
Survey and Mapping	Validate transaction	Full Node
Land Valuation	Validate transaction	Full Node
Buyers	Perform transactions	Light Node
Sellers	Perform transactions	Light Node

The government agencies will have the responsibility of validating and accepting transactions submitted by buyers and sellers before it is added to the blockchain. While the buyers and sellers will only perform transactions without any validation functions.

Figure 3. Our Proposed Land Administration Blockchain System (LABS)

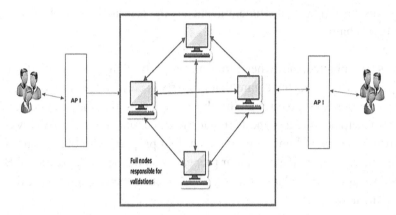

In the proposed system, as shown in figure 3, buyers and the seller (using light nodes) interact with the blockchain technology using an application programming interface (API), such as Ethereum, whiles the government agencies (using full nodes) will be responsible for validation all transaction received from the buyers/sellers. To be able to connect to the blockchain network as a buyer or a seller, you must download a client application know as a wallet, which will contain the keys that can be used to interact with the blockchain network. A client with light nodes does not have to download the full copy of the blockchain database except the government agencies responsible for validations.

How the Proposed System Will Work

As has been established, there will be three key players in the ecosystem, sellers, buyers, and validators. In this design, we also proposed a distributed peer-to-peer (P2P) public blockchain network to have more transparency and trust.

For the process to work, all land properties must be registered on the blockchain and represented as a token so that it can be traded on the platform, and the owner of a property, that is the primary owner, has the responsibility of tokenizing the property. The following process will be used to register a property on the blockchain for the first time:

1. The owner must connect to the Land Administration blockchain System (LABS) through his or her wallet.
2. The owner creates a token to represent the land properties in a process called "minting". Minting token is the process of creating a new token to represent an asset on the blockchain network. Here we adopt non-fungible token since land properties have unique characteristics. The token will contain information about the land property such as the previous owner, current owner, the value

of the property and other important information. This information will be used to create a digital land title.

3. The activities in step 2, will raise a transaction, which will be broadcast to the full nodes connected to the blockchain network.

4. The next step is the validation of the transaction. The full nodes must validate and confirm the information provided by the creator of the transaction. Once the information is confirmed by these full nodes, in this case, these government agencies, the transaction will be accepted and securely added to the blockchain.

Once this process is completed, the ownership of the property cannot be tampered with once it has been verified, and any person who wants to acquire that property is certain about the digital ownership of the property. All new properties must go through the above process so that they can be traded on the LABS.

Now if a buyer wants to acquire a property, he or she can connect to the LABS, via his or her wallet and confirm the current owner and previous owners of that property without relying on any third party or on the seller. The entire history of a particular property will be available on the LABS. If the buyer is satisfied and agreed to purchase the land property, the current owner must transfer the token representing that property to the new owner.

In order to complete the transfer, the current owner must burn his or her token representing the asset, and the token will go through a transformation process. The "transform event" accepts the burnt tokens and updates it with the new owner's information to create a new token. This process also represents a new transaction that must be validated by the full nodes based on a consensus rule or algorithm. If the validation process fails, the transaction will not be accepted.

Our proposed solution will address the following challenges in the current land system:

1. **Verification Of Ownership Of A Land Property:** With our blockchain-based land system, a potential buyer can verify the ownership of a property by simply login on to the blockchain system. The buyer will not only rely on the words of the seller.

2. **Double Spending:** Double spending, in this context, is when a token representing a land is spent in more than one transaction. With our solution, a land token cannot be issued more than once from a seller to a buyer.

3. **Immutability**: Because the land database is spread across multiple nodes and secure with a cryptographic hash algorithm, it makes the land database temper resistance. Any authorized modification will be detected and rejected.

4. **Synchronization**: With our proposed solution, the land records will be up to date and synchronized across different nodes representing the various stakeholders involved in the land administration.

5. The proposed system also brings transparency and trust in land transactions between parties.

CONCLUSION

Our proposed LABS addresses the main issues raised in the introduction section, that is, unauthorized modification, proof of ownership, transparency, and trust.

The LABS prevents unauthorized modification of records. Once the property is registered on the LABS it is immutable because the record is secured with a cryptographic that has a function that resists against unauthorized modification. When an attempt is made to change a record, all the nodes participating in the network will be alerted and it will reject the change. Secondly, since the entire history of a property is stored permanently on the blockchain, the customer can track and identify the right owner of a digital asset. Furthermore, since all transactions are available in the public domain, and any person can connect to the LABS to verify any transaction, there is transparency and trust. Stakeholders will not rely on a trusted third party, but rather the trust is placed in the underlying cryptographic protocols.

REFERENCES

Antonopoulos, A. M. (2014). *Mastering Bitcoin: unlocking digital cryptocurrencies*. O'Reilly Media, Inc. Retrieved from: https://github.com/bitcoinbook/bitcoinbook

Antonopoulos, A. M., & Wood, G. (2018). *Mastering ethereum: building smart contracts and dapps*. O'Reilly Media. Retrieved from https://github.com/ethereumbook/ethereumbook

Beedham, M. (2019, March). *All you need to know about Bitcoin network nodes*. Retrieved from: https://thenextweb.com/hardfork/2019/03/01/bitcoin-blockchain-nodes-network/

Bitconist. (n.d.). *Bitcoin vs Ethereum: Differences, Advantages and Disadvantages – Which is Better?* Retrieved from: https://bitcoinist.com/bitcoin-vs-ethereum/

Brakeville, S., & Perepa, B. (2018, March). *Blockchain basics: Introduction to distributed ledgers*. Retrieved from: https://developer.ibm.com/tutorials/cl-blockchain-basics-intro-bluemix-trs/

Casino, D., Dasaklis, T. K., & Patsakis, C. (2019). A systematic literature review of blockchain-based applications: Current status, classification and open issues. *Telematics and Informatics*, *36*, 55–81. doi:10.1016/j.tele.2018.11.006

ConsenSys. (2019). *Blockchain: Foundations and Use Cases*. Retrieved from: https://www.coursera.org/learn/blockchain-foundations-and-use-cases

Curran, B. (2019, August). *What Are Non-Fungible Tokens? Unique & Authentic Digital Assets*. Retrieved from: https://blockonomi.com/non-fungible-tokens/

Devan. (2018, October). *How Blockchain Technology is Revolutionizing Data Provenance*. Retrieved from: https://medium.com/blockpool/how-blockchain-technology-is-revolutionizing-data-provenance-e47610019390

Esatya. (n.d.). *Whose land Is It Anyway?: land Registry Powered by Blockchain*. Retrieved from: https://esatya.io/news/land-registry-powered-by-blockchain/

Etoro. (2019, January). *What is tokenization and what are the different types of tokens available?* Retrieved from: https://www.etoro.com/blog/market-insights/what-is-tokenization-and-what-are-the-different-types-of-tokens-available/

Hackernoon. (2019, July). *Blockchain Technology Explained: Introduction, Meaning, and Applications.* Retrieved from: https://hackernoon.com/blockchain-technology-explained-introduction-meaning-and-applications-edbd6759a2b2

Kaushik, M., Gola, K. K., Khan, G., & Rathore, R. (2016). Detection of Sybil Attacks in Structured P2P Overlay Network. *International Journal of Computers and Applications*, *975*, 8887.

King, R. (2019, July). *Ethereum vs Bitcoin: Is Ethereum a Better Bitcoin Alternative?* Retrieved from: https://www.bitdegree.org/tutorials/ethereum-vs-bitcoin/

Lisk. (n.d.). *What is Decentralization?* Retrieved from: https://lisk.io/academy/blockchain-basics/benefits-of-blockchain/what-is-decentralization

Markunas, J. D. (2019, July). *The Impact of Blockchain Technology on the Surveying Industry, Cadastre and Land Registry Systems.* Retrieved from: https://landportal.org/fr/blog-post/2019/08/impact-blockchain-technology-surveying-industry-cadastre-and-land-registry-systems

O'Neal, S. (2019, June). *Tokenization Explained.* Retrieved from: https://cointelegraph.com/explained/tokenization-explained

Oxcert. (2018, April). *Fungible vs non-fungible tokens on the blockchain.* Retrieved from: https://medium.com/0xcert/fungible-vs-non-fungible-tokens-on-the-blockchain-ab4b12e0181a

Stefanović, M., Pržulj, D., Ristic, S., & Stefanović, D. (2018, November). *Blockchain and Land Administration: Possible applications and limitations.* Retrieved from: https://www.researchgate.net/publication/329650717_Blockchain_and_Land_Administration_Possible_applications_and_limitations

Themistocleous, M. (2018). Blockchain Technology and Land Registry. *The Cyprus Review*, *30*(2), 195–22.

Vos, J. A. C. O. B., Beentjes, B., & Lemmen, C. (2017). *Blockchain based land administration feasible, illusory or a panacea.* Paper prepared for presentation at the 2017 World Bank Conference on Land and Povertry, Washington, DC.

Vujičić, D., Jagodić, D., & Ranđić, S. (2018, March). Blockchain technology, bitcoin, and Ethereum: A brief overview. In *2018 17th International Symposium INFOTEH- JAHORINA (INFOTEH)* (pp. 1-6). IEEE. 10.1109/INFOTEH.2018.8345547

Williams, I., & Agbesi, S. (2019). Blockchain, Trust and Elections: A Proof of Concept For The Ghanaian National Elections. In Handbook on Ict in Developing Countries (vol. 2). River Publishers.

Chapter 7
Blockchain in the Insurance Industry:
Use Cases and Applications

İsmail Yıldırım
Hitit University, Turkey

ABSTRACT

New technologies that will be developed in the future will determine the place of Blockchain technology in our lives. It is certain that blockchain technology, which has the potential to be used in every field from smart phones to the health sector, will be a technology that will be frequently encountered in the future rather than simply being used in some sectors. What will determine the areas of use of Blockchain technology and how much it can be used depends on what future security, cost, and speed it can do. Blockchain, which can be used in the insurance sector, will help to keep track of accidents, material, and moral losses during the insurance period and keep track of all records very easily. It is expected that this technology, which is expected to be useful in eliminating the minute information problems in the insurance sector, can be very helpful in preventing insurance frauds, and it is expected to have a preventive effect in defrauding insurance and citizens. This chapter discusses how blockchain technologies will transform the insurance sector and their future uses.

INTRODUCTION

In the current new world order driven by digitalization, technological changes should not only be in the fields of people and business, but also in the public spheres. The reason why many transactions are still recorded as printed documents in the late 2010s is the lack of electronic storage of such transactions and the lack of trust in digital services (Deloitte, 2018). Blockchain technology changes the entire document storage structure by providing a secure system that everyone can access and view all records over the Internet (Decker and Wattenhofer, 2015). It is necessary to examine the basic features provided by Blockchain, whether it is possible to secure a system that is essentially open to everyone. Mainly Blockchain; distributed databases where all copies of a transaction or any other process for data validation are

DOI: 10.4018/978-1-7998-3632-2.ch007

retained by all participants. It is not possible for participants to change any information in the system; if one copy is compared with other copies, any changes made can be detected. However, it should be kept in mind that this technology is still in its early stages, and the serious challenges and risks involved, both technical and regulatory, must be addressed before it is widely adopted. Potential uses can truly benefit the global market and generate a new generation of services; however, many legal uncertainties that need to be resolved to facilitate the mass adoption of this technology are still surrounding the area.

Although Blockchain technology was only used for crypto currency software in the early periods, it was discovered that this new structure could be used in different areas over time. Both crypto currencies have started to change the way of doing business in different branches of trade, and the advantages of using this structure for other transactions independent of money and financial activities have started to emerge (Beck et all., 2016). Every day, especially in the world of economics and finance, a different field has begun to explore ways to adapt Blockchain technology to its own processes. This technology, which eliminates the need for central authorities, promises time saving and freedom in this context, has become one of the most popular discussion topics. Both the applications and experiences of the organizations and institutions in different fields using the Blockchain platform and the products produced by the academic, intellectual and cultural circles that produce ideas about this field show that this technology is a revolutionary and transformative innovation similar to the discovery and use of the internet by the societies. In this context, it is useful to discuss the social and structural effects that Blockchain technology may cause.

One of the sectors to be transformed by Blockchain technology is the insurance sector. Blockchain technology can also open the door to many innovations in the field of digital insurance. This technology, which will prevent fraudulent transactions, will ensure the registration of belonging of physical and digital assets. Because of this situation, insurance companies will be able to prevent the cost losses experienced every year.

WHAT IS BLOCKCHAIN?

There is no clear definition of Blockchain. Satoshi Nakamoto's first introduced the concept when he was disseminating the concept of Bitcoin in 2008. He defined Blockchain as information blocks connected by encryption (Jacobovitz, 2016). The essence of Blockchain technology is the collection of previously secured data into a technical schema. This technical scheme consists of blocks formed by the encryption of multiple and distinct nodes in the system. Therefore, Blockchain is also referred to as a chain of blocks. There are many blocks in the Blockchain. These blocks are connected to each other in a linearly and chronologically. These blocks have digital fingerprints that confirm the validity of the information stored in each block (Tian, 2016). Each block also contains a block sequence, a block header summary, a summary of the title of the linked block and the preceding block, the difficulty value, the time stamp of the time the block was formed, the random value, and the values of the transfer operations (Figure 1). All transactions can be monitored by all stakeholders in the network.

Figure 1. How Blockchain Works?
Source (Social Rush, 2018)

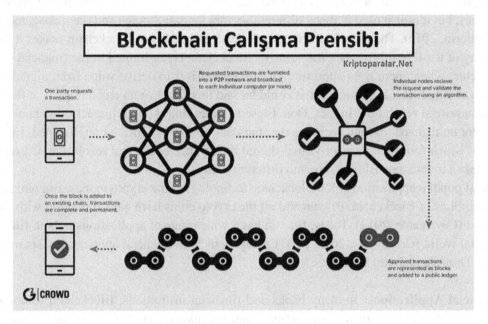

Blockchain, a chain of blocks, is a distributed database system that provides encrypted transaction tracking. In money transfers, each step forms a block (Swan, 2015). For example, each information such as the sender's name and the amount sent is a block. These blocks created during the transfer process are encrypted, they can never be changed and made unbreakable (Zaninotto, 2017). These blocks are distributed all over the network, and everyone has the same encrypted information. Blockchain's principle of decentralization is based on this technological design. The buyer and the seller can only process the information on the block. In addition, Blockchain technology is transparent, anyone can review blocks that have accumulated already.

Figure 2. Blockchain Technologies

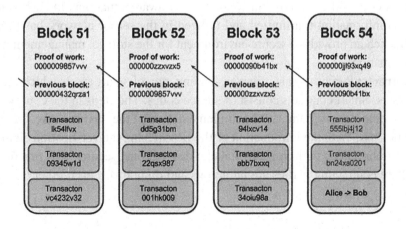

Blockchain technology provides individual users with unprecedented control over digital identity. Therefore, Blockchain (which is an open global account book) is use not only in the production of crypto money, but it is also used in many different sectors for data storage and the management of data storage (Buterin, 2015). The digital identity possibilities embedded in Blockchain makes it the key to the economy of trust. In this respect, the value of Blockchain is not limited to the financial sector, but to other sectors where there is an opportunity to for enterprises to derive value from digital technologies (Catlin et all., 2015). In this respect, it could be said that Blockchain technology is at the center of the fourth industrial revolution. In fact, Don Tapscott states that the real impact of technology in our lives will not be realized through social media, big data, robots or artificial intelligence. He says that Blockchain, which forms the basis of virtual-digital money, drives the real revolution. Currently steps are being taken to integrate Blockchain, into different sectors.

The most popular application of the Blockchain technology is the crypto money, Bitcoin. As a result of the capabilities of Blockchain, Bitcoin and all the crypto coins have gained traction with low maintenance cost (Cavalcante, 2013). Today, Bitcoin has a wide range of applications in both financial and non-financial world (Crosby, M., 2015, p.7). Examples include financial applications, smart property, Internet of Things and Smart Contracts.

1. **Financial Applications:** In many banks and financial institutions, Blockchain technology was utilized first in international money transfer and international trade finance applications. Then it was later utilized for payment transactions, money transfers, buying / selling platforms, insurance, clearing management, authorization, verification, digital identity management, document management (Credit Suisse, 2016).

2. **Smart Property:** Through smart technology, tangible assets (such as cars, houses, white goods, offices) and intangible assets (such as patents, property titles, brands, company shares) can be integrated and recorded. With this record, information about either a persons or establishment that are allowed as relevant asset can be kept in the book together with the contract details. Authorized persons or organizations can easily access this information via smart keys. Smart property reduces the risk of fraud, mediation and questionable activities; and further increases confidence and productivity.

3. **Internet of Things**: IoT implies the delivery of software programs, RFID tags, sensors, triggers, and networked smart phones, etc., over an internet-based network of objects. The Internet of Things, which is defined by its ability to enable interaction between people machines and objects using sensor networks provides the possibility for context aware situations. In such situation, valuable human based information transmitted and utilized in the sensor network has to be accurate and secured. Blockchain provides a secure environment for the storage, management and transmission of such information.

4. **Smart Contracts:** Purchase, sale, transfer, lending, etc. of smart assets which are mostly used as smart contracts. Smart contracts consist of source codes. The steps in the contract go through the control of a computer program and the implementation of the contract takes place automatically during the process. With the introduction of the Blockchain, the verification element of the chain ensures that transactions with insecure stakeholders become secure. This practice is particularly suitable where contracting parties are numerous and do not trust each other (Würst and Gervais, 2017).

INSURANCE INDUSTRY

Throughout history, people have encountered different forms of risks. These risks are natural, social or managerial in nature. The desire to take precautions against these risks gave birth to the concept of insurance. In return for a certain premium, the insurance covers the losses that may arise as a result of these and other risks (Acer, 2017). Thus, it enables people to priorities safety in life more. The basis for insurance is thought to have started with the maritime trade and was enacted as a measure taken to protect goods against attacks by pirates at sea (Çipil, 2017). Approximately 4000 years ago, the Babylonian civilization has a similar system to the modern insurance system we have today. In those days when loan sharks lent to merchants and caravans, who were eventually robbed and their goods damaged, they had already received a certain amount of money from the merchants to cover such risk.

The Babylonian ruler Hammurabi legalized this system. The special feature of this law was that the cost in damages incurred by the damaged caravan should be shared between the other caravans. This is the first example of risk sharing in road transport. We see that insurance practices were also applied intensively in Venice, Genoa, Florence and other Italian cities advanced in the maritime trade.

The concept of insurance as we know it today began in the 14th century. This was a result in the rise in commerce and overall economic developments. For example as mentioned earlier, the growth in maritime trade was the catalyst for the emergence of Insurance in Italy. The cargo of the ship SantaClara, which departed from the port of Genoa in Italy on 23 October 1347, was protected by a contract. This contract historically is the first insurance policy. Similarly, in the UK, as maritime trade increased, the UK merchants adopted the Italian practice of insuring their goods. In the UK, an insurance office was established for the first time in 1574 to carry out insurance business.

UK took it a step further and enacted insurance regulations, making it a British law, in 1601. Initially there were no insurance companies as traders carried out their own bilateral insurance business in the UK until the 17th century. In the 17th century, insurance companies emerged. This was because of the growth in size of the maritime trade and the growing demand for marine insurance. However, the advantages of insurance did transcend the maritime trade. For example, the Great London fire in England destroyed many houses and churches in the 17th century. The result was the financial loss incurred by many people as a result of the fire. After this event, insurance companies were established in London to specifically deal with risks associated to destruction by fire. Among other commercial centers in the world, London became a leader in world insurance after 17th century. The UK once again broke new ground in insurance, and became the meeting point for traders who wanted to insure their cargo and secure their cargo in a coffee shop run by Edward Lloyd in London. The ensemble was later named Llyod's. The British Parliament later adopted a law (Llyod's Law) for this community in 1871.

The period in which insurance companies were established in the modern sense was 1700-1900.Since then significant improvements have been made with respect to fire insurance after the Great London fire in the UK. The demand for insurance at the advent of the industrial age in the 19th century made industry insurance more prominent. As a result, today, the insurance sector has become a sector operating in every sector and has an important place in the national income of the countries.

BLOCKCHAIN AND INSURANCE RELATIONSHIP

Blockchain offers basic technology that supports trust, transparency and stability. These solutions do not cover all of the problems that insurers face. But Blockchain offers a variety of alternatives towards reducing the difficulties of insurance transactions and contribution to the sector. These alternatives are Security, Big Data, Third Party Transactions, Smart Contracts, Reinsurance (KPMG, 2017).

1. **Security:** Through the use of general ledger, Blockchain can log each transaction and eliminate suspicious and duplicate transactions. Through its decentralized digital repository, it can verify the authenticity of customers, policies and transactions by providing historical records. This makes it difficult for hackers to corrupt and steal files. Numerous policies are issued in the insurance industry. More accurate and error-free regulation of policies will be possible with the detection of suspicious policies, especially with Blockchain technology. Prevention of insurance abuses is possible by identifying suspicious policies. Insurance companies issue thousands of insurance policies daily. Blockchain technology will make it easier to identify suspicious and untrue policies.
2. **Big Data**: More and more connected devices are being used every day, leading to an increase in the amount of data that insurance companies have to handle. Blockchain can properly manage, share, and make large amounts of data. The benefit of this is that the technology can store static records and/or data in a decentralized manner. The decentralization enables the data to be viewed by all parties. Data is saved to the Blockchain by creating a digital fingerprint using the date and time stamp that provides both security and transparency. Facilitated data can also make risk assessment more accurate and more accurate.
3. **Third-Party Transactions:** Blockchain may increase third-party transactions and claims made on personal digital devices. Blockchain helps reduce administrative costs by automatically verifying claim / payment data from third parties (Morini, 2016). Now, insurance companies can quickly view historical claim transactions registered with Blockchain for easy reference. This provides a higher level of trust and loyalty between the insurance company and the customer.
4. **Smart Contracts**: Personalized contracts now exist in the insurance sector. These contracts link real-time information from multiple systems to physical documents and activities that trigger accurate transactions. Such transactions include claims, payments, and quick and accurate refunds. This gives the customer a better experience and it saves time and money for the insurance company (Larimer, 2016).
5. **Reinsurance:** Within the reinsurance area, the Blockchain can make accurate reserve calculations based on existing contracts. This helps property and casualty insurers who need to know how much money is available when they claim compensation. Blockchain may allow them to rebalance exposure risks to specific risks. Insurance companies are now confident in their daily business operations (Morisse, 2015).

Insurance companies work in a high-risk environment. At the same time insurance is dealing with uncertainties. Blockchain technology has the potential to accelerate insurance assessment, forecasting and processing of claims. Within a few years, the insurance industry should have the knowledge to bring back centuries of ineffective pen and paper applications with a cheaper, more reliable and more effective system (Larimer, 2016).

Blockchain technology, that connects customers, agents and insurance institutions in real-time and creates a secure bond by keeping data on distributed records, is of great interest to insurers. In the insurance sector, Blockchain technology is rapidly moving from being a concept to becoming a useful application in the insurance sector. In a world where all stakeholders could have the same risk data at the same time, the data is carried in a fully automated process using digital contracts. These digital contracts are protected by an advanced encryption algorithm; they are secure; open to all kinds of auditing; enable end-to-end allocation and damage management will no longer be a dream (Nakamoto, 2008). While keeping the data highlighted by Blockchain on a distributed trial is not technically a new concept, it is a technique that has become feasible as a result of the current level of the technology.

Blockchain-based solutions connect customers, agents, insurance agencies in real-time and create a secure bond by keeping data on the distributed network. What are the advantages of this solution to insurers?

1. Real-time decision-making becomes a reality.
2. Processes can be completed at a quicker pace and there is reliably as well as cost-efficiency on smart contracts.
3. A data ecosystem is being established and all stakeholders involved can benefit from this advantage under equal conditions.
4. Billing can be done without delay and it increases financial efficiency.
5. Stakeholders can offer new services through this data platform and increase the scope of the application regardless of cost increases.
6. Last, but not least, audits of controls and contracts can be conducted internationally and in many different dimensions.

It is important to take the right steps together to fully exploit the potential of Blockchain technology. Blockchain in the insurance industry will become a win-win model for everyone when all stakeholders participate. Many common problems, such as multiple and dirty data, reconciliation, data transfers and prolongation of process completion times due to transaction volumes, can thus be eliminated (Larimer, 2016). The smart contract structure has the potential to define the sector from the beginning. The fact that the rules can be defined digitally and can be changed dynamically provides a very high operational efficiency potential. Many innovative solutions such as peer-to-peer insurance, pay-as-you-go, and fragmented payment can be implemented at very low costs on common platforms. Since insurance regulators will also play an important role in the transition phase of Blockchain technology, it is important that the business models are defined at the beginning. These business models should make common sense to the institutions.

What should insurance companies do about new business models with Blockchain? The following steps come to the fore.

1. A good understanding of the technology and the mapping of the value proposition that can be derived from the technology is an important issue. When selecting a Blockchain, it should be clear whether it is public, private or hybrid Blockchain; who will be in possession; what transactions will occur and be included in the Blockchain; the advantages the Blockchain will provide and how the Blockchain will be presented to the customer.

2. Creating an ecosystem and establishing the right collaborations are another important points. This is because new generation and game changing technologies do not seem to gather to develop the structure by which it will be supporting by itself. Humans and organization have to decide how the technology will operate and support their business operations. For this purpose, it is important to increase cooperation with startups and academic innovation centers and to establish collaborations with institutions from different sectors. These collaborations in formulating the right value proposition to the customer will at some point determine the competitive advantage.

3. Blockchain is not only an IT subject but requires the integration of business model, accounting, tax and basic insurance functions. How and where these technologies will be used; and which collaborations are needed should be determined by the direction and work of the team integrating the Blockchain into business processes.

4. It is important to see the next steps in terms of business model and to act 'by seeing where the ball is going, not where the ball is going'. It is necessary to consider the changes in the insurance business model; the changes in the service model and the impact of artificial intelligence applications deployed together with Blockchain on the insurance business.

5. Operational implementation is another point to emphasize. It is theoretically not possible to advance Blockchain and similar technologies at a go. It is critical to start with small experiments and see how the structure works in practice. As with big data, analytics and similar applications, the company's experimentation in this area is an effective way to visualize new business opportunities. Blockchain is a technology that is likely to become mainstream. Companies that identify early business models and value suggestions for this technology will provide a major competitive advantage in the new business models to which insurance will go.

BLOCKCHAIN USAGE EXAMPLES AND APPLICATIONS IN INSURANCE SECTOR

Blockchain will have several different uses in insurance. These includes the detection of insurance abuses, insurance damage management, customer loyalty applications, effective pricing and agentless operations.

1. **Detection of Fraud:** Particularly in the case of accidents involving a large number of parties, there may be situations where information sharing between insurers is insufficient. This may increase the risk of fraud. Given the fact that fraud damages are assumed to be within the range of 5-10% worldwide, it is clear how important it is to enact any action that will prevent them. However, the main issue here is the difficulty in sharing information between companies. Thanks to its distributed structure, the heap chain appears to be the perfect tool for keeping track of damage records as these records are shared with different parties. Blockverify's solutions for luxury products or Everledger diamonds are tagged to save the production and sales history of the tagged products in the same manner as a Blockchain, preventing counterfeiting and the sale of stolen goods, etc.

2. **Damage Management:** Insurance companies, that use automation in some of their damage processing activities, see significant differences in processing times and quality. But these companies are rare. Nevertheless, the results of the automation processes are much faster and the frequency of errors decreases. Damage processes managed by artificial intelligence has another advantage that is not visible at first glance. Systems using artificial intelligence show great success in preventing

abuses. These abuses are detrimental to the global insurance industry resulting in an average loss of $ 40 billion annually. Instead of manually identifying inconsistent damage files, artificial intelligence uses special algorithms to scan data for specific patterns of abuse and achieve a high level of success in detecting abuses.

There appear to be several different uses here with respect to Blockchain. These are:

a. Automated confirmed damage notification processes via sensors in vehicles or mobile devices.
b. Facilitation and automation of issues such as rights ownership inquiry through tracking of identity records through the heap chain.
c. Benefits from contractual corporate management, payment management, etc., facilitated by cluster chain records that provide payment when you go to a particular service.
d. Decrease in expertise costs by evaluating the above.

3. **Customer Loyalty Practices:** The secure structure of the heap chain makes it easier to protect personal information. A structure in which identity information and medical records are registered in the heap chain and can only be shared with third parties with the consent of the person if necessary; is much more than an environment in which data is transmitted to the insurer. This paper circulates by hand and has to be entered by both the insured and the insurer repeatedly. Seem to be reliable. Even such applications do not even require the registration of personal information in the heap chain, it is sufficient to register a code confirming identity information such as mobile signature applications today (such Know Your Customer (KYC) data, where companies like Tradle are trying to produce solutions through the heap chain).

4. **Effective Pricing:** Companies and in particular actuaries have to work with an increasing amount of data. Although concepts such as Big data have emerged, they are increasingly used for telematics applications and the Internet of things to keep a considerable amount of data distributed from a single center rather than from a decentralized center, and to (partially automated) pricing studies on this data. Blockchain will enable easy access to Big data records, thereby reducing the search cost allocated to working with Big data.

5. **New Product and Distribution Channels**: The use of the heap chain will require various product designs to be operated with IOT(such as airline ticket policies with automatic cancellation and cancellation compensation offered by InsureETH), both for micro-insurance applications in developing countries, and so on.

6. **Non-intermediary Transactions**: Both the reduction of loss appraisal costs with the above mentioned automatic damage processes and the reduction of deintermediation in both bid and damage processes and automation (deintermediation) can provide cost savings to companies.

Examples of new platforms that implement Blockchain technology in the insurance industry are Black Insurance. Black Insurance is a decentralized intermediary digital insurance company. It will eliminate unnecessary transactions, correspondence and waste of time and speed up transactions. Without intermediaries, transactions will accelerate and the premiums will not swell. The main objective of this platform is to empower insurance companies to establish their own virtual insurance companies and thus merge them directly with equity. Black Insurance promises to revolutionize the world of digital insurance by using Blockchain to transfer risks to customers directly to lenders. In addition, it makes the management of insurance policies with the Blockchain ecosystem much easier and more efficient, so these products will be much cheaper and provide more profit.

Figure 3. Insurance System Using Blockchain

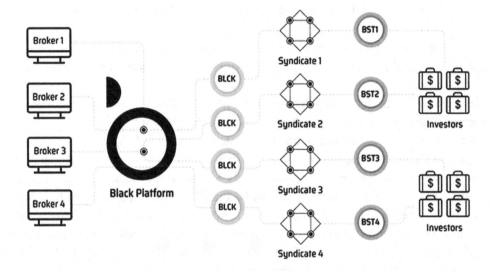

In short, the Black approach is a platform that create single Blockchain-backed insurance products that address the largest and most inefficient part of the current insurance industry with a market value of around $ 4 trillion. The platform also integrates the insurance entrepreneurs with capital to address the most important challenges in this sector. It is a platform that minimizes all inefficiencies; securely stores all data in the Blockchain; creates transparent business operations with Smart contract and develops faster innovations by Platform members.

This is how the Black platform works,

1. Entrepreneurs provide a list of insurance products.
2. Investors can create and benefit from trade unions by investing in tokens and allocating a certain amount of capital between different products.
3. Policies are written in a transparent and fully secure Blockchain ecosystem as smart contracts.
4. Users can access and evaluate invariable data (premiums sold, claims, profits) on the platform.
5. Earned profits are distributed automatically among Token owners.

FUTURE EXPECTATIONS AND TRENDS

The digitalization of all links in the insurance value chain is ongoing. It is not possible for companies to offer the perfect solution to all the rings within the value chain by themselves. Instead, companies that create a collaborative environment with insurtech initiatives and implement common platforms will come to the fore. This is because insurtech ventures offer companies important opportunities not only in the sales to the customer, but also in providing optimum solutions to all segments of the insurance value chain.

The general view is that cooperative models will create a more effective than disruptive competition in the insurance sector. As a reflection of this, insurtech ventures are currently focusing on solutions that create value for companies and customers through B2B and B2B2C models. They are not focusing on existing players and thereby demolishing structures. Another important topic in recent times is ecosystems and platforms. Since insurance products are integrated into many aspects of the life cycle of individual and corporate customers, insurance companies and entrepreneurs need to think beyond the insurance field and be open to becoming part of a wider ecosystem and platform.

Along with digitization and insurtech ecosystems, it is possible to gather the developments that are expected to occur in the insurance sector in the coming period under 3 headings. These are, access to personal data will be easier; artificial intelligence applications will increase; and traditional operational business models will change.

Resources such as mobile communications, wearable devices, smart gadgets, smart homes and the Internet of things will provide a larger, more up-to-date and more personalized large data set for companies to use. As a result, the traditional database will replace data mining applications with a much different information platform. Moreover, with the introduction of artificial intelligence and robotic technologies, data usage and pricing methodologies will gain a very different dimension. In addition, with the expansion of Blockchain applications, there will be fundamental changes in business models and operational structures. More flexible, more agile, more sharing and collaborative models will come to the fore.

The interaction with the customer will increase and product structures in a customizable manner and service models integrated into life will come to the fore;

New generation customers now prefer to be in contact with product and service providers in a much more flexible, instant and easy way. This trend will change the patterns towards tariff setting in the insurance sector, product packaging, paper working structures. New insurance consumers will demand more customizable products that is based on personal pricing. In addition, instead of standard annual maturities, flexible products can be purchased at the time when needed and whose collateral can be stopped if desired. These products will be of interest. Instead of following many maturity policies, it will become popular to meet the needs with a single product in an "all-inclusive" structure. Insurers will start to offer different services that complement their main functions and add value to their customers, or will cooperate with those who provide this service. This will increase the number of insurance services and practices integrated into the lives of individuals.

Traditional insurtech initiatives with fast-paced insurance companies will try to create a common ground;

Corporate and traditional global companies are looking for ways to adapt to the startup ecosystem. Some of them are trying to prepare themselves for this new era by adapting to the environment in Silicon Valley as well as establishing an innovative labor laboratory. In addition, a significant portion of the investments in insurtech ventures are made by insurance and reinsurance companies. On the other hand, new e-enterprise companies, which are much faster, agile and creative, are implementing new platforms and applications for the insurance sector. As a result, these two groups are exploring ways to meet on a common ground. Players will be able to take advantage of this collaboration and integration in the fastest and most agile way.

CONCLUSION

Blockchain technology, which is regarded as one of the most powerful technologies of the 21st century, enables the coding of digital pieces of data that make up the data blocks. These blocks contain information such as date, time, amount, user's digital identity of the transaction, with a coding system called "hush benzeri. After the digital information recorded with this code is converted to alphanumeric characters, the block is added to the data chain. The data stored in Blockchain is stored in a shared and constantly updated database, copied by all computers on the network and accessible to all. It is not possible to change this data, which is copied to millions of computers and not collected in a central location.

Blockchain technology is actually the creation of an index of records called blocks, which are linked together using cryptography. The Merkle tree, which was developed in 1979 is used to verify the integrity of large data groups. These large data groups are used in the field of cryptography and their data structures in computer technology. The Hash chain developed in 1981 for reliable chronological sequencing of events is the cornerstones of Blockchain technology.

Although Blockchain's first application was money transfer, it is now used in many areas outside the financial world. These areas are almost unlimited but foreign trade, international transfer transactions, insurance, supply chain management, health, voting and election systems, internet of objects, money transfers, cyber security, creation and storage of valuable documents, e-commerce and digital payments, smart contracts, forecasting applications, copyright are some of the use cases.

Blockchain is a new system that is still under development. The biggest problem with this system is that it is difficult to implement because it is open source and lacks standardization. But because it is a promising high-security system, large corporations and major banks around the world have begun to use Blockchain technology. Blockchain enables them to overcome problems in existing processes or improve upon business processes. Furthermore, investments in the development of this technology have been on the increase.

Blockchain has also introduced crypto-based payment solutions. These payment solutions work differently from the online payment systems currently available. This technology eliminates intermediaries, making bank transfer fees inexpensive, especially in international transactions.

The insurance sector is one of the leading sectors to be transformed by Blockchain technology. With Blockchain, insurers can save big money. By implementing a block chain, the global insurance market can achieve operational cost savings of between $ 20 billion and $ 50 billion each year. According to the report of the block chain solution provider R3 and ChainThat, it can save 10% to 25% or 20 billion to $ 50 billion in operational costs each year by applying block chains to the global reinsurance market. According to the news in insurancejournal, about 30 per cent to 60 per cent of the savings in accounting and solution (A & S) will be created. These processes lead to many interactions between counterparties (such as brokers and insurers) that they first accept their debts and authorize, implement and reconcile payments between each other. Complexity and operational challenges arise from coordinating actions and information between different organizations and systems.

A block chain or distributed book can serve as a shared record between the counterparties and can coordinate and reduce complexity in common A & S processes. Thus, technology can reduce operating costs and speed up the processing process along this insurance distribution chain. In the report, reconciliation and liquidation of payment means that it can be realized through fiat money book representation and therefore directly on block bridge-based platforms, meaning that there is no need to use digital currencies such as Bitcoin and Ethereum.

REFERENCES

Acer, F. (2017). *Sigorta Sektörü Insurtech ile Gelişecek* [Insurance Sector to Develop with Insurtech]. Retrieved from https://www.bankasurans.com.tr/sigorta-sektoru-insurtech-ile-gelisecek/

Beck, R., Czepluch, J. S., Lollike, N., & Malone, S. (2016). Blockchainthe Gateway to Trust-Free Cryptographic Transactions. *European Conference on Information Systems.*

Buterin, V. (2015). *On Public and Private Blockchains.* Retrieved from https://blog.ethereum.org/2015/08/07/on-public-and-private-Blockchains/

Cavalcante, S. A. (2013). Understanding the impact of technology on firms' business models. Enhanced Profitability, Lower Costs and Stronger Customer Loyalty. *European Journal of Innovation Management, 16*(3), 285–300.

Çipil, M. (2017). *"Blockchain" sigortacılığı nasıl etkileyecek?* [How will Blockchain affect the insurance?]. Retrieved from https://www.dunya.com/kose-yazisi/Blockchain-sigortaciligi-nasil-etkileyecek/344612

Credit Suisse. (2016). *Blockchain - The Trust Disrupter.* Retrieved from https://www.finextra.com/finextra-downloads/newsdocs/document-1063851711.pdf

Decker, C., Wattenhofer, R. (2015). A fast and scalable payment network with bitcoin duplex micropayment channels. *Stabilization, Safety, and Security of Distributed Systems, 9212.*

Deloitte. (2018). *Deloitte Blockchain Lab.* Retrieved from https://www2.deloitte.com/ie/en/pages/technology/topics/Blockchain-lab.html

Jacobovitz, O. (2016). *Blockchain for identity management. Technical Report.* Beer Sheva, Israel: The Lynne and William Frankel Center for Computer Science Department of Computer Science, Ben-Gurion University.

KPMG. (2017). *Sigortacılık, Teknolojiyle Yeniden Doğdu* [Rebirth of Insurance with Technology]. Retrieved from https://home.kpmg.com/tr/tr/home/media/press-releases/2017/07/sigortacilik-teknolojiyle-yeniden-dogdu.html

Larimer, D. (2016). *Blok zinciri ve Sigorta* [Blockchain and Insurance]. Retrieved from https://www.blokzinciri.org/yazi/blok-zinciri-vesigorta/

Morini, M. (2016). From 'Blockchain hype' to a real business case for financial markets. *Journal of Financial Transformation, 45,* 30–40. doi:10.2139srn.2760184

Morisse, M. (2015). Cryptocurrencies and bitcoin: charting the researchlandscape. *21st Americas conference on information systems.*

Nakamoto, S. (2008). *Bitcoin: A Peer to Peer Electronic Cash System.* Retrieved from https://bitcoin.org/bitcoin.pdf

Social Rush. (2018). *Tracking food supply with blockchain.* https://thesocialrush.com/tracking-food-supply-with-blockchain/

Swan, M. (2015). *Blockchain: Blueprint for a New Economy.* Newton, MA: O'Reilly Media.

Tian, F. (2016). An agri-food supply chain traceability system for china based on RFID & Blockchain technology. In *Service Systems and Service Management (ICSSSM), 13th International Conference on*. IEEE.

Wüst, K., & Gervais, A. (2017). Do you need a Blockchain? *ACR Cryptology ePrint Archive*.

Zaninotto, F. (2017). *The Blockchain Explained to Web Developers, Part 3: The Truth*. Retrieved from http://marmelab.com/blog/2016/06/14/Blockchain-for-web-developers-the-truth.html

KEY TERMS AND DEFINITIONS

Autonomous Administration: Cyber-physical systems are the ability to make their own decisions within smart factories.

Cloud Computing: For computers and other devices, which can be used at any time and enabling shared computing resources between users, is the general name of internet-based information services.

Insurance: A connection agreement with an organization that deals with this business in order to compensate for any future damage that may be incurred by someone or something in return for a pre-paid premium.

Internet of Things: A network of physical objects connected to each other or to larger systems. It is envisaged that the objects can work together over the Internet infrastructure by marking them with a single key and thus creating values greater than the sum of the small parts.

Modularity: Provides flexible adaptation system to intelligent factories for changing requirements of individual modules.

Real-Time Capability: Ability to collect and analyze data. This structure makes fast understanding.

Service Orientation: Cyber-physical systems, people and smart factory services are offered via the Internet of Services.

Smart Contracts: It was introduced by Nick Szabo in 1994 according to some sources and in 1996 according to some sources. Szabo, which is both a legal and programming infrastructure, defines the term "contract" as dizi a series of agreements or promises between agents/agents."

Chapter 8
Developing Use Cases of Blockchain Technology:
Value Creation Perspectives

Ezer Osei Yeboah-Boateng
https://orcid.org/0000-0002-1355-8586
Ghana Technology University College, Ghana

Stephane Nwolley, Jnr.
Npontu Technologies Ltd., Ghana

ABSTRACT

Technology innovation creates value and competitive advantage. Blockchain has been used to resolve existing problems and offer efficient operations. Blockchain is applied in education, healthcare, automation, etc. Blockchain with permanence and reliability attributes has created trust in digital assets with high integrity and availability to leverage on innovative transactions. Indeed, a plethora of blockchain use cases and value propositions are documented. That notwithstanding, there is dearth of literature on transforming some legacy systems and creating value. To harness the potential, a deeper understanding of use cases and future opportunities is imperative. So, how can blockchain be harnessed for best value creation? What strategies could be adopted by SMEs to leverage? The study explicated on taxonomy of use cases in taxation, e-voting, AI and IoT, and analyzed some value creation perspectives to identify opportunities, in particular, smart contracts used to enforce regulatory compliance. It implies that blockchain use cases could create future opportunities for SMEs.

INTRODUCTION

The essence of technology innovation is either to create value or to leverage on competitive advantage in the market. A number of studies indicate that Blockchain technology usage can provide invaluable solutions to resolving existing problems, whilst harnessing operations (Bauer, Leisibach, Zavolokina, & Schwabe, 2018). Blockchain, although not a new technology, had been relatively unpopular until 2008

DOI: 10.4018/978-1-7998-3632-2.ch008

when Satoshi Nakamoto invented the first widely used cryptocurrency based on Blockchain technology. Named Bitcoin, Nakamoto's digital currency sought to implement the transfer of value between two "untrusting" parties without the need for a trusted central authority, as is the case for traditional money system. According to Nakamoto (2008), Bitcoin is a peer-to-peer electronic cash system. The first major implementation of Blockchain technology occurred in 2009 when Nakamoto released his breakthrough crypto-based digital currency, the Bitcoin. Since then, the technology has gained public traction and many are advocating for the application of Blockchain technology to areas beyond cryptocurrency such as Education, Healthcare, Insurance, Supply Chain, Asset Management, etc. In Estonia, for example, the Keyless Signatures Infrastructure (KSI) Blockchain technology is used to police Estonian e-services such as the e-Health Record, e-Prescription database, e-Law, and e-Court systems, e-Police data, e-Banking, e-Business Register, and e-Land Registry (Cullell, 2019).

Blockchain in its most basic form may be defined as a time-stamped sequence of tamper-proof record of data that is handled by a cluster of computers which do not belong to any one individual or entity (Shuhada, 2019). The record of data blocks are linked securely to one another by underlying cryptographic principles. Among the core attributes of Blockchain is a distributed ledger in which identical copies of data is shared among network participants and each participant has the ability to independently validate the shared data without the need for central authority, as required in the traditional transactional value exchange. A failure at one node does not affect operation of the network, thereby making a Blockchain network highly available. As a digital technology, manual processing of data is completely eliminated. Blockchain transactions are chronological and time-stamped ensuring that each block of data is intricately and securely linked to the previous one, leaving behind a traceable trail of historical records. Data stored in a Blockchain is cryptographically signed. This makes Blockchain immutable or tamper-proof to a very large extent. Blockchain could only be tampered if more that 50% of the network-computing power is controlled and all previous transactions are rewritten (Carson, Romanelli, Walsh, & Zhumaev, 2018).

As a result of these enticing characteristics of Blockchain technology, there is tremendous interest in the technology by public and private sector operators, various interest groups and individuals alike. The following startling statistics buttress this point: The Blockchain domain is expected to grow by 42.8% by 2020; the entire market capitalization of cryptocurrencies at the end of 2017 was $600 billion (World-Press, 2017); from 2017 to 2018, the number of Blockchain related jobs on LinkedIn tripled; Global spending on Blockchain solutions equaled $2.1 billion in 2018 (NewGenApps, 2018). In recent years, the hype for Blockchain has been nothing less overwhelming. Within a spade of two years from 2016 to 2018, there were a half a million publications on Blockchain, which also accounted for 3.7 million Google search results (Carson, Romanelli, Walsh, & Zhumaev, 2018). By 2027, it is anticipated that 10 percent of global GDP will be kept on Blockchain according to a World Economic Forum (2015) survey.

Several Blockchain use cases and future opportunities have been suggested and documented across the globe. Many more publications on Blockchain continue to pour out on daily basis. Carson et al. (2018) identified six broad classes of Blockchain use cases which address two fundamental necessities of today's world: they are record keeping and transactions. Ranging from broad categories of Static and Dynamic Registries to Identity Assurance, Smart Contracts to Payment Infrastructures, several use cases such as supply chain management, land title registration, identity records, insurance claim payouts and cross-border payment systems, etc. have been proposed. Countless use cases and future opportunities are being advanced within the Blockchain space today.

However, much of the present literature on Blockchain use cases and future opportunities appear to scratch the surface of the subject. The essential details of each use case vis-à-vis current legacy implementations, identifiable shortcomings and Blockchain potential improvements, are dearth or not sufficient. Consequently, this study seeks to bridge the knowledge gap by analyzing some of the already proposed Blockchain use cases in detail and suggesting other future opportunities. There is no doubt on the potential benefits of Blockchain across multiple industries today. Nonetheless, in order to realize the prospects of the technology, businesses require a proper understanding of its potential and applicability to business. The primary objective of this study is to contribute to the discourse on Blockchain use cases, whilst given some value propositions for businesses, particularly SMEs in developing economies. A survey conducted by Deloitte (2018) identified low awareness and understanding as one of the challenges confronting Blockchain adoption. According to the executive survey, 39 percent of senior executives at big US organizations had limited or no knowledge of Blockchain. Therefore, the importance of this study, in so far as understanding Blockchain use cases and future opportunities is concerned, cannot be overemphasized.

It is anticipated that the findings here will add to the body of knowledge in the use cases and future opportunities domain of Blockchain technology. In particular, deeper insights will be gained in application areas such as Education and Academia, Supply Chain Management, Healthcare, Real Estate, Insurance, Cloud Storage and Computing, Music and Entertainment, Land Title Registration, Identity Management, Banking and Finance, among dozen others.

Blockchain is poised to disrupt any human activity that requires time-stamped record-keeping and transaction of services (Grech & Camilleri, 2017). It is now almost an established fact that Blockchain presents a great potential to transforming multiple facets of the world of business and society today. Similar to how the Internet revolutionized the very concept of information exchange in the 90s, Blockchain is poised to challenge and transform conventional notions of "value" (Deloitte Insights, 2018). There is currently a plethora of Blockchain use cases and future opportunities propounded and documented across the globe. Pisa & Juden (2017) posit that Blockchain has the potential for eliminating intermediaries in transactions, thus adding value of effectiveness and efficiency. Indeed, proponents and/or enthusiast of Blockchain technology are upbeat about the prospects of its use cases, but they somewhat lack the requisite understanding of some implications of security and as a disruptive technology (Pisa & Juden, 2017).

Furthermore, the essential details of each use case regarding current legacy implementations, identifiable shortcomings, such as the lack of universal protocols accustomed with the Internet, and Blockchain potential improvements, are dearth or not sufficient, especially amongst developing economies. In order to reap potential benefits of Blockchain technology, a deeper understanding of current use cases and future opportunities is required (Grech & Camilleri, 2017).

The other question is how can Blockchain technology be harnessed for best value creation? Inspire of the enormous potentials of Blockchain technology for businesses in developing economies, SMEs, most especially, would need to exploit these value propositions in order to realize these benefits. However, these SMEs lack the strategy to adopt and harness these opportunities (Bauer, Leisibach, Zavolokina, & Schwabe, 2018). In this study, we endeavor to assist business leaders with some insights on prospects of Blockchain and how to harness its value for competitive advantage.

The primary goal of this study is to enhance deeper understanding of Blockchain use cases and future opportunities, with the end result of enabling industry's or business leaders' realistic assessment of the technology for possible deployment. In this regard, the study delivers a thorough review of contemporary literature on Blockchain use cases and future prospects. Furthermore, the research delves deeper and uncover crucial details regarding current legacy implementations, identifiable shortfalls and potential improvements to be realized by introducing Blockchain. Quite apart from these, in examining the current use cases and future prospects of Blockchain, attention is given to scrutinize the differences which exist in the context of Africa, the Middle East, Europe and North America. In summary, the study seeks to achieve the following objectives:

1.   To explore and enumerate Blockchain use cases and future opportunities with value propositions;
2.   To explicate the use cases and future prospects of Blockchain in relation to current legacy implementations, identifiable shortfalls and Blockchain potential improvements;

The result of this study will be valuable in enhancing the understanding of industry practitioners and academia on Blockchain use cases and future opportunities. It will in no doubt add to the body of knowledge and serve as reference material for future researchers on the subject matter.

This introductory section dealt with overview of Blockchain technology and value creation aspects of appropriating use cases. Followed by related works on Blockchain uses cases. Techniques employed to source literature are discussed. By explicating the available literature we discussed a number of use cases and their inputs towards value creation. Specific strategic value creation appropriation techniques are also discussed, and then conclusion and recommendations.

LITERATURE REVIEW: BLOCKCHAIN USE CASES AND FUTURE OPPORTUNITIES

In systems engineering, use cases are a set of objectives or intended system behavior, used in system design analysis to identify, clarify and classify system functional requirements. They depict the possible system interactions between end-users and the system (Yeboah-Boateng & Nwolley, 2019). Use cases are a form of writing that can be used in different situations, to describe (Cockburn, 2000):

1.   A business work process;
2.   To focus discussion about software system requirements, but not the requirements description;
3.   To document the design of the system; and
4.   They may be written in a small, close-knit group, or in a formal setting, or in a large distributed group.

The year 2008 may go down history as a year in which one of the world's most disruptive technologies was given birth to, known as Bitcoin, its inventor, Satoshi Nakamoto first proposed the crypto technology in a whitepaper he released in 2008. The dawn of 2009 then saw the initial implementation of Bitcoin based on Blockchain (Nakamoto, 2008). It must be noted that Bitcoin and Blockchain are closely related but not the same. Whereas Bitcoin is just but one cryptocurrency application of Blockchain technology, the functionality of Blockchain extends beyond cryptocurrency into many other areas of application (Carson, Romanelli, Walsh, & Zhumaev, 2018).

In basic terms, Blockchain is a time-stamped sequence of tamper-proof record of data that is handled by a cluster of computers which do not belong to any one individual or entity (Shuhada, 2019). The recorded blocks of data or transactions are contained in a digital distributed ledger, which spans a network of computers or nodes. The blocks of data are linked together in a chainlike fashion through underlying cryptographic hash functions. Before a new block of transactions is persisted to the end of the "chain", it must be independently and cryptographically validated by each node through a consensus algorithms or mechanism (Deloitte Insights, 2018).

Key characteristics of Blockchain are Decentralization, Persistency, Anonymity and Auditability (Zheng, Xie, Dai, Chen, & Wang, 2018). These core attributes underpin the attractiveness of Blockchain technology to many use cases around the world. Because the Blockchain is decentralized, performance constraints which is akin to centralized systems, is mitigated. By persistency, a Blockchain transaction is practically impossible to falsify since transactions are append only and impracticable to reverse. Anonymity preserves some form of privacy on Blockchain transactions, but this is not a guarantee. Auditability on the other hand means that Blockchain transactions are completely traceable and can be proven.

Blockchain seems to signify the beginning of a new era in several ways, as it transforms how we store and exchange value; it can be regarded as one of the greatest technology inventions in recent past, akin to the dawn of the Internet in the early 1990s (Deloitte Insights, 2018). Started as the foundation for cryptocurrencies such as Bitcoin, Blockchain technology is now spanning a myriad of industries throughout the world (CBINSIGHTS, 2019). Today, there are many use cases of Blockchain which extend far beyond the initial in banking and cryptocurrency. Many businesses and industries are beginning to leverage the power of Blockchain. We examine the following use cases and future prospects of Blockchain in the ensuing sections.

Taxation

Some of the key attributes of Blockchain such as transparency, control, security and real-time information make the technology potentially suited for application in the tax regime (PricewaterhouseCoopers LLP, 2016). By design, Blockchain transactions are transparent, traceable and can be proven, which are all useful in tax administration. Control is achieved through the concept of permissioned networks in Blockchain, whereby data access is granted to only registered users. This is consortium Blockchain which is most suitable for this use case. A tax authority can implement Blockchain over its area of administration, allowing both the authority and the tax payer to reap the shared benefits of Blockchain.

Taxation in the informal sector is particularly more challenging especially in developing economies where a greater percentage of the workforce falls within that sector. As a result of the sheer numbers, tax authorities lack the needed resources or human capacity to implement, monitor and enforce tax laws (Joshi & Ayee, 2002). According to PricewaterhouseCoopers LLP (2016), while Blockchain may not be a panacea for all problems in the taxation system, the administrative liability and the cost associated with tax collection, as per transaction costs, could be reduced by applying Blockchain to some areas of the system.

E-Voting

Voting to elect political leaders in many countries around the world is bedeviled with issues of electoral fraud and vote rigging or gerrymandering. In order to produce a credible winner in an election, it is required to authenticate each voter's identity, securely record and track votes, as well as produce trusted tallies. Some countries have employed biometric verification devices to authenticate the voter's credentials, but it has its problems. Given the capabilities of Blockchain, it is possible to design an e-voting system based on the technology, to allow secure casting, tracking and casting of votes in an election (Sumana & Anitha, 2019). It is anticipated that Blockchain technology, utilizing homomorphic encryption, could be used to analyze the results, whilst preserving the sanctity of votes cast (Jones, Johnson, Shervey, Dudley, & Zimmerman, 2019).

Land Title Registration

In most developing economies, land ownership is a big problem and has potential for causing conflict. The reason is as a result of multiple sale of the same parcel of land to different people due to lack of proper data on land ownership. Deployment of Blockchain, with associated traceability and auditability attributes, is very much needed to achieve sanity in the land registry space (Oprunenco & Akmeemana, 2018).

Ghana recently launched a mapping application known as GhanaPostGPS. It is Ghana's official digital property addressing system which demarcates the entire land mass of Ghana (GhanaPosts, 2018). This mapping application could be integrated with Blockchain to produce a digital land register which eliminates the problems associated with manual processing of title documents. For this to succeed however, stakeholders such as the Lands Commission, Government and prospective land owners need a clear understanding of how Blockchain will fit into the current state of affairs. A painstaking exercise will have to be undertaken by the Lands Commission to scan and archive all present documentation to be used as input to the Blockchain digital ledger. Government on its part must be ready to provide the needed funding to support the deployment. Finally, prospective land owners need to exercise patience and go through due process to realize the first implementation.

Blockchain in AI and IoT

Many Organizations will develop their applications on Blockchain technology, going beyond the concept stage and rather adopting it as a start to realize the cost savings and enhanced security they can achieve. In fact, it's predicted that Blockchain application development will revolutionize technological advancement (Iansiti & Lakhani, 2017) (Gogan, 2018). These apps might have broad use such as cybersecurity or be niche-focused, as in our fantasy football example above. Blockchain technology will improve the Internet of Things (IoT) where apps must run anywhere by building trust, reducing risk, decreasing costs, and speeding up transactions.

Artificial Intelligence (AI) needs data to function, and the faster the AI can access bigger volumes of data, the better. With Blockchain, data can be authenticated more reliably and faster, making it possible for AI to access Big Data, thereby vastly improving the performance of the AI (Ernst, Merola, & Samaan, 2019).

METHODOLOGY

This is an exploratory study on the use cases of Blockchain technology and its prospects of value creation. We herewith adapted the Agile Scrum approach, wherewith Blockchain use cases were sourced and analyzed using value creation principles to enhance adoption decision-making (Batrinca & Treleaven, 2015). Sources of datasets employed are mainly global literature on Blockchain use cases and associated value creation analytics.

In this study, we carried out site scraping or web data extraction, which involved collecting online data from online repositories and academic database (Batrinca & Treleaven, 2015). We also conducted extensive literature review of key articles, databases, repositories, and authorities, with the view to assessing use cases necessary for value creation when using Blockchain technologies for competitive advantage.

Theoretically, systems development principles are employed to evaluate or assess the potentials of various use cases and to explore the value additions accruing therefrom. Indeed, the value created as insights could aid in Blockchain adoption decision-making.

VALUE CREATION PERSPECTIVES

As discussed in the preceding sections, Blockchain technologies can be harnessed various use cases or applications to create value in business and in society. Here we posit that the value is created through the process of Blockchain technology utilization, such as optimization of transaction costs, effective and secured records keeping or storage, as well as offering high-level privacy with auditability.

Typically, a study carried out by Sunil (2018) on value creation through Blockchain technology in supply chain management (SCM) – highlights the potential value accruing from securing enormous data entries or transactions, detecting fraudulent transactions, and ultimately building customer confidence in the SCM operations.

Integrity and Availability, as exhibited as data security and reliable access respectively, are amongst the cyber-security CIA triad or bedrock; these are some of the value creation from using Blockchain technologies. They could be used to facilitate the tracking of products and services being offered to customers in real time.

Blockchain technology is typically based on offering transactional ledger for products and services as information assets (Sunil, 2018). Value could be further harnessed by transforming existing service level agreements (SLAs) into smart contracts and processing them using associated consensus algorithms (Ruta, Scioscia, Leva, Capursola, & Sciascio, 2017). In essence, smart contracts are codified legal agreement which are computer executable; thus, smart contracts are able interact with other computer systems and other contracts, to execute formal verification and/or validation as well as enforcement of regulatory compliance requirements (Treleaven, Galas, & Lalchand, 2013).

Across industries, from healthcare to software development, Blockchain technology can also be harnessed to create value with reduction in dissemination of corrupted information, elimination of unnecessary intermediaries in supply chain management of products and services, as well as its avowed attribute of transparency and efficiency in operations (Morini, 2017) (Brunner, et al., 2017).

In summary, the value proposition for this study is first the taxonomy of Blockchain use cases; then key attributes of Blockchain technology – namely, decentralization, persistency, anonymity and auditability. The SMEs in developing economies could harness these potentials. In practice, these values could be modeled by way of adoption and implementation of Blockchain applications into existing and/or new services and products to realize the benefits of optimized transaction costs and improved operations with reliability (Yeboah-Boateng, 2017).

Blockchain is meant to create a variety of business opportunities. In other words, Blockchain undoubtedly can add value, but the question is how can this value be articulated, queried (Warren & Treat, 2019). The World Economic Forum (WEF) Blockchain Value Framework espouses that the tenets of rethinking business models, rethinking business relationships and associated strategic focus (Warren & Treat,

2019). This is collaborated by the Treacy and Wiersema's Value Disciplines – of product leadership, customer intimacy and operational excellence ((Treacy & Wiersema, 1993) as cited (Bauer, Leisibach, Zavolokina, & Schwabe, 2018)).

CONCLUSION

Any and every future technology must grapple with the issues of trust and data privacy. The very nature of how blockchain technology works makes it a much better option for adoption by companies in their deployment of essential solutions that enrich the lives of their clients. Whilst it is still early days yet, the adoption and usage of Blockchain technology like the bitcoin reveals its potential to offer and deliver on a much more efficient structure in the software development phase, besides the taxonomy of use cases dealt with in this text.

Blockchain is a technology whose prospects are so high, enabling it to function as a peer-to-peer reorganized "digital ledgers" that can play a major role in reducing the dissemination of corrupted information, eliminating unnecessary intermediaries across almost every industry, increasing transparency, witnessing multiplied efficiency in countless processes (Morini, 2017).

Blockchain being a subset of supply chains, will effortlessly record each touchpoint of an element, heighten production transparency for buyers who wish to make more cognizant purchase decisions. Blockchain technology also has a space to accommodate the industry of governance, as it is poised to decentralize the voting process while maintaining trustworthiness and integrity to prevent election hacks. The Real estate industry, also has its share in this phenomenal technology by ensuring estate asset record histories stored on Blockchain will annihilate time invested in due diligence and financial verifications.

At the individual level, Blockchain technologies will enable you to more easily authenticate your identity, share your health records, augment gains from your financial assets, and track the origins of your every purchase.

Blockchain technology at the societal level, will catalyze a sweeping shift away from tiered structures towards democratized networks at larger scales than ever before experienced by humankind. Blockchain would be the groundbreaking new order that serves the next-generation as an indispensable tool capable of maintaining trust in large populations.

In conclusion, the outcome of this study will be an enhanced understanding of Blockchain use cases and future opportunities. Nevertheless, it is far from truth to state that this research is conclusive; the field of technology is ever expanding and Blockchain is no exception. Future studies are thus expected to build on the findings achieved here.

REFERENCES

Batrinca, B., & Treleaven, P. C. (2015). Social Media Analytics: A Survey of Techniques, Tools and Platforms. *AI & Society*, *30*(1), 89–116. doi:10.100700146-014-0549-4

Bauer, I., Leisibach, F., Zavolokina, L., & Schwabe, G. (2018). *Exploring Blockchain Value Creation: The Case of Car Ecosystem*. Academic Press.

Brunner, A., Abderrahmane, N., Muralidharan, Halpap, P., Sume, O., & Zimprich, S. (2017). Trade Finance Disrupted: A Blockchain Use Case. *The CAPCO Institute Journal of Financial Transformation, 45*, 41-48.

Carson, B., Romanelli, G., Walsh, P., & Zhumaev, A. (2018, June). *Blockchain Beyond the Hype: WHat is the Strategic Business Value?* Retrieved from McKinsey Digital: https://www.mckinsey.com/business-functions/mckinsey-digtal/our-insights/blockchain-beyond-the-hype-what-is-the-strategic-business-value

CBINSIGHTS. (2019). Banking Is Only The Beginning: 55 Big Industries Blockchain Could Transform. *CBINSIGHTS*. Retrieved from www.cbinsights.com

Cockburn, A. (2000). *Writing Effective Use Cases*. Addison-Wesley.

Cullell, L. M. (2019). Is e-Estonia Built on Blockchain Technologies? *Hackernoon.com*. Retrieved from www.hackernoon.com/e-estonia-is-not-on-blockchain/

Deloitte Insights. (2018). *Blockchain: A Technical Primer*. Deloitte.

Ernst, E., Merola, R., & Samaan, D. (2019). Economics of Artificial Intelligence (AI): Implications for the Future of Work. *IZA Journal of Labor Policy, 9*(4), 1–35.

GhanaPosts. (2018). *My Digital Address*. Retrieved November 30, 2019, from www.ghanapostgps.com

Gogan, M. (2018, August 17). *Blockchain Technology in the Future: 7 Predictions for 2020*. Retrieved November 29, 2019, from AiThority: https://www.aithority.com/guest-authors/blockchain-technology-in-the-future-7-predictions-for-2020/

Grech, A., & Camilleri, A. F. (2017). Blockchain in Education. In A. Inamorato dos Santos (Eds.), JRC Science for Policy Report. European Union (EU).

Iansiti, M., & Lakhani, K. R. (2017, February). The Truh About Blockchain. *Harvard Business Review (HBR)*. Retrieved from https://hbr.org/2017/01/the-truth-about-blockchain

Jones, M., Johnson, M., Shervey, M., Dudley, J. T., & Zimmerman, N. (2019, August). Privacy-Preserving Methods for Feature Engineering Using Blockchain: Review, Evaluation and Proof of Concept. *Journal of Medical Internet Research, 21*(8), e13600. doi:10.2196/13600 PMID:31414666

Joshi, A., & Ayee, J. (2002). Taxing for the State? Politics, Revenue and the Informal Sector in Ghana. *IDS Bulletin, 33*(3), 1–9. doi:10.1111/j.1759-5436.2002.tb00030.x

Morini, M. (2017). From "Blockchain Hype" to a Real Business Case for Financial Markets. *The CAPCO Institute Journal of Financial Transformation, 45*, 30–40.

Nakamoto, S. (2008). *Bitcoin: A Peer-to-Peer Electronic Cash System*. bitcoin.org. Retrieved from www.bitcoin.org/bitcoin.pdf

NewGenApps. (2018). *8 Experts on the Future of Blockchain Technology and Applications*. Retrieved from www.newgenapps.com/blog/future-of-blockchain-technology-applications

Oprunenco, A., & Akmeemana, C. (2018, April 13). Using Blockchain to Make Land Registry More Reliable in India. In *Information & Technology: Sustainable Development Goals*. United Nations Development Programme (UNDP). Retrieved November 30, 2019, from https://blogs.lse.ac.uk/business-review/2018/04/13/using-blockchain-to-make-land-registry-more-reliable-in-india/

Pisa, M., & Juden, M. (2017). *Blockchain and Economic Development: Hype vs. Reality.* Center for Global Development. Retrieved from www.cgdev.org

PricewaterhouseCoopers LLP. (2016). *How Blockchain Technology Could Improve the Tax System.* PwC.

Ruta, M., Scioscia, F., Leva, S., Capursola, G., & Sciascio, D. (2017). Supply Chain Object Discovery with Semantic-Enhanced Blockchain. In *15th ACM Conference on Embedded Networked Sensor Systems*. Delft, The Netherlands: ACM. 10.1145/3131672.3136974

Shuhada, N. (2019, July 24). *What is Blockchain?* Retrieved from Techcryption: www.techcryption.com/2019/07/24/what-is-a-blockchain/

Sumana, C., & Anitha, G. (2019, May). Blockchain Enabled Secure E-Voting System. *International Journal for Research in Applied Science and Engineering Technology*, 7(5).

Sunil, K. (2018). Value Creation Through Blockchain Technology in the Supply Chain Management (SCM). *Journal of Information Technology & Software Engineering*.

Treacy, M., & Wiersema, F. (1993, Jan.-Feb.). Customer Intimacy and Other Disciplines. *Harvard Business Review*, 12.

Treleaven, P., Galas, M., & Lalchand, V. (2013). Algorithmic Trading Review. *Communications of the ACM*, 56(11), 76–85. doi:10.1145/2500117

Warren, S., & Treat, D. (2019). *Building Value with Blockchain Technology: How to Evaluate Blockchain's Benefits.* The World Economic Forum (WEF).

World Economic Forum. (2015). *Deep Shift: Technology Tipping Points and Societal Impact.* The World Economic Forum (WEF).

WorldPress. (2017, October 4). Back in Business. *Financial Advisors*. WorldPress.

Yeboah-Boateng, E. O. (2017). Cyber-Security Concerns with Cloud Computing: Business Value Creation & Performance Perspectives. In A. K. Turuk, B. Sahoo, & S. K. Addya (Eds.), Resource Management & Efficiency in Cloud Computing Environment (pp. 106-137). IGI Global Publishers.

Yeboah-Boateng, E. O., & Nwolley, J. S. (2019). Developing Use Cases for Big Data Analytics: Data Integration with Social Media Metrics. In K. E. Skouby, I. Williams, & A. Gyamfi (Eds.), *Handbook on ICT in Developing Countries: Next Generation ICT Technologies (Vol. Series in Communications)*. Rivers Publisher.

Zheng, Z., Xie, S., Dai, H. N., Chen, X., & Wang, H. (2018). Blockchain Challenges and Opportunities: A Survey. *International Journal of Web and Grid Services*, 14(4), 352. doi:10.1504/IJWGS.2018.095647

Chapter 9
Blockchain Smart Contracts and Empathy Trade–Off:
Is Africa Ready?

Cephas Paa Kwasi Coffie

University of Electronic Science and Technology of China, China & All Nations University College, Ghana

Hongjiang Zhao

School of Management and Economics, University of Electronic Science and Technology of China, China

Benjamin Kwofie

Koforidua Technical University, Ghana

Emmanuel Dortey Tetteh

ⓘ https://orcid.org/0000-0002-7522-5752

University of Electronic Science and Technology of China, China & Koforidua Technical University, Ghana

ABSTRACT

Contracts have emerged as an appropriate expanse for the application of Blockchain to eliminate human mediation perceived to be mired by weaknesses. Smart contracts date back to the 1990s, but the proposed Blockchain technology makes it a great force economically. Beyond the transactional processing qualities of blockchain, industries envisage the technology to resolve divergent human-related complications with traditional contracts. Per literature, smart contracts offer superior economic value with respect to legality, formation, deployment, execution, and cost. These qualities of smart contract ensure performance and eliminate risk. Criticised on the inhumane aspect of the technology in terms of contract amendments and the current influx of foreign-based blockchain companies in Africa limiting indigenous design considerations, the application of smart contracts in continent could be hindered by contract renegotiations strongly embedded in cultural values of empathy. Nonetheless, a trade-off would resolve the contractual bottlenecks in Africa.

DOI: 10.4018/978-1-7998-3632-2.ch009

INTRODUCTION-EVOLUTION OF CONTRACTS

Evolutionary, humans have devised resourceful revenues for the formation and enforcement contracts. Aside written evidences either on paper, stones and or woods, most countries in Africa occasionally revert to the use of eggs, schnapps, and other traditional means of establishing contracts to avoid breach, Chiefs revered traditionally in Africa also played crucial roles in contract mediation until the era of foreign colonization. This led to the adoption of civil law making contracts enforceable at the law court. Currently, the practice of primitive methods of contract formation and enforcement in Africa co-exist alongside civil law because of the perceived limitations of civil procedure. A traditional contract is a written or oral (or partly written and partly oral) promise exchanged for another promise or for a performance that the law enforces (Mik, 2017). Although traditional contracts are backed by the laws of specific jurisdiction, holdups like breach and re-negotiations leading to delayed and extra cost of enforcement plaques this type of contracts. Consequently, Nick Szabo in 1990 proposed computer-based smart contracts to resolve the holdups concomitant with contracts. The promise of smart contract includes but not limited to; the elimination of erroneous interpretation by human judges, corruption and bribery, and possible delayed enforcement. This concept did not attract much attention until the introduction of Blockchain by Nakamoto in 2008. Fairfeld (2014) defines Blockchain-based smart contracts as automated program transferring digital assets within the Blockchain upon certain triggering conditions. Although smart contracts are supported by several technologies, current literature refer to smart contracts as Blockchain-based because of the offerings of the technology over others (Zheng *et al.*, 2020;Szabo *et al.*, 2017). Blockchain offers; decentralization, records are shared across various networks resulting in a mediation free dissemination process. This prevents information asymmetry and eliminates the possibility of altering records without the approval of all parties (Catchlove, 2017). Transparency, Blockchain provides all-around transparency due to the use of public ledger. The contents of contracts can be made visible and opened to all stakeholders. Holden and Malani (2017) indicate that it is absolutely impossible for signatories to a smart contract to dispute the terms of the contract once established. Accurate records, error free interpretation of contracts depend on details establishing the contract. Blockchain interprets contracts based on the error free records shared between parties. Speed, Blockchain has an added advantage of executing contracts quickly as a triggered condition leads to a corresponding response (Clack, Bakshi & Braine, 2016). Ultimately, trust, Blockchain executes autonomously without the intervention of humans and therefore trust is assured. Accordingly, the application of Blockchain is wide-spread supporting initial coin offerings (ICOs), crowdfunding contracts, and various cryptocurrency trades. Still at an early stage, smart contract is conceptualized (Savelyev, 2017; Zheng et al., 2020) to have the ability to transform contract formation and execution at peer-to-peer (P2P), business-to-customer (B2C), business-to-business (B2B) levels, and in public survives. However, the application of Blockchain in Africa lags significantly compared to other continents because of the perceived cost associated with the technology (Yermack, 2018), and the prevalence of mobile money running on simpler mobile phones (Coffie *et al.*, 2020). Nonetheless, recently, the uptake of cryptocurrencies in Africa continues to surge with countries like Kenya, Nigeria, and South Africa as the front-runners. Consequently, Africa is earmarked as a region with the highest prospect for Blockchain diffusion (Yermack, 2018), therefore, smart contract could become a reality in Africa in the coming years. In preparation, how should the continent handle smart contract from the perspective of empathy to generate trust and ultimately boost diffusion?

EMAPTHY AND SMART CONTRACT

According to Mead (1991) empathy is the ability to take the role of the other and to embrace alternative standpoint. This explains the capacity to consider how others feel, or the condition others find themselves and putting yourself in a similar position. Empathy revolves around uncertainties, sincerity to unknown consequences, and the likelihood of changes. Empathy is an essential aspect of endeavour; Ford Motors Company simulated the "empathy belly" on their male engineers to allow them appreciate the experience of pregnancy symptoms. While this simulation proved to be useful, it also proved that failing to acknowledge the limits of empathy can affect performance and also erode ethics (Waytz, 2016). Smart contracts execute upon the trigger of a predefined condition. There is no room for renegotiations in case a party to a contract cannot fulfil part or all the conditions of the contract. This has led to the criticism of smart contracts for the lack of empathy. PayPal became an example of the empathy-lacking machine criticism when it sent a message to Lindsay Durdle's husband for a breach of contract in $ 4,200 over the death of her wife (Tribune media wire). In all negotiations, there must be an agreement between parties based on compromise and therefore the fulfilment of party A's conditions should ideally trigger the fulfilment of party B's. However, in most cases, unforeseen circumstances obstruct this process resulting in much needed renegotiations. Smart contracts struggles in this regard and any attempt to alter the conditions of the already established contract would automatically lead to the creation of an entirely new contract. However, different continents have distinct cultural values leading to divergent views on empathy. These are salient factors influencing policy formulation, institutional structures, and the design of technology related applications. In Africa, empathy is deeply rooted in cultural values. Contractual disputes only end up at the law court when family members, the Church, community elders, and Chiefs are unable to amicably resolve the matter. Worse, criminal cases like rape and murder can be kept from the law on the grounds of empathy because the perpetrator is a family member or a close relative. Human mediation is still preferred because empathy forms the basis for renegotiation of contracts. Considering this phenomenon, the application of smart contracts in the sub-region could be greatly hindered. For example, the introduction of the Computer School Selection and Placement System (CSSPS) in Ghana which autonomously select and place junior high school students into respective senior high schools across the country based on test scores has been marred by the distrust for the system by parents. Parents believe in the old system where they can pay bribe and influence heads of these schools to select and place their wards in the school of their choice. Nonetheless, the introduction of the CSSPS has greatly reduced corruption, saved cost and improved efficiency in the Ghana Education Service over the short period of operation. Consequently, the diffusion of smart contracts in Africa is possible with the optimal design of contracts fabricated on healthy balance between empathy, law and, technology.

ECONOMIC FORCE OF SMART CONTRACT

Economically, smart contracts provide value for contracting parties in the following ways;

- **Legality of Smart Contract***s:* The legality of contracts depend on the laws of a nation. Therefore, what is legal in one country might not be in another. Contracts derive their legality from their enforcement via law and so the inability of the law to enforce a contract makes it nullified. Contracts are established on key principles (offer, acceptance, consideration, mutuality of obligation, written instrument, and capacity) and therefore, legal enforceability is derived from these pillars. Smart contracts have the capability to absorb all these principles and can fulfil the requirement for its enforceability by law. In the Africa where physical infrastructure is limited and many reside in rural communities, the legality of smart contracts provide support to the legal system by reducing the number of processed cases at the law court thereby reducing administrative cost. Nonetheless, many believe that the job of lawyers might be disrupted by this technology (Mik, 2017). There is an on-going debate as to the real meaning of smart contracts with relation to legality in the real world. While countries like the USA, Canada, South Africa, Kenya, and Singapore have favourable regulations governing Blockchain related applications, others like South Korea, China, Namibia, Zimbabwe, Zambia, Morocco, Algeria, and Libya have placed bans on Blockchain applications and initial coin offerings (ICOs), classifying it as non-compliance to both civil and security and exchange regulations (Enyi, & Le, 2017; Baker, 2019) Smart contracts are not the same as e-commerce and thus understanding this difference is key to uncovering the legality of smart contracts (Mik, 2017). So far as Blockchain technology is the underlying technology of smart contracts, the legality for enforceability greatly depends on laws of a specific country.

- **Mode of Establishing Smart Contract**: Smart contracts is similar to traditional contracts with regards to the formation. Contracts have components: offer, acceptance, consideration, mutually of obligation competence, capacity and sometimes written instrument (Mik, 2017). This is the same with smart contracts, parties and other stakeholders to a smart contract must duly spell out the terms and conditions of the contract with the help of a lawyer. This means that economically, the speculation that the jobs of lawyers could be disrupted by Blockchain is unsubstantiated. The only moment that the involvement of lawyers might not be required is the enforcement stage. Given the nature of smart contracts, the terms and conditions of the contract should be accurately spelled out for parties to avoid errors during the coding of the contract.

- **Deployment of Smart Contract**: Contracts are established when parties sign written documents or verbally exchange promise to execute specific acts in the formation phase. After, the terms and conditions agreed to by all parties is then transformed into computer readable codes and uploaded onto the Blockchain. Coding is another way of writing digitally and this does not disqualify a smart contract from being acknowledged by the law court. Economically, the cost of storing digital information over the years has proven to be much cheaper and safer than using paper (Wiles, 2015). Again verbally established contracts could be problematic and create dispute in future but digitized contracts establish the intention of the parties and this is difficult to disprove (Fairfeld, 2014). Throughout the lifetime of a smart contract, changes cannot be made and the process is fully automated to avoid human interferences (Riseley, 2016). The Blockchain promotes decentralization (Benkler, 2006), centralization is discouraged due to its negative effect of slowing down processes and not being able to provide real-time information.

- **Mediation of Smart Contract:** When contracts are established, normally parties depend on the law for enforcement. Traditional contracts are mediated by humans while smart contracts are mediated by Blockchain. The Blockchain famously nicknamed the "trust machine" came into existence as a remedy to the perceived human weakness in mediation. The tendency to amend conditions of a contract to favour a party exist but with smart contracts, there is no avenue for human intervention and for that matter the computer executes the commands once the condition is satisfied (Holden and Malani, 2017).

- **Enforceability of Smart Contract**: Contracts failure results in breach and parties need to seek redress at the law court. Traditional contracts have high rate of default due to human mediation. Parties may require extra days to fulfil their debt obligations under traditional contracts mediated by humans but they cannot ask Blockchain for extensions. Under the smart contract, once a condition is satisfied a corresponding action is executed. Blockchain is programmed to work according to strict instructions and nothing can change their response to a trigger (McGuinness, 2006). According to Atta-Krah (2016) smart contracts are self-enforcing and require no human assistance to make it happen. The smart contracts ensure that humans cannot have their away by interfering with execution. It should be understood however that, enforceability of smart contracts can be achieved via either legal or programmed codes within the smart contract (Clack, Bakshi, and Braine, 2016). Economically, the delays in processing court cases in Africa due to limited infrastructure and resources can be resolved through Blockchain enforcements.

- **Cost of Smart Contract:** Blockchain is perceived to be expensive compared to other forms of technology (Pilkington, 2015). Therefore, traditional contracts look cheap from the onset but when there is the need for enforceability where a breach of contract is imminent, the cost associated with traditional contracts can be exorbitant. Smart contracts might be expensive when it comes to computing power, but the average cost associated with enforceability and execution of the contract on a smart contract is cheaper compared to traditional contracts. Consequently, cost should be discussed as the total amount spent on an establishment, execution, and enforcement of contracts. Economically, Africa can eradicate the high cost associated with compensations for delays in payment for public contracts.

BLOCKCHAIN APPLICATION DEVELOPMENTS FRAMEWORK FOR SMART CONTRACTS IN AFRICA

Smart contract is years away from practicality in Africa. However, proposed and practical applications of Blockchain are evidence across different industries in Africa. Aside the high uptake in cryptocurrencies leading to the installation of Bitcoin ATMs in South Africa, Kenya, Zimbabwe, and Djibouti (Coinatmradar), Kenya and Nigeria have plans to streamline regulations to forester cooperation with the private sector to boost Blockchain applications diffusion (Osato, 2019). Further, to improve record keeping, safety and insurance claim processing, the Nigeria Union of Road Transport Workers (NURTW) has launched a Blockchain-scheme to resolve the infrastructural deficiencies in the transport industry. In Botswana, the Satoshi Centre has developed a mobile-based Blockchain application (PLAAS) to help farmers manage daily agricultural production and stock to improve food security in the country. In the area of land registry, the Bitland project has successfully resolved land disputes since 2016 in Ghana. Rwanda provides similar solution via WiseKey's WiseID apps and Microsoft's Azure cloud. Kenya has also initiated a Blockchain and artificial intelligence (AI) task force for the purpose of integrating Blockchain within the countries existing economic framework to resolve land disputes, voting, and other areas prone to corruption. The Swiss company, Agora has successfully piloted and proven in Sierra Leone that Blockchain technology can mitigate election risk (Finextra). Mauritius has established a Regulatory Sandbox License (RSL) as a framework to guide the development of Blockchain applications by investors. In funding, the Funds Aid in South Africa is successfully used as the underlying technology of crowdfunding to solicit and transfer donations effectively. In Tanzania, the Humaniq app running on mobile devices supports peer-to-peer transactions in an effort to reach the unbanked. While the progress of Blockchain applications in Africa is promising, the influx of foreign-based companies in the industry raises argument on the optimal design of applications based on the African settings.

The optimal design of smart contract is necessary to stimulate mass diffusion, eliminate challenges and to achieve greater economic returns. As Africa prepares for the uptake of Blockchain technology in various industries such as financing, investment, and the sharing-economy; it is prudent to understand the cultural environment of Africa in the design of smart contracts. The continent stands to benefit greatly from smart contracts because of the infrastructural deficiencies making it difficult to provide equal opportunities for all. Again, the high number of unprocessed court cases in the region due to contract breach could also be resolved by the application of smart contracts. Better, corruption, bribery, and discrimination based on religion, tribe, and or political affiliations can also be eradicated with the elimination of human mediation. Nonetheless, the acceptance of smart contract in Africa would greatly depend on the ability of smart contracts to absorb empathy to an extent.

- **The Formation of Contract**: Blockchain is fundamentally immutable making smart contracts unable to be modified after deployment. Consequently, the terms of the contract should be discussed thoroughly by all parties and stakeholders to account for unforeseen circumstances. To avoid breach of contract and or the call for future renegotiations, parties should make provisions for what if situations and design the contract to cater for different options which may arise as a result of situations requiring empathy. Garbage in garbage out; what is fed to the Blockchain is what is executed at the end of the day. The only point where empathy could be considered in the design of smart contracts is at the point of formation, beyond that nothing can be done. Nevertheless, a healthy limit of empathy is required to avoid defeating the purpose of smart contracts.
- **Deployment of Contracts**: Pre-Agreed terms and conditions should be coded according to the details. Frantz and Nowostawski (2016) suggested a semi-automated translation scheme that transforms human-readable contract into computer programs. The coding should strictly fulfil the requirements of the parties without errors before uploading unto the Blockchain. For example, the CSSPS of the Ghana Education Service was criticised for posting girls into strictly boys' schools. Issues like this create distrust and could jeopardize the purpose of the system. This is a problem which could be avoided at the programming and data capture stage of the contract. However, human errors either intentional or unintentional can affect smart contracts, therefore, public source code, reverse engineering tools (Erays), and human readable codes provide useful avenues for verification (Zheng et al., 2020).
- **Execution of the Contract**: Implementation stage is central to smart contracts as it governs the concluding state of smart contracts. At this stage the trigger of a condition produces a corresponding reaction following the predefined terms of the contract. This autonomous execution would resolve any form of delays which may arise from human mediation. In a continent where millions of dollars are lost each year through the payment of compensations for delayed public contracts, smart contracts provides a suitable solution to this menace.
- **Post-execution**: Smart contracts do not end with execution, all records related to the contract is safely stored and distributed to all nodes on the network. The smart contract should be designed to suit the needs of the parties. Blockchain can utilize pseudonymous public keys to support anonymity of transactions preventing others from knowing the identity of parties. However, making

transactions visible or invisible is a decision which should be made during the design phase of the contract. See figure 1.

Figure 1.

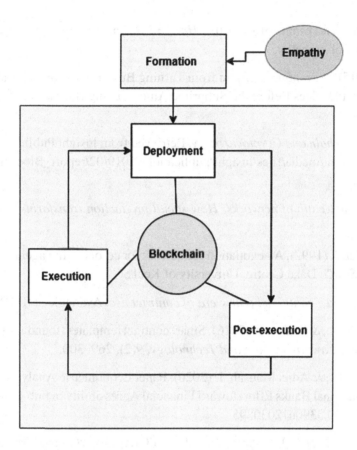

CONCLUSION

Currently, there is a high optimism on the prospects of smart contracts globally given the economic offerings over traditional contracts; however, what constitutes a legal smart contract remains debatable given the legal framework of different countries. Again, smart contract is criticised on the grounds of lacking empathy and in Africa where empathy is deeply rooted in culture, the optimal design of contracts considering empathy at the time of negotiations is a critical factor to boost mass diffusion. Nonetheless, most of the companies currently engaged in the deployment of Blockchain technology in Africa are foreign-based; this could limit the consideration of cultural values in the design of Blockchain applications in the continent. While, the application of smart contracts in Africa is still undergoing legal deliberations to fit into the civil law and the exchange and security laws of countries, the development of indigenous Blockchain companies should be encouraged to stimulate the customization of Blockchain applications to the settings African. Subsequently, Africa can rely on Blockchain applications to resolve issues in copyright and patent, insurance, supply chain management, mortgages, employment contracts, and the delivery of public services.

REFERENCES

Adam, W. (2016, Jan.). The Limits of Empathy. *Harvard Business Review.* Accessed from https://hbr.org/2016/01/the-limits-of-empathy

Atta-Krah, K. D. (2015). Preventing A Boom from Turning Bust: Regulators Should Turn Their Attention to Starter Interrupt Devices Before the Subprime Auto Lending Bubble Bursts. *Iowa Law Review, 101*, 1187.

Baker, M. (2019). *Blockchain and Cryptocurrency.* Retrieved from Insight Publications website: https://www.bakermckenzie.com//media/files/insight/publications/2019/02/report_Blockchainandcryptocurrencyreg_feb2019.pdf

Benkler, Y. (2006). *The wealth of networks: How social production transforms markets and freedom.* Yale University Press.

Bussman, S., & Muller, J. (1992), A negotiation framework for co-operating agents. In S.M. Deen (Ed.), *Proceedings of CKBS-SIG.* Dake Centre, University of Keele.

Catchlove, P. (2017). *Smart contracts: a new era of contract use.* Available at SSRN 3090226.

Clack, C. D., Bakshi, V. A., & Braine, L. (2016). Smart contract templates: foundations, design landscape and research directions. *Law, Innovation and Technology, 9*(2), 269–300.

Coffie, C. P. K., Zhao, H., & Adjei Mensah, I. (2020). Panel Econometric Analysis on Mobile Payment Transactions and Traditional Banks Effort toward Financial Accessibility in Sub-Sahara Africa. *Sustainability, 12*(3), 895. doi:10.3390u12030895

Enyi, J., & Le, N. D. Y., (2017). Regulating Initial Coin Offerings ("Crypto-Crowdfunding"). *J. Int'L Banking & Fin. L.,* (8), 495.

Fairfield, J. A. (2014). Smart contracts, Bitcoin bots, and consumer protection. *Washington and Lee Law Review Online, 71*(2), 36.

Finextra. (2018). African countries open for Blockchain acceptance. *Blogposting.* Retrieved from https://www.finextra.com/blogposting/15656/african-countries-open-for-Blockchainacceptance

Frantz, C. K., & Nowostawski, M. (2016, September). From institutions to code: Towards automated generation of smart contracts. In *2016 IEEE 1st International Workshops on Foundations and Applications of Self* Systems (FAS* W)* (pp. 210-215). IEEE.

Fuslier, G. D. (1988). Hostage negotiation consultant: Emerging role for the clinical psychologist. Professional Psychology: Research and Practice, 19, 175-179.

Hogan, R. T. (1969). Development of an empathy scale. *Journal of Consulting Psychology, 33*(3), 307–316. doi:10.1037/h0027580 PMID:4389335

Holden, R., & Malani, A. (2017). Can Blockchain Solve the Holdup Problem in Contracts? *Biz Journal*. https://www.bizjournals.com/bizjournals/howto/technology/2017/09/businessadvantages-of-Blockchain-smart-contracts.html

Holden, R. T., & Malani, A. (2019). *Can Blockchain Solve the Hold-up Problem in Contracts? (No. w25833)*. National Bureau of Economic Research. doi:10.3386/w25833

McGuinness, D. (2006). *Early reading instruction: What science really tells us about how to teach reading*. MIT Press.

Mead, G. H. (1993). *Mind, self, and society*. Chicago: University of Chicago Press.

Mik, E. (2017). Smart contracts: Terminology, technical limitations and real world complexity. *Law, Innovation and Technology, 9*(2), 269–300. doi:10.1080/17579961.2017.1378468

Osato, A. N. (2019, September 15). Africa using Blockchain to drive Change. *Cointelegragh*.

Pilkington, M. (2015). *Blockchain Technology: Principles and Applications*. Research Handbook on Digital Transformations. doi:10.4337/9781784717766.00019

Reik, T. (1949). *Listening with the third ear: The inner experience of the psychoanalyst*. New York: Grove.

Riseley, W. J. (2016). *Blockchain-A link to future law reform: Factors for a regulatory framework response to disruptive technologies*. Academic Press.

Savelyev, A. (2017). Contract law 2.0: "Smart" contracts as the beginning of the end of classic contract law'. *Information & Communications Technology Law, 26*(2), 116–134. doi:10.1080/13600834.2017.1301036

Szabo, N., (1996). Smart contracts: building blocks for digital markets. *EXTROPY: The Journal of Transhumanist Thought, (16)*.

Toris, C. (1994), A negotiation model of empathy. *9th International Balint Federation Congress*.

Tribune Media Wire. (2018, July). *Paypal tells dead woman she is in breach of contract because she is dead*. https://www.fox43.com/article/news/local/contests/paypal-tells-dead-woman-she-is-in-breach-of-contract-because-she-died/521-1558ca22-c198-4835-95bd-cca1a1f30fb7

Wiles, N. (2015). *The radical potential of Blockchain technology*. Academic Press.

Yermack, D. (2018). *FinTech in Sub-Saharan Africa: What Has Worked Well, and What Hasn't. New York University (NYU)*. doi:10.3386/w25007

Zheng, Z., Xie, S., Dai, H. N., Chen, W., Chen, X., Weng, J., & Imran, M. (2020). An overview on smart contracts: Challenges, advances and platforms. *Future Generation Computer Systems, 105*, 475–491. doi:10.1016/j.future.2019.12.019

Chapter 10

Cross–Chain Blockchain Networks, Compatibility Standards, and Interoperability Standards:
The Case of European Blockchain Services Infrastructure

Idongesit Williams
https://orcid.org/0000-0002-5398-3579
Aalborg University, Denmark

ABSTRACT

This chapter explains the role and how interoperability standards and compatibility standards will enable the development of cross-chain blockchain networks. Blockchain currently lacks standardization. There are different initiatives aimed at facilitating interoperability between different blockchains. But if there are no uniform interoperability and compatibility standards, that will cause a problem for the development of cross-chain blockchain networks. In the EU, there is an initiative to facilitate a continental cross-chain blockchain network. Interoperability and compatibility standards are an integral aspect of the initiative. This chapter uses the case of the EU as a basis for explanation on how blockchain service providers can work together to develop these standards.

INTRODUCTION

This chapter highlights the need for interoperability and compatibility standards in the development of cross-chain Blockchain networks. Interoperability here implies the ability for two systems to communicate and exchange data (Wegner 1996). This is different from compatibility, which is about two different systems working together in the same environment without disrupting the functions of one another

DOI: 10.4018/978-1-7998-3632-2.ch010

(Braunstein and White 1985). The Cross-chain Blockchains of interest to this chapter are networks of heterogeneous Blockchain platform that are compatible and can exchange data with one another (Zhao and Li 2020). One could also call it an Internet of Blockchains. The idea and the concept is novel. This is because end users can connect to a service provider and benefit from the services of many other service providers who from different Blockchain networks collaborate with a service provider to deliver a service. Technically this is possible. In fact, as will be mentioned in this chapter, some Blockchain service providers are developing these solutions.

Although this idea sounds interesting, there is a lot going against this idea. The first is that Blockchain is not a standardized technology. There are different types of Blockchains technologies operating under different technical specifications (Sharma 2019). This has resulted in the existence of Blockchains that are not interoperable and not compatible due to the absence of universally accepted interoperability and compatibility standards for Blockchains (Kot 2018) (Lima 2018) (Chang, Lakovou and Shi 2018). This makes the idea of creating Cross-chain Blockchains challenging. Blockchain service provider are currently trying to solve this problem but their efforts are geared towards enabling interoperability between the major Public Blockchain Platforms such as Bitcoin and Ethereum etc. They do not necessarily consider different private Blockchains that are not operating on the aforementioned platforms. Hence, the challenge of random Blockchain platforms becoming interoperable and compatible with other random platform still exists. This implies that there is the need for universally accepted interoperability and compatibility standards that will enable the exchange of data and enable compatibility between any two Blockchain platforms.

The development of cross-chain Blockchain platforms that will be of regional or global significance will be a daunting task. One of the major barriers will be regulatory barriers. These regulatory barriers could be either sectoral, national or regional in nature. A current example is the challenge posed by privacy laws such as the European General Data Protection Regulation (GDPR) (CMR 2019). Currently this law does have an impact on single platform Blockchains at the national and at the cross-border level. It definitely has the potential of scaring away organizations from adopting Blockchains. This is because Blockchain does not grant anonymity to the stakeholders on the platform. As will be mentioned in this chapter, certain services do require anonymity of the client. Therefore, privacy laws will be a problem. This problem will still exist when cross-Chain Blockchains come into existence. This dilemma led to the investigation that resulted in this chapter.

The guiding question this chapter aims at providing answers for is: how can cross-chain Blockchains be standardized to enable technical interoperability and compatibility and still become useful to different organizations operating in different sectors of the economy in the midst of barriers such as regulation? To answer that question, there was no other place to turn to than the European Union (EU). The EU the home of the GDPR and they have a vision and are working to achieve the vision of facilitating a continental cross-chain Blockchain networks. It is therefore interesting to see how they navigate these challenges and what lessons one can learn that will be beneficial for the development of global technical and compatibility standards for Cross-chain Blockchains.

This chapter is divided into 5 sections. The introduction is followed by a brief overview on the necessity of interoperability and compatibility standards. The third section highlights the EU Blockchain initiative and the role of Interoperability and compatibility standards in the process. The fourth section provides a discussion on how the initiative can inspire the development of interoperability and compatibility standards for Cross-chain Blockchain networks. The final section is the conclusion.

WHY STANDARDS

Standards are normative rules, requirements or conventions adopted by an ecosystem aimed at the harmonization on how to perform an action (Cargill 2011). These norms could be created either via consensus among stakeholders, a dominant industry player or by government agencies. The stakeholder group could consist of Non-Governmental Organizations, Government agencies and industry players. Standards created by consensus among stakeholder groups are either called voluntary standards or private standards or de facto standards (Smith 2009) (David and Greenstein 1990). Voluntary standards are not mandatory but if dominant players or stakeholders promote them they are likely to become widely accepted, though without sanctions in the event of non-compliance. On the other hand, mandatory standards, also known as de jure standards, are those standards incorporated in to law and require compliance (David and Greenstein 1990).

There are different forms of standards. However, the standards of interest to this chapter are technical standards or standards governing technical systems. Most technical standards are de facto standards. The importance of technical standards dates back to the early days of the industrial revolution (Ping 2011). Since then, the need for technical standards has been on the increase. The initial idea behind the development of technical standards was to harmonize the specifications for the development of different category of technical tools and equipment used in the industrial age. An example is the harmonization how the sizes of screw thread (ibid).

Technical standards are generally developed to either:

1. Ensure the minimum quality needed for efficient and secure technical systems (minimum quality standard) (David and Greenstein 1990);
2. Serve as a reference on how different aspects of technical equipment can be developed (reference standard) (ibid);
3. Ensure technical compatibility between components of two or more technical systems (compatibility standards) (ibid);
4. or ensure the interoperability between two technical systems (interoperability or open standards) (Hunter 2001).

Compatibility standards and interoperability standards are similar in that they enable two systems to work together. However, they are also slightly different in how and in what form they enable the systems work together. Nevertheless, compatibility standards and interoperability standards are the reasons certain technologies gain widespread adoption and others do not. This is because compatibility standards and interoperability standards enable distinct technical systems to work together as well as exchange data respectively.

Compatibility standards impedes technology users from experiencing lock-in effects to a particular technology provided by a single technology provider (Succi, et al. 1998). Compatibility standards enables technology users to be able to choose which brand of technology suits their operational and economic situations. It also enable manufacturers to adopt alternative brand of spare parts that support the operations of a machine. Interoperability standards also provides the user with the ability to choose any service provider of their choice, as long as the technology can exchange data with either legacy systems or systems from another brand manufacturer.

An example can be seen in the case of 2nd Generation mobile telephony (digital telephony). In the early years of digital telephony, there were different standards but only one of them enabled network interoperability and compatibility. That technical standard was the European Telecommunications Standards Institute (ETSI) developed Global System for Mobile Communications (GSM) (Bartosch and Braun 2009). As a result, the GSM standards dominated Europe, South America and Africa and 75% of the mobile market (Boretos 2007). This was in contrast with the CDMA standard's global market share of 25% (Oluwatoyin 2015). CDMA had better voice quality than GSM but it did not support interoperability and network compatibility. Hence GSM became the network of choice for telecom network operators. GSM Networks were successful was because GSM is an interoperability and compatibility standard (Pelkmans 2001) (Bartosch and Braun 2009). This implies that the GSM standard supported the forward and backward compatibility of GSM mobile networks. Forward compatibility implies that an existing network can operate alongside its upgrade, which is developed based on another standard (Choi 1994). Backward compatibility implies that the new upgrade is compatible with the legacy technology (ibid). Forward and backward compatibility enabled mobile network operators to maintain the customer base on the legacy network, while they gradually built up the customer base for the upgraded network. This market arrangement was possible because, the network operator could use the same core network to support enhanced Radio Access Networks while maintaining the legacy Radio Access Networks. This made the networks compatible. Furthermore, the new GSM standards enabled technical interoperability. This was because the GSM network is able to exchange data between the legacy Radio Access Networks and the new radio Access networks. This operational strategy enables the mobile operator to offer product differentiated value added services in a manner in which different classes of people will afford. This strategy among other factors has been the reason for the wide spread adoption of mobile telephony.

Other areas where the positive effect of compatibility and interoperability standards are important is in development of hardware and software solutions in an Information technology (IT) system and other technical systems (Succi, et al. 1998) (Adams 2015). These standards provide specifications for making software and hardware products and compatible. Hence, interoperability and compatibility standards are critical to the success or failure of a product in the market. As mentioned earlier, it enables choice and competition on the demand side of the market.

In the early days in the development of IT systems, compatibility standards were more significant than interoperability standards. However today, due to the growth in the reliance on data driven economies, interoperability standards are becoming more significant. This standard now determines business models, as the connectedness of different stakeholders in the data driven business ecosystem grows. This significance was recognized in the early parts of the 21st century. Faber et al (2003) in their attempt to analyse the emerging business model enabled by the mobile telephony created the Service, Technology, Organization and Financial (STOF) business model framework (Faber, et al. 2003) (De Vos and Haaker 2018). In their model, the technological setup is an integral part of the business model. This is because mobile telephony did not just enable voice calls, it enabled wireless broadband internet, which further enabled the development of business ecosystems supported by Information and Communication Technologies (ICT). This required organizations conducting remote transactions, which required interoperability of different ICT systems. Today the ICT set-up is becoming complex and becoming more embedded in the operations and processes in organizations. This obviously requires the interoperability of different ICT systems within the organization and between organizations. These technical support systems are critical to the business model. Companies that do not embrace these webs of technical interactions in their operations could lose competitive advantage to those who do. Nevertheless, the possibility for the complex web of interoperability of these technical systems are enabled by different universally or regionally accepted technical standards, depending on the scope of collaboration between the different organizations. Hence, technical interoperability standards have an effect on emerging business models.

Nevertheless, for technical interoperability and compatibility standards to become of value, they have to be widely accepted either in a country, region or globally by the relevant stakeholders. These stakeholders include equipment manufacturers, organizations adopting the technology and other interest groups and associations. Otherwise, such standards can only gain traction if it is a de Jure standard. This implies that the fact that a technical interoperability and compatibility standard exist does not imply that the technology will be widely adopted (David and Greenstein 1990). There is need for consensus among the various stakeholders. In this chapter, an example is provided with the case of the EU.

However, before explaining the EU approach, it is important to understand that one take away from global experiences on interoperability and compatibility standards, is that consensus on these standards enhances the network effect of technologies that interconnect organizations or individuals. This is evident with standards governing Internet technologies, telephony technologies, and other Information technologies. However, the level of network effect the technology will create is technology dependent and not standard dependent. Bearing this in mind, this section has provided an insight into some of the reasons why interoperability and compatibility standards are important. However, does Blockchain have the potential to produce network effects if it becomes standardized to become interoperable and compatible with each other? In the next sub-section, the potential effect of interoperability and compatibility standards on the network effect produced by Blockchain will be discussed.

Blockchain, Network Effects, Technical Interoperability and Compatibility Standards

The current global uptake of Blockchain is low. The lack of technical interoperability and technical compatibility between different Blockchain technologies is one of the reasons for the slow and low uptake of the technology (Chang, Lakovou and Shi 2018). As mentioned in the previous sub-section, interoperability standards and compatibility standards can enhance the network effects for technical systems that interconnect people or organizations. The examples provided in the previous sub-section was that of Information and Communication Technologies. Blockchain is a technology that interconnects organization and people for transactional purposes. Hence, there is potential economic value in its network effect. The network effect of Blockchain and how it can be enabled can be viewed in two ways. The first is the network effect created by a single Blockchain platform and the second is the network effect enabled by homogenous and heterogeneous Cross-chain Blockchain platform.

Let us discuss the first network effect enabled by a single Blockchain Platform. A single Blockchain platform hosts a finite number of stakeholders or computer nodes performing a common transactional activity. The Blockchain platform could either be open to anyone (public Blockchain); restricted to a selected interest group (private Blockchain); or owned by a selected interest group but open for other parties (hybrid Blockchain) (Williams and Agbesi 2019). The network effect in each of these platforms vary. The network effect is greater in the public Blockchain than in the private or hybrid Blockchain. This is because additional random node that signs up enhances the value proposition of public Blockchain. For the private and hybrid Blockchains, the value proposition is not enhanced by a random node. Rather this is either a node that will provide additional support that is lacking to the Blockchain network in the case of a private Blockchain or a node that belongs to a class of unrestricted nodes in the case of a private

Blockchain. Examples of the network effect of public Blockchains is evident with cryptocurrency platforms. Example of network effect of private Blockchains is evident in initiatives such as is the initiative between Maersk and IBM (Mearian 2019) and EU initiatives in the maritime sector (i-Scoop 2017).

However, the network effect of single Blockchain platforms can be enhanced if it is developed to become homogenous cross-chain Blockchain networks. This implies that different business ecosystems, either in the same or different sector have decided to collaborate. The collaboration will imply data exchange between both platforms and operational compatibility between both platforms in order to synchronize their Blockchain operational processes. The enhancement of the network effect is made possible because both Blockchain platforms will become interoperable and compatible. This is because Blockchain platforms using the same technology will be compatible to one another. That is not the case if the underlying technology between both Blockchain platforms are different. In that case there will be no collaboration and the potential enhancement of the network effect of the Blockchain would not exist.

The second type of network effect is enabled by heterogeneous cross-chain Blockchain platforms. This is because such platforms have the potential of interconnecting different stakeholders in different Blockchain ecosystems nationally, regionally and across the globe. However, heterogeneous cross-chain Blockchains are rare. Nevertheless, the rarity in the interoperability and compatibility of heterogeneous cross-chain Blockchains will not exist for a long time. There are attempts by different Blockchain backed organizations to enable the interoperability and compatibility of Blockchain application networks such as that of Ethereum and Bitcoin. There are examples of such initiatives from WanChain (Reecer 2018) and RSK (Baker 2020). In practice, these initiatives will result in greater collaboration and enhance limited network effects which will revolve around organizations using both technics. However, the interoperability posed by technology centricity will leave out other Blockchain technologies, using neither Bitcoin nor Ethereum, which could be customized for specific industries and sectors. That would limit potential cross-sectoral collaboration thereby becoming a barrier to business model innovation.

Aside the efforts from Blockchain Platform manufacturers, The International Standards Organization (ISO) hopes to have some standards ready by 2020 and 20201 (Morris 2018). This is good news but one waits to see how ISO envisages the interoperability and compatibility standards for Blockchain. How they approach it will depend on their vision for Blockchains.

So based on the analysis presented in this subsection, interoperability and compatibility standards do enhance the network effects of Blockchains. However, in order not to be too utopic, it is important to note that the extent to which these standards will enable the network effect of heterogeneous cross-chain Blockchains might be determined by competing technologies. This is because deploying a Blockchain network alongside some of these technologies might be cost effective and cheaper than having end-to-end heterogeneous cross-chain Blockchain solutions. An example of such a cost effective technology that can be integrated into Blockchain solutions are cloud-based solutions (Rimba, et al. 2017) (Rijmenam 2019). This deployment possibility is also driven by the fact that there is no evidence that companies that are not using Blockchains are gaining lesser Return on Investment with the technologies they adopt than those using Blockchain. On the contrary is the case (Chang, Lakovou and Shi 2018). Hence, some organizations, contrary to popular report are not so keen on adopting Blockchain (Pawczuk, Massey and Schatsky 2018). They view the technology as overhyped (ibid). This challenge is not something the interoperability and compatibility of Blockchains will solve.

Having said that, one could also indicate that someday-decentralized business models and solutions will be needed to facilitate business transactions. Blockchain or some other phenomena could influence this change. In such a scenario, Blockchain platforms will be required as a decentralized solution for transactions (Rijmenam 2019). Then interoperability and compatibility standards will be required to enable heterogeneous cross-chain Blockchain platforms. Such a change is taking place in the EU. In the next section, an overview of this change and the role of Interoperability and compatibility standards will be highlighted.

THE EU APPROACH

The EU approach towards standardizing heterogeneous cross-chain networks is based on their long tradition of promoting interoperability for technologies with potential for cross-border service delivery. In this section, the explanation will highlight the initiatives adopted in the EU in the past and how has served as an enabler for the development of the EU Blockchain infrastructure and standards. It will further provide an insight into the organization behind the EU Blockchain infrastructure.

EU Interoperability and Compatibility Initiatives

Long before the conception of the Blockchain initiative, the EU has a history of promoting cross-border interoperability for ICT infrastructure. The driver for this process has always been the delivery of cross-border e-government services. In order for such services to be enabled and delivered to business and citizens, different government systems ought to be able to exchange data. Hence, over the years, the EU have promoted different technical interoperability standards to enable the delivery of cross-border e-government services. This section highlights some of these initiatives. It further highlights how these initiatives serve as a foundation for Blockchain related interoperability standards for the EU Blockchain initiative.

In 2015, the EU launched the Digital Single Market (DSM) policy (Eur-lex 2015). The idea behind the policy is to facilitate intercontinental Digital infrastructure, regulations, standards and initiatives that will enable the continent operate as one market and not different independent markets as it is today. Since 2015 the EU has been setting up continental institutions, facilitating cross-border digital infrastructure development and passing regulations that will ease the free movement of businesses, citizens and services within the EU (Williams, Falch and Tadayoni, Internationalization of e-Government Services 2018). The backbone to the DSM is the digital infrastructure. The digital infrastructure requires for the digital single market is not defined. Hence, government agencies and private sector entities in member states can adopt the technologies they see fit to deliver. Nevertheless, despite the propensity towards technology neutrality in the EU, efforts has been made by the European Commission (EC) and the EU member states to ensure that the different national infrastructure are interoperable, technically, operationally, legally and at the semantic level (ISA[2] 2016). From the perspective of technical interoperability, the European Commission have developed a set of building Blocks. These building blocks are backed by EU e-government policies and regulations aimed at facilitating the Digital single market. These building blocks are de jure standards backed by either EU laws or directives by which member states have to abide. But these de jure standards are aimed at public services. However for the private sector, the building blocks are de facto standards. They are not forced to use it, but they choose to adopt it. These standards are technical interoperability and compatibility standards respectively. They come in the form of technical specifications. The standards are not aimed at modifying national service delivery infrastructures; rather they are aimed at:

1. Enabling the interoperability of different national technical infrastructure in order to enables access, data exchange and data processing possibilities to a service provider and a cross-border end user.
2. Enabling the compatibility of national technical infrastructure with common EU required infrastructure necessary for routing data within a country and across border.

These Building Blocks often called the Connecting Europe Facility (CEF building blocks) include:

1. eArchiving (data preservation and transmission),
2. Big Data Test Infrastructure (Virtual testbed for big data tools),
3. Context Broker (for centralization and consolidation of data),
4. eDelivery (data exchange),
5. eID (electronic identification of business and citizens),
6. eInvoicing (cross-border invoice delivery),
7. eSignature (verification),
8. eTranslation (machine language translation standard),
9. European Blockchain Services Infrastructure (EBSI) (Cross chain cross-border Blockchain networks)
10. and the Once Only Principle (cross-border data reuse standards) Source (CEF Digital 2020)

The eID and e-signature standards backed by the eIDAS regulations (Williams, Falch and Tadayoni, Internationalization of e-Government Services 2018), allows the mutual recognition of eIDs across member states. Therefore, persons from different EU member states do not have to be onboarded to each other's national infrastructure whenever they intend to access a service. They eID is mutually recognized, once the eID infrastructure complies with the eIDAS regulation and standards. The eIDAs standards are de jure standards.

The context broker consolidates, filters and redistribute data. The data sources are from government services, the private sector and user service consumptions patterns extracted from services providers. The context broker sorts and filters this data and makes it available as a service delivered by government agencies and the private sector. Due the freedom of movement of business and citizens in the EU, these set of data does have value to government agencies and businesses that need information about the member state, where the context broker is domicile. Hence there is the need for the different context brokers in EU member state to exchange data and that is possible if both context brokers are technically and semantically interoperable. This will enable government agencies and businesses to deliver value added services using this data.

The eDelivery infrastructure routes data between different government agencies and private organizations at the national level and between EU member states. Finally the eArchives preserve the data and also transmits the data from the national registers, company databases etc to where it is needed. These set of building blocks are the fundamental building blocks designed for the development of the continental infrastructure. These building Blocks have to work together and ought to be integrated in national service infrastructures in order to enable cross-border service delivery.

It is based on the existence of these interoperability and compatibility standards governing eID, e-signature, context broker and edelivery that the EU commission decided to EU saw the possibility of delivering the other CEF building blocks. These building blocks are namely: Big Data test infrastructure, European Blockchain Services Infrastructure (EBSI) and the Once Only Principle. These three building Blocks are also backed by technical standards aimed at ensuring that each of them are interoperable and compatible across national EU borders.

In the case of Big Data solutions, the idea is to ensure a harmonized approach towards cross-border processing and delivery of Big-Data. Public authorities and innovators are provided with a standardized test environment, where they can test their Big Data ideas. Successful ideas will obviously be backed by the technical standard of the underlying Big Data technology used in the test environment. Hence, when different public services and innovators in EU member states deploy the solution, the technology will be able to exchange data across border.

The European Blockchain initiative is enabled by interoperability standards (CEF Digital 2019). It will also make use of other standards from other Building blocks such as; eID, Context broker, Big data and edelivery. Furthermore, the Once Only Principle block is a standard that ensures that once a citizen or business provides data once to the system of an EU member state, the data attributes follow the eID as it accesses other systems. Hence, the citizen or business representative does not have to provide the same information repeatedly as they are onboarded to new systems in new countries. The standards for the Once Only Principle standard will support the European Blockchain Initiative.

Aside Blockchain, Once Only Principle and Big Data, Public and private sector organizations are adopting these building Blocks (CEF Digital 2020)(Williams, Falch and Tadayoni 2018). Although in some cases, public agencies in EU member states are coerced to adopt these building blocks because of EU regulations the private sector organizations have embraced these building blocks. For the private sector, these building blocks enable them to extend their services to different EU member states as well allow any EU resident to access their services from anywhere. This would not be possible if it were not for the investment by the EU in ensuring that infrastructure that serves the public good in the continent are interoperable and compatible.. The next section explains the organizational framework towards facilitating Interoperability and compatibility of cross-chain Blockchains.

The EU Blockchain Initiative

The idea on the development of an EU Blockchain initiative was pushed by EU member states. Over the years different public services in EU member states have either piloted, tested or implemented Blockchain solutions to enable specific transactions in certain sectors (Allessie, Sobolewski and Vaccari 2019). However, these initiatives not many. Nevertheless, the potentials exhibited by these initiatives led different member states to collaborate to set up the European Blockchain Partnership (EBP). The formal declaration creating the partnership was signed in 2018 (DG Connect 2020). The signatories were 21 EU member states and Norway and later grew to 30. The idea behind the partnership was to cooperate to establish the European Blockchain Service Infrastructure (EBSI) (ibid). This infrastructure was originally meant for public sector services (ibid).

However before the EBP was formed, the EU also envisaged the creation of interoperability standards that will enable heterogeneous cross-chain Blockchain networks in the continent. In 2019, they created the International Association for Trusted Blockchain Applications (INATBA) (Chandler 2019). The association consist of equipment manufacturers, non-profit, large enterprises, medium enterprises and small enterprises across different sectors in the EU. Their tasks is focused on creating sectoral and cross-sectoral technical interoperability Blockchain framework for public and private organizations within the EU (INATBA 2020).

This association works in collaboration with European Blockchain Partnership (EBP). The major reasons for this collaboration is to create harmonized interoperability standards as well as standards that enable the technical compliance of the GDPR. In this manner, the GDPR will not become an impediment to the use of heterogeneous cross-chain Blockchains. A bi-product of this collaboration is the EBSI standards (specifications) mentioned in the previous section. Also as mentioned in the previous section, it became part of the CEF building Block on Blockchain. The technical specifications of the EBSI contains protocols governed by technical and compatibility standards. The resuable software serves as a reference model. Hence, EU institution and public institutions in member states do not have to develop their own software based on national centric specifications alone. That is because it would present technical interoperability and compatibility challenges, which would defeat the vision behind the infrastructure.

This collaboration between EBP and INATBA opened up the possibility for allowing companies, start-ups, investing into Artificial intelligence to utilize the EU Blockchain infrastructure developed by EBP (Köpman 2019). The infrastructure is enabled by the Blockchain CEF building block. However the collaboration between EBP and INATBA will enable heterogeneous Blockchains in different ecosystems, interoperate to enable the delivery of public and private service. Furthermore, EBP, in addition to the collaboration with INATBA to create interoperability standards are also developing legal frameworks that will enable the interoperability of the ecosystems (ibid). EBP is also developing use-cases, infrastructure functionality, infrastructure architecture and the governance framework for cross-border public services using this infrastructure.

To get the infrastructure up and running, the CEF and Horizon 2020 funding facilities are used as funding instruments. CEF is utilized because, existing Building Blocks are aimed at enabling cross-border service delivery and these building Blocks are standards that can enable some of the points of interoperability. For example, eID and eSignature user access and authentication. Furthermore the utilization of CEF and Horizon 2020 funding schemes enables different industry players in different sectors to develop their different solution using a standard that enables cross-chain interoperability. Aside that the utilization of a Public Private Partnerships consortium in the development of applications and services. These consortiums often include knowledge institutions, private sector institutions and in this case public sector institutions as well. In such a consortium, knowledge institutions will be able to provide up to date knowledge on the technical solutions; public institution present the use cases and the context with which the solution will operate; and the private sector actually developes the solution and leads in the piloting process. Hence they can examine how Blockchains, owned by, Private Organizations, could interface with those of public institutions to deliver cross-border service delivery.

The promotion of the collaboration in the funding regime is critical as it simulates actual service delivery. This is because, in most cases, the public sector collaborate with private sector organizations to deliver public services. An example of such a private sector organizations are financial institutions. This is because financial institutions enable most transactions between citizens and governments. However aside financial institutions, there are third party contractors that provide support services to public institutions. An example include digital mail services (not email), expense account handlers (providers of cloud based electronic invoices and receipts), consultants, Non-governmental associations, external auditors and digital service providers to mention a few. These agencies would obviously own Blockchains where they store relevant data. Therefore, their collaboration in the project provides an environment where the solutions can created and tested without destabilizing the existing public service infrastructure. So when the solution becomes stable, it can then be gradually integrated into the public service infrastructure.

The EU Blockchain initiative is the first of its kind in the world. There is no other country (EU is not a country) or region that has envisioned the delivery of either a nationwide or regional Blockchain solution.

DISCUSSION

There are four aspects to the EU initiatives. The first is consensus between member states on the need for such an infrastructure. The second is the emphasis on interoperability and compatibility. The third is the selection of a focal point that will enable wide spread usage of the Blockchain. The fourth aspect is the consideration of regulatory risks in the development of the standards and infrasturcture. These aspects presents lessons and implications to the development of cross-chain Blockchain networks.

On the first aspect, it is obvious that the EU commission would not be able to coerce EU member states to adopt an infrastructure they have developed. Yes, it is true that the EU parliament has the powers to make laws and the EU commission has to execute what is enshrined in law. However, such an approach will result in member states having radically modify their existing infrastructure in order to accommodate fulfil the law. That would result in the waste of taxpayers' money and possibly a revolt from the member states. Therefore, the idea did not originate a good outcome from the EU but from the member states. This is because; the member states themselves have identified the relevance of Blockchain to their national and cross-border operations and have found a way to collaborate.

However, the EU, though a microcosm of the world is not a reflection of how the rest of the world thinks with respect to Blockchain s. Secondly, the approach to Blockchain outside the EU is mostly private sector driven. Despite these differences, the first lesson from the EU is the need for a broad consensus for cross-chain Blockchain networks by Blockchain Service providers. Currently, as mentioned earlier, there are initiatives aimed at creating cross-chain networks. However, if these solutions do not gain widespread acceptance within an economic in the same scale as Microsoft, Apple or CISCO products, to name a few, it will be difficult for them to become standards. This is because there will be other solutions that will also deliver interoperability for that sector and that will pose a problem. It is very unlikely that Blockchain standards outside the EU will be de jure standards. They will be de facto standards. Hence, the development of a broad stakeholder group that will arrive on a consensus on the technical interoperability and compatibility standards are crucial. Some organization with the potential of coming together to produce such a consensus include the Global Blockchain Business Council, and the Enterprise Ethereum Alliance and other alliances supporting different Blockchain platforms.

On the second aspect, the EU puts much emphasis on technical specifications for interoperability and compatibility. In their case, they are building on over 20 years' experience towards achieving interoperability. Their vision coincides with the existence of supporting infrastructure described in the CEF building Blocks with promotes interoperability. Unlike the EU, Blockchain service providers working on interoperability are doing so with limited vision. As mentioned in one of the examples, the interoperability is aimed at specific two block chain technologies (bitcoin and Ethereum) exchanging data. This idea though novel excludes other platforms and newer Blockchain technologies that might emerge as required by specific use cases. Although it is important to enable the two platforms work together, what should be important is to have a technical specification that will enable any two Blockchain network, irrespective of their technological and functional differences, become interoperable and compatible.

Therefore, Blockchains serving different ecosystems could be different but when it comes to the incorporation of newer Blockchain networks that should be feasible. To develop such standards, the first aspect on consensus becomes very critical. This is because if the standards is to gain global acceptance, then the consensus should have a semblance of global representation.

In the third aspect, the EU's vision though aimed at continental adoption utilizes cross-border public services delivery as a starting point. So far it could be said that Blockchain platforms delivering cryptocurrencies has been the starting point towards facilitating cross chain interoperability. This idea is novel, but let us be honest cryptocurrency has not impact on different sectors of the economy. In certain jurisdictions, it is seen as a threat to current legal tenders, it is limited in supply and it is actually struggling as a legal tender. The good thing about Blockchains is that it enables the storage and transactions of digital assets. Hence, not everything has to be about cryptocurrencies. Therefore, what is important tis to find out an aspect of society that has an influence on other aspect of society. In the EU, digital governance is the key towards developing interoperable Blockchain networks. For Blockchain service providers, the starting point could be by facilitating Blockchain interoperability between supply chains and their associated support service providers in two or more industries, where the different supply chains own different block chain technologies. Therefore, different supply chains can decide to collaborate and if the collaboration breaks down, they can stop sharing data. But in case it does not breakdown, these supply chains then have the possibility to modify their business models around the Block chain. Obviously developing such standards would be a difficult but not an impossible task. But it will still require consensus.

One way of generating the concensus on the relevant interoperability and compatibility standards would be to borrow a leave from Internet regulations, specifically the assignment of IP addresses. In such a scenario, there would be a global Blockchain standards body consisting of relevant stakeholders from the seven continents of the world. The global bodies will provide an overarching Blockchain interoperability and compatibility framework; different working groups representing different sectors of the economy in the seven continents will work on sectoral interoperability and compatibility standards; while another group works on cross-sectoral interoperability and compatibility parameters. Inputs from different regional stakeholders from the seven regions would be directed to the central working committee, who will deliberate and arrive on a consensus on the various standard needed for Blockchain interoperability. This approach will result in voluntary standards that are accepted by all Blockchain technology manufacturers. Organizations adopting the Blockchain will find the technology to be of value and useful and the network effect of using the technology for transactions will grow.

The final aspect is the consideration of the regulatory risk. In the case described in this chapter, the EU considered the risk posed by GDPR in the development of the standards for Blockchain. This is critical for stakeholders involved in the development of standards. Hence, wherever possible, cross-chain Blockchains should actually enable the law. For example, Block chain should prevent money laundry, tax evasion where necessary, at least technically that is possible. The tricky part is the fluidity of laws and user privacy laws. These could impede on cross-border transactions as an example. Nevertheless, neglecting the law all together might not be a good idea, as organizations might not find value for cross-chain Blockchains. But where ethically possible, such standards body should engage with government agencies to do away with laws that neither harms the economy nor the citizens of the country. An example is the move from the post world war 2 Keynesian economic driven laws to that of neo-liberalization. The Keynesian economic paradigm was not bad, but doing away with it was not unethical. Different governments around the globe embraced neo-liberalization and in most cases it was because they wanted to promote ICTs in their country. Such change might be needed for cross-chain Blockchains to thrive.

CONCLUSION

Based on the lessons from the EU, one could say that the development of cross-chain Blockchains, that will gain global traction, requires a great deal of effort from Blockchain stakeholders at a global level. These are efforts aimed at coming to a consensus on the global vision for cross-chain Blockchains; and efforts aimed at actually agreeing on which interoperability standard should be adopted, bearing in mind that there are ongoing efforts in this direction.

The efforts made today by different Blockchain alliances are novel. They offer practical tips, which could become useful suggestions development of interoperability and compatibility standards for cross-chain Blockchains. But the most important is the creation of the forum for consensus on the de facto standards and taking regulatory risks into consideration in the development of the standards.

Cross-chain Blockchains have the potential of becoming the next Internet as well as produce great network effects. It has the potential to enable sectoral and multi-sectoral usage of Blockchains. However this will not happen without universally accepted interoperability and compatibility standards promoted by a group of stakeholders or by a big industry player.

REFERENCES

Adams, K. M. (2015). *Non-functional Requirements in Systems Analysis and Design*. Springer.

Allessie, D., Sobolewski, M., & Vaccari, L. (2019). *Blockchain for digital government*. European Commission. https://joinup.ec.europa.eu/sites/default/files/document/2019-04/JRC115049%20blockchain%20for%20digital%20government.pdf

Baker, P. (2020). RSK Launches Interoperability Bridge Between Bitcoin and Ethereum. *Coindesk*. https://www.coindesk.com/rsk-launches-interoperability-bridge-between-bitcoin-and-ethereum

Bartosch, A., & Braun, J. (2009). *EC Competition and Telecommunications Law*. Kluwer Law International B.V.

Boretos, G. P. (2007). The future of the mobile phone business. *Technological Forecasting and Social Change, 74*(3), 331–340. doi:10.1016/j.techfore.2005.11.005

Braunstein, Y., & White, L. J. (1985). Setting technical compatibility standards an economic analysis. *Antitrust Bulletin, 30*, 337–356.

Cargill, C. F. (2011). Why Standardization Efforts Fail. *The Journal of Electronic Publishing: JEP, 14*(1). doi:10.3998/3336451.0014.103

CEF Digital. (2019). *The European Blockchain Services Infrastructure is on its way*. https://ec.europa.eu/cefdigital/wiki/display/CEFDIGITAL/2019/09/25/The+European+Blockchain+Services+Infrastructure+is+on+its+way

CEF Digital. (2020a). CEF Building Blocks. *CEF Digital.* https://ec.europa.eu/cefdigital/wiki/display/CEFDIGITAL/Building+Blocks

CEF Digital. (2020b). Success Stories. *CEF Digital.* https://ec.europa.eu/cefdigital/wiki/display/CEF-DIGITAL/Success+Stories

Chandler, S. (2019). *EU Launches International Blockchain Association, Bringing Crypto One Step Closer to Mainstream Adoption.* https://cointelegraph.com/news/eu-launches-international-blockchain-association-bringing-crypto-one-step-closer-to-mainstream-adoption

Chang, Y., Lakovou, E., & Shi, W. (2018). Blockchain in global supply chains and cross border trade: A critical synthesis of the state-of-the-art, challenges and opportunities. *International Journal of Production Research.*

Choi, J. P. (1994). Network ecternality, compatibility, Choice and Planned Obsolence. *The Journal of Industrial Economics*, *42*(2), 167–182. doi:10.2307/2950488

CMR. (2019). *The tension between GDPR and the rise of blockchain technologies.* CMS Legal Services.

Connect, D. G. (2020). *European Countries join Blockchain Partnership.* https://ec.europa.eu/digital-single-market/en/news/european-countries-join-blockchain-partnership

David, P. A., & Greenstein, A. (1990). The economics of compatibility standards: An introduction to recent research. *Economics of Innovation and New Technology*, *1*(1-2), 3–41. doi:10.1080/10438599000000002

De Vos, H., & Haaker, T. (2018). The STOF Model. In Mobile Service Innovation and Business Models. Springer.

Eur-lex. (2015). A Digital Single Market Strategy for Europe. *European Commission.* https://eur-lex.europa.eu/legal-content/EN/TXT/?uri=celex%3A52015DC0192

Faber, E., Ballon, P., Bouwman, H., Rietkerk, O., & Steen, M. (2003). Designing business models for Mobile ICT services. *16th Bled Electronic Commerce Conference eTransformation.* http://www.cs.jyu.fi/el/tjtse50_09/TJTSE50_Syllabus_files/Faber%20et%20al%202003.pdf

Hunter, J. (2001). MetaNet A Metadata Term Thesaurus to Enable Semantic Interoperability Between meta data Domains. *Journal of Digital Information*, *1*(8), 1–13.

i-Scoop. (2017). *Blockchain smart port case: efficient and secure container release in the port of Antwerp.* https://www.i-scoop.eu/blockchain-smart-port-project-case-container-release-port-antwerp/

INATBA. (2020). *International Association for Trusted Blockchain Applications.* https://inatba.org/organization/

ISA². (2016). Improving semantic interoperability in European eGovernment systems. *ISA² - Interoperability solutions for public administrations, businesses and citizens.* https://ec.europa.eu/isa2/actions/improving-semantic-interoperability-european-egovernment-systems_en

Köpman, H. (2019). *European Union Leadership in Blockchain.* WTO. https://www.wto.org/english/res_e/reser_e/00_b_helen_kopman_global_trade_and_blockchain.pdf

Kot, I. (2018). Lack of Standards in Blockchain Technology: What to Do? *I transition*. https://www.itransition.com/blog/lack-of-standards-in-blockchain-technology-what-to-do

Lima, C. (2018). Developing Open and Interoperable DLT/Blockchain Standards [Standards]. *Computer*, *51*(11), 106–111. doi:10.1109/MC.2018.2876184

Mearian, L. (2019). Maersk adds two big shipping firms to its blockchain ledger. *Computerworld*, *29*(May). https://www.computerworld.com/article/3398923/maersk-adds-two-big-shipping-firms-to-its-blockchain-ledger.html

Morris, N. (2018). ISO blockchain standards. *Ledger Insights*. https://www.ledgerinsights.com/iso-blockchain-standards/

Oluwatoyin, K. K. (2015). Comparative Analysis of GSM and CDMA, Strength and Weakness, Future Challenges and Practical Solutions (A Case Study of MTN and NITEL Nigeria). *Journal of Information Engineering and Applications*, *5*(5), 74–88.

Pawczuk, L., Massey, R., & Schatsky, D. (2018). *Breaking blockchain open Deloitte's 2018 Global Blockchain Survey*. Deloitte. https://www2.deloitte.com/content/dam/Deloitte/us/Documents/financial-services/us-fsi-2018-global-blockchain-survey-report.pdf

Pelkmans, J. (2001). The GSM standard: Explaining a success story. *Journal of European Public Policy*, *8*(3), 432–453. doi:10.1080/13501760110056059

Ping, W. (2011, Apr.). A Brief History of Standards and Standardization Organizations: A Chinese Perspective. *East-West Center Working Papers - Economic Series*, 1-25.

Reecer, D. (2018). Wanchain 3.0 Launches Bitcoin Bridge to Ethereum — Continues Rapid Progression in Blockchain Interoperability Mission. *Medium*. https://medium.com/wanchain-foundation/wanchain-3-0-launch-bitcoin-ethereum-erc20-7cd504f25c0c

Rijmenam, M. V. (2019). *The Organisation of Tomorrow: How AI, blockchain and analytics turn your business into a data organisation*. Routledge. doi:10.4324/9780429279973

Rimba, P., Tran, A. B., Weber, I., Staples, M., Ponomarev, A., & Xu, X. (2017). Comparing Blockchain and Cloud Services for Business Process Execution. In *Conference: ICSA'17: IEEE International Conference on Software Architecture*. IEEE.

Sharma, T. K. (2019). Top 10 blockchain platforms you need to know about. *Block Chain Council*. https://www.blockchain-council.org/blockchain/top-10-blockchain-platforms-you-need-to-know-about/

Smith, G. (2009). Interaction of Public and Private Standards in the Food Chain. OECD Food, Agriculture and Fisheries Papers. OECD Publishing.

Succi, Valerio, Vernazza, & Succi. (1998). Compatibility, Standards, and Software Production. *ACM StandardView, 6*(4).

Wegner, P. (1996). Interoperability. *ACM Computing Surveys, 28*(1), 285–287. doi:10.1145/234313.234424

Williams, I., & Agbesi, S. (2019). Blockchain, Trust And Elections: A Proof Of Concept For The Ghanaian National Elections. In Handbook on ICT in Developing Countries: Next Generation ICT Technologies. River Publishers.

Williams, I., Falch, M., & Tadayoni, R. (2018). Internationalization of e-Government Services. In *11th CMI International Conference: Prospects and Challenges Towards Developing a Digital Economy within the EU*. Copenhagen Denmark: IEEE.

Zhao, D., & Li, T. (2020). *Distributed Cross-Blockchain Transactions*. https://arxiv.org/abs/2002.11771

Chapter 11
Emerging Opportunities for Blockchain Use by Small and Medium Enterprises (SMEs) in Developing Economies

Benjamin Kwofie
Koforidua Technical University, Ghana

Emmanuel Dortey Tetteh
ⓘ https://orcid.org/0000-0002-7522-5752
University of Electronic Science and Technology of China, China & Koforidua Technical University, Ghana

ABSTRACT

The blockchain digital technology holds immense possibilities for the growth and development of developing economies such as Ghana. Since the emergence of blockchain technology, many developing economies have as yet to tap into its limitless possibilities with Ghana being no exception. In this chapter, the authors explore the possibilities for the blockchain for SMEs in developing economies like Ghana with a view to identifying the properties of a blockchain ecosystem that will facilitate their development, adoption, and use by SMEs.

THE BLOCKCHAIN TECHNOLOGY - AN INTRODUCTION

The Blockchain technology is an information technology based distributed record book (ledger) that keeps accounts of, authenticates and enforces transactions performed by any two or more parties. It allows transactions to be tracked using an encrypted digital technology. It uses cryptography to allow each participant on the network to use the ledger in a secured way. Blockchain can further considered as a disruptive technology that shifts control of financial transactions data and processes from centralized traditional financial institutions like banks to the parties engaged in these transactions. These transactions

DOI: 10.4018/978-1-7998-3632-2.ch011

are recorded, verified and enforced in real time creating an easy to follow trail for internal and external audits by governmental and other agencies. The technology guarantees the accuracy of data, removing the need for collecting available data from various sources for evidence. According to Kuczwara (2017), there are four key reasons why Blockchain affords a better solution than other traditional tools for record keeping. First, is its immutability which allows them to be unchangeable once accepted as part of the ledger. Second is its verifiability which requires all participants on the ledger to agree on what is recorded, helping to build a consensus. Third is its embedding of privacy which ensures that transactions are secure, verifiable and authenticated without the need for the exchange of identity; and finally, Blockchain enables all assets on the ledger to be traced back to their origin. Essentially therefore, the Blockchain technology provides a safe, secure and trusted solution for any two or more parties engaged in a business transaction using state of the art technology with embedded encryption that safeguards the interests of the parties involved. Aside the technology's ability to solve myriad financial challenges posed by the rigid structures and requirements of the existing financial systems of most countries, its potential for addressing other business processes such as contract formation and execution, identity confirmation, monitoring of supply chain makes its application in Small and Medium Enterprises (SMEs) particularly in developing economies a timely consideration. SMEs all over the world and in developing economies in particular, e.g. Ghana, have challenges with financing their businesses. In the last three decades since the emergence of the internet and other online technologies, many SMEs in developing economies have been unable to integrate IT to support their operations both at a local or international level. Advocates of the Blockchain technology argue that Blockchain solutions can be utilized to pay employees and business partners locally and at international levels, fulfil contractual agreements through smart contracts, accept payments from customers by verifying identities digitally, store data in the clouds, etc. SMEs in developing economies can leverage this technology to develop new business models that can address many of their challenges, potentially enabling them to compete effectively with larger businesses across the world. This would require an understanding of, trust in and acceptance of the technology by all stakeholders at a national and international level. In this paper we review the literature on the state of art of Blockchain technologies, existing posture of SMEs in developing economies and how Blockchain solutions can benefit them, the inherent constraints with this technology and their possible solutions. The rest of the paper looks at the global perspectives on Blockchain technologies, global perspectives on SMEs and their challenges, SMEs in developing economies with a focus on Ghana's SME environment and Blockchain development.

PERSPECTIVES ON BLOCKCHAIN ADOPTION AND USE

Many experts, developers and reviewers of the Blockchain technology all over the world generally agree that Blockchain solutions are versatile and capable of helping parties involved in transactions secure digital assets, manage multicurrency transactions, facilitate the monitoring of supply chains, etc. (Uzialko, 2018). Blockchain use for cryptocurrency solutions or other business operations such as transactions, supply chain management, digital identity management, smart contracts or global fundraising has indeed taken the global financial sector by storm. This view is widely believed to have been afforded by properties of Blockchain technology such as trust, verifiability, traceability, immutability, digital identifiability, distributed and decentralized nature that have facilitated the technology's quick adoption and transformation of the global trade environment.

There is general acceptance among the proponents of Blockchain solutions that the technology can be used in trade among businesses in the traditional settings such as Business-to-Business (B2B), Business-to-Consumer (B2C), and Business-to-Government (B2G) payments. The details of such transactions are kept in an indisputable ledger accessible to every user. These details are tamper-proof as tampering with such information is believed to be impossible due to the decentralized and distributed nature of the Blockchain ledger, unlike the traditional centralized systems.

There is also widespread agreement that Blockchain solutions can be used to make supply chain processes transparent to all stakeholders. Distributors, suppliers, processors, or retailers, can utilize Blockchain solutions to make every step of the supply process transparent in order to build trust among business partners. From the origination of a transaction to its destination, every step in the process can be made transparent.

Again, a wide consensus exists about the capability of Blockchain solutions for managing and verifying digital identities with promises to deepen the trust and usage of the technology among businesses. With lots of transactions taking place online within and across countries involving businesses and individuals, a lot of concerns tend to plague online platforms in terms of security. People's identities can be falsified, stolen, personal information hacked, etc. contributing to the skepticism held about online transactions by many users, existing and potential, especially in developing economies. However, with the Blockchain solutions, there is widespread belief that with the multiple information needed for verifying a user's identity captured securely and unalterably in the ledger, trust and security of transactions are guaranteed. This will enable businesses to authenticate their users securely and allow compliance with know-your-customer and anti-money-laundering regulations, while avoiding making sensitive information accessible to third parties.

Another generally accepted usage potential for Blockchains is in Smart contracts. Many proponents believe that Smart contracts allow the execution of transactions to be preset on the Blockchain. When the required information is entered into the ledger, it automatically triggers a corresponding action to complete the transaction without the intervention of either party. Since the contracting parties can both see the Blockchain in real time, both can verify that indeed the transaction has been executed from both ends, and subsequently allows convenience and trusts to be built.

Among the early adopters of Blockchain technologies worldwide, Blockchain has demonstrated the potential to help raise capital for startup financing through initial coin offerings (ICO). Although some scams have been experienced in this respect, with many countries such as the US being skeptical and others like China banning outright usage, there are situations where ICOs have been used to raise huge sums of money to support ambitious projects though it remains an unregulated terrain. Businesses and startups can utilize Blockchains to raise funds where the traditional mediums have proved challenging or uninterested.

Despite its growing recognition and acceptance, Blockchain is beset by several challenges that threaten its widespread adoption. According to Deloitte (Browne, 2018), there is the need for increased performance, interoperability, reduced complexity and cost, supportive regulation and more collaboration if widespread adoption is to be achieved. Deloitte argued that the processing power of the Blockchain technology compared to some legacy systems still remains relatively slow at an average of 3 to 15 transactions per second making large scale application an unlikely event. Existing legacy systems with centralized architectures are able to process thousands of transactions per second rendering this new technology a little obsolete despite its great potential. This slow performance is as a result of the so-called miners on the network working out complex mathematical problems in order to validate transactions. Their work ensures there is a consensus on the network about the validity of a transaction before it sails through. This increases the time taken for a transaction to settle in the process.

Furthermore, it has been contended that with the many players in the industry, developers of Blockchain technologies will arise one day to realize that their solutions cannot communicate with other platforms without assistance. With the many different coding languages, protocols, consensus mechanisms and privacy measures being deployed by over 6000 Blockchain projects on one coding site alone (Browne, 2018), there will be attendant integration difficulties. This will obviously create more challenges than solutions for businesses in general. Again considering the cost of mining a single Blockchain being on the high side, coupled with the need to pay these miners, the cost of validating transactions could be a potential problem for widespread adoption of the technology for commercial business purposes. This high cost is present in the creation and maintenance of Blockchain networks. Aside this inherent cost, Blockchain technologies tend to be fraught with a lot of complexities.

It has also been argued that that there is the need for a supportive regulatory environment to back and facilitate the growth and adoption of Blockchain solutions. Whereas the sale of some digital tokens and the offerings of initial coins have been banned in some countries e.g. China, South Korea, with the United states Securities and Exchange Commission charging the Floyd Mayweather-backed cryptocurrency initial coin offering, there are other areas e.g. smart contracts, where no regulation still exist. This delay in developing regulation for Blockchain adoption and use is what can result in slow adoption of the technology across borders.

The absence of more collaborative engagements among developers, businesses and countries is also believed to be disadvantaging Blockchain growth. Such collaborations are necessary to ensure that solutions created using Blockchain technologies can communicate across platforms without difficulty else such solutions will serve no good. It has also been contended that the need for increased collaborative efforts in the Blockchain industry was critical if any progress is to be made in widespread adoption. Such collaborations must include stakeholders such as enterprises, technology providers, regulators, and the government in order to hasten such developments. (Browne, 2018).

Quite evidently, the Blockchain technology has seen massive acceptance in developed economies such as the United States and Europe. Although many will argue that this acceptance is still in its embryonic stages, impressive growth in usage for cryptocurrencies and other financial transactions has been equally observed. These economies have advanced in digital technology development and usage in both social and business arenas. Constantly at the frontiers of new digital solutions, their experiences with different technologies in centralized and decentralized contexts have informed subsequent decisions to adopt and use new technological solutions like the Blockchain. Developed economies possess a huge stock of well-trained digital technology developers who are resourced and inspired to continue to search for solutions that work in the best interest of their economies. With the support from their governments and other philanthropic organizations interested in their solutions, growth in the adoption and use of digital solutions as the Blockchain can be predicted to grow with the right ecosystem support.

Same cannot be said for developing economies. These economies struggle with the much needed infrastructure to develop and drive digital solutions use. Although much progress have been made developing digital solutions and platforms, these economies basically consume solutions developed for other contexts. In other words, many of these digital solutions found on the market have been developed for contexts where the ecosystems are already in place and supportive of the solutions and so in many cases inappropriate for developing economy contexts. It is important therefore, in coming out with a solution suitable for developing economies SMEs, to consider factors that will facilitate the development and use of these solutions for the benefit of such economies.

PERSPECTIVES ON SMALL AND MEDIUM ENTERPRISES (SMES)

SMEs all over the world provide the backbone support of many economies through employment and the provision of over 50% of their GDPs. In the Netherlands for instance, SMEs constitute over 90% of all business and contribute 60% of their GDP. Similar observations are made in Ghana where 90% of registered businesses are SMEs, and contribute about 70% of the GDP. All over the world, SMEs face a major challenge with access to bank loans, lack market information to conduct efficient businesses, and suffer from inefficient processes and procedures.

According to a World Bank report, SMEs are an indispensable tool for job creation and income generation in most economies and in particular, developing economies. They account for a majority of businesses worldwide, represent 90% of businesses and more than 50% of employment worldwide. The report also indicated the crucial need for SME development in developing economies as most formal jobs in emerging markets, are created by SMEs (about 7 out of 10). It also indicated that a major constraint to SME growth is access to finance, the second most cited factor obstructing SME growth in emerging economies. According to the report, a major function of the World Bank is to improve SMEs' access to finance and identify innovative solutions to unlock sources of capital. With the huge funding gap requirement by both formal and informal SMEs and the inability of financial institutions to meet these needs, innovative solutions as the use of Blockchain technologies in closing this funding gap is worth considering. The requirements by financial institutions for granting funds is so stringent that many SMEs are unable to comply. Trust is central to this relationship between the financial institutions and the SMEs, with information being the critical driver of this trust. This information is often stored and shared among cooperating financial institutions making it difficult once rejected by one financial institution to be considered by another. This necessitates the consideration of a better solution that will enable SMEs occupy their potential position in emerging economies as drivers of development.

Blockchain solutions are generally considered expensive for businesses and in particular SMEs. Some have advanced the argument that SMEs will be slow in adopting Blockchains, and will adopt such solutions only as needed since they envisage no real need for Blockchain technologies. It is important to note that the existing market that serves these SMEs with the standard software for conducting their business operations offer no real competitive prices for these SMEs. This is particularly more so in developing economies like Ghana. The various charges on these transactions and for software solutions do not necessarily vary with the size of the business. Hence larger companies tend to benefit more in comparison to SMEs. Blockchain technologies have the potential to enable SMEs leverage competitively with larger organizations by providing affordable and competitive prices in a transparent, traceable and more secured manner.

SMEs in Developing Economies

SMEs all over the world have challenges with financing of their businesses, scaling their operations, processing their payments as well as engaging other ancillary services needed for growth or internationalization. SMEs in developing economies need easy and reliable access to credits in order to generate new jobs and facilitate the much economic growth (De Meijer, 2019). Unfortunately very few Blockchain solutions exist in these economies to support access to funding.

Another major challenge faced by entrepreneurs and SMEs in developing economies, is with securing loans from banks for starting or growing their businesses. This is a major cause of many new or ongoing SMEs collapsing after a while in business. It is estimated that almost 30% of SMEs shut down in the first three years of operation as a result of lack of funding. These banks however cannot be blamed entirely as their experiences with market crises over the years have caused an all-time low lending to SMEs. It is estimated that while the credit demand by SMEs all over the world stands at $2.38 trillion, only about 15% get their requested loans from the banks. With Blockchain solutions still under development and awareness creation underway in some developing economies, trust is still an issue and so its benefits cannot immediately be tapped into.

Trade finance also poses a major challenge to the internationalization of many SMEs in developing economies. Although trade has changed over the last couple of decades, financing trade, much like other forms of credit, has failed to match this development. The current trade finance deficit of $1.5 trillion is believed to be caused by data shortfalls as much of the operations of SMEs is still paper-based and follows outdated procedures and processes. Traditional trade finance operations are as a result time-consuming, bureaucratic and just too expensive for new SMEs. This disproportionately impacts SMEs in developing economies yet to integrate any form of digital technology into their business. The emergence of Blockchain therefore, coupled with their lack of knowledge about it, its cost and how it can add value to their businesses combine to make Blockchain's prospect an illusion.

The lack of understanding, competency and capacity to use the Blockchain technology, the cost implications coupled with the absence of tests cases to learn from all make Blockchains adoption and use an uphill task for many SMEs in developing economies. The scale (resources, market, funds, etc.) of operation for many of these SMEs compared to large organizations is relatively smaller and as such makes it imprudent for SMEs to engage in their acquisition and use. Whereas large organizations can quickly acquire, experiment and develop new products and services using latest digital and automation solutions, many SMEs cannot respond in the same vein. For instance many SMEs cannot afford to have an IT team that will develop new strategies based on some of these new technologies.

Developing Economies – The Case of Ghana in Context

Many developing economies are yet to experience a deep level of digital technological integration into their SME businesses. Telecommunication companies have been very instrumental in the present level of technology use both at a social and business level. Many of these countries have seen a high penetration of mobile phones and internet data. This development is good for business development using online solutions as it has laid some foundation for potential customers' use of digital technologies for engaging in transactions. The challenge here however is the cost of the services provided by the telecom companies compared to similar services offered in developed economies. Ghana is one such economy where telecommunication giants such as MTN and Vodafone had facilitated the development of infrastructure for IT usage in homes and businesses. Nonetheless, the cost of these services are discouragingly high and can potentially threaten any benefits that can be gained by SMEs. With regards to SMEs and digital technology innovations, what exists in developing economies can best be described as still in the infantry and awareness stages. With many SMEs still not integrating digital solutions into their businesses or even taking advantage of internet solutions to reach a wider market, the advent of new digital solutions such as the Blockchain will only serve to widen the gap between developed and developing economies irrespective of their benefits. In a survey of 70 SMEs in the Eastern region of Ghana, none had integrated any digital solution or planned to in order to grow their businesses. Their levels of operation seldom utilizes these digital technological innovations either for B2B or B2C. As such, despite the increasing innovations in the digital space, the ability and capacity of these SMEs to adopt and use these solutions cannot be compared with those of developed economies. In as much as affordable digital solutions for SMEs in developing economies such as Ghana are scarce and relatively expensive for businesses, many business owners and their employees also lack the necessary knowledge and skill to use many of these technological solutions. And although there is a growing population of digital technology users in these developing economies, SME businesses that deploy digital solutions are yet to make any meaningful impact in this space.

Although the market for Blockchain adoption and deployment is potentially huge for SME business growth and development in these economies, the prevailing conditions needed to push for adoption and use appears to be still developing. The environment in developed economies appear to be more prepared and ready to leapfrog their current levels of development than are developing economies. In the next section we take a closer look at Ghana's SME environment and the development of Blockchain solutions.

Ghana's SME Sector

SMEs constitute about 90% of registered businesses in Ghana and contribute an estimated 70% of the GDP. They play a major role in Ghana's local as well as international trade activities. As in other parts of the world, SMEs in Ghana face severe challenges with funding and credit financing from financial institutions. It is also a well-established fact that SMEs in Ghana exhibit poor governance practices, lack risk management practices, have poor record keeping practices, etc. Businesses in this sector are classified under micro, small and medium with about 70% being informal SMEs. Business transactions in this sector cut across B2C, B2B and B2G. The B2C transactions are usually undertaken locally with little evidence of direct transactions between some of these businesses and some external market outside Ghana. In the case of B2B, these transactions are often carried out both locally and internationally with a well-established international market engaged in trade with local business men and women. Funding for all forms of trade is difficult to access by SMEs along with unnecessary delays in the processing of transactions from traditional banking institutions. SMEs involved in international trade often experience unnecessary delays in the transfer of payments to their international partners. The cost of transactions charged by these banks are so exorbitant these SMEs have no option than to transfer those costs to customers causing the prices of their products to be higher than in other parts of the world. In addition, the high taxes regime in Ghana, when added to the high cost of loans, credit transfers, and bank charges on payments and transfers for SMEs causes many SMEs to be discouraged. This is an area where new technologies such as Blockchain solutions can provide a game-changing opportunity for SMEs in Ghana, especially those engaged in international businesses. Financing trade can be made more efficient through the transparency and consensus mechanisms offered by these technologies that have the potential to replace the multiple instances of verification and checking done by traditional banks that lead to delays. It has been identified that the impact on the global finance gap by Blockchain solutions would be greatest felt by emerging markets and SMEs as they have the ability to harness these technologies beyond well-established markets and organizations. It is also believed that this global trade finance gap which stands at $1.5 trillion, could be reduced by $1 trillion through an efficient deployment of Blockchain technologies.

BLOCKCHAIN DEVELOPMENTS IN GHANA

Ghana is known for its ambition to go paperless with the integration of digital solutions in all sectors of the economy. Since 2017, led by the vice president of the country, Dr. Bawumiah, the country has embarked on several digitization projects notable amongst them being the paperless port, the Ghana Post GPS, online business registration, online passport application, digital DVLA, etc. In other developments, the government of Ghana is reported to be piloting a project with Bitland, a local not-for-profit organization engaged in Blockchain development, to record land title deeds in Kumasi, the regional capital of the Ashanti Region, using Blockchain to reduce fraud and allow for a more efficient mortgage lending (Oxford Business Group, 2019). It has been reported that Blockchain technologies can enable Ghana leapfrog infrastructure and institutions in developed economies allowing it to reach similar levels of development at lower costs and at higher speeds.

In addition, there have been series of conferences and training programmes on Blockchain technologies organized in the country to educate and build a community of developers and users to ensure Ghana does not miss out on this new technology and ensure sustainability. The conferences for example have been running since 2017, and in 2019 had its 3rd event with the theme: "Blockchain for Digital Transformation", (Business Ghana, 2019).

There are also efforts from renowned personalities at the forefront of digitization for the country to embrace the Blockchain technology. One such personality, Prof. Nii Narku Quaynor advocated for Blockchain' adoption in 2018. He contended that the technology was capable of improving financial inclusion and facilitating ease of doing business. Blockchain has been identified to have the potential for use in various sectors of Ghana's young economy such as manufacturing, retail, financial services, legal, healthcare, insurance, energy and government business (Joy Online, 2018).

In other developments, it has been reported that the bank of Ghana, as announced by its governor, is planning on introducing an 'e-cedi' although it is unclear what technology would be behind it (Coindesk, 2019). However in a related development, a first deputy governor of the central bank of Ghana assured delegates of the 2nd Blockchain conference organized in Ghana, of the bank's commitment to providing supportive regulatory environment without undermining the stability of the country's financial system (jbklutse.com, 2018).

The potential for Blockchain's usage in the supply chain environment and logistics for Tilapia, a popular fish product used in meals in Ghana, has also been identified (Rejeb, 2018). The telecommunication giant, Vodafone, has also been instrumental in training and challenging Ghanaian university students to identify and develop Blockchain solutions. Their intention is to make Ghana a leading player in the African Blockchain environment (NewsLogical, 2019).

The opportunities afforded by Blockchain technologies for SMEs requires a conducive environment with the right support, regulation, developers etc. to be successful. In the next section we take a look at a Blockchain ecosystem that will enable SMEs in Ghana tap into the affordances of Blockchain.

A Blockchain Framework for Ghana

If Ghana will benefit from any introduction of Blockchain solutions, a Blockchain ecosystem needs to be implemented. This ecosystem must include an infrastructure that can support the development of Blockchain solutions by encouraging information technology companies and SMEs to experiment with, identify areas for potential use and gradually adopt such technologies. The infrastructure must include an information base where all kinds of questions by SMEs can receive appropriate answers regarding how Blockchain solutions can add value and enhance the competitiveness of these SMEs. These solutions need to cut across the various sectors of the economy where SMEs operate in order to enable them become competitive enough to compete on a global scale while increasing their operational efficiencies and funding opportunities. These solutions can also potentially strengthen the trust most Ghanaians are developing in online transactions which has the potential of ensuring convenience and ease of use for customers of SMEs. This ecosystem should also house open source collaborative platforms that will enable SMEs build customized solutions instead of allowing them struggle to find solutions on their own (must be led by a government/business with government support). The platform should allow easy access to trade financing and credit for both domestic and international transactions by connecting all the parties involved. This will enable these businesses to enter into new markets and establish new business partnerships both locally and internationally. The platform should also enable people who have excess funds lend to SMEs through a proof-of-concept from anywhere in the country, eventually spilling over to other partner Blockchain solutions around the world. This will help direct available funds to where they are most needed with the highest return on investments. The platform can also provide a functionality for helping banks get access to public credit data to enable them identify SMEs that are not prone to defaulting in payment of loans advanced to them. In addition, an advisory committee can be put in place to monitor and advise the government and other stakeholders on best paths and strategies for getting the most out of this new technology.

CONCLUSION

The Blockchain technology is still under trial all over the world even though its potential to transform the global trade finance and business has been clearly demonstrated. SMEs in developing economies stand to gain the most as this technological solution will afford them the opportunity to raise funds, access credit, make payments, engage in smart contracts, monitor supply chain, manage digital identities and so much more in an unprecedented way. Cost of Blockchain solutions is however essential, especially for SMEs in developing economies. This is where the greatest impacts can be made as it will allow these businesses to operate and compete on comparable levels with larger enterprises all over the world. Equally of great importance is the development of a regulatory framework that will guide implementation, create assurance and trust as well as ensure recognition. All of these can be achieved through the creation and development of a Blockchain ecosystem for SMEs in developing economies. Only time will tell how far this solution will go in the not too distant future.

REFERENCES

Browne, R. (2018). *Five Things That Must Happen for Blockchain to See Widespread Adoption, According To Deloitte*. Retrieved from: https://www.cnbc.com/2018/10/01/five-crucial-challenges-for-Blockchain-to-overcome-deloitte.html

Business Ghana. (2019). *Ghana to Host third Blockchain Conference*. Retrieved from: https://www.businessghana.com/site/news/general/197826/Ghana-to-host-third-Blockchain-conference

Coindesk. (2019). *Ghana May Issue Digital Currency in 'Near Future,' says Central Bank Chief.* Retrieved from: https://www.coindesk.com/ghana-may-issue-cbdigital-currency-in-near-future-says-central-bank-chief

D'Aliessi, M. (2016). *How Does the Blockchain Work? Blockchain Technology Explained in Simple Words.* Retrieved from: https://onezero.medium.com/how-does-the-Blockchain-work-98c8cd01d2ae

De Meijer, C. R. W. (2019). *Blockchain: A game-changer for Small and Medium-Sized Enterprises.* Retrieved from: https://www.finextra.com/blogposting/17380/Blockchain-a-game-changer-for-small-and-medium-sized-enterprises

Furlong, J. (2017). *What is Blockchain Technology?* Retrieved from: https://www.businessnewsdaily.com/10390-what-is-Blockchain-technology.html

Jbklutse.com. (2018). *Bank of Ghana Promises Policy Support for Blockchain Innovations.* Retrieved from: https://www.jbklutse.com/bank-of-ghana-promises-policy-support-for-Blockchain-innovations/

Joy Online. (2018). *Computer Scientist Urges Ghana to Embrace Blockchain Technology.* Retrieved from: https://myjoyonline.com/business/2018/september-18th/computer-scientist-urges-ghana-to-embrace-Blockchain-technology.php

Keskin, H., Senturk, C., Sngur, O., & Kiris, H. M. (2010). *The Importance of SMEs Developing Economies, 2nd International Symposium on Sustainable Development.* Retrieved from: https://utica.libguides.com/c.php?g=291672&p=1943019

Kuczwara, D. (2017). *3 Ways Blockchain Can Help Businesses Today.* Retrieved from: https://www.businessnewsdaily.com/10407-Blockchain-changing-small-business.html

NewsLogical. (2019). *Vodafone Initiates Blockchain Program in Ghana Institutions.* Retrieved from: https://newslogical.com/Blockchain-adoption-ghana/

Oxford Business Group. (2019). *Blockchain Technology Provides Multiple Opportunities for The Developing World.* Retrieved from: https://oxfordbusinessgroup.com/overview/building-blocks-Blockchain-technology-has-applications-could-revolutionise-trade-and-4

Rejeb, A. (2018). Blockchain Potential in Tilapia Supply Chain. *Acta Technica Jaurinensis, 11*(2), 104–118. doi:10.14513/actatechjaur.v11.n2.462

Small And Medium Enterprises (SMEs) Finance, Improving SMEs Access to Finance and Finding Innovative Solutions to Unlock Sources of Capital. (n.d.). Retrieved from: https://www.worldbank.org/en/topic/smefinance

Uzialko, A. C. (2017). *Beyond Bitcoin: How Blockchain is Improving Business Operations.* Retrieved from: https://www.businessnewsdaily.com/10414-Blockchain-business-uses.html

Uzialko, A. C. (2018). *Can Your Business Trust a Block Chain Service.* Retrieved from: https://www.businessnewsdaily.com/10938-Blockchain-business-trust.html

Chapter 12

When Trust is not Enough to Mobilize Blockchains:
A Mobilization–Decision Theory Perspective

Idongesit Williams

(iD) https://orcid.org/0000-0002-5398-3579

Aalborg University, Denmark

ABSTRACT

The Mobilization Decision theory provides an insight into why mobilization occurs and the factors that result in mobilization. In the last decade, blockchain technology has been touted as a technology that facilitates trust between unknown parties. Trust is at the core of all human interaction, be it commercial or social. However, the global adoption of blockchain is low. At a global scale, relatively few organizations have mobilized blockchain to either handle or support their organizational processes. In order to understand why this is the case, the mobilization decision theory is used to explain why the global adoption of blockchain is low and what needs to change to facilitate its widespread adoption at a global scale.

INTRODUCTION

Blockchain technology has evolved from being a hype to a technology being used by public and private sector players to deliver different services. The technology has also evolved from Blockchain 1.0 to now Blockchain 3.0. Blockchain 1.0 enabled cryptocurrencies; Blockchain 2.0 was upgraded to support different forms of transactions in different commercial operations in various sectors of the economy; while Blockchain 3.0 enabled transactions in social services, public services and other areas such as the arts etc (Momo, et al. 2019). There is great deal of literature highlighting the potentials of Blockchain towards the transformation of business ecosystems as we know today. It is believed that the technology will someday have the same impact as the Internet on the way and manner commercial transactions are conducted (Shaikh and Lashari 2017). Obviously these are ideas that will either one day materialize or

DOI: 10.4018/978-1-7998-3632-2.ch012

otherwise. However, beyond these ideas on the significance of Blockchain to organizational activities and processes, Blockchain has a basic characteristic (facilitating trust). Trust is critical in every commercial transaction. Therefore the inventors designed Blockchain, to among other things, facilitate trust between different partners or stakeholders who do not trust themselves (Prasad, et al. 2018) (Brown 2018) (Williams and Agbesi 2019). In some cases Blockchain has been identified as an architecture of trust (Werbach 2018). This characteristic makes Blockchain a unique technology.

In principle, this characteristic (trust) should be enough to enable the rapid adoption of Blockchains. Unfortunately, today (Year 2020), the global adoption of Blockchain is low (Clohessy and Acton 2019). Furthermore, the amount of global investment towards propping up the Blockchain market is also low (Stastista (c) 2019). What makes the low adoption of Blockchain intriguing is that decision makers in companies making over 100 million in their global revenue are aware of the technology (Pawczuk, Massey and Schatsky 2018). However, there is no sense of urgency towards adopting Blockchain by these decision makers. In some cases, organizations who adopted Blockchain have discontinued the use of the technology (PWC 2018). The low adoption of Blockchain is also prevalent and even lower in developing countries (Clohessy and Acton 2019).

Adoption theories have often contended that the usefulness of technologies moderates the behavioral intention towards technology adoption (See some classic adoption theorists (Oliver 1980) (Venkatesh, et al. 2003) etc). Nevertheless, in the case of Blockchain, one could contend that its usefulness is not pronounced to companies. This is because most companies have already adopted competing technologies and they find have these competing technologies to be useful for their operational processes. The existence of these competing technologies diminishes the need for adoption of Blockchain (Pawczuk, Massey and Schatsky 2018). One could also say that facilitating trust in a business ecosystem or commercial encounters should be a strong motivation for organizations to adopt Blockchain. However, as presented in the methodology and findings of this chapter, facilitating trust is not a strong enough motivation for organizations to adopt Blockchain. Therefore, although Blockchain has its unique usefulness in enabling trust in a business ecosystem, this usefulness has not resulted in the mass adoption of Blockchain technology. Therefore current adoption theories seem to be inadequate towards analyzing why organizations are not adopting this Blockchain. In this chapter another theory, the Mobilization-Decision theory, will be used to explain why the adoption of Blockchain is low and what can be done about it.

The Mobilization-Decision theory by Williams (2021) is used as the theoretical framework for searching and explaining why organizations are not adopting Blockchain. The theory provides an explanation on why mobilization occurs. This theory is used for this exercise, because as mentioned earlier, cooperation and some SMEs (McKinsey 2017) are aware of Blockchain (Pawczuk, Massey and Schatsky 2018). Some of them are piloting Blockchain (ibid). They believe that the technology has some usefulness. Hence, usefulness is not an issue; it is the decision to mobilize resources to adopt the technology that is the issue. This is where the mobilization-decision theory comes in handy. The theory will also be used as a basis for providing suggestions on how make more organizations adopt Blockchain.

The chapter has six sections. The first section is the introduction, followed by the theoretical background, which gives an overview of the Mobilization-Decision Theory. The third section provides an insight into the methodology used in gathering and analyzing data. The fourth section and the fifth section provides insights into the findings. These findings are further explained using the mobilization-decision theory. The seventh and eighth chapters are the findings and conclusions.

THEORETICAL BACKGROUND

This section provides an overview of the Mobilization-Decision theory. Furthermore, the Mobilization-Decision theory is used to explain how humans mobilize technologies to perform actions.

Mobilization-Decision Theory from Concept to Theory

Mobilization-Decision theory is a social theory developed by Williams (2021), to explain why the decision to mobilize resources in order to perform an action occurs. The theory is based on the premise that mobilization is not a spontaneous act but a result of a rational process, which occurs when certain conditions are fulfilled. The theory was inspired by Community Based Network Models (CBNM) were developed by Williams (2015). The CBNM models was a result of a Grounded Theory analysis, which was aimed at explaining how and why the inhabitants of rural communities around the globe develop rural broadband networks (ibid). In each of the CBNM models, it was evident that there was a tipping point where the various organizations decided to mobilize themselves to perform an action. The action in this case was the development of rural broadband network. From 2015 onwards, the model was utilized to highlight the potentials of developing Broadband network and services in developing countries (Williams 2018) (Williams 2018).

The "decision to mobilize", as presented in the CBNM models was limited to the development of Broadband Infrastructure and services. Nevertheless, it was evident from theories such as the Actor Network Theory, Community Mobilization theory and social movement theories, that mobilization was not a spontaneous event. This is because there were preconditions, which trigger the "decision to mobilize" before mobilization occurs. The CBNM models was an obvious framework that explained this "decision to mobilize". Hence, it was reanalyzed, using the aforementioned social theories to decontextualize the model and make it applicable to everyday life. This analysis was successful as there were bits and pieces of elements of social theories that provided a universal context to the constructs of the CBNM models. The upgrade of the CBNM models, grounded in social theories, resulted in the emergence of the Mobilization-Decision Theory. This theory has the ability to provide a universal explanation as to why the "decision to mobilize" occurs.

The Mobilization-Decision theory was derived from social theories as mentioned earlier. The influence of these social theories enabled the Mobilization-Decision Theory to provide explanations on why humans mobilize other human resources to perform an action. But this theory is not limited to human-to-human mobilization. It also has the potential to explain why humans decide to mobilize machines (technology) to perform an action. It also has the potential to explain why machines decide to mobilize machines to mobilize an action. This is a subject for another chapter. For human-to-human interaction, the theory is applicable to free will mobilization but not when a human is being coercively mobilized. However, for human-to-machine (technology) interactions, the Mobilization-Decision theory does not equate humans to technology, rather technology is seen as a tool that should be mobilized in order to perform an action. In machine-to-machine interaction, the theory is applicable in a master-slave relationship as well as master-master or Slave-slave relationship. However, in this chapter the theoretical focus is on the human-to-machine (in this case Blockchain) Interaction. How the theory works in this type of relationship is explained in the next sub-section.

Mobilization-Decision Theory and Human-to-Technology Interaction

The mobilization-decision theories states thus:

the decision process towards either mobilizing a person or group of persons or being mobilized to perform a certain action will occur if the following conditions are satisfied. These are the evidence of needed resources, the mental congruence between the mobilizer and the mobilized; the evidence of either actual or potential cooperativeness between the mobilizer and the mobilized and the perception of individual value to be derived between the mobilizer and the mobilized from the action to be performed. (Williams 2021)

As indicated earlier, this theory was formulated from a human centric perspective. However, in the case of human-machine interaction, it is more of a master-slave relationship or principal-agent relationship. That is if one were to borrow a thought from the Agency theory (Asare, Beldona and Nketia 2019). Hence in this case the mobilizing agent is the human and the technology is the mobilized agent. The Mobilization-Decision theory identifies the mobilizing agent as "the visionary" and the mobilized agent as "the mobilized" (Williams, 2021). But when discussing the theory within the context of human-to- machine (technology) interaction, the mobilizing agent and the mobilized agent are preferred terms used in describing the "master" and the "slave". Nevertheless, by virtue of the unequal power relations between "the mobilizing agent (the master)" and the "mobilized (the slave)", the decision to mobilize lays squarely on the mobilizing agent. The mobilized agent has no say and cannot present objections against being mobilized. Therefore within the context of human-machine (technology) interaction, the Mobilization-Decision theory can be restated thus:

The decision process governing a humans' decision to mobilize a machine (technology) to perform an action will occur if the following conditions are satisfied:

1. there is evidence of resources needed to mobilize the machine (technology) to perform the action;

2. there is perceived congruence between desire of the mobilizing agent and the advertised potential of the machine (technology);

3. there is evidence of either actual or potential cooperativeness between the machine(technology) and its intended task;

4. and there is a perception of value to be derived by the human when the machine(technology) is utilized. (Williams 2021).

Based on this theory, the 4 factors that result in the decision for the human to mobilize the technology to perform an action includes, "resource availability", "congruence", "cooperativeness" and "value".

Figure 1.
Source: (Williams, Mobilization - Decision Theory 2021)

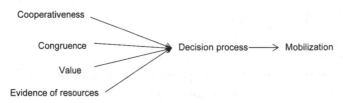

1. Evidence of available resources: What is mobilized in order to perform an action are resources. Resource Mobilization theories provide an explanation on how and when to acquire resources (McCarthy and Zaid 1977). The CBNM models on the hand does not explain how to mobilize resources. It takes that process for granted. The CBNM Models indicates that mobilization will occur when the vital resources needed to perform the action is available (Williams 2015). As an offshoot of the CBNM models, the Mobilization-Decision theory points in the same direction but with a Nuance. In the cases studied in order to develop the CBNM models the decision to mobilize occurred once the needed resources were in place. However, for the visionaries in the Mobilization-Decision theory, their decision to mobilize was not based on the availability of resources. Rather it was based on the evidence of the possibility of acquiring these resources. In other words, this was an evidence that the resources could be harnessed. Hence, in the Mobilization-Decision theory, the evidence of available resources was considered as one of the reasons to mobilize others to perform an action.

However, the same principle holds for the mobilization of machines (technology). Machines (Technology) can be mobilized either by manufacturing them or by acquisition as a finished product. In order to do so, the human needs the resources to either acquire, develop, deploy or operate the machine. Example of such resources include, financial resources, material resources, human resources (in most cases) etc. Furthermore, in the deployment of the machine (technology), that machine becomes a resource used in the performance of other actions. Hence, the mobilizer (the human) has a dual thought process. The first being the mobilization of resources to either develop or adopt a machine (technology). The second being the mobilization of the machine in order to perform an action. In both processes, the decision to mobilize to either develop, adopt or deploy a machine (technology) will not occur if there is no evidence of the resources needed to mobilize the machine.

2. Congruence: The use of the word congruence in the Mobilization-Decision theory implies similarity in thought processes between the mobilizing agent and the mobilized. However in the case of human-to-machine (technology) interaction, congruence also implies similarity. This is not a similarity of thought as machines do not think. However, machines (technologies) are designed to either support certain operations, processes and tasks within organizations. When these technologies are advertised by their manufacturers, the adverts are either centered on the operations, processes and tasks they perform. The challenge though is that the advertisements does not often provide a full picture of the efficiency of the machine in the performance of the said operations, tasks and processes. In some cases, the organization adopting the technology either act as innovators piloting the technology to see if it performs as advertised. If the technology performs as advertised, then

there is congruence on how the technology actually operates. If the result is negative, then there is no congruence on how the technology performs. That will result in the decision not to mobilize the technology. However, there are organizations with limited resources. They cannot afford to pilot the technology. Hence, they rely on referrals from industry experts, as well as testimonies and reviews from competing organization. If the technology facilitates efficiency in the processes, tasks and processes in competing company, then congruence is revealed. This implies that the technology performs as advertised. If the other competitors question the potential of the technology, then there is congruence. This implies that the performance of the technology and the expectations of the mobilizing agency matches.

3. Cooperativeness: Cooperativeness as used in the Mobilization-Decision theory implies "the willingness to work together". It is a personality trait. However, when discussing mobilization within the context of human-to-machine (technology), cooperativeness is not a personality trait. This is because machines (technologies) do not possess personalities. However, there is some element of cooperativeness, if one considers the interaction between humans and machines (technology). For example, imagine trying to use a mobile phone application to purchase gas in the early 1980s. That would not be possible as those analogue mobile telephones were not designed to facilitate financial transaction. Hence, the analogue telephone then would never cooperate with the human in order to perform financial transactions. However, in the 21st century, payment with mobile phones became possible. Today mobile phones are used to perform transactions. Some of these transactions are performed by accessing a payment gateway using mobile internet networks. Furthermore, other transactions are performed using mobile money solutions. Hence, today, the mobile telephone is enabled to cooperate with humans in making financial transactions.

Cooperativeness as presented in the Mobilization-Decision theory is about the compatibility of the machine (technology) with the intended task. Cooperativeness can be likened to the task-fitness concept as described in the task-technology fitness theory (see (Goodhue and Thompson 1995)). Although both concepts are similar, they are not exactly alike. Both are similar in that they refer to the compatibility between the machine (technology) and the intended task. However, task-fitness enhances either organizational or individual performance as they use the technology. However, cooperativeness enhances task efficiency when the technology is deployed. The enhancement of task efficiency may or may not enhance organizational or individual performance. This is because individual or organizational performance on task(s) depends on other factors such as the organizations business model, the organizational culture, and the types of organizational incentive etc. Hence, both concepts differ slightly.

4. Value: In the Mobilization-Decision theory, value is an economic term. Nevertheless, in the Mobilization-Decision theory, value is derived from the incentives inherent in the action to be performed after the mobilization process. Value is critical for the mobilizing agent and the mobilized. However, in human-technology interaction, the technology (the mobilized) does not derive value but provides value to the human when action is performed. Humans are value driven entities, hence the decision to mobilize the technology to perform an action is also value driven. For example, the reason a company adopts a technology is because the technology enables profitability, efficiency in their operations and grants the company competitive advantage over their competitors (Porter 1990). Without these incentives, the technology has no value to the human-led organization. For this reason, evidence of resources, congruence and cooperativeness are not enough to trigger

the decision to mobilize a technology. A practical example can be found in the current desire for Artificial Intelligence and industry 4.0. The value propositions for these technologies is in their potential to ultimately contribute to the profitability of the organization. As a result, an organization can deploy sensors and robots to perform the task a human would have performed. In this case, the company does not have to pay high salaries, holiday allowance etc. to humans since very few of them will be required. The maintenance cost of the sensors will be far lower that of human resources and in addition these technologies will enable an increase in efficiency and production beyond the capacity of humans. As a result, the value of AI and Industry 4.0 in this case becomes high for decision makers in organizations.

All four factors have to be fulfilled in order for the decision to mobilize to be in the affirmative. If the decision to mobilize is yes, mobilization to perform an action occurs. However, the decision to mobilize is no, then mobilization will not occur as represented in the figure above.

Although Mobilization-Decision theory provides some form of explanation for technology adoption, it is not solely a technology adoption theory. It is a theory that explains why the decision to mobilize occurs. In this chapter, it will be used to explain the plausible reason for the low adoption of Blockchain s globally. The premise adopted in this chapter is that service providers have for one reason or the other decided not to adopt Blockchain.

METHODOLOGY

A mix of an inductive and deductive exploratory research are used as the methodological approach in the gathering and analysis of the empirical data used in this chapter. These are empirical evidence from consultancy and academic studies that identify challenges encountered by organizations in their bid to decide whether or not to adopt Blockchain. This chapter relies on these secondary data sources. The idea is not to validate the challenges to Blockchain identified in these reports, but to use the Mobilization-Decision theory as the explanatory basis as to why the challenges identified in these reports and literature exist and what can be done about them. The consultancy reports were identified via a snowballing method. The starting point for the search was Statista. In Statista, web links to consultancy reports on the status and challenges encountered in adopting Blockchain, provided by Deloitte, PriceWaterhouseCoopers (PWC), Mckinsey and Accenture were identified. The overview of the sample size of data; respondents and their organizational portfolio; is presented in Table 1. Table 1 provides an overview of the respondents represented in the reports from Deloitte, Mckinsy and PriceWaterhouseCoopers. The data extracted from the Accenture report was from expert opinion. The reports were supplemented with academic literature. Industries represented the consultancy report and academic literature include the service, construction, health, logistics and supply chain management. The literature sources are indicated in the tables in the next section.

The sample size from the reports and the profile of the respondents are presented in the table below.

Table 1. Sample size and Profile of organizations from secondary data sources

	Deloitte*	PWC	Mckinsey
Sector (s)	Non Sector specific	Non-sector specific	Finance (Insurance)
	Big sized companies	Executives	Start ups, venture capitalits
Number of participating organizations	1386	600	Feb 2016 – 35 persons** May 2016 – 15 persons
Number of adopters (live)	24%	15%	6%**
Number of those piloting	-	10%	26%**
Number of those in development	-	32%	
Number of those in research	-	20%	
Number of those not adopting/wait and see	3%	14%	50%**
Number of those Paused	-	7%	
Perception of Blockchain as Overhyped	43%	-	-
Will not be relevant	3%	-	-
Not a strategic priority	14%		
Not in the top 5 strategic priority	27%		
Coverage	Brazil, Canada, China, Germany, Hongkong, Israel, Luxemburg, Singapore, Swtizerland, UAE, UK and US	Worldwide	Undefined
Year	2019	2018	2016
Portfolio of participants	Senior executives	Organization executives	

* These were companies with US$ 500 million or more for US correspondents and US$100 million or more in annual revenue for companies outside US: The respondents had a broad understanding of Blockchain and were able to comment on their organization's investment plans.

Sources: Deloitte (Pawczuk, Massey and Schatsky 2018) (PWC 2018) (McKinsey 2017);

In these reports, it was clear that the affinity towards adopting Blockchain was low, but the awareness about the technology was high among the respondents. The report from academic literature were mostly analysed qualitatively by their respective authors. However, in the works of Hackius & Peterson, 2017, 152 SMEs in the supply chain and logistics were surveyed. These were European (Germany Switzerland, France) and US SMEs.

The inductive method used in this chapter was via documentary analysis guided by thematic analysis. Each document were read through; the challenges related to Blockchain were coded, and memos created. These codes are named "implications of the barriers" in Tables 2 to 7. Seventy barriers were identified in all. This were 44 unique barriers. 26 codes were generated in the process. The axial or cross-sectional coding process resulted in six different themes. These are named as "barrier categories" in Tables 2 to 7. These barrier categories are technical, process/operational capacity, ecosystem, market and privacy/ security.

At the end of the inductive process, a deductive process was utilized. In this process, the Mobilization-Decision theory was used to identify each challenge. Based on the outcome of the secondary data, it was clear from the reports and literature that very few respondents adopted Blockchain. This implied that the challenges they identified were those that inhibited their decision to mobilize resources towards adopting Blockchain. Based on this background, the constructs of the Mobilization-Decision theory were mapped to the cross-sectional codes. This mapping is presented in section "Mobilization-Decision theory and challenges of Blockchain". The findings of these processes are discussed in the next section.'

FINDINGS – CHALLENGES TO THE ADOPTION OF BLOCKCHAIN

The explanation of the 6 categories of barriers identified are as follows:

Technical Barriers

These are barriers posed by the technical characteristics of the Blockchain technology. The technical barriers analyzed were those from non-specific sectors, and specific sectors. These specific sectors included as supply-chain and logistics, construction, energy and the health sector as indicated in the Table 2. In the bid to categorize the barriers, the implication of each barrier was analysed inductively.

The overall implication of the technical barriers were that Blockchain technology, had no technological value; was technically deficient; was operationally constraining; was resource intensive; has technical constraints; and operational constraints.

1. The lack of technological value is because the technology is unproven and immature within the sectors represented by the respondent.
2. The technical deficiencies highlights the shortcomings of the technology. These deficiencies included security threats plaguing the organizations; the lack of interoperability between different Blockchain systems, which is a result of lack of standardization; and the low scalability of Blockchains.

These deficiencies are significant as they reveal the incompatibility between Blockchain and the organizational operations and processes of the represented industry respondent. Therefore, the lack of value of the technology and the technical deficiency of the technology becomes an impediment to the outright adoption of Blockchain.

3. The operational constraints also highlights the technical deficiencies of Blockchains. However, the data sources highlighted specific technical deficiencies in specific operations. These operational constraints were experienced in the transactional and storage operations. The data sources indicated that Blockchain transactions were slow, which is a negative in an era of rapid online transactions. They also indicated that the finality function of Blockchain inhibited refunds or reallocation of funds as it is practiced now in e-commerce. These challenges trump the potentials of Blockchain because other technologies that facilitate much faster transactions exist (Mingxiao, et al. 2017). Furthermore, feedback from data, as seen in the table above, indicates that Blockchain is unable to process Big data for some of the respondents. Hence, industries that rely on analytics of algorithms, Internet of Things (IOT) and industry 4.0 are unable to actually integrate Blockchain into their core operations due to this deficiency (Alladi, et al. 2018).

Table 2. Technical barriers to the adoption of Blockchain

Barrier Category	Sector	Barrier Identified From Data	Implication of Barrier	Sources
Technical	Non Specific sector	Technology is unproven"	No technological value	Deloitte (Pawczuk, Massey and Schatsky 2018)
	Supply chain and logistics	Immature technology	No technological value	(Hackius and Petersen 2017)
	Non sector specific	Potential security threats	Technical deficiency	Deloitte (Pawczuk, Massey and Schatsky 2018)
	Non Specific sector Energy sector	Separate Blockchain s not working together	Technical deficiency	(PWC 2018) (Brilliantova and Thurner 2019)
	Non-specific sector Service sector Construction sector Health sector Energy sector	Inability to scale	Technical deficiency	(PWC 2018) (Biswas and Gupta 2019) (Perera, et al. 2020) (McGhin, et al. 2019) (Brilliantova and Thurner 2019)
	Health sector	Lack of standardization	Technical deficiency	(McGhin, et al. 2019)
	Service sectors Energy sector	The challenge posed by irreverable transaction-transaction finality	Operational constraints	(Biswas and Gupta 2019) (Brilliantova and Thurner 2019)
	Service sectors Construction sector Health sector Energy sector	Low in transaction / computation processing capabilities	Operational constraints	(Biswas and Gupta 2019) (Perera, et al. 2020) (McGhin, et al. 2019) (Brilliantova and Thurner 2019)
	Construction sector	Latency in processing transactions	Operational constraints	(Perera, et al. 2020)
	Construction sector	Inability to store big data	Operational constraints	(Perera, et al. 2020)
	Service sectors	High energy demand for the Blockchain	Resource intensive	(Biswas and Gupta 2019)
	Energy sector	Blockchain cannot be used as a standalone system in delivering electricity	Deployment constraint	(Brilliantova and Thurner 2019)

4.   Blockchains, as indicated in the table above, are technically designed to be resource intensive. This challenge is a subset of the operational constraints. However, it is described separately because the resources here refers to that which is used to operate the Blockchain. As mentioned in the table

above, Blockchain requires a lot of energy resources. It is common knowledge that industries and organizations in almost all sectors rely on energy to power their equipment. Nevertheless, such industries also gun towards saving the cost of energy and its associated cost (US Congress, Office of industrial assessment 1993). Therefore, the energy consumption of Blockchains goes against this trend, resulting in the technology being shunned by organizations that would have adopted the technology.

5. The final challenge identified by the respondents are the deployment constraints of Blockchain. Most industries that adopt Blockchains do not use it as an end-to-end solution, but they rather try to integrate it with existing solutions (Pawczuk, Massey and Schatsky 2018) (Williams and Agbesi 2019). This is often because Blockchain is unable to perform the tasks in which supporting technologies are capable to perform. In other cases, the task to be performed by Blockchain can be performed by the other solution, often a cloud-based solution. Hence, in order to save cost, companies often opt for cloud-based solutions in the place of Blockchains. These technical barriers are some of the hindrances inhibiting the adoption of Blockchains in certain industries.

Process/Operational Capacity Barriers

These are perceived and explicit barriers related to the capacity of the organization to adopt Blockchain. Insights from the data sources point to operational and process capacity challenges. These operational and process capacity challenges are highlighted in the table below. Just as in the case of the technical barriers, the implication of each barrier were analysed inductively.

Table 3. Process barriers to the adoption of Blockchain

Barrier Category	Sector	Barrier	Implication of Barrier	Sources
Process/operational Capacity	Non sector specific	Audit/compliance concerns	Task unfriendly	(PWC 2018)
	Non sector specific	Implementation (replacing or adapting existing legacy systems)	Implementation difficulties	Deloitte (Pawczuk, Massey and Schatsky 2018)
	Non sector specific	Lack of in house skills / understanding	Lack of competent personnel	Deloitte (Pawczuk, Massey and Schatsky 2018)
	Supply chain and logistics	Dependence on Blockchain operators	Lack of competent personnel	(Hackius and Petersen 2017)
	Energy sector	Skills requirement	Lack of competent personnel	(Brilliantova and Thurner 2019)
	Service sector Energy sector	High sustainability and operational cost	High operational cost	(Biswas and Gupta 2019) (Brilliantova and Thurner 2019)
	Energy sector	lack of intuitive interface	Low user experience	(Brilliantova and Thurner 2019)

The implication of the operational/process capacity barriers to the adoption of Blockchain were, task unfriendliness; implementation difficulties; lack of competent personnel; high operational cost and Low user experience. Task unfriendliness implies that the technology does not support certain tasks related to the service enabled by Blockchain. For example, in as indicated in the table above, Blockchains do not support auditing. This is mostly because the auditor is a third party who is not a party to the Blockchain. It is also challenging to grant an auditor that access because new Blockchains has to be created for new auditors. Furthermore, in most cases the Blockchain will host other parties with no obligation to the auditor. Hence adding the auditor to the Blockchain breaches the privacy of third parties with no contract with the auditor. This example also provides a bit of an insight into the second barrier, which is the difficulty in implementing/deploying Blockchain. However, the difficulty in implementing Blockchain is not only associated with their party tasks but to internal tasks. For example, the adoption of end-to-end Blockchain solutions by electoral agencies has not been successful (Williams and Agbesi 2019). Trials have been discontinued because the Blockchain does not support certain tasks, such as the successful transfer of votes from polling stations to collation centers. Internet based technologies, though not very secured, have been more efficient in the process.

Aside the deployment challenges, another major concern is the lack of competent personnel to both operate and maintain the Blockchain. Hence, as mentioned in the table above, organizations rely on Blockchain operators who are not knowledgeable about the organizational task the Blockchain is used for. These operators are expensive. Coupling the operator's cost with the high cost of maintain the Blockchain makes the operating Blockchain a luxury for most organizations.

The final operational/process barrier identified in the secondary data is the aesthetic aspect of Blockchain's user interface. Many service providers either provide or rely on data driven services. Unfortunately, Blockchain, as it is now, cannot cater enable the needed aesthetic feel that makes the data driven service user friendly. One of such industry, that requires clarity and aesthetic feel in data presentation, is the energy sector as mentioned in the table above. Hence, this becomes an impediment to the adoption of Blockchain.

Privacy and Security Challenges

It is ironic that Blockchain possesses privacy and security issues. That being that Blockchains are designed to ensure security and a certain level of privacy. Although for certain organizations this is a plus, the organizations (whose data driven services involves the re-analysis of external data) actually see this feature as inadequate for their service delivery processes. This is because persons not authorized to such data, but are nodes on the Blockchain platform, will have access to this third party data. This results in the transparency of Blockchains becoming problematic. These challenges are highlighted in the table below.

Table 4. Privacy barriers to the adoption of Blockchain

Barrier Category	Sector	Barrier	Implication of Barrier	Sources
Privacy and Security	Non sector specific Construction industry	Concerns over sensitivity of competitive information	Lack of data privacy	Deloitte(Pawczuk, Massey and Schatsky 2018) (Perera, et al. 2020)
	Service sector Energy sector	Lack of anonymity and Linking DLT addresses to real identifiers	Lack of data privacy	(Biswas and Gupta 2019) (Brilliantova and Thurner 2019)
	Energy sector	Absence of identity management standards	Does not support trust services	(Brilliantova and Thurner 2019)
	Supply chain and logistics Health sector	Data security concerns	Low data security	(Hackius and Petersen 2017) (McGhin, et al. 2019)
	Non sector specific	Intellectual property concerns	Low data security	(PWC 2018)
	Construction sector	50% vulnerability	Low data security	(Perera, et al. 2020)

As seen in the table above, the level of transparency (even in private Blockchains) impedes anonymity. Once either an organization or an individual gains access to a Blockchain, they have access to view and access confidential materials. Hence, the lack of data privacy and the overt transparency of Blockchain becomes a problem for organizations in certain sectors. However, that is not all; Blockchains are not hack-proof. As indicated in the table above, if an organization has access to 50% of the nodes, then the Blockchain can be hacked. Hence, the inbuilt privacy and security features of Blockchains are not suitable for all industries, hence resulting in the low adoption of Blockchains. Another privacy and security challenge is the lack of standards needed to manage trust services on Blockchains.

Ecosystem Barriers

Every organization belongs to a commercial ecosystem. The ecosystem could be a value chain or a network of complementary service providers who collaborate to deliver their services. Some of these ecosystems are galvanized by a business model, which enables them to share resources (revenue inclusive). In most cases these ecosystems are necessary as they often result in the reduced cost of access to the service as well as the reduced cost of service delivery. The reduction is cost of access is enabled by the fact that the operational cost of each party in the production of the service is low. Hence they can deliver the service in such a way that the end user, pays less and the ecosystem mechanism enables the collaborating service provider to share revenue. This is evident in the telecom industry, service industry etc. Nevertheless, some of these ecosystems pose problems to the adoption of Blockchain. The major challenge is in the fact that Blockchain is not compatible with the business models governing the ecosystem. This has resulted in social challenges that impede the adoption of Blockchain by ecosystems. Some of these challenges, identified by the respondents, are highlighted in the table below.

Table 5. Ecosystem barriers to the adoption of Blockchain

Barrier Category	Sector	Barrier	Implication of Barrier	Sources
Ecosystem	Non sector specific Financial sector	Inability to bring together stakeholders or foster collaboration in the supply chain network or sector.	Inability to build trust between stakeholders	(PWC 2018) (McKinsey 2017) (Hackius and Petersen 2017)
	Non sector specific	Lack of trust among users	Inability to build trust between stakeholders	(PWC 2018)
	Energy sector	Low potential for decentralization in the oil and Gas sector	Ecosystem unfriendly	(Brilliantova and Thurner 2019)
	Energy sector	Generating consensus for the usage of Blockchain in an existing decentralized electricity grid is challenging.	Ecosystem unfriendly	(Brilliantova and Thurner 2019)
	Energy sector	There is the risk of eliminating intermediaries if Blockchain is adopted	Disrupts ecosystem	(Brilliantova and Thurner 2019)

Blockchain as indicated in the table above has the tendency to disrupt ecosystems. Theoretically, Blockchain has the potential to do away with the middlemen in the ecosystem. On the other hand, Blockchain can be utilized in these ecosystems, but as indicated by the respondents in the secondary data, these ecosystems are not built to facilitate trust. External parties such as banks who handle the distribution of the revenue to the accounts of the different parties electronically facilitate trust already, where it matter. Hence, inorder to deploy Blockchain as it is today, the ecosystem has to disrupted. This could be by doing away with middlemen or by including different trust organizations, who are not currently in the Ecosystem, as nodes on the Blockchain. This will give rise to issues such as privacy, security, trust issues as well as the high cost of maintaining the growing Blockchain. These barriers become more pronounced, if the ecosystem is an international ecosystem. As will be mentioned in the next point (market barrier), national regulations becomes a problem. These challenges may not necessary affect ecosystems consisting of wealthy organizations, be they local or international. This is because, they can bear the cost of deploying the Blockchain at least nationally. If companies in such ecosystems have international branches, they can use that structure to deploy the Blockchain as internal organizational infrastructure. Furthermore, they can grant access to other members of the ecosystem with international branches as well. However, as some of the respondents from the sources cited in the table above were SMEs. Such ecosystem comprising of start-ups will definitely encounter the ecosystem challenges mentioned here.

Table 6. Market Barriers to the adoption of Blockchain

Barrier Category	Sector	Barrier	Implication of Barrier	Sources
Market	Non sector specific	Uncertain ROI	Not profitable	Deloitte(Pawczuk, Massey and Schatsky 2018)
	Non sector specific Financial sector Service sector Energy sector	Regulatory issues (national and cross-border regulatory barriers).	Susceptible to regulatory risk	Deloitte;(Pawczuk, Massey and Schatsky 2018) (PWC 2018) (McKinsey 2017) (Biswas and Gupta 2019) (Brilliantova and Thurner 2019)
	Non sector specific	Lack of compelling application of the technology	No use case	Deloitte (Pawczuk, Massey and Schatsky 2018)
	Non sector specific	Not a current business priority	No market value	Deloitte (Pawczuk, Massey and Schatsky 2018)
	Financial sector	Lack of clear business case to justify the transaction cost.	No market value	(McKinsey 2017)
	Supply chain and logistics	Lack of acceptance in industry	No market value	(Hackius and Petersen 2017)
	Service sector	Either low or no transaction fees for service providers in the supply chain (Erosion of revenue in the ecosytem)	Parasitic to resources	(Biswas and Gupta 2019)
	Energy sector	Cloud computing is already delivering the needs of the industry.	Competing technology	(Brilliantova and Thurner 2019)
	Service sector	Uncertain revenue models for miners	Uncertain business model	(Biswas and Gupta 2019)
	Supply chain and logistics	Benefits of the technology is not clear	Unclear value of technology	(Hackius and Petersen 2017)

Table 7. Uncertainty barriers to the adoption of Blockchain

Barrier Category	Sector	Barrier	Implication of Barrier	Sources
Uncertainty	Nonspecific sector	Other non-assessed issues	General uncertainty	Deloitte(Pawczuk, Massey and Schatsky 2018)
	Nonspecific sector	Technical uncertainties		(Accenture 2016)
	Nonspecific sector Logistics and supply chain. Service sector	Regulatory uncertainties (including taxation uncertainties)		(Accenture 2016) (Hackius and Petersen 2017) (Biswas and Gupta 2019)
	Non specific sector	Lack of governance	Regulatory uncertainty	(PWC 2018)
	Service sector	Market based risks	Market uncertainty	(Biswas and Gupta 2019)

Market Barriers

As indicated in the table below, regulations are one of the challenges facing Blockchain. These include national and cross-border regulations. These regulatory challenges were:

1. Industry specific regulations, privacy regulations (such as the EU General Data Protection Regulation (GDPR)) and geography specific regulations (Pawczuk, Massey and Schatsky 2018),
2. Cross-country regulations (PWC 2018).

These regulatory challenges create an uncertainty in the market. The uncertainty has an indirect negative effect on the projected Return on Investments by the responding organizations.

Furthermore, data extracted from the secondary sources imply that most organizations do not see either the market value of Blockchain, the clear value of the technology, its use-case or its profitability. Hence, they have decided not to join the market and in most cases do not foresee themselves joining the Blockchain market (Pawczuk, Massey and Schatsky 2018). In some other instances, those who can identify with the value of Blockchain are unable to either identify a business model that would result in the profitability of adopting Blockchains or are already satisfied with a competing technology. Furthermore, for other, Blockchain does not improve upon the revenue they receive from their ecosystems. So rather, than deploy Blockchain and lose their revenue to a stronger competitor, they rather not adopt Blockchains.

Uncertainty Barriers

For respondents who neither adopted Blockchains nor had plans to do so, they were plagued by uncertainty. For a technology with technical, market, process/operational and ecosystem barriers, there was no certainty in deriving organizational value in the adoption of Blockchain. Some of these uncertainties included, regulatory, market and technical uncertainty. Hence investing in Blockchain was a risky venture.

The findings reported in this section highlights the fact that Blockchain is not a one-technology-fit-all solution. Blockchain as it is, is not compatible with the operations, processes and not market ready for a lot of organizations in various economic sectors. As a result, some large cooperation's and many SMEs globally are unable to mobilize their resources to adopt the technology. If Blockchain is to be of value to SMEs, then certain changes has to occur. Hence, it is not yet the next big thing as publicized.

In the next section, these challenges will be explained within the context of the mobilization decision theory. This will be followed with discussion on what should change with Blockchain in order to improve upon its technical, operational, process, ecosystem, privacy and security abilities in different sectors of economies.

MOBILIZATION DECISION THEORY AND THE CHALLENGES OF BLOCKCHAIN

The challenges in the previous section highlight resource challenges, congruence challenges, cooperativeness challenges, and value challenges. How these challenges are categorized are presented in the Table 8.

Table 8. Mobilization –Decision theory Reasons for organizations rejecting Blockchain

Barrier Category	Barriers	Mobilization-Decision Theory Barriers
Technical	Resource intensive	Available resources
Process/operational Capacity	Incompetent personnel High operational cost	
Market	Parasitic to resources	
Uncertainty	General uncertainty	
Technical barrier	Technical deficiency Deployment constraint	Lack of congruence
Process/operational Capacity	Difficult to implement	
Privacy and Security	Does not support trust services Low data security	
Ecosystem	Inability to build trust between stakeholders	
Market	Not profitable Susceptible to regulatory risk Uncertain business model	
Uncertainty	General uncertainty Technical uncertainties Regulatory uncertainties	
Technical barrier	Operational constraints	Lack of cooperativeness
Process/operational Capacity	Task unfriendly Low user experience	
Privacy and Security	Lack of data Privacy	
Ecosystem	Ecosystem unfriendly Disrupts ecosystem	
Technical barrier	No technological value	Lack of Value
Market	No use cases No market value Competing technology Unclear value of technology	
Uncertainty	General uncertainty Market uncertainty Regulatory uncertainty Technical uncertainty	

1. **Resource Challenges:** The resource challenges are technical, process/operational, market and uncertainty. In principle, most of the respondents either lack the resources to deploy Blockchain or feel that Blockchain will deplete their resources. As seen in the table below, obviously there is an uncertainty towards the availability of resources and the potential to access these resources. One of such resources is human resources. These challenges denote lack of resources. Furthermore, there is the perception that Blockchain could erode their resources as it is resource intensive and it could disrupt the revenue flow in the ecosystem. Hence rather than earning from Blockchain, they could be spending more because of Blockchain.

2. **Congruence Challenges**: Based on the challenges analysed, it is evident that some organizations see Blockchain as a hype. What is advertised is not what some organizations observe and experience in the piloting process. For example, in the table 1, there are indications that certain organizations have stopped their use of Blockchain and very few are really deploying the technology. The challenges analyzed indicate that the lack of congruence is as a result of technical deficiency, deployment constraint, implementation difficulties, privacy and security challenges, ecosystem unfriendliness, uncertain business model and other uncertainties. Some of these challenges are failed promises of the technology. Blockchain promised technical solutions towards, enhancing transactions (Examples (Vo, Kundu and Mohania 2018) (Banafa 2017)); support of operation and processes (examples (Akyuz and Gursoy 2019) (Moreno, et al. 2020)); and privacy and security (example (Zyskind, Nathan and Pentland 2015)). However, these billed value for Blockchain does not hold in practice in some industries and in most cases it causes disruption of business models and ecosystems (Banafa 2017) (Pawczuk, Massey and Schatsky 2018). This is because Blockchain has been envisaged to create new ecosystems and business models (ibid). This has resulted in the failure of congruence between the human and the technology resulting in the decision not to mobilize. In a nutshell, for certain organizations in certain sectors, the technology has not performed in the way it was hyped.

3. **Challenges With Cooperativeness:** For organizations that actually tested the technology in certain sectors, it did not support the tasks. Technically, there were operational constraints. When adopted for operations and processes, it was task unfriendly and its user experience was low. For tasks in the service sector, that required anonymity and data privacy, the technology was deficient. Furthermore, when deployed in ecosystems it rather disrupted the tasks and nature of the ecosystem rather than enhance them. Hence, the technology in those instances did not fit the tasks, operations and processes of those organizations. Hence, it was not adopted by some of the responding organizations.

4. **Value Challenges**: The findings indicate that in some sectors and organizations, Blockchain has not technological and market value. In some cases, other technologies provide value but may not be as efficient as Blockchain. The lack of value is made worse by market uncertainty, regulatory uncertainty and other unforeseen uncertainties.

Hence, these challenges are explainable from the perspective of the Mobilization-Decision theory with respect to human- machine interaction. The Mobilization-Decision theory highlights the fact that the absence of one of its constructs will result in a negative decision, which is the decision not to mobilize (Williams 2021). This implies that the decision to mobilize in order to perform an action can only occurs if all the constructs are satisfied. It is actually interesting to see that organizations that have adopted Blockchain did not just adopt it. They had to go through the piloting phase, where they validated the four constructs of the Mobilization-Decision theory. It is also interesting to realize that organizations have also stopped their utilization of Blockchain once their initial expectations were not realized at the deployment stage (Andersen and Vogdrup-Schmidt 2018, McKinsey 2017). This implies that the decision to mobilize is a short-lived action, which does not actually influence the long-term utilization of what has been mobilized. However, it could be said that the short-lived action can be re-initiated once all the constructs are satisfied.

In the same way, the Mobilization-Decision theory can be used to diagnose the decision to mobilize; it can be used to coerce technology to do the bidding of the human as mentioned earlier. This in respect to Blockchain is discussed in the next section.

DISCUSSION– REMODELING BLOCKCHAIN WITH MOBILIZATION –DECISION THEORY

Based on the Mobilization-Decision theory, four factors has to be in place before the decision to mobilize can occur. The decision to mobilize is a precursor towards the actual adoption and implementation of a technology, Blockchain inclusive. Nevertheless, it is not in every instance that these four factors occur because of chance. Proactivity by the mobilizing agent in facilitating the availability of these factors might be necessary.

At the dawn of the industrial age, organizations were actively and directly involved in mobilizing technology towards performing an action. However, by the dawn of the 21st century, more than a century after the dawn of the industrial age, the value chain in technology mobilization changed. In the value chain were technology producers, technology suppliers and the technology adopting organization. The technology producer produced the technology either as a whole or in parts.

Figure 2. The mobilizer and the mobilized in the modern industry value chain
Source: (Williams 2021)

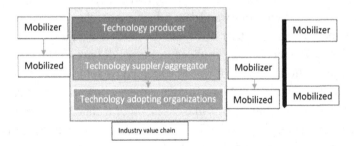

The technology supplier either aggregates the different parts of the technology and resells it or serves as the market bridge between the producer and the adopting organization. The technology adopting organization adopts and utilizes the technology to facilitate, operations, processes and tasks. Each class of technology stakeholder are technology mobilizers. However, it is the technology suppliers and the technology adopting organizations who are mobilized, by the preceding class of technology stakeholder, to reassemble/resell and to adopt the technology respectively. The implication of the 21st century value chain is that the organization adopting the technology is spoilt with choice. Therefore, the technology adopting organization, unlike at the dawn of the industrial era, has no incentive to coerce (by amending or manufacturing) a technology to perform actions. They go for technologies that have value, performs as billed (congruence), fits the organizational tasks (cooperativeness) and can be deployed with the available resources. This implies that it is not up to the technology adopting organizations to promote the global adoption of a technology. This task falls to the technology producer.

Therefore, the technology producer decides, either voluntarily or involuntarily, if a technology gains traction globally. This implies that it is the duty of the technology producer to coerce the technology to fit the needed sectoral tasks. That is a tall order but achievable. If one thinks on the data used in this chapter, technology-adopting organizations might be willing to adopt Blockchain if the four factors of the Mobilization-Decision theory held true in the sector in which they operate. Hence, the technology producers of Blockchain ought to:

1. Rethink their technology design requirements along industry and sectoral needs. This will be the first step towards providing market and technical value for Blockchains. This approach towards the design of Blockchain technologies would result in congruence and cooperativeness of the technology. If this is not achieved at the first go, it can be achieved by continuous upgrades of the technology along sectoral, cross-sectoral and industry requirements.
2. Rethink the computational, resource and scalability requirements also along industry and sectoral needs. Obviously, there are organizations in sectors and industries in which the current requirements are suitable. This is why there is some level of adoption of Blockchains. However, organizations in sectors and industries that cannot 1.) accept the current computational parameters; 2.) accept the current resource utilization and 3.) scalability parameters of Blockchain prefer to stay away. This is either because they do not have the available resources or prefer not to risk their available resources.
3. Rethink the designing Blockchain as an enabler to current ecosystems rather than a disrupter of such ecosystems. This implies preserving or enhancing the revenue models and overall business model of the ecosystem. The advantage of enabling ecosystems is because ecosystems enable the synergic adoption of technologies. These synergies will result in the reduction in cost of deployment of the Blockchain. This will be of great value to SMEs.

The adoption of these initiatives by the technology producer will set the trend for the technology supplier/aggregator and will make Blockchain appealing to the technology adopting organizations. Therefore, using the constructs of the Mobilization-Decision theory as the basis for designing sector-based Blockchains, will enable different organizations in different sectors to find the technology useful after piloting the technology. It will also reduce market and technical uncertainties that adversely affect the decisions of the organizations in the adoption of Blockchain.

An aspect that the Mobilization-Decision theory will not able to address are the regulations governing the different use cases of Blockchain. However, regulatory uncertainty in the adoption of technologies is not limited to Blockchain. However, if one could take a lesson in the liberalization and deregulation of the telecoms industry in the 1990s and 2000s (Hills 1989), it is evident that the significance of a technology towards society can result in deregulations. The deregulation of the telecoms industry occurred when the telecom technology had matured to the extent that its positive network externality was of value to organizations and society. Hence, the technology had value, visible congruence and cooperativeness, but it was resource intensive. Hence, the liberalization and deregulations were aimed at releasing resources to enable the rapid diffusion of the technology.

In the case of Blockchain as mentioned in the introduction, one of the characteristics of the technology is to facilitate trust. In the findings, it was clear that some stakeholders were not convinced that Blockchain could facilitate trust in their industry. Assuming, technology producers adopt the recommendations made in this chapter and are able to facilitate trust, and there is traction for the technology in all sectors, that will attract the attention of policy makers. This is because they will identify with the value, congruence, and cooperativeness of Blockchain. They will need the Blockchain as well to promote large-scale trust-driven e-governance initiatives, nationally and cross border. This will trigger policy makers to revisit regulations that plague the utilization of Blockchain s within sectors, nationally and across border. The new regulations will enable the provision of financial resources and market incentives needed to deliver Blockchain.

CONCLUSION

This chapter began with the quest to undertstand why the adoption of a technology that facilitates trust was very low. Using the Mobilization-Decision theory, it has been discovered that Blockchain as it is does not provide value, congruence, cooperativeness for organizations in some sectors. Furthermore, it is resource intensive. Hence, the fact that the technology facilitates trust is not enough to gain traction in the global market.

The chapter calls for the re-engineering of Blockchain along sectoral, cross-sectoral and industrial lines. Such an attempt will produce congruence, cooperativeness between the human-led organization and the technology. It will also result in the visibility of the value of the technology towards different organizations. Furthermore, the chapter also calls for a re think with respect to resource consumption of Blockchain; and the resources needed to acquire as well as deploy the Blockchain. This will rethink by the Blockchain manufacturers will lower the adoption barrier that currently exists in the adoption of Blockchain.

Finally, this chapter has extended the Mobilization-Decision theory from human centricity towards human-to-machine interaction. It has highlighted that the decision to mobilize is critical to the adoption and utilization of machines (technology).

REFERENCES

Accenture. (2016). *Blockchain Technology: Preparing for change.* Accenture. https://www.accenture.com/t20160608T052656Z__w__/us-en/_acnmedia/PDF-5/Accenture-2016-Top-10-Challenges-04-Blockchain-Technology.pdf

Akyuz, G. A., & Gursoy, G. (2019). Transformation of Supply Chain Activities in Blockchain Environment. In Digital Business Strategies in Blockchain Ecosystems. Contributions to Management Science. Springer.

Alladi, T., Chamola, V., Parizi, R. M., & Choo, K. R. (2018). Blockchain Application for Industry 4.0 and Industrial IOT: A review. *IEEE Access : Practical Innovations, Open Solutions, 7,* 176935–176951. doi:10.1109/ACCESS.2019.2956748

Andersen, O., & Vogdrup-Schmidt, L. (2018). *Rivals reject blockchain solution from Maersk and IBM.* https://shippingwatch.com/carriers/Container/article10602520.ece

Asare, E. K., Beldona, S., & Nketia, J. (2020). The Principal, the Agent, and the Culture: Potential Impacts of Culture on Financing Contracts. *The International Trade Journal*, *34*(1), 30–54. doi:10.108 0/08853908.2019.1693450

Banafa, A. (2017). IoT and Blockchain Convergence: Benefits and Challenges. *IEEE Internet of Things*. https://iot.ieee.org/newsletter/january-2017/iot-and-blockchain-convergence-benefits-and-challenges. html

Biswas, B., & Gupta, R. (2019). Analysis of barriers to implement blockchain in industry and service sectors. *Computers & Industrial Engineering*, *136*, 225–241. doi:10.1016/j.cie.2019.07.005

Brilliantova, V., & Thurner, T. W. (2019). Blockchain and the future of energy. *Technology in Society*, *57*, 38–45. doi:10.1016/j.techsoc.2018.11.001

Brown, R. G. (2018). The Corda Platform: An Introduction. *Corda White Paper*. https://docs.corda. net/_static/corda-platform-whitepaper.pdf

Clohessy, T., & Acton, T. (2019). Investigating the influence of organizational factors on blockchain adoption: An innovation theory perspective. *Industrial Management & Data Systems*, *119*(7), 1457–1491. doi:10.1108/IMDS-08-2018-0365

Glisic, S., & Makela, J. (2006). Advanced Wireless Networks: 4G Technologies. *2006 IEEE Ninth International Symposium on Spread Spectrum Techniques and Applications, Manaus-Amazon*, 442-446. 10.1109/ISSSTA.2006.311811

Goodhue, D. L., & Thompson, R. L. (1995). Task-Technology Fit and Individual Performance. *Management Information Systems Quarterly*, *19*(2), 213–236. doi:10.2307/249689

Hackius, N., & Petersen, M. (2017). Blockchain in Logistics and Supply Chain: Trick or Treat? *Hamburg International Conference of Logistics*.

Hills, J. (1989). Universal Service LIberalization and Privatization of telecommunications. *Telecommunications Policy*, *3*(1), 129–144. doi:10.1016/0308-5961(89)90038-4

Jang, K., Han, M., Cho, S., Ryu, H., Lee, J., Lee, Y., & Moon, S. B. (2009). 3G and 3.5G wireless network performance measured from moving cars and high-speed trains. In *MICNET '09: Proceedings of the 1st ACM workshop on Mobile internet through cellular networks September 2009*. ACM. 10.1145/1614255.1614261

McCarthy, J. D., & Zaid, M. N. (1977). Resource Mobilization and Social Movements: A partial Theory. *American Journal of Sociology*, *82*(6), 1212–1241. doi:10.1086/226464

McGhin, T., Choo, K. R., Liu, C. Z., & He, D. (2019). Blockchain in healthcare applications: Research challenges and opportunities. *Journal of Network and Computer Applications*, *135*(1), 62–75. doi:10.1016/j.jnca.2019.02.027

McKinsey. (2017). *Blockchain Technology in the Insurance Sector*. McKinsey & Company. https://www. treasury.gov/initiatives/fio/Documents/McKinsey_FACI_Blockchain_in_Insurance.pdf

Mingxiao, D., Xiaofeng, M., Zhe, Z., Xiangwei, W., & Qijun, C. (2017). A review on consensus algorithm of blockchain. *2017 IEEE International Conference on Systems, Man, and Cybernetics (SMC)*, 2567 - 2572. 10.1109/SMC.2017.8123011

Mohammed & Guennoun. (2010). Wireless Mobile Evolution to 4G Network. *Wireless Sensor Network*, *2010*(2), 309-317.

Momo, Schiavi, Behr, & Lucena. (2019). Business Models and Blockchain: What Can Change? *Revista de Administração Contemporânea, 23*(2).

Moreno, J., Serrano, M. A., Fernandez, E. B., & Fernandez-Medina, E. (2020). Improving Incident Response in Big Data Ecosystems by Using Blockchain Technologies. *Applied Sciences (Basel, Switzerland), 10*(2), 724. doi:10.3390/app10020724

Oliver, R. L. (1980). A Cognitive Model of the Antecedents and Consequences of Satisfaction Decisions. *JMR, Journal of Marketing Research, 17*(4), 460–469. doi:10.1177/002224378001700405

Pawczuk, L., Massey, R., & Schatsky, D. (2018). *Breaking blockchain open Deloitte's 2018 Global Blockchain Survey.* Deloitte. https://www2.deloitte.com/content/dam/Deloitte/us/Documents/financial-services/us-fsi-2018-global-blockchain-survey-report.pdf

Perera, Nanayakkara, Rodrigo, & Senaratne. (2020). Blockchain technology: Is it hype or real in the construction industry? *Journal of Industrial Information Integration, 17*.

Porter, M. (1990). The Competitive Advantage of Nations. *Harvard Business Review.* https://hbr.org/1990/03/the-competitive-advantage-of-nations

Prasad, S., Shankar, R., Gupta, R., & Roy, S. (2018). A TISM modeling of critical success factors of blockchain based cloud services. *Journal of Advances in Management Research, 15*(4), 434–456. doi:10.1108/JAMR-03-2018-0027

PWC. (2018). *PWC'S Global Blockchain Survey.* PriceWaterhouseCoopers. https://www.pwccn.com/en/research-and-insights/publications/global-blockchain-survey-2018/global-blockchain-survey-2018-report.pdf

Shaikh, Z. A., & Lashari, I. A. (2017). Blockchain technology, the new Internet. *International Journal of Management Science and Business Research, 6*(4), 167–177.

Stastista. (2019). *Blockchain adoption phases in organizations worldwide as of April 2018, by industry.* https://www.statista.com/statistics/878748/worldwide-production-phase-blockchain-technology-industry/

US Congress, Office of Industrial Assessment. (1993). *Industrial Energy Efficiency.* Washington, DC: US Government Printing Office.

Venkatesh, V., Morris, M. G., Davis, G. B., & Davis, F. D. (2003). User acceptance of Information Technology: Towards a unified View. *Management Information Systems Quarterly, 27*(3), 425–478. doi:10.2307/30036540

Vo, H. T., Kundu, A., & Mohania, M. (2018). Research Directions in Blockchain Data management and Analytics. *21st International Conference on Extending Database Technology (EDBT)*. http://www.dke.jku.at/general/news/res/N000026/Mohania%20EDBT%20paper-227.pdf

Werbach, K. (2018). *The Blockchain and the New Architecture of Trust*. MIT Press. doi:10.7551/mitpress/11449.001.0001

Williams, I. (2015). *Analysis of Public Private Interplay Frameworks in the Development of Rural Telecommunications Infrastructure: A Multiple-Case Study*. Aalborg: Aalborg University Press.

Williams, I. (2017). Community Broadband network and the opportunity for e-government services. In Encyclopedia of Information Science and Technology, Fourth Edition Hershey, PA: IGI.

Williams, I. (2018). Community Based networks and 5G Wifi. *Ekonomiczne Problemy Uslug*, *2*(131), 321-334.

Williams, I. (2021). Mobilization - Decision Theory. In Encyclopedia of Information Science and Technology, Fifth Edition. Hershey, PA: IGI Global.

Williams, I., & Agbesi, S. (2019). Blockchain, Trust And Elections: A Proof Of Concept For The Ghanaian National Elections. In Handbook on ICT in Developing Countries: Next Generation ICT Technologies. River Publishers.

Zyskind, G., Nathan, O., & Pentland, A. (2015). Decentralizing Privacy: Using Blockchain to Protect Personal Data. *IEEE Symposium on Security and Privacy Workshops (SPW)*, 180 - 184. 10.1109/SPW.2015.27

Compilation of References

Accenture. (2016). *Blockchain Technology: Preparing for change.* Accenture. https://www.accenture.com/t20160608T052656Z__w__/us-en/_acnmedia/PDF-5/Accenture-2016-Top-10-Challenges-04-Blockchain-Technology.pdf

Acer, F. (2017). *Sigorta Sektörü Insurtech ile Gelişecek* [Insurance Sector to Develop with Insurtech]. Retrieved from https://www.bankasurans.com.tr/sigorta-sektoru-insurtech-ile-gelisecek/

Adams, K. M. (2015). *Non-functional Requirements in Systems Analysis and Design.* Springer.

Adam, W. (2016, Jan.). The Limits of Empathy. *Harvard Business Review.* Accessed from https://hbr.org/2016/01/the-limits-of-empathy

Agrawal, H. (2019). *Understanding Blockchain Technology: What is Blockchain and how it works.* Retrieved August 12, 2019, from https://coinsutra.com/Blockchain/

AhIman. (2016). *Finish city partners with IBM to validate blockchain application in logistics.* https://cointelegraph.com/news/finish-city-partners-with-ibm-to-validate-blockchain-application-in-logistics

Akyuz, G. A., & Gursoy, G. (2019). Transformation of Supply Chain Activities in Blockchain Environment. In Digital Business Strategies in Blockchain Ecosystems. Contributions to Management Science. Springer.

Albeyatti, A. (2018). *White paper: MedicalChain.* MedicalChain self-publication.

Alladi, T., Chamola, V., Parizi, R. M., & Choo, K. R. (2018). Blockchain Application for Industry 4.0 and Industrial IOT: A review. *IEEE Access : Practical Innovations, Open Solutions, 7,* 176935–176951. doi:10.1109/ACCESS.2019.2956748

Allessie, D., Sobolewski, M., & Vaccari, L. (2019). *Blockchain for digital government.* European Commission. https://joinup.ec.europa.eu/sites/default/files/document/2019-04/JRC115049%20blockchain%20for%20digital%20government.pdf

AlOmar, A., Rahman, M. S., Basu, A., & Kiyomoto, S. (2017, December). Medibchain: A Blockchain based privacy preserving platform for healthcare data. In *International conference on security, privacy and anonymity in computation, communication and storage* (pp. 534-543). Springer. 10.1007/978-3-319-72395-2_49

Al-Saqaf, W., & Seidler, N. (2017). Blockchain technology for social impact: Opportunities and challenges ahead. *Journal of Cyber Policy., 2*(3), 338–354. doi:10.1080/23738871.2017.1400084

Anascavage, R., & Davis, N. (2018). *Blockchain Technology: A Literature Review.* https://papers.ssrn.com/sol3/papers.cfm?abstract_id=3173406

Andersen, O., & Vogdrup-Schmidt, L. (2018). *Rivals reject blockchain solution from Maersk and IBM.* https://shippingwatch.com/carriers/Container/article10602520.ece

Androulaki, E., Barger, A., Bortnikov, V., Cachin, C., Christidis, K., De Caro, A., & Muralidharan, S. (2018). Hyperledger fabric: a distributed operating system for permissioned Blockchains. In *Proceedings of the Thirteenth EuroSys Conference* (p. 30). ACM. 10.1145/3190508.3190538

Andrychowicz, M., Dziembowski, S., Malinowski, D., & Mazurek, L. (2014). *Secure Multiparty Computations on Bitcoin* (pp. 443–458). SP.

Antonopoulos, A. M. (2014). *Mastering Bitcoin: unlocking digital cryptocurrencies.* O'Reilly Media, Inc. Retrieved from: https://github.com/bitcoinbook/bitcoinbook

Antonopoulos, A. M., & Wood, G. (2018). *Mastering ethereum: building smart contracts and dapps.* O'Reilly Media. Retrieved from https://github.com/ethereumbook/ethereumbook

Anwar, H. (2018). *Consensus Algorithms: The Root of the Blockchain Technology.* Retrieved August 25, 2108, from https://101Blockchains.com/consensus-algorithms-Blockchain/#1

Arunkumar, S., & Muppidi, S. (2019). *Secure your Blockchain solutions.* Retrieved from https://developer.ibm.com/articles/how-to-secure-Blockchain-solutions/

Asare, E. K., Beldona, S., & Nketia, J. (2020). The Principal, the Agent, and the Culture: Potential Impacts of Culture on Financing Contracts. *The International Trade Journal*, *34*(1), 30–54. doi:10.1080/08853908.2019.1693450

Asayag, A., Cohen, G., Grayevsky, I., & Leshkowitz, M. (2018). *Helix: A Scalable and fair Consensus Algorithm.* https://pdfs.semanticscholar.org/0d19/de4e8c825164e1306b362ce6a1d43e1c5480.pdf

Atlam, H. F., & Wills, G. B. (2018). Technical aspects of Blockchain and IoT. *Advances in Computers.* doi:10.1016/bs.adcom.2018.10.006

Atta-Krah, K. D. (2015). Preventing A Boom from Turning Bust: Regulators Should Turn Their Attention to Starter Interrupt Devices Before the Subprime Auto Lending Bubble Bursts. *Iowa Law Review*, *101*, 1187.

Atzori, L., Iera, A., & Morabito, G. (2010). The Internet of Things: A survey. *Computer Networks*, *54*(15), 2787–2805. doi:10.1016/j.comnet.2010.05.010

Azaria, A., Ekblaw, A., Vieira, T., & Lippman, A. (2016). Medrec: Using Blockchain for medical data access and permission management. *2016 2nd International Conference on Open and Big Data (OBD)*, 25–30.

Baker, M. (2019). *Blockchain and Cryptocurrency.* Retrieved from Insight Publications website: https://www.bakermckenzie.com//media/files/insight/publications/2019/02/report_Blockchainandcryptocurrencyreg_feb2019.pdf

Baker, P. (2020). RSK Launches Interoperability Bridge Between Bitcoin and Ethereum. *Coindesk.* https://www.coindesk.com/rsk-launches-interoperability-bridge-between-bitcoin-and-ethereum

Bamasag, O., Munshi, A., Alharbi, H., Aldairi, O., Altowerky, H., Alshomrani, R., & Alharbi, A. (2020). Blockchain and Smart Contract in Future Transactions—Case Studies. In *Decentralised Internet of Things* (pp. 169–198). Cham: Springer. doi:10.1007/978-3-030-38677-1_8

Bambara, J. J., Allen, P. R., Iyer, K., Madsen, R., Lederer, S., & Wuehler, M. (2018). *Blockchain: A Practical Guide to Developing Business, Law, and Technology Solutions* (Rev. ed.). McGraw-Hill Education.

Banafa, A. (2017). IoT and Blockchain Convergence: Benefits and Challenges. *IEEE Internet of Things.* https://iot.ieee.org/newsletter/january-2017/iot-and-blockchain-convergence-benefits-and-challenges.html

Banafa, A. (2019). *Blockchain and AI: A Perfect Match?* Retrieved May 6, 2019, from https://www.bbvaopenmind.com/en/technology/artificial-intelligence/Blockchain-and-ai-a-perfect-match/

Banker, S. (2016). *Will blockchain technology revolutionize supply chain applications?* https://logisticsviewpoints. com/2016/06/20/will-block-chain-technology-revolunize-supply-chain-applications/

Bartosch, A., & Braun, J. (2009). *EC Competition and Telecommunications Law.* Kluwer Law International B.V.

Batrinca, B., & Treleaven, P. C. (2015). Social Media Analytics: A Survey of Techniques, Tools and Platforms. *AI & Society, 30*(1), 89–116. doi:10.100700146-014-0549-4

Bauer, I., Leisibach, F., Zavolokina, L., & Schwabe, G. (2018). *Exploring Blockchain Value Creation: The Case of Car Ecosystem.* Academic Press.

Bayer, D., Haber, S., & Stornetta, W.S. (1993). *Improving the Efficiency and Reliability of Digital Time- Stamping.* Academic Press.

Beck, R., Czepluch, J. S., Lollike, N., & Malone, S. (2016). Blockchainthe Gateway to Trust-Free Cryptographic Transactions. *European Conference on Information Systems.*

Beedham, M. (2019, March). *All you need to know about Bitcoin network nodes.* Retrieved from: https://thenextweb. com/hardfork/2019/03/01/bitcoin-blockchain-nodes-network/

Benet, J. (2014). *IPFS - Content Addressed, Versioned, P2P File System.* arXiv preprint arXiv:1407.3561

Benet, J. (2015). *IPFS - Content Addressed, Versioned, P2P File System.* Retrieved from https://arxiv.org/abs/1407.3561

Benkler, Y. (2006). *The wealth of networks: How social production transforms markets and freedom.* Yale University Press.

Berberich, M., & Steiner, M. (2016). Blockchain Technology and the GDPR-How to Reconcile Privacy and Distributed Ledgers. *Eur. Data Prot. L. Rev., 2*(3), 422–426. doi:10.21552/EDPL/2016/3/21

Bernard, R. (2018). *Private vs. Public Blockchain: What are the Major Differences?* Retrieved December 17, 2018, from https://medium.com/luxtag-live-tokenized-assets-on-Blockchain/private-vs-public-Blockchain-what-are-the-major-differences-d92a504f3a4a

Bharadwaj, R. (2019). *AI in Blockchain – Current Applications and Trends.* Retrieved August 13, 2019, from https://emerj.com/ai-sector-overviews/ai-in-Blockchain/

Bhargavan, K., Delignat-Lavaud, A., Fournet, C., Gollamudi, A., Gonthier, G., Kobeissi, N., & Zanella-Béguelin, S. (2016). Formal verification of smart contracts: Short paper. In *Proceedings of the 2016 ACM Workshop on Programming Languages and Analysis for Security* (pp. 91-96). ACM. 10.1145/2993600.2993611

Biswas, B., & Gupta, R. (2019). Analysis of barriers to implement blockchain in industry and service sectors. *Computers & Industrial Engineering, 136,* 225–241. doi:10.1016/j.cie.2019.07.005

Bitconist. (n.d.). *Bitcoin vs Ethereum: Differences, Advantages and Disadvantages – Which is Better?* Retrieved from: https://bitcoinist.com/bitcoin-vs-ethereum/

Bogetoft, P., Christensen, D. L., Damgård, I., Geisler, M., Jakobsen, T. P., Kroigaard, M., . . . Toft, T. (2009). Secure Multiparty Computation Goes Live. *FC,* 325–343.

Bonneau, J., Narayanan, A., Miller, A., Clark, J., Kroll, J. A., & Felten, E. W. (2014). Mixcoin: Anonymity for bitcoin with accountable mixes. In *Financial Cryptography and Data Security - 18th International Conference, FC 2014, Revised Selected Papers 8437* (pp. 486-504). Springer Verlag. 10.1007/978-3-662-45472-5_31

Boretos, G. P. (2007). The future of the mobile phone business. *Technological Forecasting and Social Change, 74*(3), 331–340. doi:10.1016/j.techfore.2005.11.005

Brakeville, S., & Perepa, B. (2018, March). *Blockchain basics: Introduction to distributed ledgers.* Retrieved from: https://developer.ibm.com/tutorials/cl-blockchain-basics-intro-bluemix-trs/

Braunstein, Y., & White, L. J. (1985). Setting technical compatibility standards an economic analysis. *Antitrust Bulletin, 30,* 337–356.

Brilliantova, V., & Thurner, T. W. (2019). Blockchain and the future of energy. *Technology in Society, 57,* 38–45. doi:10.1016/j.techsoc.2018.11.001

Brown, R. G. (2018). The Corda Platform: An Introduction. *Corda White Paper.* https://docs.corda.net/_static/corda-platform-whitepaper.pdf

Browne, R. (2018). *Five Things That Must Happen for Blockchain to See Widespread Adoption, According To Deloitte.* Retrieved from: https://www.cnbc.com/2018/10/01/five-crucial-challenges-for-Blockchain-to-overcome-deloitte.html

Brunner, A., Abderrahmane, N., Muralidharan, Halpap, P., Sume, O., & Zimprich, S. (2017). Trade Finance Disrupted: A Blockchain Use Case. *The CAPCO Institute Journal of Financial Transformation, 45,* 41-48.

Budko, D. (2018). *How Blockchain can Transform Artificial Intelligence.* Retrieved February 13, 2018, from https://dzone.com/articles/how-Blockchain-can-transform-artificial-intelligence

Bulk. (2018). *How Blockchain can transfer the world of indirect tax.* Retrieved from https://www.ey.com/en_gl/trust/how-Blockchain-could-transform-the-world-of-indirect-tax

Buren, W. V. (2017). *The Potential of Blockchain Technology Application in the Food System.* https://www.beefresearch.org/CMDocs/BeefResearch/.../Potential of Blockchain.pdf

Burts, I. Q. (2017). *Bringing Health to Life Whitepaper.* Retrieved from: https://www.burstiq.com/

Business Ghana. (2019). *Ghana to Host third Blockchain Conference.* Retrieved from: https://www.businessghana.com/site/news/general/197826/Ghana-to-host-third-Blockchain-conference

Bussman, S., & Muller, J. (1992), A negotiation framework for co-operating agents. In S.M. Deen (Ed.), *Proceedings of CKBS-SIG.* Dake Centre, University of Keele.

Buterin, V. (2015). *On Public and Private Blockchains.* Retrieved from https://blog.ethereum.org/2015/08/07/on-public-and-private-Blockchains/

Cargill, C. F. (2011). Why Standardization Efforts Fail. *The Journal of Electronic Publishing: JEP, 14*(1). doi:10.3998/3336451.0014.103

Caro, M. P., Ali, M. S., Vecchio, M., & Giaffreda, R. (2018). *Blockchain-based traceability in Agri-Food supply chain management: A practical implementation. In IoT Vertical and Topical Summit on Agriculture - Tuscany* (pp. 1–4). Tuscany: IOT Tuscany.

Carson, B., Romanelli, G., Walsh, P., & Zhumaev, A. (2018, June). *Blockchain Beyond the Hype: WHat is the Strategic Business Value?* Retrieved from McKinsey Digital: https://www.mckinsey.com/business-functions/mckinsey-digital/our-insights/blockchain-beyond-the-hype-what-is-the-strategic-business-value

Casado-Vara, Prieto, Prieta, & Corchado. (2018). How Blockchain improves the supply chain: case study alimentary supply chain. *Procedia Computer Science, 134,* 393-398. doi:10.1016/j.procs.2018.07.193

Casino, D., Dasaklis, T. K., & Patsakis, C. (2019). A systematic literature review of blockchain-based applications: Current status, classification and open issues. *Telematics and Informatics, 36,* 55–81. doi:10.1016/j.tele.2018.11.006

Catchlove, P. (2017). *Smart contracts: a new era of contract use*. Available at SSRN 3090226.

Cate, F. H., Kuner, C., Lynskey, O., Millard, C., Loideain, N. N., & Svantesson, D. (2018). Blockchain versus data protection. *International Data Privacy Law, 8*(2), 103–104. doi:10.1093/idpl/ipy009

Cavalcante, S. A. (2013). Understanding the impact of technology on firms' business models. Enhanced Profitability, Lower Costs and Stronger Customer Loyalty. *European Journal of Innovation Management, 16*(3), 285–300.

CBINSIGHTS. (2019). Banking Is Only The Beginning: 55 Big Industries Blockchain Could Transform. *CBINSIGHTS*. Retrieved from www.cbinsights.com

CEF Digital. (2019). *The European Blockchain Services Infrastructure is on its way*. https://ec.europa.eu/cefdigital/wiki/display/CEFDIGITAL/2019/09/25/The+European+Blockchain+Services+Infrastructure+is+on+its+way

CEF Digital. (2020a). CEF Building Blocks. *CEF Digital*. https://ec.europa.eu/cefdigital/wiki/display/CEFDIGITAL/Building+Blocks

CEF Digital. (2020b). Success Stories. *CEF Digital*. https://ec.europa.eu/cefdigital/wiki/display/CEFDIGITAL/Success+Stories

Chakraborty, S. (2018). *Introduction to Blockchain – II (History). Blockchain architecture design and use cases*. Retrieved from https://nptel.ac.in/courses/106/105/106105184/

Chandler, S. (2019). *EU Launches International Blockchain Association, Bringing Crypto One Step Closer to Mainstream Adoption*. https://cointelegraph.com/news/eu-launches-international-blockchain-association-bringing-crypto-one-step-closer-to-mainstream-adoption

Chang, Y., Lakovou, E., & Shi, W. (2018). Blockchain in global supply chains and cross border trade: A critical synthesis of the state-of-the-art, challenges and opportunities. *International Journal of Production Research*.

Charles. (2018). *Blockchain and HR: How They Intertwine*. https://hropenstandards.org/wp-content/uploads/2018/04/Charles-St-Louis.pdf

Chase, M. (2007). *Multi-authority Attribute Based Encryption*. Doi:10.1007/978-3-540-70936-7_28

Chaum, D., & van Heyst, E. (1991). Group Signatures. In D. W. Davies (Ed.), Lecture Notes in Computer Science: Vol. 547. *Advances in Cryptology -EUROCRYPT '91. EUROCRYPT 1991*. Berlin: Springer.

Chen, I.-R., Guo, J., & Bao, F. (2014). Trust management for service composition in SOA-based IoT systems. *Proceedings of the IEEE Wireless Communications and Networking Conference (WCNC)*, 3444-3449.

Cheng, R., Zhang, F., Kos, J., He, W., Hynes, N., Johnson, N.M., Juels, A., Miller, A., & Song, D. (2018). *Ekiden: A Platform for Confidentiality-Preserving, Trustworthy, and Performant Smart Contract Execution*. CoRR abs/1804.05141

Chen, Y., Ding, S., Xu, Z., Zheng, H., & Yang, S. (2019). Blockchain-based medical records secure storage and medical service framework. *Journal of Medical Systems, 43*(1), 5. doi:10.100710916-018-1121-4 PMID:30467604

Chethan Kumar, G. N. (2018). *Artificial Intelligence: Definition, Types, Examples, and Technologies*. Retrieved August 31, 2018, from https://medium.com/@chethankumargn/artificial-intelligence-definition-types-examples-technologies-962ea75c7b9b

Chikara, A. (2019). *Introduction to Blockchain Technology*. Retrieved October 8, 2019, from https://www.3pillarglobal.com/insights/introduction-to-Blockchain-technology?unapproved=124382&moderation-hash71e3560ea105cf114152a7d-186sc24c#comment-124382

Choi, J. P. (1994). Network ecternality, compatibility, Choice and Planned Obsolence. *The Journal of Industrial Economics*, *42*(2), 167–182. doi:10.2307/2950488

Chung, C. S. (2015). *The Introduction Of E-Government In Korea : Development Journey, Outcomes And Future.* Retrieved from https://www.cairn.inforevue-gestlon-et-managcment-public-2015-2-page-107.htm

CIOReview Team. (2019). *India Looks To Blockchain For E-Governance.* Retrieved November 4, 2019, from https://www.cioreviewindia.com/news/india-looks-to-Blockchain-for-egovernance-nid-3284-cid-135.html

Çipil, M. (2017). *"Blockchain" sigortacılığı nasıl etkileyecek?* [How will Blockchain affect the insurance?]. Retrieved from https://www.dunya.com/kose-yazisi/Blockchain-sigortaciligi-nasil-etkileyecek/344612

Clack, C. D., Bakshi, V. A., & Braine, L. (2016). Smart contract templates: foundations, design landscape and research directions. *Law, Innovation and Technology*, *9*(2), 269–300.

Clohessy, T., & Acton, T. (2019). Investigating the influence of organizational factors on blockchain adoption: An innovation theory perspective. *Industrial Management & Data Systems*, *119*(7), 1457–1491. doi:10.1108/IMDS-08-2018-0365

CMR. (2019). *The tension between GDPR and the rise of blockchain technologies.* CMS Legal Services.

Cockburn, A. (2000). *Writing Effective Use Cases.* Addison-Wesley.

Coffie, C. P. K., Zhao, H., & Adjei Mensah, I. (2020). Panel Econometric Analysis on Mobile Payment Transactions and Traditional Banks Effort toward Financial Accessibility in Sub-Sahara Africa. *Sustainability*, *12*(3), 895. doi:10.3390u12030895

Coindesk. (2019). *Ghana May Issue Digital Currency in 'Near Future,' says Central Bank Chief.* Retrieved from: https://www.coindesk.com/ghana-may-issue-cbdigital-currency-in-near-future-says-central-bank-chief

Connect, D. G. (2020). *European Countries join Blockchain Partnership.* https://ec.europa.eu/digital-single-market/en/news/european-countries-join-blockchain-partnership

ConsenSys. (2019). *Blockchain: Foundations and Use Cases.* Retrieved from: https://www.coursera.org/learn/blockchain-foundations-and-use-cases

Credit Suisse. (2016). *Blockchain - The Trust Disrupter.* Retrieved from https://www.finextra.com/finextra-downloads/newsdocs/document-1063851711.pdf

Cullell, L. M. (2019). Is e-Estonia Built on Blockchain Technologies? *Hackernoon.com.* Retrieved from www.hackernoon.com/e-estonia-is-not-on-blockchain/

Curran, B. (2019, August). *What Are Non-Fungible Tokens? Unique & Authentic Digital Assets.* Retrieved from: https://blockonomi.com/non-fungible-tokens/

D'Aliessi, M. (2016). *How Does the Blockchain Work? Blockchain Technology Explained in Simple Words.* Retrieved from: https://onezero.medium.com/how-does-the-Blockchain-work-98c8cd01d2ae

Daley, S. (2019). *Tastier Coffee, Hurricane Prediction and Fighting The Opioid Crisis: 31 Ways Blockchain & Ai Make A Powerful Pair.* Retrieved September 24, 2019, from https://builtin.com/artificial-intelligence/Blockchain-ai-examples

Damani, Verma, Harbour, Gross, Nigam, Lalwani, & Daniels. (2018). *Healthcare Ecosystem.* White Paper. Retrieved from: https://www.minthealth.io

David, P. A., & Greenstein, A. (1990). The economics of compatibility standards: An introduction to recent research. *Economics of Innovation and New Technology*, *1*(1-2), 3–41. doi:10.1080/10438599000000002

De Meijer, C. R. W. (2019). *Blockchain: A game-changer for Small and Medium-Sized Enterprises*. Retrieved from: https://www.finextra.com/blogposting/17380/Blockchain-a-game-changer-for-small-and-medium-sized-enterprises

De Vos, H., & Haaker, T. (2018). The STOF Model. In Mobile Service Innovation and Business Models. Springer.

Decker, C., Wattenhofer, R. (2015). A fast and scalable payment network with bitcoin duplex micropayment channels. *Stabilization, Safety, and Security of Distributed Systems, 9212*.

Deloitte Insights. (2018). *Blockchain: A Technical Primer*. Deloitte.

Deloitte. (2018). *Deloitte Blockchain Lab*. Retrieved from https://www2.deloitte.com/ie/en/pages/technology/topics/Blockchain-lab.html

Devan. (2018, October). *How Blockchain Technology is Revolutionizing Data Provenance*. Retrieved from: https://medium.com/blockpool/how-blockchain-technology-is-revolutionizing-data-provenance-e47610019390

Dhillon, V., Metcalf, D., & Hooper, M. (2017). *Blockchain-Enabled Applications: Understand the Blockchain Ecosystem and How to make it Work for You* (Rev. ed.). Gent, Belgium: Academia Press. doi:10.1007/978-1-4842-3081-7

Dickson, B. (2016). *How Blockchain can help fight cyberattacks*. Retrieved from https://techcrunch.com/2016/12/05/how-Blockchain-can-help-fight-cyberattacks/

Dinh, T. N., & Thai, T. (2018, September). AI and Blockchain: A Disruptive Integration. *IEEE Computer Society, 51*(9), 48–53. doi:10.1109/MC.2018.3620971

Dob, D. (2018). *Permissioned vs Permissionless Blockchains: Understanding the Differences*. Retrieved July 17, 2018, from https://blockonomi.com/permissioned-vs-permissionless-Blockchains/

DuPont, J., & Squicciarini, A. C. (2015). Toward De-Anonymizing Bitcoin by Mapping Users Location. CODASPY, 139–141.

El Moutaouakil, S., & Richard, C. (2017). *Blockchain, a catalyst for new approaches in insurance*. PWC.

Emrify Inc. (2018). *Health Passport: a decentralized personal health record platform to deliver trusted health information to the right hands at the right time anywhere in the world*. Retrieved from: https://www.emrify.com/hit/assets/Whitepaper.pdf

Enyi, J., & Le, N. D. Y., (2017). Regulating Initial Coin Offerings ("Crypto-Crowdfunding"). *J. Int'L Banking & Fin. L.*, (8), 495.

Ernst, E., Merola, R., & Samaan, D. (2019). Economics of Artificial Intelligence (AI): Implications for the Future of Work. *IZA Journal of Labor Policy, 9*(4), 1–35.

Esatya. (n.d.). *Whose land Is It Anyway?: land Registry Powered by Blockchain*. Retrieved from: https://esatya.io/news/land-registry-powered-by-blockchain/

Ethereum Revision 7709ece9. (2019). *Solidity language documentation*. Retrieved from https://solidity.readthedocs.io/

Etoro. (2019, January). *What is tokenization and what are the different types of tokens available?* Retrieved from: https://www.etoro.com/blog/market-insights/what-is-tokenization-and-what-are-the-different-types-of-tokens-available/

Eur-lex. (2015). A Digital Single Market Strategy for Europe. *European Commission*. https://eur-lex.europa.eu/legal-content/EN/TXT/?uri=celex%3A52015DC0192

Faber, E., Ballon, P., Bouwman, H., Rietkerk, O., & Steen, M. (2003). Designing business models for Mobile ICT services. *16th Bled Electronic Commerce Conference eTransformation.* http://www.cs.jyu.fi/el/tjtse50_09/TJTSE50_Syllabus_files/Faber%20et%20al%202003.pdf

Fabiano, N., & Fabiano, S. L. (2018). Blockchain and Data Protection: the value of personal data. IMCIC 2018-9th International Multi-Conference on Complexity, Informatics and Cybernetics.

Fairfield, J. A. (2014). Smart contracts, Bitcoin bots, and consumer protection. *Washington and Lee Law Review Online, 71*(2), 36.

Fan, K., Wang, S., Ren, Y., Li, H., & Yang, Y. (2018). Medblock: Efficient and secure medical data sharing via Blockchain. *Journal of Medical Systems, 42*(8), 136. doi:10.100710916-018-0993-7 PMID:29931655

Fatz. (2019). Towards Tax Compliance by Design: A Decentralized Validation of Tax Processes Using Blockchain Technology. *2019 IEEE 21st Conference on Business Informatics (CBI),* 559-568.

Fenwick, M., & Vermeulen, E.P.M. (2018). *Technology and Corporate Governance: Blockchain, Crypto, and Artificial Intelligence.* Retrieved November 7, 2018, from https://papers.ssrn.com/sol3/papers.cfm?abstract_id=3263222

Finck, M. (2018). Blockchains and data protection in the European union. *European Data Prot. L. Rev., 4*(1), 17–35. doi:10.21552/edpl/2018/1/6

Finextra. (2016). *Everledger secures the first bottle of wine on the blockchain.* https://www.finextra.com/pressaritcle/67381/everledger-secures-the-first-bottle-of-wine-on-the-blockchain

Finextra. (2018). African countries open for Blockchain acceptance. *Blogposting.* Retrieved from https://www.finextra.com/blogposting/15656/african-countries-open-for-Blockchainacceptance

Francisco, J. (2018). *Blockchain land registry to help resolve ownership problems.* Retrieved from: https://businessBlockchainhq.com/business-Blockchain-news/Blockchain-land-registry-to-help-resolve-ownership-problems/

Frankowski, Barańsk, & Bronowska. (2017, Dec.). *Blockchain technology and its potential in taxes.* Deloitte.

Frantz, C. K., & Nowostawski, M. (2016, September). From institutions to code: Towards automated generation of smart contracts. In *2016 IEEE 1st International Workshops on Foundations and Applications of Self* Systems (FAS* W)* (pp. 210-215). IEEE.

Furlong, J. (2017). *What is Blockchain Technology?* Retrieved from: https://www.businessnewsdaily.com/10390-what-is-Blockchain-technology.html

Fuslier, G. D. (1988). Hostage negotiation consultant: Emerging role for the clinical psychologist. Professional Psychology: Research and Practice, 19, 175-179.

Garg, S., Gentry, C., Halevi, S., Sahai, A., & Waters, W. (2013). *Attribute-Based Encryption for Circuits from Multilinear Maps.* Academic Press.

Ge, L., Brewster, C., Spek, J., Smeenk, A., Top, J.L., Diepen, F.V., Klaase, B., Graumans, C., & Wildt, M.D. (2017). *Blockchain for agriculture and food: Findings from the pilot study.* Academic Press.

Gentry, C. (2009). Fully Homomorphic Encryption Using Ideal Lattices. STOC, 169–178.

GhanaPosts. (2018). *My Digital Address.* Retrieved November 30, 2019, from www.ghanapostgps.com

Ghosal, M. (2019). *What Is AI - Weak AI and Strong AI with examples.* Retrieved July 26, 2019, from https://spotle.ai/feeddetails/What-Is-AI-Weak-AI-Strong-AI-with-examples-Key-disciplines-and-applications-Of-AI-/3173

Glisic, S., & Makela, J. (2006). Advanced Wireless Networks: 4G Technologies. *2006 IEEE Ninth International Symposium on Spread Spectrum Techniques and Applications, Manaus-Amazon,* 442-446. 10.1109/ISSSTA.2006.311811

Goertzel, B. (2017). *SingularityNET: A decentralized, open market and inter-network for AIs. Thoughts, Theories & Studies on Artificial Intelligence (AI).* Research.

Gogan, M. (2018, August 17). *Blockchain Technology in the Future: 7 Predictions for 2020.* Retrieved November 29, 2019, from AiThority: https://www.aithority.com/guest-authors/blockchain-technology-in-the-future-7-predictions-for-2020/

Goldreich, O., Micali, S., & Wigderson, A. (1987). How to Play any Mental Game or A Completeness Theorem for Protocols with Honest Majority. *STOC,* 218–229.

Goldwasser, S., Micali, S., & Rackoff, C. (1985). The Knowledge Complexity of Interactive Proof-systems. *STOC,* 291–304.

Gonfalonieri, A. (2018). *Blockchain + AI: Towards Mode Decentralization & Less Data Oligopoly.* Retrieved July 16, 2018, from https://medium.com/predict/Blockchain-ai-towards-more-decentralization-less-data-oligopoly-e0a2b2781082

Goodhue, D. L., & Thompson, R. L. (1995). Task-Technology Fit and Individual Performance. *Management Information Systems Quarterly, 19*(2), 213–236. doi:10.2307/249689

Gorbunov, S., Vaikuntanathan, V., & Wee, H. (2013). Attribute-based Encryption for Circuits. *Proceedings of the Forty-fifth Annual ACM Symposium on Theory of Computing In STOC,* 545–554.

Government I. T. Initiatives. (2019). Retrieved November 4, 2019, from https://www.gsa.gov/technology/government-it-initiatives

Grech, A., & Camilleri, A. F. (2017). Blockchain in Education. In A. Inamorato dos Santos (Eds.), JRC Science for Policy Report. European Union (EU).

Grut, O. W. (2016). *WEF: Blockchain will become the 'beating heart' of finance.* Retrieved from http://uk.businessinsider.com/world-economic-forum-potential-of-Blockchain-in-financial-services-2016-8

Gubbi, J., Buyya, R., Marusic, S., & Palaniswami, M. (2013). Internet of Things (IoT): A vision, architectural elements, and future directions. *Future Generation Computer Systems, 29*(7), 1645–1660. doi:10.1016/j.future.2013.01.010

Gupta, N. (2018). *Permissionless Blockchain vs Permissioned Blockchain – What's Your Pick.* Retrieved September 14, 2018, from https://akeo.tech/blog/Blockchain-and-dlt/permissionless-permissioned-Blockchain

Gupta, S., & Sadoghi, M. (2018). Blockchain Transaction Processing. Springer International Publishing AG. *Part of Springer Nature, 2018.* doi:10.1007/978-3-319-63962-8_333-1

Haber, S., & Stornetta, W. S. (1991). How to time-stamp a digital document. *Journal of Cryptology, 3*(2), 99–111. doi:10.1007/BF00196791

Hackernoon. (2019, July). *Blockchain Technology Explained: Introduction, Meaning, and Applications.* Retrieved from: https://hackernoon.com/blockchain-technology-explained-introduction-meaning-and-applications-edbd6759a2b2

Hackius, N., & Petersen, M. (2017). Blockchain in Logistics and Supply Chain: Trick or Treat? *Hamburg International Conference of Logistics.*

Hassan, F., Ali, A., Latif, S., Qadir, J., Kanhere, S., Singh, J., & Crowcroft, J. (2019). *Blockchain and the Future of the Internet: A Comprehensive Review.* https://arxiv.org/pdf/1904.00733.pdf

Hearn, M. (2011). Smart property. *Bitcoin Wiki, 5.* https://en.bitcoin.it/wiki/Smart_Property

Hills, J. (1989). Universal Service LIberalization and Privatization of telecommunications. *Telecommunications Policy*, *3*(1), 129–144. doi:10.1016/0308-5961(89)90038-4

Hintze, A. (2019). *Understanding the four types of Artificial Intelligence*. Retrieved November 14, 2018, from https://www.govtech.com/computing/Understanding-the-Four-Types-of-Artificial-Intelligence.html

Hogan, R. T. (1969). Development of an empathy scale. *Journal of Consulting Psychology*, *33*(3), 307–316. doi:10.1037/h0027580 PMID:4389335

Holden, R., & Malani, A. (2017). Can Blockchain Solve the Holdup Problem in Contracts? *Biz Journal*. https://www.bizjournals.com/bizjournals/howto/technology/2017/09/businessadvantages-of-Blockchain-smart-contracts.html

Holden, R. T., & Malani, A. (2019). *Can Blockchain Solve the Hold-up Problem in Contracts? (No. w25833)*. National Bureau of Economic Research. doi:10.3386/w25833

Hudson, S., & Sloan, B. (2019). *Death, Lies, and Land Registration*. Hart Publishing. doi:10.5040/9781509921409.ch-016

Hulseapple, C. (2015). *Block Verify uses blockchains to end counterfeiting and making world more honest*. https://cointelegraph.com/news/block-verify-uses-blockchains-to-end-counterfeiting-and-make-world-more-honest

Hunter, J. (2001). MetaNet A Metadata Term Thesaurus to Enable Semantic Interoperability Between meta data Domains. *Journal of Digital Information*, *1*(8), 1–13.

Iansiti, M., & Lakhani, K. R. (2017, February). The Truh About Blockchain. *Harvard Business Review (HBR)*. Retrieved from https://hbr.org/2017/01/the-truth-about-blockchain

Iftemi, A. (2018). *Exploring the different types of Blockchain*. Retrieved July 9, 2018, from https://blog.modex.tech/exploring-the-different-types-of-Blockchain-10395da93a51

Ikeda, K. (2018). Security and Privacy of Blockchain and Quantum Computation. *Blockchain Technology: Platforms, Tools and Use Cases*, 199–228. doi:10.1016/bs.adcom.2018.03.003

INATBA. (2020). *International Association for Trusted Blockchain Applications*. https://inatba.org/organization/

Inera, A. (2017). *Bosch, Cisco, BNY Mellon, other launch new blockchain consortium*. https://www.reuters.com/article/us-blockchain-iot-idUSKBN15B2D7

Insights, L. (2019, October). *Iota Launches Decentralized Industry Marketplace Miranda Wood*. Retrieved from https://www.ledgerinsights.com/iota-decentralized-industry-marketplace/

Iryo. (2017). *Global participatory healthcare ecosystem - Whitepaper*. Retrieved from: https://iryo.io/iryo_whitepaper.pdf

ISA². (2016). Improving semantic interoperability in European eGovernment systems. *ISA² - Interoperability solutions for public administrations, businesses and citizens*. https://ec.europa.eu/isa2/actions/improving-semantic-interoperability-european-egovernment-systems_en

i-Scoop. (2017). *Blockchain smart port case: efficient and secure container release in the port of Antwerp*. https://www.i-scoop.eu/blockchain-smart-port-project-case-container-release-port-antwerp/

Ivan, D. (2016, August). Moving toward a Blockchain-based method for the secure storage of patient records. In *ONC/NIST Use of Blockchain for Healthcare and Research Workshop*. Gaithersburg, MD: ONC/NIST.

Jacobovitz, O. (2016). *Blockchain for identity management. Technical Report*. Beer Sheva, Israel: The Lynne and William Frankel Center for Computer Science Department of Computer Science, Ben-Gurion University.

Jang, K., Han, M., Cho, S., Ryu, H., Lee, J., Lee, Y., & Moon, S. B. (2009). 3G and 3.5G wireless network performance measured from moving cars and high-speed trains. In *MICNET '09: Proceedings of the 1st ACM workshop on Mobile internet through cellular networks September 2009.* ACM. 10.1145/1614255.1614261

Jbklutse.com. (2018). *Bank of Ghana Promises Policy Support for Blockchain Innovations.* Retrieved from: https://www.jbklutse.com/bank-of-ghana-promises-policy-support-for-Blockchain-innovations/

Jones, M., Johnson, M., Shervey, M., Dudley, J. T., & Zimmerman, N. (2019, August). Privacy-Preserving Methods for Feature Engineering Using Blockchain: Review, Evaluation and Proof of Concept. *Journal of Medical Internet Research, 21*(8), e13600. doi:10.2196/13600 PMID:31414666

Joshi, A. P., Han, M., & Wang, Y. (2018). A survey on security and privacy issues of Blockchain technology. American Institute of Mathematical Sciences, Kennesaw State University. doi:10.3934/mfc.2018007

Joshi, A., & Ayee, J. (2002). Taxing for the State? Politics, Revenue and the Informal Sector in Ghana. *IDS Bulletin, 33*(3), 1–9. doi:10.1111/j.1759-5436.2002.tb00030.x

Joy Online. (2018). *Computer Scientist Urges Ghana to Embrace Blockchain Technology.* Retrieved from: https://my-joyonline.com/business/2018/september-18th/computer-scientist-urges-ghana-to-embrace-Blockchain-technology.php

Jung, T., Li, X. Y., Wan, Z., & Wan, M. (2013). Privacy preserving cloud data access with multi-authorities. INFOCOM, 2625–2633.

Jurgen, G. (2018). *Introducing Blockchain Technology to the world of Tax.* Retrieved from https://medium.com/@jurgeng/an-introduction-to-Blockchain-technology-tax-567e536767ec

Kadiyala, A. (2018). *Nuances between Permissionless and Permissioned Blockchains.* Retrieved February 18, 2018, from https://medium.com/@akadiyala/nuances-between-permissionless-and-permissioned-Blockchains-f5b566f5d483

Kalodner, H., Goldfeder, S., Chen, X., Weinberg, S. M., & Felten, E. W. (2018). Arbitrum: Scalable, private smart contracts. USENIX Security, 1353–1370.

Kamilaris, A., Fonts, A., & Prenafeta-Boldú, F. X. (2019). The rise of Blockchain technology in agriculture and food supply chain. Trends *Food Science & Technology, 91*, 640-652. doi:10.1016/j.tifs.2019.07.034

Kaushik, M., Gola, K. K., Khan, G., & Rathore, R. (2016). Detection of Sybil Attacks in Structured P2P Overlay Network. *International Journal of Computers and Applications, 975*, 8887.

Keskin, H., Senturk, C., Sngur, O., & Kiris, H. M. (2010). *The Importance of SMEs Developing Economies, 2nd International Symposium on Sustainable Development.* Retrieved from: https://utica.libguides.com/c.php?g=291672&p=1943019

Kim, N. (2016, July). IBM pushes blockchain into the supply chain. *Wall Street Journal.*

Kim, H. M., & Laskowski, M. (2018). Agriculture on the Blockchain: Sustainable Solutions for Food, Farmers, and Financing (December 17, 2017). In D. Tapscott (Ed.), *Supply Chain Revolution.* Barrow Books.

Kim, H., Song, H., Lee, S., Kim, H., & Song, I. (2016, July). A simple approach to share users' own healthcare data with a mobile phone. In *2016 Eighth International Conference on Ubiquitous and Future Networks (ICUFN)* (pp. 453-455). IEEE.

King, R. (2019, July). *Ethereum vs Bitcoin: Is Ethereum a Better Bitcoin Alternative?* Retrieved from: https://www.bitdegree.org/tutorials/ethereum-vs-bitcoin/

Knezevic, D. (2018). Impact of Blockchain Technology Platform in Changing the Financial Sector and Other Industries. *Montenegrin Journal of Economics. 14*(1), 109-120.

Köpman, H. (2019). *European Union Leadership in Blockchain*. WTO. https://www.wto.org/english/res_e/reser_e/00_b_helen_kopman_global_trade_and_blockchain.pdf

Kosba, A., Miller, A., Shi, E., Wen, Z., & Papamanthou, C. (2016). *Hawk: The Blockchain Model of Cryptography and Privacy-Preserving Smart Contracts*. Paper presented at 2016 IEEE Symposium on Security and Privacy (SP). 10.1109/SP.2016.55

Kot, I. (2018). Lack of Standards in Blockchain Technology: What to Do? *I transition*. https://www.itransition.com/blog/lack-of-standards-in-blockchain-technology-what-to-do

Kovach, A., & Ronai, G. (2018). *MyMEDIS: a new medical data storage and access system*. Academic Press.

KPMG. (2017). *Sigortacılık, Teknolojiyle Yeniden Doğdu* [Rebirth of Insurance with Technology]. Retrieved from https://home.kpmg.com/tr/tr/home/media/press-releases/2017/07/sigortacilik-teknolojiyle-yeniden-dogdu.html

Kuczwara, D. (2017). *3 Ways Blockchain Can Help Businesses Today*. Retrieved from: https://www.businessnewsdaily.com/10407-Blockchain-changing-small-business.html

Kumar, A. (2018). *Is Blockchain a Linked List like Data Structure?* Retrieved from https://vitalflux.com/Blockchain-linked-list-like-data-structure

Larimer, D. (2016). *Blok zinciri ve Sigorta* [Blockchain and Insurance]. Retrieved from https://www.blokzinciri.org/yazi/blok-zinciri-vesigorta/

Lastovetska, A. (2019). *Blockchain Architecture Basics: Components, Structure, Benefits & Creation*. Retrieved January 31, 2019, from https://mlsdev.com/blog/156-how-to-build-your-own-Blockchain-architecture

Lemieux, V. L. (2017, December). A typology of Blockchain recordkeeping solutions and some reflections on their implications for the future of archival preservation. In *2017 IEEE International Conference on Big Data (Big Data)* (pp. 2271-2278). IEEE. 10.1109/BigData.2017.8258180

Leng, K., Bi, Y., Jing, L., & Fu, H.-C. (2018). Research on agricultural supply chain system with double chain architecture based on Blockchain technology. *Future Generation Computer Systems*, *86*, 641-649. doi:10.1016/j.future.2018.04.061

Lewko, A., & Waters, B. (2011). Decentralizing Attribute-based Encryption. EUROCRYPT, 568–588.

Liang, X., Zhao, J., Shetty, S., Liu, J., & Li, D. (2017, October). Integrating Blockchain for data sharing and collaboration in mobile healthcare applications. In *2017 IEEE 28th Annual International Symposium on Personal, Indoor, and Mobile Radio Communications (PIMRC)* (pp. 1-5). IEEE. 10.1109/PIMRC.2017.8292361

Lima, C. (2018). Developing Open and Interoperable DLTVBlockchain Standards [Standards]. *Computer*, *51*(11), 106–111. doi:10.1109/MC.2018.2876184

Lin, Y.-P., Petway, J. R., Anthony, J., Mukhtar, H., Liao, S.-W., Chou, C.-F., & Ho, Y.-F. (2017). Blockchain: The Evolutionary Next Step for ICT E-. *Agriculture. Environments*, *4*, 50.

Lisk. (n.d.). *What is Decentralization?* Retrieved from: https://lisk.io/academy/blockchain-basics/benefits-of-blockchain/what-is-decentralization

Li, X., Jiang, P., Chen, T., Luo, X., & Wen, Q. (2017). A survey on the security of Blockchain systems. *Future Generation Computer Systems*. doi:10.1016/j.future.2017.08.020

Lu, Z. (2019). Bis: A Novel Blockchain based Bank-tax Interaction System in Smart City. *2019 IEEE Intl Conf on Dependable, Autonomic and Secure Computing, Intl Conf on Pervasive Intelligence and Computing, Intl Conf on Cloud and Big Data Computing, Intl Conf on Cyber Science and Technology Congress*, 1008-1014. 10.1109/DASC/PiCom/CBDCom/CyberSciTech.2019.00183

Mahjabin, T., Xiao, Y., Sun, G., & Jiang, W. (2017). A survey of distributed denial-of-service attack, prevention, and mitigation techniques. *International Journal of Distributed Sensor Networks*, *13*(12), 155014771774146. doi:10.1177/1550147717741463

Makridakis, S., Polemitis, A., Giaglis, G., & Louca, S. (2018). Blockchain: The Next Breakthrough in the Rapid Progress of AI. *Robotics & Automation Engineering Journal*, *2*(4), 1-12.

Markunas, J. D. (2019, July). *The Impact of Blockchain Technology on the Surveying Industry, Cadastre and Land Registry Systems*. Retrieved from: https://landportal.org/fr/blog-post/2019/08/impact-blockchain-technology-surveying-industry-cadastre-and-land-registry-systems

Marr, B. (2018). *Artificial Intelligence and Blockchain: 3 Major Benefits of Combining These Two Mega-Trends*. Retrieved March 2, 2018, from https://www.forbes.com/sites/bernardmarr/2018/03/02/artificial-intelligence-and-Blockchain-3-major-benefits-of-combining-these-two-mega-trends/#3ce781f64b44

Marwala, T., & Xing, B. (2018). *Blockchain and Aritificial Intelligence*. University of Johannesburg. Auckland Park. Republic of South Africa. https://arxiv.org/pdf/1802.04451

Maxwell, G. (2013). *CoinJoin: Bitcoin privacy for the real world*. bitcointalk.org

McCarthy, J. D., & Zaid, M. N. (1977). Resource Mobilization and Social Movements: A partial Theory. *American Journal of Sociology*, *82*(6), 1212–1241. doi:10.1086/226464

McFarlane, C., Beer, M., Brown, J., & Prendergast, N. (2017). *Patientory: A Healthcare Peer-to-Peer EMR Storage Network v1*. Addison, TX: Entrust Inc.

McGhin, T., Choo, K. R., Liu, C. Z., & He, D. (2019). Blockchain in healthcare applications: Research challenges and opportunities. *Journal of Network and Computer Applications*, *135*(1), 62–75. doi:10.1016/j.jnca.2019.02.027

McGuinness, D. (2006). *Early reading instruction: What science really tells us about how to teach reading*. MIT Press.

McKinsey. (2017). *Blockchain Technology in the Insurance Sector*. McKinsey & Company. https://www.treasury.gov/initiatives/fio/Documents/McKinsey_FACI_Blockchain_in_Insurance.pdf

Mead, G. H. (1993). *Mind, self, and society*. Chicago: University of Chicago Press.

Mearian, L. (2019). Maersk adds two big shipping firms to its blockchain ledger. *Computerworld*, *29*(May). https://www.computerworld.com/article/3398923/maersk-adds-two-big-shipping-firms-to-its-blockchain-ledger.html

Meng, W., Tischhauser, E. W., Wang, Q., Wang, Y., & Han, J. (2018). When Intrusion Detection Meets Blockchain Technology: A Review. *IEEE Access: Practical Innovations, Open Solutions*, *6*, 10179–10188. doi:10.1109/ACCESS.2018.2799854

Mik, E. (2017). Smart contracts: Terminology, technical limitations and real world complexity. *Law, Innovation and Technology*, *9*(2), 269–300. doi:10.1080/17579961.2017.1378468

Mingxiao, D., Xiaofeng, M., Zhe, Z., Xiangwei, W., & Qijun, C. (2017). A review on consensus algorithm of blockchain. *2017 IEEE International Conference on Systems, Man, and Cybernetics (SMC)*, 2567 - 2572. 10.1109/SMC.2017.8123011

Ministry of Electronics and Information Technology. (2019). *Government of India | Home Page*. Retrieved November 4, 2019, from https://meity.gov.in/

Mohammed & Guennoun. (2010). Wireless Mobile Evolution to 4G Network. *Wireless Sensor Network, 2010*(2), 309-317.

Momo, Schiavi, Bchr, & Lucena. (2019). Business Models and Blockchain: What Can Change? *Revista de Administração Contemporânea, 23*(2).

Moniz, H., Neves, N. F., Correia, M., & Verissimo, P. (2006). Experimental Comparison of Local and Shared Coin Randomized Consensus Protocols. SRDS, 235-244.

Moon, M. J. (2002). The Evolution of E-Government among Municipalities: Rhetoric or Reality? *Public Administration Review, 62*(4), 424–433. doi:10.1111/0033-3352.00196

Moreno, J., Serrano, M. A., Fernandez, E. B., & Fernandez-Medina, E. (2020). Improving Incident Response in Big Data Ecosystems by Using Blockchain Technologies. *Applied Sciences (Basel, Switzerland), 10*(2), 724. doi:10.3390/app10020724

Morini, M. (2016). From 'Blockchain hype' to a real business case for financial markets. *Journal of Financial Transformation, 45*, 30–40. doi:10.2139srn.2760184

Morini, M. (2017). From "Blockchain Hype" to a Real Business Case for Financial Markets. *The CAPCO Institute Journal of Financial Transformation, 45*, 30–40.

Morisse, M. (2015). Cryptocurrencies and bitcoin: charting the researchlandscape. *21st Americas conference on information systems.*

Morris, N. (2018). ISO blockchain standards. *Ledger Insights.* https://www.ledgerinsights.com/iso-blockchain-standards/

Nakamoto, S. (2008). *Bitcoin: A Peer to Peer Electronic Cash System.* Retrieved from https://bitcoin.org/bitcoin.pdf

Nakamoto, S. (2008). *Bitcoin: A Peer-to-Peer Electronic Cash System.* bitcoin.org. Retrieved from www.bitcoin.org/bitcoin.pdf

Nakamoto, S. (2008). *Bitcoin: A Peer-to-Peer Electronic Cash System.* www.Bitcoin.org

Nakamoto, S. (n.d.). *Bitcoin: A peer-to-peer electronic cash system.* https://bitcoin.org/bitcoin.pdf

Nakamoto. (2008). *Bitcoin: A peer-to-peer electronic cash system.* Academic Press.

Namahe. (2018). *How to Actually Combine AI and Blockchain in One Platform.* Retrieved July 7, 2018, from https://hackernoon.com/how-to-actually-combine-ai-and-Blockchain-in-one-platform-ef937e919ec2

Neisse, R., Steri, G., & Nai-Fovino, I. (2017). A Blockchain-based approach for data accountability and provenance tracking. In *Proceedings of the 12th International Conference on Availability, Reliability and Security* (p. 14). ACM. 10.1145/3098954.3098958

Nesbitt, A. (2019). *Blockchain Technology & Artificial Intelligence — Unmasking the Mystery at the Heart of AI.* Retrieved January 20, 2019, from https://medium.com/datadriveninvestor/Blockchain-technology-artificial-intelligence-unmasking-the-mystery-at-the-heart-of-ai-b1e930a59937

NewGenApps. (2018). *8 Experts on the Future of Blockchain Technology and Applications.* Retrieved from www.newgenapps.com/blog/future-of-blockchain-technology-applications

NewsLogical. (2019). *Vodafone Initiates Blockchain Program in Ghana Institutions.* Retrieved from: https://newslogical.com/Blockchain-adoption-ghana/

O'Neal, S. (2019, June). *Tokenization Explained*. Retrieved from: https://cointelegraph.com/explained/tokenization-explained

Oliver, R. L. (1980). A Cognitive Model of the Antecedents and Consequences of Satisfaction Decisions. *JMR, Journal of Marketing Research*, *17*(4), 460–469. doi:10.1177/002224378001700405

Ølnes, S., & Jansen, A. (2017). Blockchain Technology as s Support Infrastructure in e-Government. *Lecture Notes in Computer Science*, *10428*, 215–227. doi:10.1007/978-3-319-64677-0_18

Oluwatoyin, K. K. (2015). Comparative Analysis of GSM and CDMA, Strength and Weakness, Future Challenges and Practical Solutions (A Case Study of MTN and NITEL Nigeria). *Journal of Information Engineering and Applications*, *5*(5), 74–88.

Oprunenco, A., & Akmeemana, C. (2018, April 13). Using Blockchain to Make Land Registry More Reliable in India. In *Information & Technology: Sustainable Development Goals*. United Nations Development Programme (UNDP). Retrieved November 30, 2019, from https://blogs.lse.ac.uk/businessreview/2018/04/13/using-blockchain-to-make-land-registry-more-reliable-in-india/

Osato, A. N. (2019, September 15). Africa using Blockchain to drive Change. *Cointelegragh*.

Oxcert. (2018, April). *Fungible vs non-fungible tokens on the blockchain*. Retrieved from: https://medium.com/0xcert/fungible-vs-non-fungible-tokens-on-the-blockchain-ab4b12e0181a

Oxford Business Group. (2019). *Blockchain Technology Provides Multiple Opportunities for The Developing World*. Retrieved from: https://oxfordbusinessgroup.com/overview/building-blocks-Blockchain-technology-has-applications-could-revolutionise-trade-and-4

Paillier, P. (1999). Public-key Cryptosystems Based on Composite Degree Residuosity Classes. EUROCRYPT, 223-238.

Pal, K. (2019). Algorithmic Solutions for RFID Tag Anti-Collision Problem in Supply Chain Management. *Procedia Computer Science*, 929-934.

Pal, K. (2017). Supply Chain Coordination Based on Web Services. In H. K. Chan, N. Subramanian, & M. D. Abdulrahman (Eds.), *Supply Chain Management in the Big Data Era* (pp. 137–171). Hershey, PA: IGI Global Publication. doi:10.4018/978-1-5225-0956-1.ch009

Pal, K. (2020). Internet of Things and Blockchain Technology in Apparel Supply Chain Management. In H. Patel & G. S. Thakur (Eds.), *Blockchain Applications in IoT Security*. Hershey, PA: IGI Global Publication.

Papa, S.F. (2017). *Use of Blockchain Technology in Agribusiness: Transparency and Monitoring in Agricultural Trade*. Academic Press.

Patel, A. (2018). *How Blockchain and artificial intelligence complement each other*. Retrieved November 21, 2018, from https://jaxenter.com/Blockchain-artificial-intelligence-152001.html

Paul. (2019). *Everything you need to know about Blockchain architecture*. Retrieved May 22, 2019, from https://www.edureka.co/blog/Blockchain-architecture/

Pawczuk, L., Massey, R., & Schatsky, D. (2018). *Breaking blockchain open Deloitte's 2018 Global Blockchain Survey*. Deloitte. https://www2.deloitte.com/content/dam/Deloitte/us/Documents/financial-services/us-fsi-2018-global-blockchain-survey-report.pdf

Peiró, N. N., & Martinez García, E. J. (2017). Blockchain and Land Registration Systems. *European Property Law Journal*, *6*(3). doi:10.1515/eplj-2017-0017

Pelkmans, J. (2001). The GSM standard: Explaining a success story. *Journal of European Public Policy, 8*(3), 432–453. doi:10.1080/13501760110056059

Perera, Nanayakkara, Rodrigo, & Senaratne. (2020). Blockchain technology: Is it hype or real in the construction industry? *Journal of Industrial Information Integration, 17*.

Perez. (2019). *Blockchain and AI could be a perfect match – here's why.* Retrieved February 5, 2019, from https://thenextweb.com/hardfork/2019/02/05/Blockchain-and-ai-could-be-a-perfect-match-heres-why/

Peterson, K., Deeduvanu, R., Kanjamala, P., & Boles, K. (2016, September). A Blockchain-based approach to health information exchange networks. In *Proc. NIST Workshop Blockchain Healthcare* (*Vol. 1*, pp. 1-10). Academic Press.

Phan, L., Li, S., & Mentzer, K. (2019). *Blockchain Technology and The Current Discussion on Fraud.* Academic Press.

Pilkington, M. (2015). *Blockchain Technology: Principles and Applications.* Research Handbook on Digital Transformations. doi:10.4337/9781784717766.00019

Ping, W. (2011, Apr.). A Brief History of Standards and Standardization Organizations: A Chinese Perspective. *East-West Center Working Papers - Economic Series*, 1-25.

Pisa, M., & Juden, M. (2017). *Blockchain and Economic Development: Hype vs. Reality.* Center for Global Development. Retrieved from www.cgdev.org

Pokrovskaia, N. N. (2017). Tax, Financial and Social Regulatory Mechanisms within the Knowledge-Driven Economy. Blockchain Algorithms and Fog Computing for the Efficient Regulation. *2017 XX IEEE International Conference on Soft Computing and Measurements (SCM).* 10.1109/SCM.2017.7970698

Porat, A., Pratap, A., Shah, P., & Adkar, V. (2017). *Blockchain Consensus: An analysis of Proof-of-Work and its applications.* https://www.scs.stanford.edu/17au-cs244b/labs/projects/porat_pratap_shah_adkar.pdf

Porter, M. (1990). The Competitive Advantage of Nations. *Harvard Business Review.* https://hbr.org/1990/03/the-competitive-advantage-of-nations

Postchain - the first consortium database. (2018) Retrieved from: https://chromaway.com/products/postchain/

Prahalad, C. K., & Mashelkar, R. A. (2010). Innovation's Holy Grail. *Harvard Business Review, July-August Issue, 88*(7/8), 132–141.

Prasad, S., Shankar, R., Gupta, R., & Roy, S. (2018). A TISM modeling of critical success factors of blockchain based cloud services. *Journal of Advances in Management Research, 15*(4), 434–456. doi:10.1108/JAMR-03-2018-0027

PricewaterhouseCoopers LLP. (2016). *How Blockchain Technology Could Improve the Tax System.* PwC.

PWC. (2018). *PWC'S Global Blockchain Survey.* PriceWaterhouseCoopers. https://www.pwccn.com/en/research-and-insights/publications/global-blockchain-survey-2018/global-blockchain-survey-2018-report.pdf

Ramsay, S. (2018). *The General Data Protection Regulation vs. The Blockchain: A legal study on the compatibility between Blockchain technology and the GDPR.* Academic Press.

Reecer, D. (2018). Wanchain 3.0 Launches Bitcoin Bridge to Ethereum — Continues Rapid Progression in Blockchain Interoperability Mission. *Medium.* https://medium.com/wanchain-foundation/wanchain-3-0-launch-bitcoin-ethereum-erc20-7cd504f25c0c

Reik, T. (1949). *Listening with the third ear: The inner experience of the psychoanalyst.* New York: Grove.

Rejeb, A. (2018). Blockchain Potential in Tilapia Supply Chain. *Acta Technica Jaurinensis, 11*(2), 104–118. doi:10.14513/actatechjaur.v11.n2.462

Rijmenam, M. V. (2019). *The Organisation of Tomorrow: How AI, blockchain and analytics turn your business into a data organisation*. Routledge. doi:10.4324/9780429279973

Rimba, P., Tran, A. B., Weber, I., Staples, M., Ponomarev, A., & Xu, X. (2017). Comparing Blockchain and Cloud Services forBusiness Process Execution. In *Conference: ICSA'17: IEEE International Conference on Software Architecture*. IEEE.

Riseley, W. J. (2016). *Blockchain-A link to future law reform: Factors for a regulatory framework response to disruptive technologies*. Academic Press.

Rivest, R. L., Shamir, A., & Adleman, L. (1978). A Method for Obtaining Digital Signatures and Public-key Cryptosystems. *Commun. ACM, 21*(2), 120-126.

Rivest, R. L., Shamir, A., & Kalai, Y. T. (2001). *How to Leak a Secret*. ASIACRYPT. doi:10.1007/3-540-45682-1_32

Robinson, J., & Kish, L. (2016). *Youbase White Paper*. Retrieved from: https://www.youbase.io/

Roehrs, A., da Costa, C. A., & da Rosa Righi, R. (2017). OmniPHR: A distributed architecture model to integrate personal health records. *Journal of Biomedical Informatics, 71*, 70–81. doi:10.1016/j.jbi.2017.05.012 PMID:28545835

Rohitha, E. P. (2018). *An Introduction to Blockchain Technology*. Retrieved July 5, 2018, from https://dzone.com/articles/an-introduction-to-Blockchain-technology

Ruta, M., Scioscia, F., Leva, S., Capursola, G., & Sciascio, D. (2017). Supply Chain Object Discovery with Semantic-Enhanced Blockchain. In *15th ACM Conference on Embedded Networked Sensor Systems*. Delft, The Netherlands: ACM. 10.1145/3131672.3136974

Sahai, A., & Waters, B. (2004). *Fuzzy Identity-Based Encryption*. Doi:10.1007/11426639_27

Salah, K., Rehman, M.H., Nizamudddin, N., & Al-Fuquaha, A. (2019). Blockchain for AI: Review and Open Research Challenges. *IEEE Access, 7*, 10127-10149. doi:10.1109/ACCESS.2018.2890507

Salman, S. (2019). *Why Artificial Intelligence Needs to breath on Blockchain?* Retrieved Mar 14, 2019, from https://towardsdatascience.com/why-artificial-intelligence-needs-to-breath-on-Blockchain-354d7b7027c6

Santhana, P. (2019). *Risks posed by Blockchain-based business models*. Retrieved from https://www2.deloitte.com/us/en/pages/risk/articles/Blockchain-security-risks.html

Savelyev, A. (2017). Contract law 2.0: "Smart" contracts as the beginning of the end of classic contract law'. *Information & Communications Technology Law, 26*(2), 116–134. doi:10.1080/13600834.2017.1301036

Schneider, J., Blostein, A., Lee, B., Kent, S., Groer, I., & Beardsley, E. (2016). *Blockchain: putting theory into practice*. Profiles in Innovation Report.

Schroer, A. (2019). *Artificial Intelligence. What is Artificial Intelligence? How Does AI Work?* Retrieved August, 29, 2019, from https://builtin.com/artificial-intelligence

Shaikh, Z. A., & Lashari, I. A. (2017). Blockchain technology, the new Internet. *International Journal of Management Science and Business Research, 6*(4), 167–177.

Sharma, T. K. (2019). Top 10 blockchain platforms you need to know about. *Block Chain Council*. https://www.blockchain-council.org/blockchain/top-10-blockchain-platforms-you-need-to-know-about/

Shrouf, Mere, & Miragliotta. (2014). Smart factories in Industry 4.0: A review of the concept and of energy management approached in production based on the Internet of Things paradigm. *Proceedings of the IEEE International Conference on Industrial Engineering and Engineering Management*, 679-701.

Shuhada, N. (2019, July 24). *What is Blockchain?* Retrieved from Techcryption: www.techcryption.com/2019/07/24/what-is-a-blockchain/

Sirer, E. G. (2016). *Bitcoin Guarantees Strong, not Eventual, Consistency.* Retrieved from http://hackingdistributed. com/2016/03/01/bitcoin-guarantees-strong-not-eventual-consistency/

Small And Medium Enterprises (SMEs) Finance, Improving SMEs Access to Finance and Finding Innovative Solutions to Unlock Sources of Capital. (n.d.). Retrieved from: https://www.worldbank.org/en/topic/smefinance

Smith, G. (2009). Interaction of Public and Private Standards in the Food Chain. OECD Food, Agriculture and Fisheries Papers. OECD Publishing.

Social Rush. (2018). *Tracking food supply with blockchain.* https://thesocialrush.com/tracking-food-supply-with-blockchain/

Speiser, M., Mulherin, G., King, K., & Clark, S. (2017). *Artificial Intelligence and Blockchain.* Available: https://nacm. org/pdfs/gscfm/Artificial_Intelligence-Blockchain.pdf

Spielman, A. (2016). *Blockchain: digitally rebuilding the real estate industry* (Doctoral dissertation). Massachusetts Institute of Technology.

Stastista. (2019). *Blockchain adoption phases in organizations worldwide as of April 2018, by industry.* https://www. statista.com/statistics/878748/worldwide-production-phase-blockchain-technology-industry/

Steem. (2017). *An incentivized, Blockchain-based, public content platform.* Retrieved from https://steem.com/Steem-WhitePaper.pdf

Stefanović, M., Pržulj, D., Ristic, S., & Stefanović, D. (2018, November). *Blockchain and Land Administration: Possible applications and limitations.* Retrieved from: https://www.researchgate.net/publication/329650717_Blockchain_and_Land_Administration_Possible_applications_and_limitations

Suberg, W. (2019, December 19). *First Government Blockchain Implementation For Russia.* Retrieved November 4, 2019, from https://cointelegraph.com/news/first-government-Blockchain-implementation-for-russia

Succi, Valerio, Vernazza, & Succi. (1998). Compatibility, Standards, and Software Production. *ACM StandardView, 6*(4).

Sumana, C., & Anitha, G. (2019, May). Blockchain Enabled Secure E-Voting System. *International Journal for Research in Applied Science and Engineering Technology, 7*(5).

Sunil, K. (2018). Value Creation Through Blockchain Technology in the Supply Chain Management (SCM). *Journal of Information Technology & Software Engineering.*

Swan, M. (2015). *Blockchain: Blueprint for a New Economy.* Newton, MA: O'Reilly Media.

Szabo, N., (1996). Smart contracts: building blocks for digital markets. *EXTROPY: The Journal of Transhumanist Thought,* (16).

Takyar, A. (2019, January). *Blockchain in Agriculture - Improving Agricultural Techniques.* Retrieved from https://www. leewayhertz.com/Blockchain-in-agriculture/

Tao, O., Ma, K., Tian, E., & Han, S. (2018). *Matrix Wallet App is Online.* Retrieved April 2018, from https://www.matrix.io/

Tapscott, D. (2016). *How will blockchain change banking? How won't it?* https://www.huffingtonpost.com/don.tapscott/how-will-blockchain-change_b_9998348.html

Tarasenko. (2019). *Private Blockchain vs traditional centralized database.* https://merehead.com/blog/private-Blockchain-vs-traditional-centralized-database/

Teutsch, J., & Reitwießner, C. (2017). *TrueBit: A scalable verification solution for Blockchains.* Academic Press.

Thakur, V., Doja, M. N., Dwivedi, Y. K., Ahmad, T., & Khadanga, G. (2019). Land records on Blockchain for implementation of land titling in India. *International Journal of Information Management, §§§*, 101940.

The Blockchain Council. (2019). *An authoritative group of experts and enthusiasts who are evangelizing the Blockchain Research, Development, Use Cases, Products and Knowledge for the better world.* Retrieved from https://www.Blockchain-council.org

Themistocleous, M. (2018). Blockchain Technology and Land Registry. *The Cyprus Review, 30*(2), 195–22.

Thomas. (2019). *How Blockchain technology could improve the tax system.* Retrieved from https://www.pwc.co.uk/issues/futuretax/how-Blockchain-technology-could-improve-tax-system.html

Thornton, G. (2018). *GDPR& Blockchain - Blockchain solution to general data protection regulation.* Technical report.

Tian, F. (2016). An agri-food supply chain traceability system for china based on RFID & Blockchain technology. In *Service Systems and Service Management (ICSSSM), 13th International Conference on.* IEEE.

Toris, C. (1994), A negotiation model of empathy. *9th International Balint Federation Congress.*

Treacy, M., & Wiersema, F. (1993, Jan.-Feb.). Customer Intimacy and Other Disciplines. *Harvard Business Review*, 12.

Treleaven, P., Galas, M., & Lalchand, V. (2013). Algorithmic Trading Review. *Communications of the ACM, 56*(11), 76–85. doi:10.1145/2500117

Tribune Media Wire. (2018, July). *Paypal tells dead woman she is in breach of contract because she is dead.* https://www.fox43.com/article/news/local/contests/paypal-tells-dead-woman-she-is-in-breach-of-contract-because-she-died/521-1558ca22-c198-4835-95bd-cca1a1f30fb7

Truong, N. B., Sun, K., Lee, G. M., & Guo, Y. (2019). *GDPR compliant personal data management: A Blockchain-based solution.* arXiv preprint arXiv:1904.03038

Tschorsch, F., & Scheuermann, B. (2016). Bitcoin and beyond: A technical survey on decentralized digital currencies. *IEEE Communications Surveys and Tutorials, 18*(3), 2084–2123. doi:10.1109/COMST.2016.2535718

Tse, D., Zhang, B., Yang, Y., Cheng, C., & Mu, H. (2017). Blockchain application in food supply information security. *2017 IEEE International Conference on Industrial Engineering and Engineering Management (IEEM)*, 1357-1361. 10.1109/IEEM.2017.8290114

US Congress, Office of Industrial Assessment. (1993). *Industrial Energy Efficiency.* Washington, DC: US Government Printing Office.

Uzialko, A. C. (2017). *Beyond Bitcoin: How Blockchain is Improving Business Operations.* Retrieved from: https://www.businessnewsdaily.com/10414-Blockchain-business-uses.html

Uzialko, A. C. (2018). *Can Your Business Trust a Block Chain Service.* Retrieved from: https://www.businessnewsdaily.com/10938-Blockchain-business-trust.html

van Dijk, M., Gentry, C., Halevi, S., & Vaikuntanathan, V. (2010). Fully Homomorphic Encryption over the Integers. EUROCRYPT, 24-43.

van Saberhagen, N., Meier, J., Juarez, A. M., & Jameson, M. (2012). *CryptoNote Signatures.* Academic Press.

Venkatesh, V., Morris, M. G., Davis, G. B., & Davis, F. D. (2003). User acceptance of Information Technology: Towards a unified View. *Management Information Systems Quarterly, 27*(3), 425–478. doi:10.2307/30036540

Vo, H. T., Kundu, A., & Mohania, M. (2018). Research Directions in Blockchain Data management and Analytics. *21st International Conference on Extending Database Technology (EDBT).* http://www.dke.jku.at/general/news/res/N000026/Mohania%20EDBT%20paper-227.pdf

Vogels, W. (2009). Eventually consistent. *Commun. ACM, 52*(1), 40-44. Doi:10.1145/1435417.1435432

Vos, J. A. C. O. B., Beentjes, B., & Lemmen, C. (2017). *Blockchain based land administration feasible, illusory or a panacea.* Paper prepared for presentation at the 2017 World Bank Conference on Land and Povertry, Washington, DC.

Vujičić, D., Jagodić, D., & Ranđić, S. (2018, March). Blockchain technology, bitcoin, and Ethereum: A brief overview. In *2018 17th International Symposium INFOTEH-JAHORINA (INFOTEH)* (pp. 1-6). IEEE. 10.1109/INFOTEH.2018.8345547

Wang, S., Zhang, Y., & Zhang, Y. (2018). A Blockchain-based framework for data sharing with fine-grained access control in decentralized storage systems. *IEEE Access: Practical Innovations, Open Solutions, 6,* 38437–38450. doi:10.1109/ACCESS.2018.2851611

Warren, S., & Treat, D. (2019). *Building Value with Blockchain Technology: How to Evaluate Blockchain's Benefits.* The World Economic Forum (WEF).

Wattenhofer, R. (2016). *The Science of the Blockchain* (1st ed.). CreateSpace Independent Publishing Platform.

Wegner, P. (1996). Interoperability. *ACM Computing Surveys, 28*(1), 285–287. doi:10.1145/234313.234424

Werbach, K. (2018). *The Blockchain and the New Architecture of Trust.* MIT Press. doi:10.7551/mitpress/11449.001.0001

Wiles, N. (2015). *The radical potential of Blockchain technology.* Academic Press.

Wilkinson, S., Boshevski, T., Brandoff, J., & Buterin, V. (2014). *Storj a peer-to-peer cloud storage network.* Academic Press.

Williams, I. (2017). Community Broadband network and the opportunity for e-government services. In Encyclopedia of Information Science and Technology, Fourth Edition Hershey, PA: IGI.

Williams, I. (2018). Community Based networks and 5G Wifi. *Ekonomiczne Problemy Uslug, 2*(131), 321-334.

Williams, I. (2021). Mobilization - Decision Theory. In Encyclopedia of Information Science and Technology, Fifth Edition. Hershey, PA: IGI Global.

Williams, I., & Agbesi, S. (2019). Blockchain, Trust and Elections: A Proof of Concept For The Ghanaian National Elections. In Handbook on Ict in Developing Countries (vol. 2). River Publishers.

Williams, I., & Agbesi, S. (2019). Blockchain, Trust And Elections: A Proof Of Concept For The Ghanaian National Elections. In Handbook on ICT in Developing Countries: Next Generation ICT Technologies. River Publishers.

Williams, I. (2015). *Analysis of Public Private Interplay Frameworks in the Development of Rural Telecommunications Infrastructure: A Multiple-Case Study.* Aalborg: Aalborg University Press.

Williams, I., Falch, M., & Tadayoni, R. (2018). Internationalization of e-Government Services. In *11th CMI International Conference: Prospects and Challenges Towards Developing a Digital Economy within the EU*. Copenhagen Denmark: IEEE.

Wirth, C., & Kolain, M. (2018). Privacy by Blockchain design: a Blockchain-enabled GDPR-compliant approach for handling personal data. In *Proceedings of 1st ERCIM Blockchain Workshop 2018*. European Society for Socially Embedded Technologies (EUSSET).

World Economic Forum. (2015). *Deep shift technology tipping points and societal impact survey report*. http://www3.weforum.org/docs/WEF_GAC15_Technological_Tipping_Points_report_2015.pdf

World Economic Forum. (2015). *Deep Shift: Technology Tipping Points and Societal Impact*. The World Economic Forum (WEF).

WorldPress. (2017, October 4). Back in Business. *Financial Advisors*. WorldPress.

Wüst, K., & Gervais, A. (2017). Do you need a Blockchain? *ACR Cryptology ePrint Archive*.

Xia, Q. I., Sifah, E. B., Asamoah, K. O., Gao, J., Du, X., & Guizani, M. (2017). MeDShare: Trust-less medical data sharing among cloud service providers via Blockchain. *IEEE Access: Practical Innovations, Open Solutions, 5*, 14757–14767. doi:10.1109/ACCESS.2017.2730843

Xu, X., Weber, I., & Staples, M. (2019). *Architecture for Blockchain Applications*. Springer International Publishing. doi:10.1007/978-3-030-03035-3

Yaga, D., Mell, P., Roby, N., & Scarfone, K. (2018). *Blockchain Technology over Overview*. National Institute of Standards and Technology Internal Report 8202. https://nvlpubs.nist.gov/nistpubs/ir/2018/NIST.IR.8202.pdf

Yaga, D., Mell, P., Roby, N., & Scarfone, K. (2018). *Blockchain technology overview. Technical report*. National Institute of Standards and Technology. doi:10.6028/NIST.IR.8202

Yao, A. C. (1982). Protocols for secure computations. SFCS, 160–164.

Yao, A. C. (1986). How to Generate and Exchange Secrets. *SFCS*, 162–167.

Yeboah-Boateng, E. O. (2017). Cyber-Security Concerns with Cloud Computing: Business Value Creation & Performance Perspectives. In A. K. Turuk, B. Sahoo, & S. K. Addya (Eds.), Resource Management & Efficiency in Cloud Computing Environment (pp. 106-137). IGI Global Publishers.

Yeboah-Boateng, E. O., & Nwolley, J. S. (2019). Developing Use Cases for Big Data Analytics: Data Integration with Social Media Metrics. In K. E. Skouby, I. Williams, & A. Gyamfi (Eds.), *Handbook on ICT in Developing Countries: Next Generation ICT Technologies (Vol. Series in Communications)*. Rivers Publisher.

Yermack, D. (2018). *FinTech in Sub-Saharan Africa: What Has Worked Well, and What Hasn't. New York University (NYU)*. doi:10.3386/w25007

Yli-Huumo, J., Ko, D., Choi, S., Park, S., & Smolander, K. (2016). Where Is Current Research on Blockchain Technology?—A Systematic Review. *PLoS One, 11*(10), e0163477. doi:10.1371/journal.pone.0163477 PMID:27695049

Zaninotto, F. (2017). *The Blockchain Explained to Web Developers, Part 3: The Truth*. Retrieved from http://marmelab.com/blog/2016/06/14/Blockchain-for-web-developers-the-truth.html

Zhang, J., Xue, N., & Huang, X. (2016). A secure system for pervasive social network-based healthcare. *IEEE Access: Practical Innovations, Open Solutions, 4*, 9239–9250. doi:10.1109/ACCESS.2016.2645904

Zhang, R., Xue, R., & Liu, L. (2019). Security and Privacy on Blockchain. *ACM Computing Surveys*, *52*(3), 1–34. doi:10.1145/3316481

Zhao, D., & Li, T. (2020). *Distributed Cross-Blockchain Transactions*. https://arxiv.org/abs/2002.11771

Zheng, Z., Xie, S., Dai, H. N., & Wang, H. (2017). An Overview of Blockchain Technology: Architecture, Consensus, and Future Trends. *IEEE 6th International Congress on Big Data Congress*.

Zheng, Z., Xie, S., Dai, H., Chen, X., & Wang, H. (2017). An Overview of Blockchain Technology: Architecture, Consensus, and Future Trends. *2017 IEEE International Congress on Big Data (BigData Congress)*, 557-564. doi: 10.1109/BigDataCongress.2017.85

Zheng, Z., Xie, S., Dai, H. N., Chen, W., Chen, X., Weng, J., & Imran, M. (2020). An overview on smart contracts: Challenges, advances and platforms. *Future Generation Computer Systems*, *105*, 475–491. doi:10.1016/j.future.2019.12.019

Zheng, Z., Xie, S., Dai, H. N., Chen, X., & Wang, H. (2018). Blockchain Challenges and Opportunities: A Survey. *International Journal of Web and Grid Services*, *14*(4), 352. doi:10.1504/IJWGS.2018.095647

Zyskind, G., & Nathan, O. (2015, May). Decentralizing privacy: Using Blockchain to protect personal data. In *2015 IEEE Security and Privacy Workshops* (pp. 180-184). IEEE.

Zyskind, G., Nathan, O., & Pentland, P. (2015). Decentralizing privacy: Using Blockchain to protect personal data. Security and Privacy Workshops (SPW), 180–184.

Zyskind, G., Nathan, O., & Pentland, A. (2015). Decentralizing Privacy: Using Blockchain to Protect Personal Data. *IEEE Symposium on Security and Privacy Workshops (SPW)*, 180 - 184. 10.1109/SPW.2015.27

Zyskind, G., Nathan, O., & Pentland, A. (2015). Enigma: Decentralized Computation Platform with Guaranteed Privacy. *Computer Science*.

About the Contributors

Idongesit Williams is a Post-Doctoral researcher at Center for Communication, Media and Information Technologies (CMI) located at Aalborg University Copenhagen. He holds a Bachelor in Physics, a Master degree in Information and Communications Technologies and a Ph.D. He has since 2010 researched into Knowledge Management, Organizational Learning, socioeconomic, socio-technical related to Information and Communications Technologies. He has authored and co-authored more than 30 research publications, including journal papers, books, book chapters, conference papers and magazine articles. He is the co-editor of the Books, The African Mobile Story, and the Handbook on ICT for developing countries:5G perspectives. He has organized conferences like the CMI annual conference and the CMI/GTUC conferences.

* * *

Samuel Agbesi is a PhD fellow at the Center for Communication, Media and Information technologies (CMI), Aalborg University Copenhagen. He received his Master of Philosophy in Information Technology from Kwame Nkrumah University of Science and Technology (KNUST). Samuel has over eight (8) years experience in Information Technology with specialization in database administration, sql pl/sql development, optimization, performance tuning and support for varied flavors (MySQL, Oracle 9i, 10g) of databases and Computer application programming with .Net framework (VB and C# .Net), Java and Web application development, and his research area is in e-government.

Sourav Banerjee is Dean of Engineering, Technology & Management at University of Kalyani.

Manju Biswas is pursuing PhD in Computer Science and Engg. She is working as Assistant Professor at Kalyani Government Engineering College.

Necva Bölücü is a research assistant at Computer Engineering Department, Hacettepe University. She received her B.Sc. degree from Computer Engineering Department, Mustafa Kemal University in Hatay, 2014 and M.Sc. degree from Computer Engineering Department, Hacettepe University in Ankara, 2017. Currently, she has been pursuing her Ph.D degree in Computer Engineering at Hacettepe University. She conducts research in the area of natural language processing for five years. Her current research interests are semantic parsing, and contextual representations. You may contact her by necva@cs.hacettepe.edu.tr.

Nurettin Bölücü is an embedded software engineer at Maxim Integrated. He as graduated from Hacettepe University as an electric and electronical engineer, 2015. Currently he is pursuing his B.Sc degree in Computer Engineering at Hacettepe University. He has been working for embedded firmware development and BSP driver development for several Real Time Operating Systems in his 5 years of career. He has been involved in software development for Turkish Utility Helicopter Program. You may contact him by nurettinblc@gmail.com.

Bahar Gezici is a Research Assistant in the Department of Computer Engineering at Hacettepe University. She received her M. Sc. Degree in Computer Engineering from Hacettepe University, Ankara, Turkey in 2018. She is currently pursuing her Ph. D. degree from Ankara Hacettepe University. She conducts research in the area of software engineering for three years. Her current research interests are open source software evolution, software quality, internal and external quality and software metrics.

Zhao Hongjiang is an associate professor of Finance at the School of Management and Economics, University of Electronic Science and Technology of China (UESTC). His main research interests focus on entrepreneurial finance and FinTech. He had 2 years of engineer work experience and 4 years of investment banking experience. He has published more than 30 papers including quite a few top journal papers and chaired 6 research grants at national or provincial level in China.

Nagesh Jadhav received Master of Engineering degree in Information Technology from the MIT, Pune in 2013, and pursuing PhD in Computer Science and Engineering from the MIT ADT University, Loni Kalbhor, Pune. He has been working as an Assistant Professor at the MIT School of Engineering, Pune since 2017. His current research interests include artificial intelligence, machine learning and affective computing.

Benjamin Kwofie is a lecturer at the Koforidua Technical University in Koforidua, Ghana. He is at the Computers Science Department of the Faculty of Applied Science and Technology.

Jyoti Malhotra has received her Ph.D. degree in Computer Science and Engineering from RTM Nagpur University in December 2019. She is working as an Assistant Professor with the Department of Computer Science & Engineering, School of Engineering, MIT ADT University, Pune. She has 17+ years of teaching experience. Her research interest lies in Data Storage patterns, Big Data, Software Testing, and Blockchain Technologies. She has worked in C, Java, PHP, and Linux Programming. She is a life member of the Computer Society of India, IAENG, and ISTE. She has publications in National, International conferences and Scopus Journals like IEEE conference, Springer conferences, etc.

Stephane Nwolley Jnr. holds a PhD in ICT Management (Big Data), with high level expertise in synthesizing large amounts of information into insights for strategy, innovation and business development. He was highly instrumental in creating an automated machine learning tool (snwolley) designed to make data analytics easy and affordable. He has had training in project management, Master of Business Administration in information systems from SMU and Bachelor of Applied Computer Science from Royal Melbourne Institute of Technology, Australia. His key qualities are in Big Data, Data Science, Cloud Computing, Business intelligence and ERP, UNIX/LINUX Programming, Web Application Design and Development, Project Management and Risk Analysis, Human Computer Interaction, DB

Management skills and Operating System Administration. Dr. Stephane Nwolley Jnr. has more than 13 years of practical experience in the ICT industry and previously worked with MTN and Huawei as an OSS engineer. His experience and hands on knowledge of the industry enables him proffer solutions that are both practical and innovative. Formerly, the CEO of Nalo Solutions Limited, he was the product lead for projects with clients including Ecobank, GIPC, UBA, amongst others.

Adnan Ozsoy is an Assistant Professor of Computer Engineering at Hacettepe University, Turkey. His research interests include parallel programming, high performance computing with graphics processing units, big data problems, distributed systems, Blockchain applications and cryptocurrencies. He received his PhD from School of Informatics and Computing of Indiana University, Bloomington; MSc in Computer Science from University of Texas at Austin; and BSc from Virginia Polytechnic Institute and State University.

Cephas Paa Kwasi Coffie is currently a PhD scholar at the University of Electronic Science and Technology of China. His research interest focuses on FinTech and Small Business Finance. He works as a lecturer at the All Nations University College Business School-All Nations University College Koforidua, Ghana. He has published more than 10 research papers including top journal papers.

Kamalendu Pal is with the Department of Computer Science, School of Mathematics, Computer Science and Engineering, City, University London. Kamalendu received his BSc (Hons) degree in Physics from Calcutta University, India, Postgraduate Diploma in Computer Science from Pune, India; MSc degree in Software Systems Technology from Sheffield University, Postgraduate Diploma in Artificial Intelligence from Kingston University, MPhil degree in Computer Science from University College London, and MBA degree from University of Hull, United Kingdom. He has published dozens of research papers in international journals and conferences. His research interests include knowledge-based systems, decision support systems, computer integrated design, software engineering, and service oriented computing. He is on the editorial board of international computer science journals. He is a member of the British Computer Society, the Institution of Engineering and Technology, and the IEEE Computer Society.

Martin K. Parmar has received his Diploma degree in computer in 2003 from SSPC Visnagar, Bachelor degree in Computer from Charotar Institute of Technology Changa, Gujarat University and Master degree in 2014 from and L.D. College of Engineering, Ahmedabad, Gujara. Technological University. At present, he is pursuing PhD at CHARUSAT. His areas of interest include Blockchain, Cryptocurrency, Web Application Development using PHP, ASP.Net(C#), Java, Python. He is a member of Professional Societies ACM. He has 10+ years of teaching experience at UG level and PG level. He is having good teaching and research interests. He is concurrently holding the academic position as an Assistant Professor (Jan 2010 till date), at CSPIT, CHARUSAT.

Rajneeshkaur Sachdeo-Bedi has a total of 24 years of experience in Academics. She completed her Ph.D. from State University, Amravati in 2017. Her research areas include Data Security and Privacy, natural language processing and linguistics, machine learning, data mining, Blockchain, and Wireless network. Guided around 100 students for under-graduate projects and 18 students at the post-graduate level. Currently guiding 4 Ph.D. students. She has published 45 papers in Journal and Conference and 7 published patents to her credit. Her professional membership is for ISTE, IACSIT, and CSI.

Sambhaji Sarode received BE and ME in information Technology from the SPPU university Pune in 2005 and 2010, respectively and Ph.D. in Computer Science & Technology from RTM Nagpur University India in 2019. Currently, he is working as an assistant professor with the Department of Computer Science & Engineering, School of Engineering, MIT ADT University Pune. His research interest includes wireless communications, Cognitive security and internet of Things. Also, he is a reviewer for IEEE Sensor journal, National Academy Science Letter SCI indexed Journals and many other reputed Scopus and UGC approved journals. He is recipient of best Ph.D. thesis award from Ph.D. research center across all branches of engineering. Also, He is a recipient of World Championship 2018 in Sensor Technology among 5985 nominations from 96 countries, organized by International Agency for Standards and Ratings. He is fellow of International Agency for Standards and Ratings and Recipient of Best paper award on "Nano-Computer Technology" at National level Conference held at Government College of Engineering, Karad, Maharashtra, India. Presently, he is contributing in three consultancy projects, namely, 3D Mold Design, BookMyTool, and Butterfly Garden. He has completed one research funded project entitled "Priority based approach for Sensor Network" under the scheme of BCUD SPPU Pune. Also, He has received a grant for one STTP program i.e. "Business Intelligence & Analytics" and successfully conducted at international level. He is also having patents on his name in the field of wireless communications. He has delivered many expert session in STTP programs and workshops such as "Use of Modeling in Network" in TEQIP-II STTP development program, "IoT: Sensor Network" in TEQIP-II STTP development program I, etc. He has published many papers in international conferences and journals like IEEE conference, Springer Conferences, Elsevier, etc. Also, He has published two books namely Wireless Sensor Network and Object Oriented Design and Modeling and one book chapter.

Parth Shah obtained his Bachelor's degree in Computer Engineering from C U Shah College of Engineering & Technology, Wadhwan (CCET), Gujarat in 2001; Master degree in Computer Engineering from DDU in 2004, Nadiad, Gujarat and Ph.D. in area of Information Security from CHARUSAT, Changa, Gujarat. Currently, he is working as Associate Professor at the Department of Information & Technology, CHARUSAT, Changa, Gujarat. His research interest includes Information Security, Computer Architecture and Cloud Computing. He has guided more than 30 ME/M Tech dissertations and supervisor of 6 Ph.D. scholars. He has published more than 40 papers in Journal and Conference proceedings. He has received grants of 134900.00 from GUJCOST, MHRD, and CSI. He is a member of the IEEE (Computer Society of India) since 2009. He has organized more than 20 activities under the IEEE banner as a student branch counselor of CHARUSAT. Recently he has organized International Conference on Emerging Trends in Engineering, Science and Technology (ICRISET - 2018) during December 14-15, 2018 under the IEEE.

Rekha Sugandhi is Professor and Head, Department of Information Technology, SoE, MIT ADT University, India, working in the area of Cognitive Computing and Usability Engineering for IT Solutions; Other areas of interest are Natural Language Processing and Machine Learning.

Emmanuel Tetteh is a lecturer at the Computer Science Department Of Koforidua Technical University within the Faculty of Applied Science and technology and a PhD candidate at the school of information and software engineering, UESTC, China.

Ezer Yeboah-Boateng is a professional ICT Specialist and Telecoms Engineer with a strong background in cyber-security, digital forensics, business development, change management, knowledge management, strategic IT-enabled business value creation and capabilities to develop market-oriented strategies aimed at promoting growth and market share. An Executive with 25 years of domestic and global experience conceptualizing ideas, seizing opportunities, building operations, leading highly successful new business development initiatives and ventures. A Consultant with emphasis on Cyber-security, digital forensics, telecommunications, Internet, and network integration technologies, with additional experience related to dealing with refurbished and overstock equipment, and manufacturing. Strong presentation, negotiation, and team building skills.

İsmail Yıldırım is an Assoc Professor at Hitit University, Department of Insurance and Actuary, Corum-Turkey. He received PhD in Finance with his thesis entitled as "Stress Testing In The Risk Measurement Of Insurance Companies: An Implementation in Turkish Insurance Sector". Has the title of associate professor in the field of insurance. He has published several international articles and book chapters in the field of insurance. He teaches actuarial and insurance courses at Hitit University. He carried out projects at the University for the problems of Insurance Agencies. His areas of expertise include insurance business, risk management and insurance.

Index

Recommended Reference Books

ISBN: 978-1-5225-5912-2
© 2019; 349 pp.
List Price: $215

ISBN: 978-1-5225-8176-5
© 2019; 2,218 pp.
List Price: $2,950

ISBN: 978-1-5225-7811-6
© 2019; 317 pp.
List Price: $225

ISBN: 978-1-5225-7268-8
© 2019; 316 pp.
List Price: $215

ISBN: 978-1-5225-7455-2
© 2019; 288 pp.
List Price: $205

ISBN: 978-1-5225-8973-0
© 2019; 200 pp.
List Price: $195

Do you want to stay current on the latest research trends, product announcements, news and special offers?
Join IGI Global's mailing list today and start enjoying exclusive perks sent only to IGI Global members.
Add your name to the list at **www.igi-global.com/newsletters.**

Publisher of Peer-Reviewed, Timely, and Innovative Academic Research

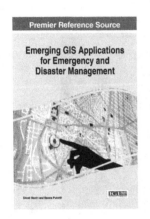
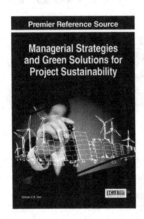

Are You Ready to Publish Your Research?

IGI Global offers book authorship and editorship opportunities across 11 subject areas, including business, computer science, education, science and engineering, social sciences, and more!

Benefits of Publishing with IGI Global:

- Free one-on-one editorial and promotional support.

- Expedited publishing timelines that can take your book from start to finish in less than one (1) year.

- Choose from a variety of formats including: Edited and Authored References, Handbooks of Research, Encyclopedias, and Research Insights.

- Utilize IGI Global's eEditorial Discovery® submission system in support of conducting the submission and blind review process.

- IGI Global maintains a strict adherence to ethical practices due in part to our full membership with the Committee on Publication Ethics (COPE).

- Indexing potential in prestigious indices such as Scopus®, Web of Science™, PsycINFO®, and ERIC – Education Resources Information Center.

- Ability to connect your ORCID iD to your IGI Global publications.

- Earn royalties on your publication as well as receive complimentary copies and exclusive discounts.

Get Started Today by Contacting the Acquisitions Department at:

acquisition@igi-global.com

Printed in the United States
By Bookmasters